The
Supreme Court
Yearbook
1995-1996

Justices assemble in the Supreme Court's conference room for an informal photograph. From left are Justices Sandra Day O'Connor, Anthony M. Kennedy, and Antonin Scalia; Chief Justice William H. Rehnquist; and Justices David H. Souter, Ruth Bader Ginsburg, Clarence Thomas, Stephen G. Breyer, and John Paul Stevens.

The
Supreme Court
Yearbook
1995-1996

Kenneth Jost

Congressional Quarterly Inc.
Washington, D.C.

Photo credits: cover, 318, R. Michael Jenkins; frontispiece, 298, 301, 313, 316, Collection, the Supreme Court Historical Society; 30, Richard Ellis (left), Senate Media Services (center); 35, AP/Wide World Photos; 40, *Richmond Times-Dispatch;* 48, AP/Wide World Photos; 55, *Denver Post;* 60, *Providence Journal-Bulletin;* 130, Scott J. Ferrell; 305, Joseph McCary; 309, Supreme Court; 315, White House.

Printed in the United States of America

ISBN   0–87187–898–4 (pbk)
ISBN   0–87187–897–6
ISSN   1054–2701

Contents

Preface

The Supreme Court moved further into the computer age in the 1995–1996 term. It established its own electronic bulletin board system (BBS), giving anyone with a personal computer online access to the Court's opinions, docket, argument calendar, and other information and publications. The telephone number for the Court's BBS is (202) 554-2570. People who have used the system describe it as user-friendly. The system is not quite in real-time, though: opinions run several days behind.

The Court announced the new development in March, just as the justices were starting to issue some of the term's major rulings. It was a term that defied easy categorization as liberal or conservative. Conservatives cheered rulings on racial redistricting, states' rights, and criminal law. Liberals were encouraged by rulings that struck down an anti–gay rights initiative in Colorado and required the all-male Virginia Military Institute to admit women. Free speech advocates on the left and right applauded several important First Amendment rulings.

Now in its seventh year, *The Supreme Court Yearbook* details the Court's work during the 1995–1996 term. Chapter 1 analyzes the justices' voting patterns and examines the possibility of an ideological shift on the Court after the 1996 presidential election. Chapter 2 gives an overview of the term's decisions and detailed accounts of the most important cases. Excerpts from these major decisions appear in the appendix. Chapter 3 contains summaries of all the Court's decisions during the term, arranged by subject categories. Chapter 4 previews the 1996–1997 term.

My thanks again go to the members of the Court's public information office, headed by Toni House, for their able assistance and to the lawyers, law professors, and other journalists whose comments and writings help inform my own coverage. At Congressional Quarterly Books, Shana Wagger, Barbara de Boinville, and Talia Greenberg provided expert editorial assistance in taking the manuscript and turning it into a finished book.

Finally, thanks to my wife, Katie White, who keeps me and my computer working properly, and to Nicole and Andrew, who fill my down time with constant pleasure and excitement.

1 | *The Center Reappears*

Bob Dole cinched the Republican presidential nomination early in the 1996 primary season and began testing themes he hoped to use in the fall campaign. So in April, he turned to a topic that had been a political issue in almost every presidential election since 1968: the Supreme Court.

Speaking to a meeting of newspaper editors, the longtime Senate Republican leader warned that a second term for President Bill Clinton could result in the most liberal Supreme Court since the Warren Court era ended almost three decades earlier. "We could lock in liberal judicial activism for the next generation, and the social landscape could change dramatically," Dole said in the April 19 speech in Washington.

Dole ran off a litany of dangers: "More federal intrusion in the lives of average Americans. More centralized power in Washington. Less freedom of religious expression. More rights for criminals—and more arrogant disregard of the rights of law-abiding citizens." And, without mentioning their names, he specifically criticized Clinton's two appointees to the Court—Justices Ruth Bader Ginsburg and Stephen G. Breyer—for being "among the most willing to use technicalities to overturn death sentences for proven murderers."

The White House responded quickly. White House counsel Jack Quinn called Dole's charges "tired, old worn-out rhetoric" and defended what he called Clinton's record of appointing "moderate, mainstream judges."

Some commentators applauded Dole's message. "Mr. Dole needs to find some way to energize his voters," wrote conservative columnist Paul Gigot of the *Wall Street Journal*, "and a battle to block a Clinton version of the Warren Court is a good bet." But many other observers and commentators said Dole had his facts wrong. "The startling aspect about President Clinton's judicial appointments has in fact been their centrist character," Anthony Lewis, the liberal columnist and one-time Supreme Court reporter for the *New York Times*, wrote a few days after Dole's speech.

The justices themselves, of course, took no official note of the partisan debate. Whatever their backgrounds before taking the bench, they swore off politics after donning their judicial robes. But over the next two months, the critics of judicial activism got some new examples to add to their list as the Court finished its 1995–1996 term.

A month after Dole's speech, the Court handed gay rights advocates a major victory by striking down a voter-approved constitutional amendment aimed at blocking laws to prohibit discrimination against homosexuals. On the same day, the Court set guidelines for overruling local juries in civil lawsuits. Then in late June, the Court threw out congressional redistricting plans drawn up by legislators in two states. In the name of equal rights for women, it ordered a state university in Virginia to fundamentally revise its admissions policies. And in the name of free speech, it threw out parts of an anti-indecency law passed by Congress, carved a new loophole in federal campaign finance laws, and gave government contractors a green light to sue state and local officials for interfering with their First Amendment rights.

But these bursts of judicial activism did not come solely—or even primarily—from the hands of liberal, Democratic-appointed justices. Justices across the ideological spectrum found legal grounds for interfering with the prerogatives of state governments and the "political branches" of the federal government. Liberal-leaning justices did provide most of the votes for overturning Colorado's anti–gay rights initiative and for ordering the all-male Virginia Military Institute (VMI) to admit women. But the decisions would not have come out the way they did without the votes of two Republican-appointed centrists: Sandra Day O'Connor and Anthony M. Kennedy.

A similar moderate-to-liberal coalition was responsible for the decision setting outer limits on punitive damage awards. But a conservative majority struck down racially drawn redistricting plans in Texas and North Carolina—once again with O'Connor's and Kennedy's votes. And some unusual crossideological coalitions formed behind the flurry of decisions extending First Amendment doctrines into new settings.

This free-wheeling activism made the Court's term difficult to describe. A year earlier, the justices left behind so many conservative decisions that some commentators said the Court's center had disappeared. The 1995–1996 term produced an ample number of conservative rulings. The Court generally backed law enforcement in criminal cases and backed states' rights on an important federalism issue—the power of Congress to authorize federal courts to hear private suits against the states. But those conservative decisions were offset by the liberal decisions in other areas.

"The Court was conservative on states' rights, crime, and race, and liberal on gay rights, women's rights, and speech," said Kathleen Sullivan, a professor of constitutional law at Stanford University. "You might say that balances out to a moderate term."

"There's certainly turning out to be a strong moderate center at the Court," said Barry Friedman, a professor of constitutional law at Vanderbilt University Law School.

Legal interest groups selectively praised the instances of judicial activism that went their way. Clint Bolick, vice president and litigation director for the conservative Institute for Justice, said the two redistricting rulings "put the nail in the coffin of racial gerrymanders." Stephen Bokat, vice president and general counsel of the U.S. Chamber of Commerce, used the same metaphor, saying the punitive damages ruling put "the nail in the coffin" of excessive jury awards.

For its part, the American Civil Liberties Union welcomed the rulings in the gay rights and VMI cases as "one of the most significant developments in equal protection law in many years." It also praised the Court's "strong defense of free speech," praise echoed by some business groups. Bokat said the Court "showed strong adherence to the First Amendment in the political sphere, which is important to business, and in the commercial sphere."

One lawyer who frequently appeared before the Court saw an increased willingness by the justices to decide cases in part on the basis of a personal sense of fairness rather than a "strict construction" of the law. "Four or five years ago, there was a stronger sense of externally imposed limits on the ability of justices to make decisions on the basis of policy judgments," Richard Taranto remarked at an end-of-term briefing sponsored by the conservative Washington Legal Foundation. "This is a Court that has at its center a very strong sense of its power to make judgments on the basis of a sometimes complex mix of factors determining what makes sense."

Other commentators detected the same trend, but viewed it less favorably. "It is becoming ever more clear that not a single member of the current Court can be called a consistent practitioner of judicial restraint," Stuart Taylor Jr., senior writer with American Lawyer Media, wrote in his wrap-up of the term. "The Court has liberals, moderates, and conservatives," Taylor, a self-described moderate, added. "But they are activists all."

"The Catbird's Seat"

With the end of the 1995–1996 term, Chief Justice William H. Rehnquist completed his tenth year in that position since President Ronald Reagan elevated him from associate justice in 1986. Clearly, Rehnquist had put his stamp on the Court in many ways. Once a lonely dissenter on the Court's far right, Rehnquist had pushed the Court in a conservative direction on a host of issues: criminal law, habeas corpus, school desegregation, voting rights, and, most recently, federalism.

Court watchers differed on whether to emphasize how far Rehnquist had brought his ideological agenda or how short he had fallen. The most controversial precedents of the Warren and Burger Courts still stood, including the Warren Court's rulings expanding protections for criminal defendants and the Burger Court's abortion-rights ruling *Roe v. Wade*. And despite his title, Rehnquist still had only one vote, and he cast it in dissent more often than several of his colleagues.

Indeed, in the 1995–1996 term—as in the past several years—it was more accurate to speak of the O'Connor-Kennedy Court than the

Table 1-1   Justices in Dissent, 1995–1996 Term

Justice	8–1/7–1	7–2/6–2	6–3	5–4	Total	Percentage
		Division on Court				
Rehnquist	—	3	4	5	12	16.0
Stevens	5	5	1	8	19	26.0
O'Connor	—	2	2	3	7	9.3
Scalia	2	4	4	5	15	20.0
Kennedy	—	2	—	4	6	8.0
Souter	—	1	2	7	10	13.3
Thomas	2	4	5	5	16	21.6
Ginsburg	—	3	2	7	12	16.0
Breyer	—	6	1	8	15	20.0

Note: The totals reflect cases where justices dissented in whole or in part. There were seventy-five signed opinions during the 1995–1996 term. Because of recusals, Justice Stevens participated in seventy-three cases, Justice Thomas in seventy-four. The count includes one 5–4 decision (*Lonchar v. Thomas*) where justices were unanimous on the result but divided on the legal reasoning.

Rehnquist Court. The two centrist justices often held the balance of power between two opposing camps: the conservative trio of Rehnquist and Justices Antonin Scalia and Clarence Thomas and the liberal-leaning bloc of Justices John Paul Stevens, David H. Souter, Ruth Bader Ginsburg, and Stephen G. Breyer.

The evidence of O'Connor's and Kennedy's pivotal roles was ample. Statistically, the two dissented less frequently than the other justices. Kennedy dissented in only six cases during the term—marking the fifth consecutive year he cast the fewest dissenting votes among the justices. O'Connor was close behind with seven dissents *(see Table 1-1).*

Moreover, O'Connor and Kennedy were almost invariably in the majority in the most important and closely divided decisions. In the fifteen or so most newsworthy of the Court's decisions, Kennedy dissented only once: in a 5–4 ruling that rejected a so-called innocent owner defense in civil forfeiture cases. In those same cases, O'Connor cast only one partial dissent, disagreeing with one part of the ruling that struck down provisions of the cable indecency law.

In the Court's 5–4 decisions, either O'Connor or Kennedy was essential to the outcome. They never were on the losing side together in a 5–4 case: one or the other was needed to make a majority. Most often, they teamed with the three conservatives. But twice each, O'Connor or Kennedy gave a critical fifth vote to the four liberals. "Certainly the moderates— Kennedy and O'Connor—still sit in the catbird's seat," Stanford's Kathleen Sullivan remarked.

In arguments, the two justices frequently asked pointed questions that gave telling clues about the likely outcome of the case. Kennedy, for example, upbraided a lawyer for the Seminole Indians who was trying to defend the federal law allowing tribes to sue states in federal courts over gambling issues. "Congress doesn't have sovereignty over the states," Kennedy told the lawyer. "That is fundamentally wrong." When the decision came out, Kennedy was with the 5–4 majority to strike the law down.

Similarly, O'Connor's questions signaled the likely outcome of the racial redistricting cases. A lawyer from the solicitor general's office defended the Texas plan by saying the racial lines were drawn to protect incumbents. "Shouldn't the state have to obey the constitutional command not to draw lines predominantly on race?" O'Connor asked curtly. But later, O'Connor was similarly short when the lawyer challenging the North Carolina plan argued that any use of race in redistricting was impermissible. "I thought we had said something different," she retorted.

When the decisions came out in late June, O'Connor wrote the principal opinion rejecting the incumbency protection defense that Texas had offered. She also wrote a pivotal separate opinion that rejected the argument that lawmakers could never deliberately create a minority-dominated district.

For Kennedy, the term inevitably was to be remembered for his majority opinion striking down Colorado's anti–gay rights amendment. It was a spare opinion, only fourteen pages long, with no footnotes. Some critics echoed the complaint made by Scalia in dissent that the opinion was legally unsupported, fashioned from whole cloth with more politics than law. But other Court watchers applauded both the result and the articulation.

"Pathbreaking decisions are not always well-crafted," said Kathleen Sullivan, who co-authored an influential brief urging the Court to strike down the law. "What was great about this decision is that it says, 'This law was so hateful, so broad, and so purposeless that we're going to strike it down, and we don't need a lot of case citations to do it.' "

Kennedy's other majority opinions were less dramatic. The most important perhaps was a precedent-setting but understated decision allowing government contractors to sue officials if they are terminated for refusing to make political contributions. But Kennedy was a strong voice in several concurring and dissenting opinions. In two decisions striking down parts of the cable indecency law and easing restrictions on campaign spending by political parties, Kennedy largely concurred in the result, but wrote separate opinions urging the Court to go further to protect First Amendment interests.

The one-time constitutional law professor also again displayed a strong commitment to fairness in the courtroom. Besides his dissent in the "innocent owner" case, he wrote an opinion allowing a fugitive defendant to contest a forfeiture proceeding even while he remained at large. And

Kennedy objected sharply when a 5–4 majority said a defendant facing multiple petty offenses had no right to a jury trial. The ruling, he wrote, "is one of the most serious incursions on the right to jury trials in the Court's history."

O'Connor's most important opinion in the term came in the Texas redistricting case. Again the decision confirmed her as the critical vote on affirmative action issues. She had written the Court's first opinion in 1994 allowing voters to challenge racial gerrymandering. A year later, she had led the same 5–4 majority in raising the standard for the federal government to justify minority preference programs for government contractors.

Just as she had done in those earlier cases, O'Connor used strong rhetoric in the Texas redistricting opinion to declare racial classifications unacceptable, but stopped short of barring all race-conscious government policies. Her studious ambivalence drew a measure of criticism. "Make up our mind, Justice O'Connor," read the headline on an op-ed article in the *New York Times* written by Jeffrey Rosen, legal editor of the *New Republic.* And the criticism was heightened by her unusual decision in the Texas case to write a separate concurring opinion — in effect, concurring with herself.

O'Connor wrote in the separate opinion that states can deliberately create majority-minority districts in some circumstances, and she laid out a four-part test to determine how. No one else joined the opinion, but some observers said O'Connor gave lawmakers some useful guidance. "I thought O'Connor set out a reasonably workable standard," David Savage of the *Los Angeles Times* remarked at an end-of-term panel discussion with other Supreme Court reporters.

Although she did not write the decision, O'Connor could take much of the credit for another of the term's major rulings: the 5–4 decision striking down a "grossly excessive" $2 million punitive damage award approved by Alabama courts. For several years, O'Connor had been the strongest voice on the Court urging action to limit punitive damage awards. In 1991, she had been the lone dissenter in a decision that refused to limit jury discretion in setting punitive damages. Now, in the new case, the Court did lay down some guidelines for judges and juries to use in such cases.

O'Connor also laid the groundwork for the decision in the VMI case. O'Connor wrote the Court's first ruling on single-sex schools: a 1982 decision ordering an all-female state nursing school to admit men. Ginsburg, who wrote the VMI decision, relied heavily on O'Connor's opinion and placed special stress on her phrase requiring an "exceedingly persuasive justification" for treating men and women differently under the law. As Ginsburg announced her opinion from the bench, she paused at that point and glanced at O'Connor, who looked up from a memo pad to return the acknowledgment.

On either side of the O'Connor-Kennedy axis stood two generally cohesive ideological blocs. The conservatives Rehnquist, Scalia, and

Table 1-2   Justices' Alignment, 1995–1996 Term

This table shows the percentage of decisions in which each justice agreed with each of the other members of the Court. On the seventy-five signed opinions for the 1995–1996 term, thirty-one (or 41 percent) were unanimous.

The voting pattern depicts two fairly cohesive blocs—three conservatives and four liberal-leaning justices—with Justices O'Connor and Kennedy not closely aligned with either grouping. On the conservative side, Chief Justice Rehnquist and Justices Scalia and Thomas each voted with each of the others in at least 80 percent of the nonunanimous decisions and nearly 90 percent of all decisions.

Among the liberals, with the exception of one pairing, Justices Stevens, Souter, Ginsburg, and Breyer voted with each of the other three in at least 70 percent of the divided cases and 80 percent of all cases. Stevens and Ginsburg had the weakest alignment among the liberals, voting together in 62 percent of divided cases and 78 percent of all cases.

O'Connor and Kennedy voted more often with each other than with other members of the Court. O'Connor was next most closely aligned with Rehnquist, Kennedy with Souter.

Souter and Breyer had the closest alignment for the term—voting together in almost 91 percent of all cases. The justices least often in agreement were Stevens with Scalia and Thomas: Stevens voted with each in fewer than one-fifth of the nonunanimous decisions.

	Rehnquist	Stevens	O'Connor	Scalia	Kennedy	Souter	Thomas	Ginsburg	Breyer
Rehnquist		26.2	70.4	80.0	68.1	47.7	81.4	59.1	36.4
		57.5	82.7	88.0	81.3	69.3	88.0	76.0	62.7
Stevens	26.2		45.2	19.0	57.1	71.4	19.5	62.0	71.4
	57.5		68.6	53.4	75.3	83.6	54.2	78.0	83.6
O'Connor	70.4	45.2		63.6	70.5	63.6	65.1	68.1	59.1
	82.7	68.6		78.7	82.7	78.7	79.7	81.3	76.0
Scalia	80.0	19.0	63.6		61.4	40.9	81.4	47.7	34.1
	88.0	53.4	78.7		77.3	65.3	89.2	69.3	61.3
Kennedy	68.1	57.1	70.5	61.4		70.4	58.1	68.1	59.1
	81.3	75.3	82.7	77.3		82.7	75.7	81.3	76.0
Souter	47.7	71.4	63.6	40.9	70.4		37.2	72.7	84.1
	69.3	83.6	78.7	65.3	82.7		63.5	84.0	90.7
Thomas	81.4	19.5	65.1	81.4	58.1	37.2		44.2	25.6
	88.0	54.2	79.7	89.2	75.7	63.5		67.6	56.8
Ginsburg	59.1	62.0	68.1	47.7	68.1	72.7	44.2		71.4
	76.0	78.0	81.3	69.3	81.3	84.0	67.6		81.3
Breyer	36.4	71.4	59.1	34.1	59.1	84.1	25.6	71.4	
	62.7	83.6	76.0	61.3	76.0	90.7	56.8	81.3	

Note: The first number in each cell represents the percentage of agreement in divided cases. The second number represents the percentage of agreement in all signed opinions.

Thomas each voted with the other in almost 90 percent of the signed opinions. On the left, Stevens, Souter, Ginsburg, and Breyer were slightly less unified. But except for one pairing, each one voted with the other at least 80 percent of the time. Stevens and Ginsburg agreed 78 percent of the time (*see Table 1-2*).

The ideological groupings could be seen clearly in the Court's 5–4 decisions. The three conservatives voted together in every 5–4 ruling, whether in the majority or in dissent. And at least three of the four liberal-leaning justices also stayed together in every 5–4 decision.

The Conservative Justices

As chief justice, Rehnquist had the prerogative to assign opinions when he was in the majority. He took for himself several of the term's most important decisions, and they reflected his longstanding positions favoring law enforcement and states' rights.

A year earlier, Rehnquist had written a 5–4 decision striking down a federal law banning possession of firearms near schools; he said Congress had exceeded its power to regulate interstate commerce. This term Rehnquist led the same 5–4 majority in striking down a part of an Indian gambling law that allowed tribes to sue states in federal court. The decision, based on a broad reading of the Eleventh Amendment and sovereign immunity principles, overturned a 1989 precedent that had allowed Congress to authorize suits against states in U.S. courts. Rehnquist had been among the four dissenters in the earlier case, along with O'Connor, Scalia, and Kennedy. Now he declared that the previous ruling "deviated sharply from our established federalism jurisprudence" and had to be overruled.

The chief justice also led a 5–4 majority in refusing to require an "innocent owner" defense in civil forfeiture cases. His opinion harked back to nineteenth century cases upholding the seizure of pirate ships and discarded any suggestions in more recent cases that owners should be allowed to argue that they were not responsible for their property being put to an illegal use. Later in the term, he led an 8–1 majority in a similarly unbending rejection of an argument that criminal prosecution and civil forfeiture together amounted to multiple punishments in violation of the Double Jeopardy Clause.

Rehnquist's other votes and opinions reflected similar conservative stands. He authored opinions making it harder for defendants to make out a claim of racial discrimination in prosecutions and upholding a new law limiting federal habeas corpus for state inmates. And he joined with Scalia and Thomas in dissenting from the decision to strike down the Colorado anti–gay rights initiative. But he split with Scalia and Thomas in some other cases. He joined in the pair of 7–2 decisions extending First Amendment protections to government contractors. And he left Scalia to dissent alone in the VMI case. (Thomas recused himself.)

For Scalia, the term was to be remembered not for his majority opinions, but for his dissents. Always a fervid writer, Scalia seemed to reach new rhetorical heights in his dissenting opinions during the term. In the Colorado gay rights case, he accused the majority of taking sides in a "Kulturkampf" (German for culture war) and lining up with "the elite class" and against "traditional American moral values." Scalia emphasized his dissent by reading it from the bench. Observers said the other justices sat stone-faced as Scalia spoke.

In the VMI case, Scalia wrote sneeringly of "this most illiberal Court," which he accused of writing "current preferences of the society . . . into our Basic Law." A few days later, he dissented bitterly in the government contractor cases, complaining that the rulings upset an established tradition of political patronage. "The Court must be living in another world," Scalia complained. "Day by day, case by case, it is busy designing a Constitution for a country I do not recognize."

Some conservatives cheered Scalia's stands. "He is doing this as the moral compass or the moral conscience of the Court," Jay Alan Sekulow, counsel to the conservative American Center for Law and Justice, told the *Washington Post.* But even among conservatives, Scalia's rhetoric struck a discordant note. In an interview with National Public Radio's Nina Totenberg, Richard Epstein, a professor at the University of Chicago Law School, called Scalia's opinions "intolerant" and "overbearing." In the same broadcast, Akil Ahmar, a neoconservative at Yale Law School, said he was "disappointed that [Scalia] was more sharp than he had to be." Both men warned that Scalia's rhetoric would reduce his influence on the Court in the future.

Scalia also stoked controversy off the bench. In a speech to a Baptist Church breakfast in Jackson, Mississippi, on April 9, Scalia lamented that "modern society" views people "who adhere to . . . traditional Christian beliefs" as "simple-minded." "We must pray for the courage to endure the scorn of the sophisticated world," Scalia told the audience. News of the remarks touched off a flurry of critical comments about Scalia's views and the propriety of his remarks. "Scalia's Persecution Complex" was the headline on a critical commentary by Stuart Taylor Jr. in *Legal Times.*

By contrast, Scalia's majority opinions during the term made less news. One of the more important, written for a unanimous Court, rejected an effort to bar police from using traffic stops to investigate drug offenses or other crimes. He also wrote the majority opinion overturning a lower court order requiring Arizona officials to upgrade prison law libraries. In the process, Scalia tightened the standard for permitting inmates to file suits over their treatment and conditions.

Thomas, the least senior of the three conservatives, continued to emerge during the term as a strong but solitary voice for fundamentally re-examining established legal doctrine in a variety of areas. In the previous two years, he had called for scrapping expansive interpretations of the federal Voting Rights Act and rethinking Congress's powers to regulate interstate commerce. Now he turned to two other areas: commercial speech and campaign finance laws.

In the decision striking down Rhode Island's law banning liquor price advertising, Thomas took the strongest First Amendment position of the justices, arguing that government should never be allowed to prohibit truthful advertising of legal products or services. " . . . [A]ll attempts to dissuade legal choices by citizens by keeping them ignorant are impermissible," he wrote. Later in the term, Thomas again took the strongest First Amendment stance in an opinion that called for overturning all limits on campaign contributions. "If an individual is limited in the amount of resources he can contribute," Thomas wrote, "he is most certainly limited in his ability to associate for purposes of effective advocacy."

Thomas's opinions drew attention. "He's developing as a fairly strong believer in very strong protections under the First Amendment," Theodore Olson, a conservative Washington lawyer, commented. But Thomas's writings had no immediate impact. In each of those cases, the majority based its ruling on other grounds. And no other justice joined Thomas's opinions.

As customary for junior justices, Thomas's assignments to write majority opinions inclined toward the technical. He drew arcane topics like bankruptcy and civil procedure and specialized liability issues in railroad and maritime law. In his most noteworthy opinion, he wrote the decision that upheld the right of employers to require employees to give up potential legal claims as part of an early-buyout pension plan.

Like Scalia, Thomas drew attention off the bench, though not of his own making. He was invited in the spring to speak to an elementary school in predominantly black Prince Georges County, Maryland, just outside Washington. But the school superintendent objected because of Thomas's opposition to affirmative action and rescinded the invitation. The action touched off a sharp debate within the county and a chorus of condemnation from without. Under pressure, the school board voted, narrowly, to reissue the invitation. Thomas came to the school on June 10 and gave a well-received talk stressing self-reliance. His critics held a counterforum at the same time, but it was poorly attended.

Thomas also marked a personal milestone during the term: he returned to the Roman Catholic Church. Thomas described his reconversion to Catholicism after a twenty-eight-year estrangement in a speech June 8 at Holy Cross College, his alma mater. Although born into a Baptist family, he said he converted to Catholicism as a second-grader and attended a

Catholic seminary as a college freshman. But he left the church because of "an unsavory comment" made by a seminarian on the day Martin Luther King Jr. was killed. Despite the experience, Thomas said that Catholicism retained an appeal for him. And, as he described it, a group of Holy Cross classmates "helped me reclaim the precious gift, lost as I arrived here in 1968, my Catholic faith."

In reporting on Thomas's conversion, Tony Mauro, who covers the Court for *USA Today* and *Legal Times*, noted that for the first time in history, the Court did not have a Protestant majority. Four of the nine justices were Protestant: Rehnquist, Stevens, O'Connor, and Souter. Besides Thomas, Scalia and Kennedy were Catholics; Ginsburg and Breyer were Jewish.

The Liberal Justices

The justices on the Court's ideological left were more fractured than the conservative bloc. None of them held consistent liberal views, even in dissent.

Stevens was the strongest liberal voice on the Court and the least likely to join with the conservatives. He agreed with Scalia and Thomas only a little over half the time and with Rehnquist only slightly more often. Stevens was also the most likely of the justices to dissent—in nineteen cases, about one-fourth the time—and the most likely to dissent alone. He cast a solo dissenting vote five times.

In three of those lone dissents, Stevens sided with criminal defendants or prison inmates against the government—for example, voting to limit the government's power to seize an offender's property after a criminal prosecution. Overall, Stevens voted against the government in twenty out of twenty-five criminal law and prisoners' rights cases. The five other rulings were all unanimous.

Stevens's major opinion of the term came in the punitive damages case. His view on the issue had evolved. In 1991, he joined the 8–1 decision that had largely affirmed jury discretion to fix punitive damages. Two years later, he wrote a plurality opinion for four justices that said punitive damage awards must satisfy "a general concern of reasonableness." In the new ruling, Stevens led a 5–4 majority that, for the first time, threw out a punitive damages award. Stevens laid out three guidelines for testing such awards: the "reprehensibility" of the defendant's conduct, the ratio of the punitive damages to the actual harm suffered, and the civil penalties prescribed for similar violations.

In dissent, Scalia mocked Stevens's guidelines as providing "virtually no guidance." But tort reform advocates called the ruling helpful. "There's a lot of grist in the opinion that will help courts in assessing claims," said

Andrew Frey, the Washington lawyer who argued the case before the Court.

Stevens wrote a second of the Court's major opinions: the unanimous decision striking down Rhode Island's liquor price advertising ban. But only two other justices joined the pivotal section of his opinion, which said that laws banning truthful advertising are subject to "rigorous review" in the courts. In two other cases, Stevens wrote the main opinion, but spoke for less than a majority. He led four justices in permitting state courts to hear suits against federally regulated medical devices, but Breyer provided the fifth vote in a separate, narrower opinion. And early in the term, Stevens announced the decision to extend the federal Voting Rights Act to political party conventions, but his opinion was joined by only one other justice: Ginsburg. Breyer again wrote a narrower concurrence, joined by two other justices: O'Connor and Souter.

Among the other justices on the Court's left, the term produced an increased alignment between the two transplanted New Englanders: Souter and Breyer. The pair voted together in slightly over 90 percent of the cases—the closest alignment of any two justices during the term. Scalia and Thomas came next, agreeing 89 percent of the time.

Souter and Breyer had differing personalities and backgrounds. Both were scholarly; but Souter was quiet, Breyer outgoing. Souter was a New Hampshire Republican who came to the Court after an unheralded rise from state attorney general to federal appeals court judge. He was described as a "stealth nominee" of uncertain views on many issues. Breyer was born into a liberal Democratic family. He gained prominence early as a Harvard professor, Senate Judiciary Committee staff director, and a federal appeals court judge with influential views in two major areas, criminal sentencing and economic regulation.

The two men nonetheless shared legal outlooks. In their opinions and votes, Souter and Breyer evinced a concern for defendants' rights in criminal cases, opposition to discrimination, support for a strong federal role, and broad interpretation of statutes to fulfill congressional intent. Both joined the gay rights and VMI majorities and dissented in the racial redistricting cases. Both dissented in the states' rights ruling on the Indian gaming law. They voted together in all but one of the most narrowly divided criminal cases—siding with defendants, usually in dissent.

Souter's most memorable opinion in the term was a dissent. He wrote a massive and scholarly opinion in the Indian gaming case dissenting from the decision to bar Congress from authorizing federal court suits against the states. The ninety-two-page opinion reviewed colonial and revolutionary legal history and two centuries of constitutional history to try to demonstrate that the Court's ruling was, as he put it, "fundamentally mistaken."

Souter demonstrated a similar breadth in his dissenting opinion in the racial redistricting cases. After critiquing the rationale for the decision, he insisted that the creation of majority black or Hispanic districts could help minorities assimilate into the political mainstream—just as ethnic neighborhoods of the past did for the Irish, Italians, and Poles. "The result has been not a state regime of ethnic apartheid, but ethnic participation and even a moderation of ethnicity's divisive effect in political practice," Souter wrote.

Souter's opinions were dense with historical and academic citations in text and footnotes. "He really reads law review articles," said Yale's Akil Ahmar. "It's clear that he's read them closely and understands them." Some of his colleagues were less impressed. In the Indian gaming case, Rehnquist characterized Souter's dissent as "a theory cobbled together from law review articles and its own version of historical events."

In the term's final decision, Souter delivered a seventy-eight-page plurality opinion upholding suits against the government by savings and loan institutions for reneging on contracts in connection with the S&L bailout in the 1980s. He also wrote the Court's unanimous opinion limiting the use of juries in patent cases. Among his other opinions were two labor law decisions that reflected, along with his other votes in labor cases, a broad construction of federal labor statutes to protect workers' rights.

Breyer continued in his second term to adopt moderately liberal views on most issues. He also emerged as an especially influential figure in First Amendment cases with plurality opinions in two important, and badly fractured, decisions. In one, the Court struck down two parts of a law aimed at restricting sexually explicit materials on cable television, but upheld a third challenged section. In the other, the Court allowed political parties to spend unlimited amounts on election contests if the expenditures were not coordinated with individual candidates.

In both opinions, Breyer adopted a flexible, case-specific approach that placed him in the pivotal position between opposing camps that favored either upholding the challenged law altogether or throwing it out. Writing in the cable case, Breyer said government "may directly regulate speech to address extraordinary problems, where its regulations are appropriately tailored to resolve those problems without imposing an unnecessarily great restriction on speech." In separate opinions, Kennedy and Thomas both criticized Breyer's formulation as too flexible. Thomas called Breyer's standard "facially subjective." Kennedy complained that his opinion was "adrift."

Breyer had a pivotal role in other cases, including three that were decided by 5–4 votes. In the punitive damages case, he wrote what Akil Ahmar, a former law clerk of Breyer's, called an "exceptionally helpful concurrence" that emphasized the Alabama courts' failure to impose any effective limits on jury awards. His separate concurrences in the Voting Rights Act and medical device cases provided critical votes for the outcomes, but limited the legal effect of both decisions.

Business groups said they found Breyer an influential supporter in many of their cases. Paul Clement, a lawyer with a corporate law firm in Washington, said that along with O'Connor and Kennedy, Breyer formed the nucleus of "a nascent pro-business majority on the Court." Besides his stance in the punitive damages case, business groups cited Breyer's majority opinion in a case limiting the use of antitrust law in multiemployer labor negotiations. The ruling came in a case involving professional sports, but business advocates said the decision would protect employers in other industries, including construction, transportation, and entertainment.

In two other labor law opinions, however, Breyer sided against business. He led a unanimous Court in a decision that sanctioned the common union tactic of getting union members hired at nonunion plants to try to organize workers from within. In a second decision, he led a 6–3 majority in permitting workers to use the federal pension protection law known as ERISA to sue an employer for misleading them about health and retirement benefits. Breyer said the law—formally, the Employee Retirement Income Security Act—was "broad enough" to support the workers' claim.

Breyer wrote only rarely in criminal law cases, but he did author a significant opinion in a death row inmate's habeas corpus case. A federal appeals court dismissed the inmate's habeas corpus petition because he had waited nearly eight years after his conviction to file it. The justices unanimously agreed that the inmate was entitled to one federal habeas corpus petition, no matter how long the delay. In addition, Breyer led a five-justice majority to instruct lower federal courts that they must grant a stay of execution in death row cases whenever they needed time to rule on the merits of an inmate's plea.

Like Breyer, President Clinton's first appointee, Ginsburg, continued in her third term to take moderate-to-liberal stands. But some differences emerged between the two. In the previous term, Ginsburg and Breyer voted together 88 percent of the time. The figure fell to 81 percent this term. "I was surprised at how many times they were on different sides of the decision," Glenn Lammi, a lawyer for the conservative Washington Legal Foundation, told *Legal Times*.

The differences surfaced in three areas. In business-related cases, Ginsburg was somewhat less likely than Breyer to side with business—most notably, in rejecting constitutional limits on punitive damage awards. In criminal law, Ginsburg split with Breyer in two significant 5–4 decisions. She rejected the "innocent owner" defense in the civil forfeiture cases, and she upheld a Montana law limiting the use of voluntary drunkenness as a defense in a murder case.

In both of those areas, Ginsburg adopted a position of judicial restraint by viewing the Due Process Clause as a procedural guarantee only rather than a substantive limit on government power. "This is a judge who is restrained," said Yale's Akil Ahmar. Erwin Chemerinsky, a liberal professor at the University of Southern California Law Center, agreed. "On due process claims," he acknowledged, "Ginsburg is really with the conservatives."

In their third area of disagreement—First Amendment cases—Ginsburg took a broader view of free speech protections in two cases, but a narrower view in a third. Ginsburg favored striking down all three of the challenged provisions of the cable indecency law, while Breyer voted to uphold one. Ginsburg joined the broadest opinion in the commercial speech case, while Breyer joined O'Connor's narrower concurrence. But in the political spending case, Ginsburg voted to uphold the law limiting political parties' expenditures, while Breyer led the Court in narrowing the statute.

The two Clinton appointees nevertheless found themselves in agreement in most cases. Both took liberal positions in the term's major rulings on racial redistricting, equal protection, and states' rights. On many criminal law issues, however, they had moderate records. And although they voted in several cases to support death row inmates' challenges to their convictions or sentences, neither Ginsburg nor Breyer took the position that capital punishment was flatly unconstitutional.

Ginsburg's major opinion for the term was her ruling in the VMI case. The decision could be seen as a culmination of her life's work seeking to expand women's rights. Ginsburg designed the legal strategy that led the Court in the 1970s to hold that the Equal Protection Clause limits the government's power to treat men and women differently. Now, as a justice, she declared that those decisions established that government cannot deny to women "simply because they are women . . . equal opportunity to aspire, achieve, participate in and contribute to society based on their individual talents and capacities."

Her other opinions were a varied lot that displayed no overall ideological orientation. Two seemed most noteworthy. In one criminal case, Ginsburg led a 7–2 majority in making it somewhat easier for inmates to win a *Miranda* challenge in federal habeas corpus cases. In the other decision—a counterpoint to her stand in the punitive damages case—she said that federal courts hearing diversity-of-citizenship cases can enforce state laws limiting jury awards.

Conservatives still found Ginsburg and Breyer unacceptably liberal. Civil liberties and criminal defense groups, however, voiced disappointment with their positions. Detached observers viewed both justices, along with Stevens and Souter, as less liberal than the liberal justices of the Warren and Burger Courts. "Clinton has reinforced the moderates," said Sheldon Goldman, a professor of political science at the University of Massachusetts in Amherst who has studied judicial appointments for many years. As for Dole's criticisms of Clinton's appointments, Goldman dismissed them as "election-year rhetoric."

Future Appointments?

With the justices dispersed from Washington, a leading Republican official brought the Supreme Court back into the presidential campaign. "The next president," House Speaker Newt Gingrich declared on a television interview program in mid-July, "is going to decide the shape of the Supreme Court for a generation."

Vice President Al Gore took up the issue for the Democrats in an August 28 speech at the party's national convention in Chicago, linking the possibility of future vacancies to the volatile subject of abortion rights. Gore told cheering delegates that Republicans "want a president who will appoint the next three justices of the Supreme Court so they can control all three branches of government and take away a woman's right to choose."

Some presidents have put their ideological imprints on the Supreme Court. Abraham Lincoln was the first of a series of Republican presidents who created a solid nationalist majority on the Court in the generation after the Civil War. Beginning in his second term, Franklin D. Roosevelt remade the Court into a solid supporter of the federal government's intervention in social and economic affairs. In the late twentieth century, three GOP chief executives—Richard Nixon, Ronald Reagan, and George Bush—changed the Court's direction on a range of issues including civil rights and criminal law.

Other presidents, however, have been less successful in using their appointment power to influence the Court's direction. Dwight D. Eisenhower's disenchantment with the liberal stands of two of his appointees, Chief Justice Earl Warren and Justice William J. Brennan Jr., was well known. Byron R. White proved to be less liberal than President John F. Kennedy may have anticipated in appointing him; John Paul Stevens has certainly been more liberal than the president who appointed him, Gerald R. Ford.

In addition, presidents have no power to control the timing of an appointment. Jimmy Carter served four years in the White House without getting the chance to make an appointment to the Court. "No one knows when the Good Lord is going to call upon the members of the Court or when they will decide to resign or retire," Professor Goldman remarked.

Still, as the fall presidential campaign neared, Court watchers were speculating that any of three of the current justices might retire during the next president's term. Chief Justice Rehnquist, who was to turn seventy-two on October 1, was one possibility. He had served almost twenty-five years and suffered from a chronic back ailment that required surgery at the start of the 1995–1996 term. Stevens, at seventy-six the oldest of the justices, was a second possibility. Justice Sandra Day O'Connor, age sixty-six, was a third.

None of the three gave any public sign of leaving the Court, however. David Savage of the *Los Angeles Times* quoted Rehnquist in June as saying that his back was feeling better and he had no plans to retire soon. Stevens appeared on the bench to be in good health. So did O'Connor, despite an earlier bout with breast cancer. Of the other six justices, all were under age sixty-five and all in apparent good health.

Even if a vacancy arose, the political divisions in the country could limit the next president's discretion in choosing a nominee. Whatever his personal inclinations, the president would feel pressure to find a nominee broadly acceptable within his own party and confirmable within a Senate where neither party was likely to have a decisive numerical advantage. Moreover, Clinton's appointees, and Dole's recommended nominees for judicial positions during Republican presidencies, tended to be judicial moderates.

So, for the time being, the Court's ideological make-up seemed likely to be relatively unchanged. On many issues, the justices were expected to stick to a conservative line. "It still is a Court that has five conservatives on it," USC's Erwin Chemerinsky remarked. But, as the justices demonstrated during the past term, the ideological groupings were far from fixed. The balance of power rested with centrist-minded justices with a preference for flexibility, pragmatism, and case-by-case decision making. As Stanford's Kathleen Sullivan commented, "The middle can dominate the swing either way."

2

The 1995–1996 Term

The final week of the Supreme Court's term brings out a crowd of people who queue up outside the press room for copies of the Court's decisions. Many of those in line are messengers hired by Washington's well-heeled law firms to wait for the justices' pronouncements and rush back with the hot-off-the-press decisions.

The Court began the last week of June 1996 with a dozen decisions yet to go. Many of the cases had generated intense public interest. The government was trying to force the all-male Virginia Military Institute to admit women. Cable producers were asking to overturn a law limiting "indecency" on cable television. There was a First Amendment challenge to a law limiting campaign contributions by political parties and a case testing a new habeas corpus law aimed at restricting federal court challenges by death row inmates.

The justices convened on Monday, June 24, and issued four of the remaining decisions. Three more decisions came on Wednesday, and four more on Friday. For the reporters covering the Court, there was plenty of news. But each day the law firm messengers appeared disappointed. They called back to their offices to report: no, it's not out yet.

The big Washington law firms had to wait until after the weekend to get the decision they had been waiting for. The Court finally ended its term on Monday, July 1—a bit later than in the past few years. The final decision: a multibillion-dollar ruling that the federal government could be held liable for reneging on contracts with savings and loan institutions that had helped bail out bankrupt thrift institutions during the 1980s.

The 7–2 decision in *United States v. Winstar Corp.* was long and dense, hard to comprehend even for government contract specialists. The legal issue—whether the government had breached its contract with the healthy S&Ls by changing accounting regulations—had the appearance of a technical dispute. But the potential impact of the ruling was easy to understand. The government said an unfavorable ruling could add another $10 billion to the cost of the S&L bailout. Industry experts said the liability costs might be even higher.

Some business law advocates said the decision had ramifications beyond the S&L bailout. "The Court said they're going to apply normal contract law when the government makes a contract," commented Stephen Bokat, vice president and general counsel of the U.S. Chamber of Commerce. The ruling would force the government to keep its contracts or face liability if it did not, Bokat and other business lawyers said.

But some experts doubted the long-run impact of the decision. "The idea is that this is going to be a cure-all for all problems in the government contract field," said a veteran lawyer with experience representing the government and private companies. "I'm not sure that's going to be the case."

Certainly, the decision arose in a unique setting. Never before had the government enlisted the help of private businesses on such a massive scale and then so blatantly tried to change its deal with the companies to their disadvantage. In its distinctive aspects, though, the Winstar case resembled other cases from the 1995–1996 term. Many of them were one-of-a-kind disputes that brought forth rulings of uncertain long-term impact.

The Colorado anti–gay rights initiative that the justices struck down in May was described in the Court's opinion as unprecedented. VMI was one of only two public military colleges that refused to admit women. The habeas corpus law contained the first congressional effort to restrict the Supreme Court's own jurisdiction since Reconstruction. The racially drawn congressional districts struck down in two states were described by the majority as virtually unique in their irregular shapes.

In resolving these exceptional legal and factual disputes, the Court sometimes seemed to be striving to keep its rulings as narrow as possible. The ruling in the Colorado case made no mention of other gay rights issues. In the VMI case, Justice Ginsburg said the decision would have no effect on single-sex education. The Court crafted a ruling on the habeas corpus law that skirted the major constitutional issue. And Justice O'Connor contended in the redistricting cases that states were still free to draw majority-minority districts under some circumstances.

The result, according to some veteran Court watchers, was a term that lacked long-term impact. "My impression is that there is not a lot of lasting jurisprudence in these cases," said Douglas Kmiec, a conservative constitutional law expert at Notre Dame University. Except for the redistricting cases, Kmiec said, "the decisions don't seem to be producing any major new elements of analysis, but instead appear to be resolutions of idiosyncratic fact patterns." Erwin Chemerinsky, the liberal USC law professor, agreed. "I don't think the cases this term, with some notable exceptions, changed the law that much," he said.

Even if the disputes were idiosyncratic, however, the Court's decisions produced headlines and winners and losers in the short term. The Rehnquist Court continued to side with law enforcement in criminal law cases. In contrast to some other years, in the 1995–1996 term, business groups also fared well—in part because of a liberal-led majority that gave tort reform advocates their first clear-cut victory in attacks on punitive damage awards. First Amendment advocates also won major rulings.

The Court displayed some streaks of judicial activism. It ruled three acts of Congress unconstitutional—most notably, a law allowing Indian tribes to sue states in federal court over gambling issues. Dissenters warned

Table 2-1   Laws Held Unconstitutional

The Supreme Court issued eight decisions during the 1995–1996 term that held unconstitutional federal laws or state laws or constitutional provisions.

Decision (in chronological order)	Law ruled invalid
Federal Laws	
Seminole Tribe of Florida v. Florida [p. 122]	Indian Gaming Regulatory Act provision allowing suits against states in federal court
United States v. International Business Machines Corp. [p. 77]	Federal tax on premiums paid to foreign insurers
Denver Area Educational Telecommunications Consortium, Inc. v. Federal Communications Commission [p. 110]	Indecency provisions of 1992 cable act
State Laws	
Fulton Corp. v. Faulkner, Secretary of Revenue of North Carolina [p. 122]	Tax on stock in out-of-state (but not in-state) corporations
44 Liquormart, Inc. v. Rhode Island [p. 108]	Ban on liquor price advertising
Romer, Governor of Colorado v. Evans [p. 114]	Constitutional ban on enactment of laws to prohibit anti-gay discrimination
Bush, Governor of Texas v. Vera [p. 100]	Congressional redistricting plan
Shaw v. Hunt, Governor of North Carolina [p. 101]	Congressional redistricting plan

the decision would reduce Congress's power to enforce federal policies against the states. The justices also significantly trimmed another federal law: the Federal Election Campaign Act's limit on political party contributions to congressional candidates. And the justices threw out five state statutes or constitutional provisions on constitutional grounds, including the Colorado anti–gay rights measure and the North Carolina and Texas redistricting plans (*see Table 2-1*).

On another measure of judicial activism, the Court overruled one of its own precedents. The decision in the Indian gaming case threw out a 1989 ruling that had upheld the power of Congress to permit private citizens to sue states in federal court to enforce federal law (*see Table 2-2*). In at least three other cases, the Court significantly departed from prior rulings. It weakened a 1974 precedent guaranteeing jury trials. In the new ruling, the Court held that a defendant has no right to a jury trial when facing

Table 2-2   Reversals of Earlier Rulings

The Supreme Court issued one decision during the 1995–1996 term that explicitly reversed a previous ruling by the Court. The ruling brought the total number of such reversals in the Court's history to at least 211.

New Decision	Overruled Decision	New Holding
Seminole Tribe of Florida v. Florida	*Pennsylvania v. Union Gas Co.*	Congress cannot authorize suits against states in federal court

multiple petty counts. In a prisoners' rights case, the Court narrowed inmates' rights to legal assistance in court cases contesting their treatment or conditions. And when the Court struck down a Rhode Island law banning liquor price advertising, a majority of justices disavowed the rationale of a ruling ten years earlier upholding a Puerto Rico statute restricting advertising by casinos.

Business and industry groups had much to celebrate during the past term. Despite the declining number of signed opinions, the Court issued a relatively large number of business-related decisions. And business was on the winning side in the most important of the cases.

"The Court has shown an amazing interest in business issues," says the U.S. Chamber of Commerce's Stephen Bokat. "And we won a lot of very significant cases."

Overall, the Court backed businesses in twenty out of twenty-seven cases where companies were opposed by individuals, labor unions, or government regulators. The most significant setbacks for business groups came in labor cases, where the justices typically deferred to broadly written federal statutes and the generally pro-labor National Labor Relations Board.

The Court gave business groups their biggest victory in the 5–4 decision striking down a sizable punitive damage award won against the German automaker BMW because of a flawed paint job. Beyond the symbolic importance of the first ever decision to throw out a punitive damage award, the ruling gave businesses some general guidelines to use in challenging damage awards in future cases. "There is going to be a battleground in every case in which there is a large punitive damage award on whether these guidelines say the award is excessive or not," said Victor Schwartz, a Washington lawyer who played a prominent part in tort reformers' efforts to limit damage awards.

Business groups won a second significant liability-related ruling in a less-noticed decision. The 6–3 decision allowed federal judges to enforce state laws restricting jury awards in cases that are tried in federal courts because the parties are from different states. In another litigation-related dispute, the Court rebuffed an attempt by shareholders in a federal securities fraud suit to circumvent a Delaware state court settlement in the same dispute.

The Court protected businesses from litigation in other areas. It rejected a retired Lockheed engineer's effort to use the federal pension protection law to contest a proviso in an early-buyout plan that he give up any legal claims against the company. The Court also somewhat narrowed the federal age discrimination law by requiring plaintiffs contesting hiring or promotion decisions to show a substantial age difference with the successful applicant for the position.

The Court rejected industry arguments in another litigation area, however, by allowing state courts to hear product safety claims relating to medical devices regulated under federal law. Medical device manufacturers had argued that federal law pre-empted state court jurisdiction.

The banking industry had an especially good year, winning unanimous rulings in three significant cases. In one, the Court rejected a consumer suit to limit late payment charges and other fees on credit-card operations located in loosely regulated states. The Court also backed the right of small-town banks to sell insurance. In a third case, the justices permitted banks to freeze the accounts of depositors with outstanding loans even if the customers have gone to bankruptcy court to get protection from creditors.

Business groups counted one labor law ruling as a welcome victory: an 8–1 decision rejecting an antitrust suit by professional football players against National Football League owners. A lower court had ruled the owners violated antitrust law by unilaterally imposing a salary cap when labor talks broke down. But the Court said antitrust law generally does not apply to multiple employer negotiations. Experts said the impact of the decision would extend beyond professional sports to other areas, including the construction, transportation, and entertainment industries.

In other labor cases, however, the Court sided with union interests. The justices unanimously held that federal labor law protects workers from antiunion discrimination even if a union is paying the worker to help organize the company's workforce. The ruling gave some protection to a practice — called "salting" — that unions sometimes used in organizing drives. The Court also ruled that the federal pension protection law — the Employee Retirement Income Security Act (ERISA) — could be used to sue employers for intentionally misleading workers about health or pension benefits. And the Court said unions could bring damage suits against companies for violating the federal law requiring advance notice of plant closings or layoffs.

The Winstar decision represented business groups' biggest victory in cases against government agencies. A second government contract case went against business interests, however. The Court rejected an effort by two chemical companies to force the government to pay the cost of

Vietnam veterans' suits stemming from use of the defoliant Agent Orange during the Vietnam War.

Apart from those cases, the Court had few other clear-cut disputes between businesses and government regulators. But businesses did succeed with constitutional challenges in two tax cases. The Court struck down a federal tax on premiums paid to foreign insurers and a North Carolina levy on stock owned by out-of-state residents but not on stock owned by North Carolinians. The federal tax violated the Constitution's ban on taxing exports, the Court said, while the state levy improperly discriminated against interstate commerce.

The Court produced an unusually large number of important rulings in First Amendment cases, almost uniformly favoring free speech claims against government regulation. But, as Stanford law professor Kathleen Sullivan noted, the plaintiffs in the five cases were not the typical free speech advocates. "All the speakers were speakers with funds: liquor advertisers, public contractors, political parties," says Sullivan. "This was not a term for flag burners and soapbox orators."

Rather than carving out new free speech areas protected from government regulation, the rulings generally tinkered with existing First Amendment doctrine. The Rhode Island liquor case represented only a modest tightening of the existing standard for reviewing commercial speech regulation; only one justice, Thomas, wanted to go further and ban any law limiting truthful advertising to consumers.

The Court invoked its previous constitutional safeguard for "independent" political campaign expenditures to curb the effect of a federal law limiting political party contributions to candidates. The plurality in the fractured opinion said political parties could spend unlimited amounts in election campaigns if the expenditures were not "coordinated" with candidates.

In two other politically charged cases, the Court extended prior free speech protections for government employees to government contractors. In one case, the Court ruled that a government contractor cannot be terminated for refusing to make political contributions. In the other, the Court limited the government's ability to terminate a contractor for criticizing government agencies or officials. Dissenting in both cases, Justice Scalia said the decisions were aimed at the widespread practice of "rewarding one's allies ... [and] refusing to reward one's opponents"—which he called "an American political tradition at least as old as the Republic."

The Court's final First Amendment ruling was also the most complex and the most divided. The Court struck down two out of three challenged provisions of a 1992 law aimed at restricting "indecent" material on cable television. The justices upheld a provision allowing cable operators to prohibit sexually explicit programming on channels set aside for unaffiliated programmers. But they struck down a related provision that would have required cable operators that do not bar such material to place it all on one channel and block it from customers except upon request. The Court also struck down a third provision that authorized cable operators to ban indecent material on public access channels.

Beyond its immediate impact, the cable indecency ruling was significant for its clues about the Court's likely approach in another First Amendment case likely to be heard during the 1996–1997 term: a challenge to the Communications Decency Act, a new law aimed at keeping sexually explicit material off the Internet. Experts had different assessments. ACLU legal director Steven Shapiro — whose organization was representing the plaintiffs in the case — said the law could not survive the kind of careful scrutiny the Court gave to the cable act. But James Goodale, a media lawyer and cable expert, said the Court adopted a flexible standard that could be used to uphold the new law. "It does not take much imagination," he wrote in the *New York Law Journal,* "to see that any legislation regulating indecency would pass this hurdle."

The Court cheered civil rights advocates with its two high-profile decisions striking down the Colorado anti–gay rights amendment and requiring Virginia Military Institute to admit women or give up public funding. But minority groups strongly criticized the Court's continuing scrutiny of racially motivated redistricting plans.

Many observers saw in the Court's decisions a unified equal protection principle: opposition to government discrimination in any form. "The Court significantly strengthened the Equal Protection Clause," said Clint Bolick, litigation director for the conservative Institute for Justice. With other conservatives, Bolick was a longtime critic of racial redistricting. Unlike other conservatives, however, he said he also endorsed both the VMI and Colorado gay-rights decisions.

But Pamela Karlan, a liberal professor at the University of Virginia Law School and a lawyer working to defend the Texas redistricting scheme, complained that the Court's decisions reflected a changed attitude toward discrimination issues. "The Supreme Court is at the end of the road of protecting blacks," Karlan said. "Yet at the same time they're very expansive in other areas."

Karlan was the winning lawyer in the Court's only clear expansion of traditional civil rights legislation during the term: a 5–4 ruling extending the federal Voting Rights Act to state political party nominating conventions. In that case, too, racial discrimination was not the issue. The Court allowed a group of law students to use the federal act to challenge a registration fee imposed by the Virginia Republican Party on anyone who wanted to participate in the convention to nominate its candidate for the U.S. Senate.

Generally, the Court had a thin agenda on individual rights issues, and its rulings had mixed results. The Court backed an age discrimination plaintiff by ruling that he did not have to show that he was replaced by someone under forty, the age threshold for coverage under the law. But in another case it barred a plaintiff from recovering damages from a federal agency for violating the federal law prohibiting discrimination against disabled persons.

In an important privacy ruling, the Court recognized a psychotherapist privilege in federal courts. The 7–2 decision generally barred federal courts from requiring psychotherapists or other mental health professionals to testify or turn over records about their patients and clients. Most states already recognized a similar privilege.

The Court had no signed decisions during the term on one of the most divisive rights issues: abortion. Two unsigned decisions produced mixed results. In one, the Court upheld a lower court decision requiring the state of Arkansas to pay for abortions for poor women who have become pregnant because of rape or incest. But the Court also cleared the way for possible reinstatement of part of a Utah law prohibiting most late-term abortions. In a third action, the justices refused to hear an appeal by South Dakota seeking to reinstate its law requiring physicians performing abortions on teenagers to notify parents in advance of the procedures. Three justices—Rehnquist, Scalia, and Thomas—voted to hear the case; four were needed.

The states scored a significant victory with the Court's ruling protecting them from federal court suits under the Indian Gaming Regulatory Act of 1988. The ruling prompted a new round of predictions that the Court was fundamentally re-examining federalism issues with an eye toward shifting power from Washington to the states.

"The conservative revolution has come in challenging the accepted relationship between the states and federal governments," remarked the ACLU's Shapiro. "The big question is where is the Court going with all this."

But Notre Dame's Douglas Kmiec said other Court decisions—including the VMI and Colorado gay rights cases—suggested a lack of respect for states' prerogatives. "It's only standing up for states' rights at the level of philosophy," Kmiec complained. "At the level of practicality, they seem to be disregarding federalism principles."

States' rights issues cut different ways, though. The conservatives who supported the Court's ruling in the Indian gaming case also generally favored overriding the redistricting plans passed by the North Carolina and Texas legislatures. And most conservatives applauded the Court for tightening up the review of punitive damage awards from state courts.

The justices showed a mixed voting pattern themselves. In the racial redistricting rulings, the Court's liberal bloc protested that the majority was riding roughshod over state legislative prerogatives. But in the punitive damages case, liberals and moderates formed the majority. Three of the four dissenters who protested the ruling as an intrusion on state authority were conservatives: Chief Justice Rehnquist and Justices Scalia and Thomas; Ginsburg was the fourth.

Among the other state-federal issues the Court resolved was a dispute that literally occurs only once every decade: a challenge to the federal census. The Court rejected an effort by a number of cities to correct an undercounting of African Americans and other minority groups in the 1990 census. A recount could have affected apportionment in Congress and allocation of federal aid under population-based programs. But the Court unanimously ruled that the Bush administration had no obligation to use a statistical estimation method to correct the undercount.

The Court once again sided with law enforcement in most of the criminal law decisions during the 1995–1996 term, including virtually all of the major rulings. Out of twenty-five decisions involving criminal defendants or prison inmates, the Court backed the government in sixteen. Nine government victories were by 9–0 or 8–1 votes.

Michael Barnes, a veteran Indiana prosecutor who served as president of the National District Attorneys Association, said the Court's rulings were "generally helpful" for law enforcement. From the opposite perspective, Barbara Bergman, a professor at the University of New Mexico Law School who followed the Court for the National Association of Criminal Defense Lawyers, called the year "frustrating."

Law enforcement's most significant victories came in two rulings on forfeitures. The Court rejected efforts by criminal defendants to use the Double Jeopardy Clause to prevent the government from prosecuting offenders and seizing money or property in successive proceedings. The justices also narrowly rejected a claim that the Due Process Clause limits the government's power to seize property used in a crime from an "innocent owner"— someone with no responsibility for the property's illegal use.

The rulings reversed the Court's trend since its 1992–1993 term of checking the government's power as law enforcement agencies expanded their use of forfeiture to seize the assets of drug offenders in particular. But one law enforcement advocate said he saw nothing wrong in the Court's seeming change of heart.

"It was the recent forfeiture cases that had deviated from the previous precedent," said Kent Scheidegger of the California-based Criminal Justice Legal Foundation. "There's nothing sacred about the last word. You have to look at the whole stream of cases, and that's what they did."

The Court gave police an important victory by unanimously rejecting an argument that the Fourth Amendment limits their power to stop traffic violators when they are really looking for drugs. Law enforcement advocates were pleased, but defense-minded experts criticized the decision. "It gives police tremendous discretion," Bergman remarked.

In another setback for defendants, the Court overturned a lower court's order enabling a group of Los Angeles drug defendants to get information needed to show the government was singling out African Americans for prosecution in crack cocaine cases. The 8–1 ruling held that the defendants had failed to make a necessary showing that the government had failed to prosecute "similarly situated" white defendants.

The justices moved quickly to rule — favorably — on one part of a newly enacted law aimed at curbing the ability of death row inmates to use habeas corpus to challenge state court convictions in federal court. The law required federal appeals courts to screen out inmates' repeat habeas corpus petitions unless they raised significant legal issues, and it also barred the Supreme Court from reviewing those decisions.

The justices set the case for argument in a special session in early June and then unanimously upheld the so-called gatekeeper provision less than a month later. The ruling specified, however, that inmates can still file a habeas corpus petition directly with the Court. The case left unanswered a host of other questions about the new law.

In a divided ruling, the Court limited defendants' rights to jury trial for minor offenses. The Court had previously ruled that a defendant was entitled to a jury trial when charged with an offense carrying a sentence of six months or more. But this term the Court said no jury was required when a defendant was facing multiple minor charges even if they carried a total sentence of more than six months.

In an important prisoners' rights suit, the Court overturned a wide-ranging order requiring the Arizona corrections system to upgrade its prison law libraries. The ruling also made it harder for inmates in future cases to show that they have been unconstitutionally denied access to the courts.

The Court issued no rulings directly dealing with death penalty procedures in civilian courts, but it did uphold the military's capital punishment system. The unanimous ruling rejected a claim that President Ronald Reagan exceeded his powers in a 1984 executive order that prescribed a list of aggravating factors to be used in imposing capital sentences in military courts.

Several other criminal law rulings, however, involved death penalty cases. The results were mixed. The Court rejected two efforts by death row inmates to overturn convictions or sentences because of trial procedures. A Washington State inmate said prosecutors should have turned over the results of a polygraph examination given to an accomplice who was fingering him as the triggerman in a robbery-murder. A Virginia man convicted of a robbery-murder accused prosecutors of unfairly surprising him by introducing evidence linking him to a separate killing during his sentencing hearing. The Court divided 5–4 in rejecting both inmates' claims.

The justices, however, unanimously backed an Oklahoma death row inmate's challenge to a state law imposing a high standard — "clear and convincing evidence" — for defendants to prove they were mentally incompetent to stand trial. In a second unanimous ruling, the Court backed a Virginia inmate's right to challenge his murder conviction and death sentence on grounds he had been improperly denied a court-appointed psychiatrist at trial.

Along with the mental competency case, the Court's most noteworthy ruling in favor of criminal defendants was a decision limiting the power of federal appeals courts to second-guess trial judges' sentencing decisions. The ruling stemmed from the prosecution of two former Los Angeles police officers for the 1991 beating of motorist Rodney King. A federal appeals court had reversed a lower court judge's decision to give the two officers sentences well below levels specified in sentencing guidelines.

The justices unanimously ruled the appeals court had used the wrong standard in reviewing the judge's decision. Theoretically, the ruling could be used by prosecutors or defense lawyers alike, but experts agreed that defendants were the most likely to benefit from the added protection given to trial judges' sentencing decisions.

The Court strengthened defendants' ability to raise constitutional issues in two other cases. In one, the Court ruled that appeals courts, rather than deferring to a trial judge's decision, must make an independent determination whether police had adequate grounds for an investigatory stop or warrantless search. Similarly, the Court held that judges in federal habeas corpus cases must make their own determination of one of the crucial issues in *Miranda* cases — whether the defendant was "in custody" at the time of a statement later used as evidence at trial.

For the most part, though, defense lawyers had little good news during the past year, while prosecutors favorably compared the Rehnquist Court's decisions with those from previous eras. "Obviously, this Court has made decisions with regard to law enforcement that in an overall way have been helpful," Barnes said. Such a record, he noted, "was not always the case with previous Courts."

Reapportionment and Redistricting

Court Bars "Racial Gerrymanders" in Two States

Bush, Governor of Texas v. Vera, decided by a 5–4 vote, June 13, 1996; O'Connor wrote the plurality opinion; Stevens, Souter, Ginsburg, and Breyer dissented. (*See excerpts, pp. 199–224.*)

Shaw v. Hunt, Governor of North Carolina, decided by a 5–4 vote, June 13, 1996; Rehnquist wrote the opinion; Stevens, Souter, Ginsburg, and Breyer dissented. (*See excerpts, pp. 224–231.*)

For the third time in four years, the Supreme Court returned this term to the contentious issue of racial redistricting. And, once again, by a narrow majority and with sharp divisions, the justices rejected congressional districting plans aimed at electing minority representatives.

The decisions—striking down four congressional districts in two states, Texas and North Carolina—cheered the critics of racial line-drawing but drew bitter attacks from traditional civil rights groups. Legally, the rulings made clear that states faced added difficulties in justifying excessive use of race in drawing district lines. But they left unclear precisely when a racial districting plan crosses the line to become an improper racial gerrymander.

The factual settings for the two cases fit a now familiar pattern. Texas and North Carolina both redrew congressional districts after the 1990 census gave them additional seats in the House of Representatives. Under pressure from the Bush administration's Justice Department, both states crafted plans that included districts consciously drawn to include majority-minority populations.

North Carolina's Twelfth District—which had already been before the Court in its first racial redistricting ruling, *Shaw v. Reno* (1993)—snaked across half the state, tying together widely separate black urban centers by means of a narrow corridor no wider than the width of an interstate highway at times. In Texas, a new Thirtieth District started in predominantly black sections of Dallas, but had narrow tentacles reaching into two neighboring counties and jagged edges to skirt around white neighborhoods. Two interlocking districts in Houston—the Eighteenth and Twenty-Ninth—were configured by means of jigsaw-puzzle geometry to include majority black and Hispanic populations respectively.

Both states used detailed racial census information and sophisticated computer techniques to accomplish their tasks. But race was not the only reason for the districts' bizarre shapes. Each of the districts took on an added measure of irregularity in the interest of protecting the political fortunes of incumbent officeholders.

The political calculus was most complicated in Texas. In Dallas, an African-American state senator with ambitions for Congress, Eddie Bernice Johnson, initially proposed a plan for a relatively compact district with a black population of about 45 percent. But the plan was redrawn to accommodate the wishes of incumbent House members—one Republican, one Democrat, both white. The final plan added outlying black neighborhoods to the core of Johnson's original district. She won the House seat from the new district in the 1992 election.

In Houston, the redistricting plan increased from 35 percent to 50 percent the black population of the existing Eighteenth District, which had been represented since 1971 by a succession of African-American lawmakers. The new Twenty-Ninth District was drawn to embrace a majority Hispanic population. Again, the plans departed from more compact districts to accommodate white officeholders: an incumbent House Democrat who wanted to preserve some of his existing district and a white state rep-

Texas Congressional
District 18

Texas Congressional
District 29

Texas Congressional
District 30

The Supreme Court threw out three Texas congressional districts, saying they were based predominantly on race. Jackson-Lee, left, and Johnson, right, were elected from mainly black districts; Green—an Anglo—won in a predominantly Hispanic district.

resentative who planned to run in the Hispanic district and wanted parts of his political base included.

North Carolina also shaped its districts with incumbent House members' interests in mind. Legislators easily settled on a majority-black district in the state's northeastern region. But they balked at a similar majority-black district in the Southeast because some Democratic House incumbents would have been moved out of their existing districts.

The North Carolina case spawned the Court's first ruling limiting racial redistricting. By a 5–4 vote, the Court in 1993 agreed that white voters could use the Fourteenth Amendment's Equal Protection Clause to challenge the use of race in drawing legislative district lines. (*See* Supreme Court Yearbook, 1992–1993, *pp. 20–23.*) The ruling sent the case back to a three-judge federal district court to give the state a chance to justify the plan. But the Court said the plan had to satisfy the highest level of constitutional review—"strict scrutiny"—which required the government to show that it had a "compelling interest" in using race to draw the district lines and that it had "narrowly tailored" the plan to serve that interest.

The Court's ruling cleared the way for lower courts to decide not only the North Carolina case but similar challenges in other states, including

Georgia, Louisiana, and Texas. Two years later, the Court used the Georgia case to issue a second key ruling: another 5–4 decision backing a challenge by white voters to a majority-black district stretching halfway across the state. (*See* Supreme Court Yearbook, 1994–1995, *pp. 32–36.*)

Together, the two decisions established that race could not be the "predominant" consideration in drawing district lines, but they left unanswered a host of other questions—in particular, whether irregular shape was by itself a constitutional defect and whether other factors could justify racial line-drawing. The federal courts in North Carolina and Texas reached opposite conclusions on those questions. In North Carolina, the same court that had initially heard the case again approved the districting plan. The panel ruled by a 2–1 vote that the state had a compelling interest in overcoming the effects of past discrimination and in creating separate majority-black districts with rural and urban populations.

In Texas, however, a three-judge court unanimously struck down three congressional districts: the predominantly black district in Dallas and the majority-black and majority-Hispanic districts in Houston and Harris County. In the course of the opinion, the court said that a state could justify racial line-drawing only if the district had "the least possible amount of irregularity in shape, making allowances for traditional districting criteria."

The Court took up both cases for review on the final day of its 1994–1995 term and set them for argument on December 5. The arguments and questions were intense and animated, but they indicated no change of heart among the justices. The Court's more liberal justices— Stevens, Souter, Ginsburg, and Breyer—appeared sympathetic to the states' efforts to increase minority representation in Congress. Among the conservatives, Justice Scalia was the most openly critical of racial-line drawing, but Chief Justice Rehnquist and Justices O'Connor and Kennedy had skeptical questions as well. As usual, Justice Thomas asked no questions, but he had strongly opposed racial districting plans in the previous cases.

When the Court announced the decisions in the two cases on June 13, the justices' lineup remained unchanged: the five conservatives voted to strike down the challenged districts, over strong dissents from the four liberals. The Texas case produced a multiplicity of opinions that included, remarkably, two from O'Connor: the main opinion as well as a separate concurrence suggesting broader leeway in racial line-drawing than the other conservatives were willing to accept.

O'Connor began her plurality opinion in the Texas case by upholding the lower court's finding that race had been the "predominant" consideration in drawing the lines of the three challenged districts even though incumbency protection had also played a part. The evidence, she said, included the state legislators' open intention to create majority-minority districts, as well as the districts' "bizarre" shapes and the use of "unprecedentedly detailed racial data" to "manipulate" the lines.

The district lines therefore had to be reviewed under strict scrutiny, O'Connor said, and they failed to satisfy the test. O'Connor said the Court, as in previous cases, would leave open the question whether a state's interest in complying with the federal Voting Rights Act could ever amount to a "compelling" interest. She also rejected the lower court's rule that districts had to be as compact as possible. Still, a district must be "reasonably compact and regular," O'Connor continued, to be deemed "narrowly tailored" under the strict scrutiny test. And none of the three districts met that test, she said.

Because there was no current finding of "specific" and "identified" discrimination, O'Connor rejected the argument that the districts were needed to overcome racially polarized voting attributable to past racial discrimination. She also rejected the state's argument that the majority-black Houston district was justified to comply with the Voting Rights Act provision requiring Justice Department "preclearance" of any voting change that could result in a "retrogression" in the position of racial minorities. The state had gone further than necessary, she said, because the new plan had actually increased the black population in the district.

In a final section, O'Connor answered the arguments of the dissenters that the Court's rulings were resulting in excessive "judicial entanglement" in the redistricting process. The new rulings would help clarify the legal rules for state legislators, O'Connor responded, while re-emphasizing that voters are "more than racial statistics."

"Our Fourteenth Amendment jurisprudence evinces a commitment to eliminate unnecessary and excessive governmental use and enforcement of racial stereotypes," O'Connor concluded. "We decline to retreat from that commitment today."

Chief Justice Rehnquist and Justice Kennedy joined O'Connor's opinion. But in a concurring opinion Kennedy took issue with O'Connor's statement that an intentionally created majority-minority district did not necessarily require strict scrutiny. In a separate concurring opinion, Thomas, joined by Scalia, said that strict scrutiny should apply whenever a legislature "affirmatively undertakes to create a majority-minority district that would not have existed but for the express use of racial classifications."

O'Connor underscored the divisions among the conservatives with her unusual concurrence with her own opinion. A former Arizona legislator, O'Connor said state lawmakers were entitled to "more definite guidance" from the Court. She said she would explicitly decide that states have a compelling interest in complying with the Voting Rights Act and that they may intentionally draw majority-minority districts as long as the districts did not "deviate substantially" from "traditional districting principles" for "predominantly racial reasons."

In one of two dissenting opinions, Souter acknowledged O'Connor's stance, calling it "a very significant step toward alleviating apprehension" that the Court's decisions were in conflict with the Voting Rights Act. But he said the rulings still had resulted in "confusion" among state legislators and shifted redistricting issues to the courts—"and truly to this Court, which is left to superintend the drawing of every legislative district in the land."

Stevens gave greater emphasis in his dissent to the factual issues in the case. After a detailed examination of the Dallas districts, he insisted that they should not be subject to strict scrutiny because they were primarily "political gerrymanders" instead of "racial gerrymanders." The Houston district was a closer question, he said, but in any event it would be justified by the state's "compelling interest in creating majority-minority districts in accord with the Voting Rights Act."

Both dissents closed by insisting that the Court had failed to provide "manageable standards"—in Souter's phrase—while threatening the progress minority groups had made in political representation. "Nothing in the Constitution," Stevens wrote, "requires this unnecessary intrusion into the ability of States to negotiate solutions to political differences while providing long-excluded groups the opportunity to participate effectively in the democratic process." Ginsburg and Breyer joined both dissents.

The Court's opinion in the North Carolina case—written by Rehnquist, but announced by O'Connor because he was away at a judicial conference—paralleled the reasoning of the Texas case. The redistricting plan was subject to strict scrutiny because race was the predominant consideration in drawing the challenged Twelfth District, Rehnquist said, and the state could not justify the plan on grounds of eradicating past discrimination or complying with the Voting Rights Act. O'Connor, Scalia, Kennedy, and Thomas joined Rehnquist's opinion.

In his dissenting opinion, Stevens contended that the state's interest in complying with the Voting Rights Act and consolidating urban areas into a single district amounted to valid "race-neutral" justifications for the plan. Ginsburg and Breyer joined most of the dissent, while Souter merely cited his dissent in the Texas case to explain his position.

Interest groups reacted to the pair of decisions along familiar lines. Civil rights groups warned the decisions would reduce minority representation in Congress. "This decision could have the effect of reducing the Congressional Black Caucus so that it could fit in the backseat of a taxicab," said Elaine Jones, director-counsel of the NAACP Legal Defense and Educational Fund. But Abigail Thernstrom, senior fellow at the conservative Manhattan Institute, said minorities would be better represented in the long run if forced to forge biracial coalitions to get elected. "It's possible we're going to have some short-term pain," Thernstrom said, "but I think it's going to be long-term gain."

For the states themselves, the rulings posed a conundrum: whether to hold congressional elections in November under the redistricting plans that the Court struck down or to draw new maps in time for the general election. State officials indicated they wanted to stick with the existing districts, but the plaintiffs in the two cases said they wanted new maps drawn. The two lower courts made different decisions. In North Carolina, the judges allowed the use of the existing districts for the November elections. But in Texas, the court drew up a new plan that changed thirteen districts altogether, including the three that the justices had ruled invalid.

Meanwhile, the Court had already set the stage for yet another racial redistricting case in its coming term. The justices on May 20 agreed to hear an appeal by the Clinton administration and Georgia officials of a lower court's decision adopting a redistricting plan for the state with only one black majority district. *(See "Preview of 1996–1997 Term," pp. 125–141.)*

Gay Rights

States Cannot Ban Laws to Protect Homosexuals

Romer, Governor of Colorado v. Evans, decided by a 6–3 vote, May 20, 1996; Kennedy wrote the opinion; Scalia, Rehnquist, and Thomas dissented. *(See excerpts, pp. 177–188.)*

Americans were both divided and ambivalent about homosexuality as the gay rights debate intensified in the 1980s and 1990s. Gay rights advocates won passage of state and local laws to prohibit discrimination against homosexuals, but their efforts provoked a strong backlash from religious and social conservatives. Meanwhile, polls indicated that most Americans opposed discrimination against homosexuals, but that a majority also disapproved of what was sometimes termed "the homosexual lifestyle."

The ambivalence and divisions were reflected sharply in Colorado, where the state adopted an executive order prohibiting discrimination in employment against homosexuals, and three municipalities—Aspen, Boulder, and Denver—passed ordinances to protect homosexuals against discrimination in employment and public accommodations. Opponents of the measures responded with a successful statewide initiative in 1992 that repealed those laws and prohibited enactment of any future laws granting "protected status" to homosexuals except by a state constitutional amendment.

The measure, known as Amendment 2, never went into effect, however. Colorado courts ruled that the measure violated the U.S. Constitution's guarantee of equal protection of the laws. This term, the U.S. Supreme Court agreed, in a 6–3 decision that was hailed by gay rights advocates and bitterly denounced by opponents—and by the dissenting justices themselves.

Amendment 2's supporters said in their campaign that the measure

Attorney Jean Dubofsky hugs Priscilla Inkpen, one of the plaintiffs who challenged Colorado's anti–gay rights initiative, after the Supreme Court ruled the measure unconstitutional. Richard Evans, the first named plaintiff in the case, is at left.

would promote morality and prevent Colorado from becoming a mecca for homosexuals. But they also described it in narrow legal terms, saying in their campaign slogan that the amendment would give homosexuals "Equal Rights—No Special Rights." Opponents expected to defeat the measure, but it won with about 53 percent of the vote—a 100,000 vote margin.

Opponents promptly challenged the law in the Colorado courts. The suit was brought by six individuals—all gay men or lesbians, with Richard Evans, a Denver city administrator, as the first named plaintiff. The three cities with ordinances affected by the amendment joined the suit. The first named defendant was Gov. Roy Romer, a Democrat who had actually opposed the measure during the campaign.

The suit reached the Colorado Supreme Court twice. In its initial ruling—upholding a lower court judge's preliminary injunction against the amendment—the state high court said the amendment was subject to the highest constitutional review, "strict scrutiny," because it infringed homosexuals' "fundamental right" to participate equally in the political process. On remand, the state offered a variety of justifications to try to satisfy strict scrutiny, but Judge Jeffrey Bayless again ruled against the amendment. On appeal, the state supreme court reaffirmed its original ruling, by a 6–1 vote.

When the U.S. Supreme Court agreed to review the case in February, opponents worried that the justices would not accept the Colorado courts' rationale for striking down the amendment. The Colorado courts had relied on Supreme Court precedents overturning measures that sought to block laws against racial discrimination. But the Court had never ruled that homosexuals constituted a "suspect class" for purposes of the Fourteenth Amendment's Equal Protection Clause—entitling them to special protections against laws that singled them out for unequal treatment. In fact, the Court in a 1986 decision, *Bowers v. Hardwick*, had upheld state laws making homosexual conduct a crime. In addition, the Court's conservative majority was thought unlikely to uphold the creation of a new "fundamental right" of participation in the political process.

A group of five prominent legal scholars, led by Harvard's Laurence Tribe, sought to solve the opponents' problem by crafting a brief that took a different tack in arguing against the amendment. The short, thirteen-page brief called the amendment "a per se violation" of the Equal Protection Clause. "Never since the enactment of the Fourteenth Amendment," Tribe wrote, "has this Court confronted a measure quite like Amendment 2—a measure that, by its express terms, flatly excludes some of a state's people from eligibility for legal protection from a category of wrongs."

When the case was argued before the Court on October 10, centrist and liberal justices evidenced strong doubts about the constitutionality of the amendment. "I've never seen such a measure," Justice Kennedy told Colorado Solicitor General Timothy Tymkovich as he began his argument. A few minutes later, Justice Ginsburg echoed the concern: "I would like to know whether in all of United States history there has been any legislation like this."

Tymkovich appeared tongue-tied as he tried to answer a question from Justice Stevens about what "rational basis" the state had for the amendment. Twice, he said simply that the amendment represented "a political response" by opponents of the gay rights ordinances. When Stevens asked a third time, Tymkovich said only that the measure's supporters considered the gay rights ordinances "overintrusive."

In her turn, attorney Jean Dubofsky, a former Colorado Supreme Court justice representing the opponents of Amendment 2, faced critical questions from only one of the justices: Scalia. At one point, Dubofsky conceded that she was not asking the Court to overturn its 1986 antisodomy ruling. "If we've upheld a law that says a state can prohibit the conduct," Scalia shot back, "why can't a state take a step short of that?"

After the argument, Colorado Attorney General Gale Norton was noncommittal about the likely outcome, while Dubofsky said she was confident the opponents would prevail. Seven months later, she was proved right.

In a compact, fourteen-page opinion, Kennedy declared Amendment 2 to be an equal protection violation not for the reason given by the Colorado Supreme Court but on a rationale seemingly drawn from Tribe's brief. " . . . [T]he amendment imposes a special disability upon [homosexuals] alone," Kennedy wrote. "Homosexuals are forbidden the safeguards that others enjoy or may seek without constraint."

Kennedy rejected the argument that the amendment merely sought to deny "special rights" to homosexuals. "We find nothing special in the protections Amendment 2 withholds," he wrote. He added that the amendment could not satisfy even the least rigorous form of constitutional review — the so-called rational basis test. The amendment, he concluded, "seems inexplicable by anything but animus toward the class that it affects; it lacks a rational relationship to legitimate state interests."

Five justices joined Kennedy's opinion: his fellow centrist O'Connor and liberals Stevens, Souter, Ginsburg, and Breyer. None of the five wrote a separate concurring opinion — an indication the majority justices wanted the Court to speak with a single voice. But the dissenters were also to be heard from.

In a scathing dissent that he emphasized by reading from the bench, Scalia called the amendment "a modest attempt . . . to preserve traditional sexual mores against the efforts of a politically powerful minority to revise those mores through use of the laws." The amendment, he insisted, "prohibits *special treatment* of homosexuals, and nothing more." In striking it down, Scalia continued, the majority was taking sides in a culture war — he used the German word "Kulturkampf"— and wrongly accusing people of Colorado of prejudice against homosexuals.

Scalia insisted that Kennedy had no precedents to support his decision. "Today's opinion has no foundation in American constitutional law," Scalia declared, "and barely pretends to." The decision, he ended, "is an act not of judicial judgment, but of political will." Chief Justice Rehnquist and Justice Thomas joined his opinion.

Gay rights groups cheered the Court's decision. "This is a landmark civil rights ruling," said Suzanne B. Goldberg, a staff attorney with the Lambda Legal Defense Fund and co-counsel for the challengers of the amendment. Elizabeth Birth, executive director of the Human Rights Campaign, agreed. "This Supreme Court will not permit any state to attempt to pass laws making its gay residents second-class citizens," she said.

The amendment's supporters reacted with disgust. "Today is a truly chilling day for people of conscience across America," said Will Perkins, the executive board chairman of Colorado for Family Values, which sponsored the amendment. Perkins raised the possibility of launching a drive to impeach the six justices who voted to strike down the amendment.

Despite their elation at the decision, gay rights advocates said the ruling's long-term impact remained to be seen. Kennedy had avoided any need to consider whether homosexuals are entitled to any special protections against unequal treatment. In addition, Kennedy made no mention whatsoever of the *Bowers v. Hardwick* decision, even though Scalia cited it prominently in his dissent.

As a result, many legal experts questioned whether the decision would have any effect on two other gay rights issues pending in the courts: gays in the military and same-sex marriages. Still, many gay rights advocates said the ruling had a symbolic impact beyond its value as legal precedent. "I don't want to exaggerate," Morris Knight, a gay rights leader in Los Angeles, told the *New York Times*, "but I believe it's the capping of our liberation."

Sex Discrimination

Military School Must Admit Women or Lose Public Funds

United States v. Virginia, decided by a 7–1 vote, June 26, 1996; Ginsburg wrote the opinion; Scalia dissented; Thomas did not participate.*(See excerpts, pp. 252–275.)*

Virginia Military Institute and the Citadel in South Carolina, the nation's two surviving publicly supported all-male military colleges, fought pitched battles in the 1990s to defend their policies of refusing to admit women. The federal government went to court to support women who wanted to attend the schools. The schools fought back—cheered on by fiercely loyal alumni, conservatives who admired the schools' methods of inculcating military discipline, and some feminists who feared the dismantling of women's colleges.

The battle ended at the Supreme Court, which issued a landmark ruling this term ordering the Virginia school either to admit women or give up its public status. The ruling, authored by Justice Ruth Bader Ginsburg, a pioneer for women's rights before her appointment to the federal court in 1980, also appeared to tighten the constitutional standard for reviewing government actions that treat men and women differently. But Ginsburg went out of her way to allay fears that the decision meant the end of public or private colleges for women.

The Citadel made national headlines on the issue first by fighting a losing battle in federal court against a South Carolina woman, Shannon Faulkner, who then unexpectedly left the school in August 1995 only five days after she had finally been allowed to enroll. Meanwhile, the VMI case had been taking shape with somewhat less fanfare in Washington and Virginia.

Founded in 1839, VMI had a unique place in Virginia's public educational system and a prominent place in the state's business and political circles. First-year cadets, called rats, had to endure a rigorous seven-month regimen of harsh and demeaning treatment by upperclassmen. According to the school's philosophy, this "rat-line" regimen — or, in educational parlance, "adversative method"—helped instill the importance of strictly following rules and of closely bonding with fellow cadets.

Whatever the strengths or weaknesses of its educational philosophy, VMI succeeded in cementing a solid relationship between its students and alumni. VMI graduates comprised an influential network in Virginia, famously eager to help their fellow alumni. An active alumni foundation helped give VMI the largest per-student endowment of any public college in the country. And, as the school gained national attention, VMI's current corps of cadets with virtual unanimity defended the school to visiting reporters.

In 1990, however, a Virginia high school senior—never identified—challenged the VMI tradition by filing a complaint with the Bush administration's Justice Department. She claimed that the school's refusal to act on her application amounted to illegal sex discrimination. The department agreed. In March 1990, the government filed suit in U.S. District Court in Richmond, contending that VMI's all-male admissions policy violated the Fourteenth Amendment's Equal Protection Clause. The case reached the Supreme Court more than five years later after four rounds in lower federal courts ended with VMI's all-male status still intact.

In the initial trial, U.S. District Court Judge Jackson Kiser ruled that VMI's all-male admissions policy satisfied the test for permissible gender classifications set by the Supreme Court in a 1982 decision, *Mississippi University for Women v. Hogan.* The Court, in ordering the admission of men to an all-women's state nursing school, held that sex classifications could be justified only if they served "important governmental objectives" and were "substantially related to the achievement of those objectives."

Judge Kiser ruled in 1991 that VMI's men-only admissions policy did serve an important objective: achieving "single-gender diversity" within Virginia's system of public higher education. Further, he said, some aspects of VMI's "distinctive" character—physical training, absence of privacy, and the adversative method itself—would have to change if women were admitted. On that basis, he rejected the government's suit.

The Justice Department took the case to the Fourth U.S. Circuit Court of Appeals, where a three-judge panel unanimously set aside Kiser's ruling. The panel held that the all-male policy violated the Constitution. Instead of ordering immediate admission of women, however, the appeals court sent the case back to Kiser to give VMI a chance to offer an alternative remedy.

The school developed a plan: a military program for women, the Virginia Women's Institute for Leadership, to be established at a nearby private women's school, Mary Baldwin College, and to be financed in part by VMI alumni. Judge Kiser approved the plan, saying it provided women substantially equivalent educational opportunities. By a 2–1 vote, the appeals court agreed. "We should defer to a state's selection of educational techniques," the appeals court ruled, as long as the state did not have a "pernicious" goal. On a rehearing, the full appeals court also upheld the plan, by a 7–4 vote.

Virginia Military Institute Superintendent Josiah Bunting, left, and Board of Visitors Chairman William Berry meet with reporters to announce the board's narrow vote to admit women beginning in fall 1997. The Supreme Court ruled VMI's all-male admissions policy unconstitutional.

Both sides appealed to the Supreme Court. VMI asked to overturn the appeals court's first finding of a constitutional violation, while the government urged the justices to reject the Mary Baldwin program as an inadequate remedy. Deputy U.S. Solicitor General Paul Bender opened his argument on January 17 by saying that VMI's admissions policy rested on "a stereotypical view of women" as unqualified for the school's rigorous educational method. Justice Scalia, himself a graduate of an all-male military academy, jumped to VMI's defense. Admitting women, he told Bender, "would interfere with the kind of relationships" needed for VMI's educational philosophy.

But justices across the ideological spectrum—from Stevens, Souter, Ginsburg, and Breyer on the left to O'Connor and Kennedy in the center—appeared openly skeptical of VMI's defense. "What is it that is so important," Breyer asked VMI's lawyer, Theodore Olson, "that enables you to say to a young woman, 'I'm very sorry. I know you want to go there, but you can't'?"

Ginsburg's announcement of the Court's decision five months later was rich in drama and symbolism. "This case concerns an incomparable military college," Ginsburg began, reading a seven-page summary with a firm tone and measured cadence. Women sought admission to VMI because of its "unique program and unparalleled record," she continued, and it was "undisputed" that at least some women could meet the standards imposed on men. Under the Court's precedents, defenders of sex-based government action must demonstrate an "exceedingly persuasive justification." They cannot rely, she continued, on "overbroad generalizations . . . about the way that most women (or most men) are." The Mary Baldwin program was inadequate, she said. To cure the equal protection violation, Ginsburg concluded, "women seeking and fit for a VMI-quality education cannot be offered anything less."

The vote in the case was 7–1, with Justice Thomas not participating: his son, Jamal, was a fourth-year cadet at VMI. Chief Justice Rehnquist voted with the majority, but did not join Ginsburg's opinion. He said Ginsburg had altered the Court's sex discrimination precedents by overemphasizing an isolated phrase—"exceedingly persuasive justification"—used in some of those rulings. Still, Rehnquist agreed that VMI had been on notice since the 1982 ruling that something had to change. If educational diversity was the state's goal, Rehnquist said, "that diversity had to be available to women as well as to men."

Scalia wrote a scathing dissent of forty pages, slightly longer than Ginsburg's own opinion. "Today the Court shuts down an institution that has served the people of the Commonwealth of Virginia with pride and distinction for over a century and half," Scalia began. He excoriated the majority for overturning the lower courts' findings in VMI's favor, "drastically" revising the established standards in sex discrimination cases, and "inscribing" into the Constitution "the current preferences of society" with scant regard for history, tradition, or political process.

In her written opinion, Ginsburg included a footnote to say that the ruling would not completely bar single-sex education. "We do not question the state's prerogative evenhandedly to support diverse educational opportunities," she wrote, citing a brief filed by a coalition of twenty-six women's colleges.

But Scalia insisted the decision was a death-knell for all single-sex education in the country. No one would dare start a new single-sex public school in the face of the ruling, he warned. In addition, government assistance to private single-sex schools would be subject to challenge—just as state support of racially segregated schools had been barred in cases dating back to 1967.

The Court's decision provoked strong reactions on both sides. "Today's decision integrates VMI into the 20th century," rejoiced Sara Mandelbaum, a staff attorney with the American Civil Liberties Union's Women's Rights Project. At VMI, however, the school's superintendent, Josiah Bunting, called the decision "a savage disappointment." He also said that in complying with the ruling, the school would try to make only "minimum changes" in its curriculum and methods.

The reaction was more cooperative at the Citadel, VMI's counterpart in South Carolina, which announced two days after the decision that it would begin admitting women in the fall. Over the next two weeks, VMI officials remained noncommittal as alumni studied the possibility of raising the money needed to take the school private. The option faded, however, in the face of the financial requirements—about $35 million, it was estimated—and the need to win approval for the change from the Virginia General Assembly. On September 21, the school's Board of Visitors rejected by a 9–8 vote a proposal by alumni to become a private institution and then, by the same margin, voted to admit women beginning in 1997.

States

Federal Court Suits on Indian Gaming Barred

Seminole Tribe of Florida v. Florida, decided by a 5–4 vote, March 27, 1996; Rehnquist wrote the opinion; Souter, Stevens, Ginsburg, and Breyer dissented. (*See excerpts, pp. 154–167.*)

The Supreme Court gave states an important legal victory this term in a less-than-obvious setting: Indian gambling. The Court ruled that a federal law allowing Indian tribes to sue states in federal court violated the Eleventh Amendment, which limits federal courts' power to hear private suits against states.

Gambling on Indian reservations grew from community-center bingo games to become by the 1990s a multibillion-dollar business, with 200 tribes operating more than 100 casinos in 24 states. For the tribes, gambling represented an important source of revenue. But many states opposed the introduction of casino gambling within their borders.

The states' efforts to block gambling on Indian reservations reached both the Court and Congress in the 1980s. The Indian Gaming Regulatory Act, passed by Congress in 1988, stemmed from a Supreme Court decision the year before that states had no power to regulate gambling on Indian reservations. Within the intricate statute, one central provision required states to negotiate with tribes over gambling issues and gave tribes the right to sue states in federal court if the state refused.

The Seminole Tribe invoked the law in 1990 to start negotiations with Florida officials, but the talks broke off when the state refused to agree to casinos. The Seminoles then sued the state in federal court, claiming the state had failed to negotiate "in good faith" as required by law. Florida officials denied the allegation of bad faith, but they also insisted the law violated the Eleventh Amendment's limitation on suits against states in federal court. The Eleventh U.S. Circuit Court of Appeals agreed, setting the stage for the case to reach a Supreme Court that had twice within the past four years struck down congressional enactments in the name of states' rights.

In 1992, the Court ruled in *New York v. United States* that a federal law requiring states to take responsibility for nuclear wastes generated within their borders violated the Tenth Amendment. Then in 1995, the Court ruled that Congress had exceeded its power to regulate interstate commerce when it passed a law making it a federal crime to possess a gun near a school. Chief Justice Rehnquist wrote the 5–4 decision in that case, *Lopez v. United States*.

A few years earlier, the Court had upheld a federal law that, like the Indian gaming act, allowed individuals to sue states in federal court—in that case to recover the cost of cleaning up toxic wastes. But the Court had decided that 1989 case, *Union Gas Co. v. Pennsylvania*, by a single vote, and the author of the main opinion, Justice William Brennan Jr., retired in 1990. Meanwhile, the four dissenters in *Union Gas*—Rehnquist and Justices O'Connor, Scalia, and Kennedy—had gained, in Justice Thomas, a fifth likely vote on many states' rights issues.

The arguments in the Seminole case on October 11—in the second week of the Court's term—drew only limited attention, eclipsed by the arguments earlier that day in a closely watched case on punitive damages, *BMW of North America v. Gore. (See pp. 188–199.)* The tribe's lawyer, Bruce Rogow, a Fort Lauderdale attorney, began by saying that the Indian gaming law "carefully balances the interests of three sovereigns: the states, the United States, and the Indian tribes." But Assistant State Attorney General Jonathan Glogau argued the law infringed Florida's sovereignty. "The 11th

Amendment and our sovereign immunity prevents us from being held before a federal court without our consent," Glogau said. "That is the essence of sovereign immunity."

Some of the justices, including Stevens and Ginsburg, appeared in their questions to be shying away from the constitutional issue in the case. But Chief Justice Rehnquist and Justice Scalia seemed to be siding with the state's argument. And in Rogow's brief rebuttal, Justice Kennedy made clear his sympathy with the state's position. "The states are separate, autonomous sovereignties within their spheres," Kennedy said sharply. "Congress doesn't order states to do anything."

Rehnquist announced the Court's decision on March 27 in an understated style that belied the ruling's importance. After summarizing the statute, Rehnquist proceeded through two steps to reach the main issue in the case. First, Rehnquist said that Congress had made an "unmistakably clear statement of its intent to abrogate" Florida's sovereign immunity from federal court suit. Second, he concluded that Congress had no greater power to authorize suits against the states under the Indian Commerce Clause contained in Article I of the Constitution than under the Interstate Commerce Clause involved in the *Union Gas* case.

On that basis, Rehnquist said the Court had to consider whether *Union Gas* should be allowed to stand. The ruling lacked a clear majority, Rehnquist said, and the plurality's opinion "deviated sharply from our established jurisprudence" and undermined the Eleventh Amendment. "We feel bound to conclude," Rehnquist ended, "that *Union Gas* was wrongly decided and that it should be, and now is, overruled."

With that said, the rest of the decision was easy. "The Eleventh Amendment restricts the judicial power under Article III," Rehnquist explained, "and Article I cannot be used to circumvent the constitutional limitations placed upon federal jurisdiction." Nor could the tribe use the doctrine of a 1908 case, *Ex Parte Young*, to sue the state's governor to enforce the duty to negotiate because that was only part of the "intricate remedial scheme" set out in the law. O'Connor, Scalia, Kennedy, and Thomas joined Rehnquist's opinion.

In contrast to Rehnquist's low-key opinion, Souter's dissent was a forceful—and massive—dissertation on what he insisted was a persistent misinterpretation of the Eleventh Amendment and state sovereign immunity. The opinion ran to ninety-two pages, and Souter read a lengthy summary from the bench. The Court's decision, he began, marked the first ruling ever "that Congress has no authority to subject a State to the jurisdiction of a federal court at the behest of an individual asserting a federal right."

Souter reviewed the history of the Eleventh Amendment at length, insisting that it did nothing more than bar federal court suits against a state brought by a citizen of another state. The Court had made a mistake by extending the amendment in an 1890 decision, *Hans v. Louisiana,* to bar a federal court suit brought against a state by its own citizen, Souter said. Even so, he continued, the Court had never decided that Congress lacked the power to explicitly provide for citizen suits against a state in federal court. And the idea of state sovereign immunity that the majority found in the Constitution, he said, actually conflicted with the Framers' scheme of popular sovereignty and federal supremacy.

From that perspective, Souter concluded that the Indian gaming law's provision for federal court suits was within Congress's power. Alternatively, he said that the tribe could bring suit against the state's governor individually in federal court.

Ginsburg and Breyer joined Souter's opinion. Stevens endorsed Souter's position in a separate, shorter dissent that warned against the broader implications of the Court's decision.

The effect of the ruling, Stevens said, would not be limited to "the rather curious statutory scheme" contained in the Indian gaming law. "Rather, it prevents Congress from providing a federal forum for a broad range of actions against States," covering everything from copyright and patent law to bankruptcy, environmental law, and economic regulations.

As Stevens suggested, the Court's decision provoked reactions that went beyond the issue of tribal casinos. The ruling did not prevent federal courts from hearing suits against state officials under civil rights laws, which were justified under the post-Civil War Fourteenth Amendment. But some experts agreed that the ruling would give states a powerful weapon in other areas. "It's saying that there are some principles in the Constitution that can't be enforced in a meaningful way against states," said Michael Gerhardt, a constitutional law professor at the College of William and Mary.

States' attorneys, however, praised the decision as a weapon against congressional overreaching and judicial intrusion. The ruling "frees the states to be accountable to their own people for deciding what is a fair scheme, rather than being accountable to the courts," John Knorr, Pennsylvania's chief deputy attorney general, told the *New York Times* a few days after the ruling.

In Florida, meanwhile, the Seminoles and the state remained at loggerheads. But the Interior Department moved to take up the issue by asking for comment, in the light of the Court's decision, on its own authority to prescribe regulations for gambling on tribal lands. Rogow said the result could be to allow tribes to "bypass" the state altogether. But Glogau said Florida and some twenty other states had written letters urging the Interior Department to take no action and to leave it to Congress to rewrite the law.

In the meantime, Glogau said, the state continued to oppose casino gambling on Seminole reservations. "The people of the state of Florida three times have voted overwhelmingly against casino gambling," Glogau emphasized. The Seminoles "live in Florida," he continued, "and the federal act recognizes that the public policies and the gambling laws of the states have to be considered."

Torts

$2 Million Punitive Damage Award Called "Excessive"

BMW of North America, Inc. v. Gore, decided by a 5–4 vote, May 20, 1996; Stevens wrote the opinion; Scalia, Rehnquist, Ginsburg, and Thomas dissented. *(See excerpts, pp. 188–199.)*

Opponents of large punitive damage awards tried repeatedly through the 1980s and 1990s to get the Supreme Court to set constitutional limits on the practice. They won some procedural protections, but until this term the Court had never actually overturned a jury's punitive damage award.

Business and insurance groups thought they had their best chance ever in the case of a well-to-do Alabama doctor who won a whopping $2 million punitive damage award for a flawed paint job on a newly purchased BMW automobile. By a 5–4 vote, the Court agreed, overturning the penalty in a ruling that set new guidelines for courts to use in reviewing the size of punitive damage awards.

The story began when Ira Gore Jr., a Birmingham physician, paid $40,750.08 for a new BMW sedan in January 1990. Nine months later, when he took the car to a shop for some detailing, Gore was surprised to discover that the car had not been in mint condition when he bought it. Leonard Slick, the shop's owner, told Gore the car had been repainted after it left the factory. Over time, Slick said, the finish would deteriorate and the car's resale value would be reduced.

The cause of the damage to the original paint job was never established, but people in the automobile industry insisted it was common— and proper—to repaint cars that suffered incidental damage in transit from factory to showroom floor. Gore, however, felt "cheated and misled," as he testified later. So he filed a fraud suit against the German auto manufacturer in an Alabama state court, asking for $4,000 in compensatory damages—10 percent of the original purchase price—along with an unspecified amount in punitive damages.

BMW insisted it had done nothing wrong. The company had what it regarded as a sensible and lawful policy: it did not disclose damage to a new car if it could be corrected for less than 3 percent of the suggested retail price. The car would simply be retouched and sold as new. Damages above the 3 percent threshold would also be corrected, but the car would be sold as used. BMW said its policy conformed with laws in many states, including Alabama, that required manufacturers and dealers to disclose defects above the 3 percent threshold.

At trial, Gore's attorney, Andrew Bolt, of Anniston, Alabama, presented evidence that BMW had delivered over a ten-year period at least 983 cars nationwide, including fourteen in Alabama, that had been refinished at a cost of at least $300 without disclosure. The jury was convinced. It awarded Gore $4,000 in compensatory damages and—after multiplying that figure by 1,000—imposed a punitive damage award of $4 million.

The Alabama Supreme Court cut the punitive damage award in half, agreeing with BMW that the jury's use of a multiplier had been improper. But BMW took the case to the Supreme Court, insisting that the reduced $2 million award was so excessive as to amount to a violation of the Fourteenth Amendment's Due Process Clause.

The justices had reviewed Alabama's civil justice system once before. In 1991, the Court had upheld a $1 million punitive damage award in an Alabama case, *Pacific Mutual Life Insurance Co. v. Haslip*. The ruling stressed that juries have broad discretion in setting punitive damages. Only Justice O'Connor dissented. In two later rulings, the Court gave tort reform advocates modest victories. A fractured decision in 1993 established the limited principle that punitive damage awards must be "reasonable." Then, in 1994, the Court ruled in an Oregon case, *Honda Motor Co. v. Oberg*, that states must provide some form of review of jury awards, either at the trial or appellate level.

To present its case to the Court, BMW selected Andrew Frey, a well-known Supreme Court advocate who had argued the winning side in the Honda case. Frey told the justices that the Alabama jury had no right to consider out-of-state sales in assessing the penalty against BMW. "Alabama cannot project its law outside Alabama," he said. And the state supreme court had not cured the jury's mistake, he insisted, by merely cutting the penalty in half.

Michael Gottesman, a Georgetown University law professor representing Gore, agreed with Frey that the Alabama jury could not punish out-of-state violations, but insisted that the panel did have a right to consider the "quality and nature" of BMW's conduct in fixing the penalty. And he said the punitive damage award accomplished its purpose: BMW changed its policy within a week to require disclosure of any repairs performed on new cars after leaving the factory.

In their questions, the justices seemed divided and uncertain. Scalia and Ginsburg both appeared to question the Court's power to review jury awards in state cases, while Stevens and Kennedy both agreed with BMW's claim that it was being unfairly punished for sales beyond Alabama. Most significantly, Justice Breyer, sitting in his first major punitive damages case, cheered tort reform advocates with a suggestion that large awards should be viewed with skepticism in cases involving minimal harm.

Seven months later, the Court sided with BMW, with Stevens writing for a five-justice majority and Breyer providing a supportive concurrence.

Lawyer Andrew Bolt poses with the repainted BMW sedan purchased by Dr. Ira Gore Jr. that led to a big punitive damage award against the manufacturer. The Supreme Court overturned the award, ruling it was "grossly excessive."

Stevens began by accepting BMW's argument to limit the reach of state jury power over nationwide business practices. A state can impose "economic penalties"—whether as "legislatively authorized fines or judicially imposed punitive damages"—only in the interest of "protecting its own consumers and its own economy," Stevens declared.

Reviewing the award in that light, Stevens said the penalty against BMW was "grossly excessive." He laid out three reasons: the relatively low "reprehensibility" of BMW's nondisclosure; the "disparity" between the award and the actual harm to Gore; and the difference between the award and the civil penalties imposed in similar cases. He concluded with a warning against punishing big companies just because of their size. "The fact that BMW is a large corporation rather than an impecunious individual does not diminish its entitlement to fair notice," he wrote.

O'Connor, Kennedy, Souter, and Breyer joined Stevens's opinion. In a twelve-page concurrence, Breyer also faulted Alabama courts for their handling of punitive damage cases. The state courts had failed to enforce any standards to "significantly constrain . . . a jury's discretion" in fixing awards, Breyer said. O'Connor and Souter joined his opinion.

In separate dissents, Scalia, joined by Thomas, and Ginsburg, joined by Rehnquist, said the decision improperly intruded on states' prerogatives.

The decision, Ginsburg wrote, "unnecessarily and unwisely ventures into territory traditionally within the States' domain." Scalia also scoffed at the guidelines in Stevens's opinion, saying that they provided "virtually no guidance . . . as to what a 'constitutionally proper' level of punitive damages might be."

Business groups reacted to the ruling with glee. "This is the victory business has been waiting for," Stephen Bokat, general counsel of the U.S. Chamber of Commerce, proclaimed. Victor Schwartz, a Washington lawyer and longtime tort reform advocate, said he believed the ruling would lead to more careful review of jury awards by state court judges and in federal courts.

Trial lawyers and consumer groups voiced mixed reactions to their seeming defeat. Arthur H. Bryant, head of the Washington-based Trial Lawyers for Public Justice, called the decision "a sad ruling for justice." But the Association of Trial Lawyers of America, the biggest plaintiffs' attorneys' group, put a more favorable spin on the decision. The group's president, New York attorney Pamela Anagnos Liapakis, maintained that the ruling had "affirmed the role of juries" and "repudiated a one-size-fits-all standard" in punitive damage cases.

As for Gore, the Court sent his case back to the Alabama Supreme Court for it to decide whether to set a new award itself or let the trial court do so. And over the next few weeks, the Court signaled that it was not declaring open season on overturning punitive damage awards. More than a dozen punitive damage cases had been put on hold pending the decision in the BMW case. Tort reform advocates wanted the cases sent back for reconsideration in light of the BMW ruling. But to their disappointment, the Court ordered new proceedings in only six of the cases—including three others from Alabama—and left the rest standing.

Telecommunications

Court Edits Law to Limit "Indecency" on Cable

Denver Area Educational Telecommunications Consortium, Inc. v. Federal Communications Commission, decided by 7–2, 6–3, and 5–4 votes; June 28, 1996; Breyer wrote the main opinion; Kennedy and Ginsburg dissented from one part of the decision; Thomas, Rehnquist, and Scalia dissented from two parts of the decision, joined by O'Connor on one part. (*See excerpts, pp. 275–292.*)

Cable television subscribers who stayed up late in New York City had more to choose from than sports, movies, or shopping channels. On Channel 35, they could watch "Midnight Blue," a program offering a raunchy menu of sexually explicit film clips and lurid advertisements for telephone sex and escort services.

Around the country, some public cable channels also presented occasional R-rated material: movies with nude scenes or educational programs
discussing safe sex. Cable's ability to offer programs like these, unavailable
on commercial television networks, was welcomed by some viewers and producers. But many other people wanted to get the off-color fare off cable.

The critics of cable indecency included Jesse Helms, the conservative
Republican senator from North Carolina, who managed to get a three-part
provision dealing with the problem attached to a cable regulation bill enacted in 1992. Coalitions of cable programmers promptly brought a First
Amendment challenge to the law. This term the Supreme Court struck
down the two major parts of the indecency provision but left the third section intact.

For several reasons, the indecency case presented some exceedingly
difficult legal issues. The law itself was complex. The interests at stake—
involving cable operators, programmers, and viewers—were also complex
and diverse. Finally, neither Congress nor the Court had settled on the regulatory framework for a medium that had grown in forty years from an
adjunct of broadcasting to a pervasive presence in nearly two-thirds of the
nation's television homes.

Congress first tried to come to terms with cable in 1984, when it passed
a law freeing local cable operators from rate regulation and most local government controls. But the law also contained two access provisions tailored
to a unique aspect of the cable industry: cable operators controlled the
physical network used to distribute programs, but they did not control the
programming offered on the various channels carried on the system.

To try to promote greater programming diversity, one provision in the
1984 law—the "leased access" channel provision—required most cable systems to set aside a specified percentage of their channels for lease by "unaffiliated" cable programmers, networks with no financial ties to the cable system itself. A second provision ratified the right of local governments to
require cable systems to provide channels for "public, educational, and governmental" use—so-called "PEG" channels.

The leased access provision proved to have relatively little effect in
most markets, though a few programmers used the law to gain slots on
cable systems, notably in New York City. Meanwhile, the public access provisions helped spawn local public affairs channels, carrying local government proceedings and the like, and some public channels, featuring mostly talking-heads programs with rudimentary production values.

Sex was also available on cable. Subscribers had to pay to get premi-
um networks like the Playboy Channel. But the leased access and public
channels had to be available to all subscribers. Subscribers who did not
want that kind of stuff on their TV screens sometimes complained to cable
operators, who told their customers they had no right to bleep out the
offending material.

Helms offered his proposal to control cable indecency directly on the Senate floor without prior hearings. Briefly, the amendment gave cable operators the *option* to block out sexually explicit programming on leased access channels or on public access channels. A third provision of the law *required* cable operators that did not bar indecent material on the leased access channels to place such programming on a single channel and to block that channel from general viewer access. Subscribers could get access to the blocked channel only by making a request in writing.

The court challenge to the law was brought by the Denver Area Educational Telecommunications Consortium, which produced programming for leased-access cable channels on topics such as gay rights, AIDS, and art censorship, and the Alliance for Community Media, a coalition of public access cable producers. Initially, a three-judge panel of the U.S. Court of Appeals for the District of Columbia agreed that the provisions violated the First Amendment. But the full court decided to rehear the case and then voted 7–4 to sustain the provisions.

The arguments before the Supreme Court on February 21 were as complex as the law itself. Michael Greenberger, the Washington lawyer who represented the cable programmers, said that the law violated the First Amendment by extending government regulation to cable channels that historically had been free of editorial control by the government or the cable operator. But Justice Breyer suggested the cable operators' interests had to be considered, too. "I find this very difficult because there are First Amendment rights on both sides," Breyer said.

Still, most of the questions reflected doubts about the law. Justice O'Connor said the law amounted to an effort by the government "to eliminate certain types of protected speech." And Justice Ginsburg criticized the effect of the "segregate and block" provision requiring subscribers to make a written request to see sexually explicit programming on leased channels. The law put the customer, Ginsburg said, "in the uncomfortable position of having to identify herself to the cable operator."

When Breyer announced the decision on June 28, Court watchers had to use a scorecard to keep the rulings and the justices' votes straight. The justices held the public access provision unconstitutional by a 5–4 vote and overturned the "segregate and block" provision by a 6–3 vote. But by a 7–2 vote, the Court upheld the provision allowing cable operators to prohibit sexually explicit programming on leased channels.

Breyer began his opinion by accepting the government's interest in dealing with what he called "an extraordinarily important problem"— "protecting children from exposure to patently offensive depictions of sex." And the government, he said, may regulate speech to address "extraordinary problems" if the regulations are "appropriately tailored to resolve those problems without imposing an unnecessarily great restriction on speech."

By that standard, Breyer said, a "permissive" provision giving cable operators the right to control sexually explicit programming on leased channels was an appropriate way to accommodate their interests along with the interests underlying the access requirement. But he cautioned that the indecency provision should not be interpreted to apply to programming of "scientific or educational value," but only to seriously offensive material.

Breyer said that the blocking requirement was unconstitutional because the government had less restrictive ways of accomplishing its goal. The government, he explained, could have required cable operators to provide customers with a "lockbox" that they could use to block out specific channels or programs. He also noted that Congress had just passed a law requiring manufacturers to make TV sets with a "V-chip" that could automatically identify and block sexually explicit or violent programs. With those alternatives available, Breyer said, the mandatory blocking provision was "considerably more extensive than necessary" and therefore unconstitutional.

Finally, Breyer said the public access channel provision was unconstitutional because historically these channels had been controlled by community-based organizations rather than cable operators. Giving cable operators control would "radically change present programming relationships," he warned. In addition, the government had failed to show a need for the regulation. Congress and the Federal Communications Commission had only limited evidence—a few "borderline examples"—of questionable material on the public channels, he said.

Breyer deliberately left one issue unsettled. In its earliest cable decisions, the Court had ruled that cable could be regulated just like broadcasting. But in 1994, the Court had suggested that cable should have the broader First Amendment protection recognized for newspapers and other print media. Breyer, who joined the Court later that year, now said it was not possible to adopt "a rigid single standard, good for now and for all future media and purposes."

Only two justices, Stevens and Souter, joined all of Breyer's opinion. O'Connor joined most of it, but voted to uphold the provision giving cable operators the right to prohibit sexual material on public channels.

The other five justices split into two camps: Kennedy and Ginsburg voted to overturn all three parts of the law, while Rehnquist, Scalia, and Thomas voted to uphold all three.

In his opinion, Kennedy, joined by Ginsburg, said that Breyer's opinion was "adrift" because it failed to settle on a rationale for regulating cable. He characterized the leased and public access channels as congressionally created "public forums," where any government regulation was subject to "strict scrutiny," the most stringent constitutional standard. "It contravenes the First Amendment," Kennedy concluded, "to give Government a general license to single out some categories for lesser protection."

Thomas, joined by Rehnquist and Scalia, also faulted Breyer for failing to adopt a clear approach on regulating cable. But, unlike Kennedy, Thomas viewed the indecency law as a permissible provision aimed mainly at protecting First Amendment rights of cable operators to control programming on their systems. The provisions, Thomas said, "merely restore part of the editorial discretion an operator would have absent government regulation." But, apart from Breyer or Kennedy, Thomas said the mandatory blocking provision was a "narrowly tailored" provision to help parents control children's access to sexually explicit material.

The fractured ruling gave both sides the chance to cheer. "It's a sweeping victory for legitimate First Amendment expression," Greenberger told reporters. But Cathleen Cleaver, an attorney with the conservative Family Research Council who filed a brief defending the law, said she was "relatively pleased" because the decision gave cable operators "the right to screen pornographic programs."

Academic experts promptly began speculating about the decision's potential impact on the next indecency case: the First Amendment challenge to the newly enacted Communications Decency Act regulating indecent material on the Internet. A three-judge federal court ruled the measure unconstitutional; the law provided that an appeal would go directly to the Supreme Court. Some experts said the opinion helped opponents of the law, but others said Breyer's ad hoc approach to regulating new technologies could be used to uphold the measure.

In the short term, the practical impact of the ruling might be slight. "It's hard to predict," said Daniel Brenner, a lawyer with the National Cable Television Association, which urged the Court to uphold the law. "Operators can still leave [sexually explicit programming] on. It's possible that nothing will change in New York."

Campaign Finance

Court Backs "Independent" Spending by Parties

Colorado Republican Federal Campaign Committee v. Federal Election Commission, decided by a 7–2 vote, June 26, 1996; Breyer wrote a plurality opinion; Stevens and Ginsburg dissented. *(See excerpts, pp. 241–252.)*

Colorado Republicans had not yet chosen their candidate for the U.S. Senate in the spring of 1986 when they started their attack on the expected Democratic candidate, Rep. Tim Wirth. The state's party spent $15,000 on radio ads contrasting Wirth's election-year pronouncements with what was depicted as an inconsistent voting record in Congress.

Wirth went on to win the election in November. Meanwhile, however, the Colorado Democratic Party complained to the Federal Election Commission (FEC) that the state GOP's pre-primary spending put the party in violation of federal limits on political party contributions to congressional candidates. When the FEC agreed, the Republicans took the case to the Supreme Court, contending that political parties have a First Amendment right to spend unlimited amounts in support of candidates for the House or the Senate.

In a splintered end-of-term ruling, the Court gave the Republicans a partial victory and, in the process, created a new hole in the federal law regulating campaign spending and contributions. Four of the justices voted to strike down all limits on political party spending in congressional races. But three others joined in rejecting the FEC's stance on a narrower ground. They ruled that parties can spend unlimited amounts in congressional campaigns as long as the expenditures are completely independent of the candidates' own campaigns.

The division on the Court harked back to its first major ruling on the Federal Election Campaign Act, a law originally passed in 1971 and strengthened in 1974 in the wake of campaign funding abuses in the Watergate scandals. The law required disclosure of campaign contributions and spending by congressional and presidential candidates. It also limited the amount that candidates could spend or that individuals, political action committees (PACs), or parties could contribute to federal candidates. In addition, the act created a system of public financing for presidential candidates.

In 1976, the Court issued a long and complex decision that struck down the campaign spending limits as a violation of candidates' First Amendment rights but upheld the contribution limits as a reasonable means of combating political corruption. The ruling in *Buckley v. Valeo* also allowed any individual to make unlimited "independent" expenditures on a federal campaign. Finally, the decision upheld public campaign financing for presidential candidates and said that any candidate who accepted public funds could be bound by the spending limits set in the law.

The Court's decision left campaign finance reformers with half a loaf. With no expenditure limits, spending in congressional races continued to climb over the next two decades. The ruling also allowed wealthy candidates to spend huge sums on their own campaigns, while others had to raise money from individuals subject to the limit of $1,000 per race. Reformers in the 1980s and 1990s tried to get Congress to revise the law, but their efforts ended in partisan stalemate between Democratic plans to impose spending limits and Republican counterproposals to limit PAC contributions.

The limits on political parties' contributions to candidates formed a minor part of the debates. Party officials, supported by some academic critics of campaign finance laws, urged that the limits—which were set according to a state's population and adjusted periodically for inflation—be

Colorado representative Tim Wirth, left, campaigns in 1986 for the seat of retiring senator Gary Hart, center. A Republican campaign spot against Wirth led to an important Supreme Court ruling on campaign finance laws.

raised or eliminated altogether. They contended that political party contributions had no corrupting effects on candidates. Relaxing the limits, they said, would strengthen party discipline and accountability. Supporters countered that the limits helped contain overall spending and prevented well-to-do donors from using party committees to funnel large contributions to candidates.

In Colorado, the limit on party contributions for the 1986 Senate race was $103,000. But the state GOP had "assigned" its spending to the national party. On that basis, the FEC contended that the $15,000 the state GOP spent on its first round of radio spots amounted to a violation of the law. Initially, a federal district court in Washington rejected the FEC's complaint, narrowly ruling that the law did not cover the ads because they were not "in connection with" the general election campaign. The federal appeals court in Washington, however, disagreed, saying the spending amounted to "electioneering" covered by the law. The appeals court also rejected the party's First Amendment attack on the contribution limits.

When the case was argued before the Supreme Court on April 15, Solicitor General Drew S. Days III drew skeptical questions from several justices when he defended the contribution limits as a means of preventing corruption. "It's called party discipline," Justice Scalia said. "I have never considered it corruption." But some justices suggested the Court might decide the case on a narrow ground without completely eliminating the party contribution limits.

The justices' opinions two months later confirmed both suggestions. In the plurality opinion, Justice Breyer took the narrow approach. After detailing evidence that the state party chairman had approved the early media campaign without any consultation with any of the contenders for the senatorial nomination, Breyer concluded the spending was an "independent expenditure" constitutionally protected under the Court's precedents.

"The independent expression of a political party's views is 'core' First Amendment activity," Breyer wrote. "We are not aware," he added, "of any special dangers of corruption associated with political parties that tip the constitutional balance in a different direction."

Breyer insisted there was no need to decide the constitutionality of limiting party spending that was "coordinated" with a candidate's campaign. The issue, he said, was "complex" and needed further argument in lower courts before the Supreme Court could decide it. Justices O'Connor and Souter joined Breyer's opinion.

In separate concurring opinions, Justices Kennedy and Thomas both argued that the Court should decide the constitutional issue and strike down the party contribution limits. Kennedy argued that limiting any party expenditures — either independent or coordinated — "has a stifling effect on the ability of the party to do what it exists to do." Chief Justice Rehnquist and Justice Scalia joined his opinion.

Justice Thomas went further and called for abolishing all limits on political donations. ". . . [C]ontribution limits infringe as directly and as seriously upon freedom of political expression and association as do expenditure limits," he wrote. Rehnquist and Scalia joined other parts of Thomas's opinion, but not that section. And Breyer responded stiffly to Thomas's call for scrapping the Court's precedents. ". . . [G]iven the important competing interests involved in campaign finance issues," Breyer wrote, "we should proceed cautiously."

Only two justices — Stevens and Ginsburg — voted to uphold the contribution limits as the FEC had interpreted them to apply to any party spending in congressional races. In a three-page dissent, Stevens maintained that the contribution limits helped prevent "the appearance and the reality" of political corruption. He said the provision supplemented the law's other limits on donations by individuals and PACs and served the goal of "leveling the electoral playing field by constraining the costs of federal campaigns."

Supporters of campaign finance controls called the decision narrow and unlikely to lead to widespread new spending by parties. "Parties operate as a kind of joint venture with their own candidates," said Donald Simon, executive vice president of the lobbying group Common Cause. "The notion that a party is going to be able to engage in spending completely independent of the candidate doesn't comport with the common sense notion of how parties work."

But Jan Baran, the Washington election-law attorney who represented the Colorado Republicans before the Court, disagreed. "Representatives of both parties have indicated that they will exercise their right to engage in independent advertising to promote the parties' own views about their candidates and the candidates of opposing parties," he said.

The Court's decision had no impact on the presidential campaign finance system. The ruling returned the case to the Tenth U.S. Circuit Court of Appeals, where Baran said the Colorado GOP would again urge that the party contribution limits be struck down completely. "I don't think that anyone can read the opinions of the seven justices and read it that they are enthusiastic about spending limits," Baran insisted.

Commercial Speech

States Cannot Ban Liquor Price Advertising

44 Liquormart, Inc. v. Rhode Island, decided by a 9–0 vote, May 13, 1996; Stevens wrote the main opinion. *(See excerpts, pp. 167–176.)*

The newspaper advertisement that a discount liquor store in suburban Providence, Rhode Island, placed in newspapers in December 1991 had no earmarks of a First Amendment test case in the making. The ad listed the store's low prices for peanuts, potato chips, and mixers and, as an additional come-on, blazoned the single word "WOW" next to pictures of bottles of rum and vodka.

A rival liquor store, however, viewed the ad as a violation of a Rhode Island law that prohibited liquor stores from advertising prices. The state's liquor control administrator agreed and levied a $400 fine on the store, 44 Liquormart. After paying the fine, the store's owner, Shirley Santoro, decided to make a federal case out of the issue. And the Supreme Court, in a decision strengthening protection of commercial speech rights, agreed that the Rhode Island law violated the First Amendment.

Along with her father, John Haronian, who owned two liquor stores across the border in New Bedford and Fairhaven, Massachusetts, Santoro challenged the law in a suit filed in U.S. District Court in Providence in 1992. Haronian's stores advertised their prices in Massachusetts media, but Rhode Island's price advertising ban extended to any media within the state.

Rhode Island defended the law, passed in 1956, on the ground that, by preventing price competition among liquor stores, it helped raise liquor prices and thereby discouraged excessive consumption. A trade association of liquor stores intervened on the state's side, saying that invalidating the law would force them into "the advertising arena."

The lawyer for the liquor stores, Evan Lawson of Boston, who took on the case after other lawyers said the suit was a loser, decided to confront the state's defense head-on. He presented evidence from expert witnesses and a 1985 study by the Federal Trade Commission that advertising has little impact on alcohol consumption or abuse. Rhode Island actually ranked in the upper 30 percent of states in per capita alcohol consumption, the evidence showed.

Judge Raymond Pinette was persuaded. He ruled in August 1993 that the law was unconstitutional, saying it did not "directly advance" the state's asserted interest and was "more extensive than necessary to serve that interest." But a year later, the First U.S. Circuit Court of Appeals overturned his decision. The three-judge panel agreed with the state that banning price advertising would help keep prices high and consumption low. In addition, the court agreed that the Twenty-first Amendment, which repealed Prohibition, gave the state added leeway in regulating liquor.

At the Supreme Court, Lawson confronted an ambiguous line of cases dealing with commercial speech. The Court first extended constitutional protection to advertising in a pair of cases in 1975 and 1976 that struck down state laws limiting ads about abortion services and price advertising by pharmacists. Then in 1980, the Court crafted a four-part test to determine the constitutionality of laws regulating commercial speech.

The so-called *Central Hudson* test—named after the 1980 case—asked first whether the advertising concerned a lawful product or service and was not misleading. If so, the regulation could be upheld only if it served a substantial governmental interest, directly advanced that interest, and was no more extensive than necessary to promote the government's goal. Justices who favored stronger protection for commercial speech opposed the test, and through the 1980s the Court seemed to relax it further. In one notable case—*Posadas de Puerto Rico Associates v. Tourism Co. of Puerto Rico*—the Court in 1985 applied the test loosely to uphold a Puerto Rico law limiting advertising by casinos.

Lawson also faced two Court precedents that directly backed state control over the liquor industry. In 1982, the Court had summarily affirmed a lower court decision upholding an Ohio law banning price advertising of liquor by the drink. Even though the justices had not heard arguments in the case, the ruling counted as a binding legal precedent. In addition, the Court in 1972 had accepted the argument that the Twenty-first Amendment gave states extra power to regulate alcoholic beverages; the decision had upheld a ban on nude dancing in bars.

When the Court heard arguments in the case on November 1, several of the justices questioned Lawson's insistence that the law did not help keep liquor consumption down. "Isn't there a certain latitude allowed to the states to indulge a common-sense presumption?" Chief Justice Rehnquist asked. But some of the justices also questioned the motivation behind the law. "Would the constitutional analysis change if the real motivation were to protect small retailers" from price competition? Stevens asked.

The Court's decision six months later was simultaneously unanimous and divided. All of the justices agreed that Rhode Island's law was unconstitutional, but they split three ways in their reasoning. In the main opinion, Stevens put some additional spine into the *Central Hudson* test by saying that courts must give a "rigorous review" to laws prohibiting "truthful" commercial speech and should not uphold them if less restrictive alternatives are available. In this case, Stevens said, the state could try to discourage alcohol consumption by imposing a tax or by enacting minimum price laws—both less restrictive than banning price advertising.

In that passage, Stevens specifically rejected a critical part of the *Posadas* decision. The Court there had said that if a state can ban a product or service, it can also take the "less restrictive" step of banning advertising about it. " . . . [B]anning speech," Stevens rejoined, "may sometimes prove more intrusive than banning conduct." Stevens also rejected the state's Twenty-first Amendment argument. That provision, he said, could not overcome the free speech protections of the First Amendment.

Although all the justices agreed on the Twenty-first Amendment issue, only two—Kennedy and Ginsburg—joined all of Stevens's opinion. Thomas, in a lone concurrence, went further than Stevens. He said the government should never be allowed to ban truthful advertising in order to promote social policies. " . . . [A]ll attempts to dissuade legal choices by citizens by keeping them ignorant are impermissible," Thomas wrote.

Four other justices took a narrower approach, saying that Rhode Island's justification for the law could not satisfy the "less stringent standard" for commercial speech established in *Central Hudson*. Like Stevens, O'Connor noted that Rhode Island had less restrictive options. She noted minimum prices or sales taxes as well as limiting purchase amounts or conducting educational campaigns about alcohol abuse. On that basis, she concluded, the price-advertising ban "clearly fails to pass muster" without any "new analysis" for future commercial speech cases. Rehnquist, Souter, and Breyer joined her opinion.

Scalia joined none of the opinions, but confessed in a lone concurrence to ambivalence about the issues. He said he agreed with Stevens's "aversion

Craig Power, manager of a Providence, Rhode Island, liquor store, stands in front of a sign carrying newly added price information the day after the Supreme Court struck down a state law banning liquor price advertising.

toward paternalistic governmental policies" and with Thomas's "discomfort" with the ad hoc nature of the *Central Hudson* test. But he voiced his own discomfort in applying the First Amendment outside the area of political speech. For the time being, he concluded, he would accept the *Central Hudson* test, which, he agreed, Rhode Island's law could not satisfy.

Despite the multiplicity of opinions, First Amendment experts viewed the decision as a potential blow to government regulation of other forms of advertising—most prominently, tobacco advertising. But the Food and Drug Administration quickly insisted that proposed regulations to restrict marketing of cigarettes to young people would pass muster. "Kids can't legally buy cigarettes," an FDA spokesman told the *Wall Street Journal.* "The rules are aimed at preventing temptations for them to buy cigarettes."

The Court itself followed its ruling by sending back to lower federal courts a pair of commercial speech challenges to local ordinances in Baltimore, Maryland, limiting alcohol and tobacco billboards. In a separate case, the Court also told the federal appeals court in Philadelphia to reconsider a decision upholding Pennsylvania's ban on liquor price advertising.

In Rhode Island, Santoro celebrated the victory by adding price information the next day to the billboard outside her store. A few months later, Lawson said other Rhode Island liquor dealers were following her lead.

"Advertising is now rampant," the attorney said. "And I'm told that prices are dropping."

Forfeitures

Government Backed on Seizing Offenders' Assets

Bennis v. Michigan, decided by a 5–4 vote, March 4, 1996; Rehnquist wrote the opinion; Stevens, Kennedy, Souter, and Breyer dissented. *(See excerpts, pp. 145–154.)*

United States v. Ursery, decided by an 8–1 vote, June 24, 1996; Rehnquist wrote the opinion; Stevens dissented in part. *(See excerpts, pp. 231–241.)*

Tina Bennis had reason enough to be upset when Detroit police arrested her husband John in 1988 for having oral sex with a prostitute in the front seat of the family car. But the Wayne County prosecutor's office had one more unpleasant surprise for her. It seized the automobile, over her protests that she was a co-owner and evidently innocent of her husband's offense.

This term the Supreme Court upheld the seizure, rejecting Tina Bennis's argument that the Constitution limits the government's power to seize property from an "innocent owner." The decision marked a turnaround from the Court's recent trend of establishing constitutional safeguards in forfeiture cases.

Two months later, the Court gave prosecutors further help in going after criminals' money and property. In a pair of drug cases, the Court rejected lower court rulings that prosecutors were violating double jeopardy principles by prosecuting offenders and seizing their assets in successive actions.

The Bennises' car was one of the first to be seized under a policy adopted by Detroit police in 1988 to crack down on inner-city prostitution. Over a period of seven years, the office seized more than 9,000 cars from hapless johns. "I believe it is the only program that has been effective" in dealing with prostitution, prosecutor John O'Hair told ABC News.

Prosecutors filed motions under a "public nuisance" statute to have the Bennis car forfeited after John Bennis was convicted of gross indecency. Tina Bennis insisted she had no knowledge that her husband was going to use the car—a 1977 Pontiac recently purchased for $600—for a late-night dalliance. But Judge Michael Talbot rejected her defense, noting that the family had another car, and he refused to order the county to give Bennis half the proceeds from any sale. "There's practically nothing left minus costs in a situation like this," he said.

On appeal, the Michigan Court of Appeals reversed the decision, saying that state supreme court precedent prevented the state from "abating" Mrs. Bennis's interest in the car without proof that she knew the car would be put to improper use. But the Michigan Supreme Court took up the case and said, to the contrary, that Bennis's "innocent owner" defense was not required by state law or by the federal Constitution.

When the U.S. Supreme Court agreed to review the case, many observers and experts anticipated a ruling against the government given the Court's recent rulings in forfeiture cases. In a 1993 case, *Austin v. United States*, the Court had ruled that offenders could challenge forfeitures under the Eighth Amendment's prohibition against "excessive fines." A year later, the Court held that property owners are ordinarily entitled to notice and a hearing before seizure of assets in a civil forfeiture.

The arguments before the Court on November 29 reinforced the expectations. "Why should a person who is totally innocent be punished by having to give up their property?" Justice Breyer asked Larry Roberts, the assistant Wayne County prosecutor arguing the case.

Assistant Solicitor General Richard Seamon, arguing for the Clinton administration, which joined in urging the justices to uphold the forfeiture, fielded similar questions to the Court. "What was [Tina Bennis] supposed to do?" Justice Ginsburg asked the government lawyer. "She had no power over [her husband]. She can say anything she wants, and it won't do any good."

But the Court defied expectations with its March 4 decision. Writing for a five-justice majority, Chief Justice Rehnquist harked to precedents dating to the early nineteenth century permitting the government to seize property used for criminal purposes. The earliest case, Rehnquist said, was an 1827 decision permitting the seizure of a pirate ship. From that case on, he said, quoting a 1974 decision, "the innocence of the owner has almost uniformly been rejected as a defense."

Rehnquist said the government's interest in deterrence argued against requiring proof that an owner knew property was to be put to illegal use. As to the fairness of the procedure, he noted that the Michigan Supreme Court had expressly stated that trial judges had discretion to soften the impact of any forfeiture order.

Four justices—O'Connor, Scalia, Thomas, and, surprisingly, Ginsburg—joined Rehnquist's opinion. In a four-page concurring opinion, Thomas warned that forfeiture could be "improperly used" as a "roulette wheel . . . to raise revenue from innocent but hapless owners." But it was up to the states and "the political branches of the federal government" to prevent such abuses, he said.

Ginsburg wrote a briefer concurrence. She stressed that the car "belonged to John Bennis as much as it did to Tina Bennis." It was "uncontested" that Michigan could seize the automobile, she continued. The only issue was whether Tina Bennis was entitled to half the proceeds—likely to be an inconsequential sum, as the trial judge pointed out.

Michigan "has not embarked on an experiment to punish innocent third parties," Ginsburg ended. "Michigan has decided to deter Johns from using cars they own (or co-own) to contribute to neighborhood blight, and that abatement endeavor hardly warrants this Court's disapprobation."

Stevens opened his dissenting opinion by conjuring up the various places where prostitutes have practiced their trade—from "palaces," "luxury hotels," and "cruise ships" to "college dormitories," "truck stops," and "back seats." Not until 1988, he said, had any state tried to confiscate property based on "a single transaction with a prostitute."

" ... [E]lementary notions of fairness," Stevens continued, "require some attention to the impact of a seizure on the rights of innocent parties." Justices Souter and Breyer joined Stevens's opinion.

In a shorter dissent, Kennedy said the Court's earliest cases supporting seizure of pirate ships should not be extended to automobiles—"a practical necessity in modern life for so many people." The government's interest in preventing criminal use of property, he said, could be sufficiently met by "a strong presumption" that an owner was guilty of either "negligent entrustment or criminal complicity." But without such a finding, Kennedy concluded, a forfeiture would not satisfy due process.

Only six weeks later, the Court convened again on a forfeiture issue. This time, the question was whether the government's practice of bringing criminal prosecutions and civil forfeiture actions in drug cases violated the constitutional ban on multiple punishments in the Fifth Amendment's Double Jeopardy Clause.

The Court consolidated two cases that raised the issue. In one, a Michigan man, Guy Jerome Ursery, had been arrested by state police after a search found 142 marijuana plants growing outside his house. The federal government initiated a forfeiture action to seize his house and property; Ursery settled the case by paying $13,250. In the meantime, he was also indicted and then convicted for growing marijuana and given a sixty-three-month sentence. On appeal, however, the Sixth U.S. Circuit Court of Appeals agreed with his claim that the government's decision to prosecute him after the forfeiture action amounted to double jeopardy.

In the second case, two California men—Charles Wesley Arlt and James Wren—were indicted on drug trafficking and money-laundering offenses; the government commenced a forfeiture action five days later, seeking the return of $405,089.23 in cash along with various property that included automobiles and one airplane. The government held up the forfeiture case until after the men were both convicted and given lengthy prison sentences. At that point, Arlt and Wren claimed that the forfeitures violated double jeopardy. The Ninth U.S. Circuit Court of Appeals agreed.

The Court's decision to review the two issues cheered prosecutors, who feared the appeals courts' decisions would hamper forfeiture actions unless overturned. But the arguments before the justices on April 17 were mixed. Justices Souter and Breyer both questioned the argument by Deputy Solicitor General Michael Dreeben that forfeiture did not amount to punishment for double jeopardy purposes. Chief Justice Rehnquist and Justice Scalia appeared sympathetic to the government's arguments, but other justices appeared hard to read.

Two months later, however, the justices were nearly unanimous in upholding the law enforcement practice. The appeals courts, Rehnquist explained in the Court's opinion, had misinterpreted the Court's precedents in *Austin* and other cases to mean that forfeiture always amounted to punishment for double jeopardy purposes. " . . . [C]ivil forfeiture has not historically been regarded as punishment, as we have understood that term under the Double Jeopardy Clause," Rehnquist wrote.

The correct approach, Rehnquist said, was to examine the particular forfeiture to determine whether it was "so punitive" that it amounted to a criminal procedure. As for the drug forfeiture statutes in these cases, Rehnquist continued, Congress had "specifically structured [them] to be impersonal by targeting the property itself." And it did not matter, he concluded, that the forfeitures also had "certain punitive aspects" because they also served "important nonpunitive goals" of encouraging property owners to prevent their property from being used for illegal purposes.

Five justices—O'Connor, Kennedy, Souter, Breyer, and Ginsburg—joined Rehnquist's opinion, but Kennedy appeared to condition his agreement somewhat. "Forfeiture . . . punishes an owner by taking property involved in a crime . . . ," Kennedy wrote in a concurring opinion. "But the forfeiture is not a second *in personam* [personal] punishment for the offense, which is all the Double Jeopardy Clause prohibits." In a separate opinion, Scalia, joined by Thomas, said he agreed with the result on the basis of his previously stated view that the Double Jeopardy Clause applies only to multiple prosecutions, not to multiple punishments.

Stevens dissented alone, but even he found no objections to most of the forfeitures. He said, however, that the seizure of Ursery's house was clearly punitive because it went beyond the established practice of using forfeiture to take contraband or the proceeds of crimes. And he complained that the Court's ruling, combined with the Bennis decision, amounted to "dismantling the protections it so recently erected" in forfeiture cases.

Prosecutors welcomed the Court's rulings as well as its apparent change of heart about forfeitures. "We think we can now proceed with some degree of expectation that these kinds of actions will be viewed favorably," commented Michael Barnes, an Indiana prosecutor and president of the National District Attorneys Association.

A leading defense expert, however, questioned the importance of the rulings. David Smith, a criminal defense lawyer in Alexandria, Virginia, said that most recent forfeiture statutes included an innocent owner defense provision. As for the double jeopardy issue, he said that even if prosecutors had lost, they could have easily circumvented an unfavorable ruling—for example, by trying the criminal and forfeiture cases together.

Meanwhile, in Detroit, prosecutor Larry Roberts said the policy of seizing cars from prostitutes' clients had spread from Detroit to other jurisdictions in Wayne County. "The suburbs are now doing it too," Roberts said. "They can attempt to eradicate the problem, or they can move it [to another city]. But they pick up the cars. And these individuals call within the hour and want their cars back."

3

Case Summaries

A once-in-a-century snowstorm hit Washington in January, burying the city under a foot-and-a-half of snow and virtually shutting down the federal government. But at the Supreme Court, it was business (almost) as usual.

As the blizzard struck on Friday, January 5—three days before the Court was to return from a four-week recess—Chief Justice Rehnquist conferred with administrators about what to do. After verifying that the lawyers in the three cases to be heard on Monday were already in Washington and that the other justices had no objections, Rehnquist decided the show would go on.

The decision provoked grumbling among the Court's staff. The Court itself was short one member. With airports closed, Justice Stevens was stranded in Florida, where he lived when the Court was not in session. And Justice Souter, who saw plenty of snow in his native New Hampshire, arrived on the bench six minutes late. He gamely set out in his own car, got stuck, and had to be rescued by Court police.

Court police brought in most of the other justices too—except for Ginsburg and Breyer, who made it on their own. But the courtroom was virtually empty. "This is as lonely as it has been in a long, long time," Carter Phillips, who argued the first case, told the *Washington Post*'s Joan Biskupic afterward.

Still, Rehnquist, a Wisconsin native and a stickler for schedules, offered no comment about the weather from the bench. And the Court's only accommodation to the blizzard was to move one case scheduled for Tuesday, January 9, to the next week. The California lawyer who was to argue the case could not fly in.

Rehnquist's determination to stay on schedule might suggest that the Court's workload was so pressing that the justices simply could not afford a postponement. But the Court's argument schedule had slots to spare, and the justices' opinion-writing was relatively leisurely. In fact, the Court was on its way to producing the fewest signed opinions in more than four decades.

The Court ended its 1995–1996 term with only seventy-five signed opinions, the lowest number since the justices issued sixty-five signed opinions in the 1953–1954 term. The number was below the previous year's total of eighty-two and was only half what it was at the start of Rehnquist's tenure as chief justice. The Court issued 145 signed opinions during the 1986–1987 term. The number had fallen each year since. *(See Figure 3-1.)*

The output was even below what the Court itself apparently considered a comfortable workload. In testimony before a congressional committee on the Court's budget, Justice Kennedy described a figure of 100 signed opinions as "optimal." But the 1995–1996 term was the third in a row short of that mark.

Even the Court's total caseload was shrinking. The number of cases on the docket at the end of the 1995–1996 term stood at 7,565—a 6.6 percent decrease from the 8,100 cases on the docket a year earlier. *(See Figure 3-1.)* The drop stemmed mainly from a decrease in indigent petitions—so-called *in forma pauperis* or IFP cases. The number of new IFP cases filed during the year fell to 4,500 from 4,858, a 7.4 percent decrease. The number of new "paid cases" filed during the year fell only slightly to 2,095 from 2,138.

Observers continued to puzzle over the Court's shrinking number of decisions. By now, the suggested explanations were familiar: legislation giving the Court more control over its docket, a deliberate decision by the justices to lower the Court's profile, closer ideological alignment with lower court judges, tactical maneuvering by the justices themselves to vote against taking up cases that one or the other ideological blocs feared losing.

Court watchers said the reduced workload was not necessarily producing better crafted opinions. "I don't see any more clarity or unanimity in their decisions," commented Theodore Olson, a partner in the Washington law office of Gibson, Dunn & Crutcher who had a 2–1 record in the three cases he argued before the Court during the term. "They had opinions all over the lot in the campaign finance case. They had opinions all over the lot in the cable indecency case. They're still relying a lot on three-part tests and balancing. So I don't know that it is producing clearer and more forceful opinions."

The selection of cases was also something of a puzzle. More than a few of the disputes were numbingly technical. Even the justices took note that some decisions were of limited interest at best. "I know that was scintillating," Justice Thomas remarked one day in June as he finished announcing the first in a series of three decisions. "Wait till you hear the next one," Rehnquist interjected.

Meanwhile, the Court was, as always, leaving many interesting and important issues on the judicial equivalent of the cutting-room floor, to the disappointment of interest groups variously on the right or the left. The Court spurned a parents' rights challenge to distribution of condoms in high schools. It turned back an effort by religious groups to allow the use of a cross on a city government seal. The justices disappointed advocates of campaign finance limits by leaving in place a federal appeals court ruling striking down a tough $100 limit on campaign contributions. But the Court also refused a First Amendment plea to strike down a campaign finance regulation that barred municipal bond firms from contributing to candidates for local offices.

Figure 3-1   Supreme Court Caseload, 1960 Term–1995 Term

Total cases on docket

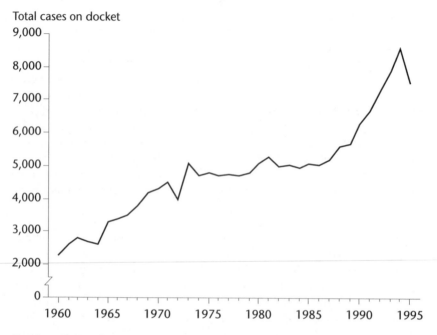

Number of signed opinions of the Court

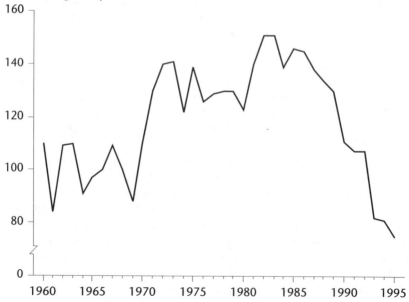

The Court gives no official explanation of its refusal to hear a case, and the action supposedly says nothing about the Court's approval or disapproval of the lower court ruling. Occasionally, however, one or more justices issue a dissenting or explanatory statement. Rehnquist, Scalia, and Thomas, for example, complained about the refusal to take up the city-seal case. They said the lower court's decision made it too easy for private citizens to bring church-state issues into court. The same trio also criticized the refusal to review a federal appeals court decision striking down South Dakota's law requiring parental notification before a teenager can have an abortion.

In a surprise move, the Court declined on the final day of the term to hear an appeal of a controversial affirmative action ruling by the federal appeals court in New Orleans. The ruling barred public colleges and universities from giving any consideration to race in their admissions policies. The Court had been thought certain to take up the case since the ruling—in a case brought against the University of Texas Law School—flatly contradicted the Court's landmark 1978 decision in *University of California Regents v. Bakke*. There, the Court had said that colleges and universities could use race as a factor in admissions policies as long as they did not set rigid quotas.

The state of Texas, civil rights groups, and the Clinton administration had all urged the justices to hear the case. As usual, the Court gave no reasons for its action. But in a brief "opinion respecting the denial of the petition for a writ of certiorari," Justice Ginsburg, joined by Justice Souter, said that the case did not present a good opportunity for deciding the issue. The law school had discontinued the admissions policy that had been challenged in the case, Ginsburg explained. "Accordingly," she wrote, "we must await a final judgment on a program genuinely in controversy before addressing the important question raised in this petition."

The justices actually did a bit more work than the low number of signed opinions indicated. Two closely watched, high-impact cases fell by the wayside after the justices heard arguments.

One of those cases—argued on the first of the Court's snow-days in January—raised the question whether federal copyright law extends to command menus in copyright software. Stevens had recused himself from the case, and the remaining justices were divided 4–4. So a week later the Court issued a one-sentence opinion saying that the lower court's opinion, which limited copyright protection, was "affirmed by an equally divided vote."

In the other case, the Court heard arguments in December on an effort by local telephone companies to overturn a federal law banning them from providing cable television service in the same area. While the case was under advisement, Congress repealed the provision as part of a broad overhaul of telecommunications law. Once the law was signed, the

Figure 3-2   Vote Divisions on Cases Decided in 1995–1996 Supreme Court Term

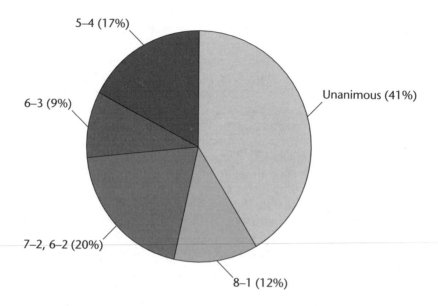

Court issued a one-sentence opinion sending the case back to a federal appeals court to determine whether it was moot.

The Court also issued six other unsigned, *per curiam* opinions on a summary basis—without hearing arguments. Typically, the Court reserves this procedure for cases where lower court rulings clearly conflict with established precedent. For that reason, *per curiam* opinions are usually unanimous. This term, however, three of the six were by divided votes, including two decided by 5–4 margins.

The degree of division among the justices was comparable to recent years. Out of seventy-five signed opinions, the Court was unanimous in thirty-one, or 41 percent, the same percentage as in the previous year. The number of 5–4 decisions was slightly lower—thirteen (17 percent) compared with seventeen (20 percent) in the previous year. Of the remaining decisions, nine were with one dissenting vote, fifteen with two dissenting votes, and seven with three dissenting votes. *(See Figure 3-2.)*

Following are summaries of the seventy-five signed opinions and eight *per curiam* opinions issued during the 1995–1996 term. They are organized by subject matter: business law, courts and procedure, criminal law and procedure, election law, environmental law, federal government, First Amendment, individual rights, labor law, states, and torts.

Business Law

Banking

Bank One Chicago, N.A. v. Midwest Bank & Trust Co., decided by a 9–0 vote, January 17, 1996; Ginsburg wrote the opinion.

Federal courts have jurisdiction over damage suits filed by one bank against another bank over dishonored checks.

The ruling involved a provision of a 1987 law, the Expedited Funds Availability Act, aimed at speeding up the check-clearing process. The act authorized federal courts to hear suits by customers against banks for failing to comply with its provisions. But the federal appeals court in Chicago interpreted a second section regarding liability in disputes between two banks as barring federal court jurisdiction.

In a unanimous decision, the Court disagreed. Ginsburg said that both of the law's liability sections "permit recovery of damages caused by a regulated party's failure to comply with the Act."

Barnett Bank of Marion County, N.A. v. Nelson, Florida Insurance Commissioner, decided by a 9–0 vote, March 26, 1996; Breyer wrote the opinion.

National banks may sell insurance from small-town branches despite state laws to the contrary.

The ruling was based on a 1916 federal law codified as section 92 of the Banking Code, which authorizes any national bank in a town with a population under 5,000 to "act as the agent for any fire, life, or other insurance company." The Florida insurance commissioner invoked a state law prohibiting banks from selling insurance to block the Barnett Bank from selling insurance in its branch office in the small town of Belleview. Two lower federal courts said the state law superseded the federal act because of a different federal law, the McCarran-Ferguson Act, which generally protects state regulation of insurance matters.

In a unanimous decision, the Court disagreed, saying the federal statute pre-empts any conflicting state law. Breyer said the 1916 act "explicitly grants" national banks power to sell insurance and "contains no indication that Congress intended to subject that power to local restriction." In addition, Breyer said the McCarran-Ferguson Act did not apply because it permits Congress to override state law if the federal statute "specifically relates to insurance." Concluding, Breyer wrote, ". . .[A] statute permitting banks to sell insurance can specifically relate to banks and to insurance."

Smiley v. Citibank (South Dakota), N.A., decided by a 9–0 vote, June 3, 1996; Scalia wrote the opinion.

National banks may impose late payment charges and other fees according to the law of their home state even if the charges violate laws in the customer's state.

The unanimous ruling rejected a class action suit brought by a California woman over late payment fees incurred on two credit cards issued by Citibank, a national bank that located its credit operations in South Dakota. The plaintiff, Barbara Smiley, said the fees violated California law. Citibank responded that the fees constituted interest that, under the National Bank Act of 1864, could be set according to the law of its home state. Two California courts agreed and dismissed Smiley's suit.

The Court agreed, but based its decision on a new federal banking regulation issued after the California courts' decisions. The rule, issued by the Comptroller of the Currency in February, defined "interest" under the law to include late fees and several other charges. Scalia said the regulation was entitled to deference because it was "obviously" a "reasonable" interpretation of an "ambiguous term" in the act.

Bankruptcy

Citizens Bank of Maryland v. Strumpf, decided by a 9–0 vote, October 31, 1995; Scalia wrote the opinion.

Banks or other creditors may temporarily withhold payment of money owed to a debtor in bankruptcy without violating the automatic stay provisions of federal bankruptcy law.

The ruling set aside a contempt finding against a Maryland bank that placed an "administrative hold" on the account of a depositor who filed for bankruptcy after defaulting on a $5,000 loan to the bank. The bank said it wanted to use the account as a "setoff" against the loan. The federal bankruptcy code generally bars creditors from taking any action to collect debts except through federal court.

Writing for the unanimous Court, Scalia said the bank's action did not amount to an improper setoff. The bank "refused to pay its debt, not permanently and absolutely, but only while it sought relief [under the bankruptcy law] from the automatic stay," he wrote.

Field v. Mans, decided by a 7–2 vote, November 28, 1995; Souter wrote the opinion; Breyer and Scalia dissented.

The Court relaxed the legal standard for creditors to collect money owed them by individuals in bankruptcy who have been guilty of false pretenses in connection with the debt.

The 7–2 decision construed a provision of the bankruptcy code — section 523(a)(2)(A) — that a debt cannot be discharged in bankruptcy if it results from "false pretenses, a false representation, or actual fraud." A New Hampshire couple who sold property to a developer who later filed for bankruptcy protection sought to use the law to enforce a $187,500 promissory note. The bankruptcy court judge agreed the developer had been guilty of fraud, but refused to apply the law because the couple had not "reasonably" relied on the misrepresentation.

Writing for the Court, Souter said the judge applied the wrong standard. He said creditors can use the law to enforce a debt if they "justifiably" rely on the misrepresentation. The federal statute did not specify a standard, Souter said, but the "less demanding" requirement was the prevailing rule at common law and in most states.

The decision returned the case to bankruptcy court for a ruling under the new standard. In a limited dissent, Breyer, joined by Scalia, disagreed with the need to remand the case. He suggested that the creditors were pursuing an "impossible dream" of recovering their money.

Things Remembered, Inc. v. Petrarca, decided by a 9–0 vote, December 5, 1995; Thomas wrote the opinion.

The Court limited appellate review of lower court decisions on whether individual lawsuits should be heard in state courts or as part of federal bankruptcy proceedings.

The unanimous decision held that federal appeals courts cannot review a lower court's decision to return to a state court a dispute originally filed in the state court and then "removed" to federal bankruptcy proceedings. Thomas based the ruling on a broad reading of the general federal "removal" statute that prohibits appellate review of "any order remanding a case to the State court from which it was removed."

The ruling backed a commercial property owner's effort to have a back-rent action heard in Ohio state court instead of in federal bankruptcy court. The company that filed the bankruptcy proceeding brought the dispute into federal court, but the property owner won a lower court ruling that the company had acted too late.

United States v. Noland, decided by a 9–0 vote, May 13, 1996; Souter wrote the opinion.

The Bankruptcy Code provision giving Internal Revenue Service claims priority over claims by other creditors cannot be altered by federal courts on general grounds of equity.

The decision, reversing rulings by three lower federal courts, stemmed from the bankruptcy liquidation of an Ohio trucking company, First Truck Lines. The IRS filed claims for taxes, interest, and penalties for unpaid Social Security and unemployment withholding taxes. The bankruptcy court judge gave the IRS priority in collecting taxes and interest, but invoked the doctrine of "equitable subordination" to put the claim for tax penalties below claims of other creditors. The district court judge and the Sixth U.S. Circuit Court of Appeals affirmed the ruling.

In a unanimous opinion, Souter said the lower courts had no authority to make a "categorical" change in the scheme of priorities Congress had established in the Bankruptcy Code.

United States v. Reorganized CF&I Fabricators of Utah, Inc., decided by 9–0 and 8–1 votes, June 20, 1996; Souter wrote the opinion; Thomas dissented in part.

A bankruptcy court was wrong to give low priority to the federal government's claim against a Utah company for an unpaid penalty for failing to make required contributions to employee pension plans. But the Court also rejected the government's argument that the penalty was entitled to high priority as an excise tax.

The ruling came in the case of a Utah manufacturing concern that filed for bankruptcy reorganization largely because of its inability to fund its employee pension plans. The government filed a claim in bankruptcy court for what it called a $1.24 million "tax" imposed by the Employee Retirement Income Security Act (ERISA) for failure to make pension plan contributions. The bankruptcy judge held the penalty was not a tax and then subordinated the government's claim below all other unsecured creditors.

The Court agreed, 8–1, that the ERISA provision was a penalty rather than an "excise tax" for purposes of the bankruptcy law. But it ruled unanimously that the bankruptcy judge had overstepped his authority in ranking the government's claim below those of other creditors. Souter cited the Court's earlier ruling in another bankruptcy case, *United States v. Noland*, limiting bankruptcy judges' power to reorder the priority of claims established by Congress. *(See above.)*

The decision sent the case back to lower courts. In a partial dissent, Thomas said the ERISA provision did amount to an excise tax, and the government's claim was entitled to priority over other creditors.

Copyright

Lotus Development Corp. v. Borland International, Inc., decided by a 4–4 vote, January 16, 1996; *per curiam* (unsigned) opinion; Stevens did not participate.

The Court deadlocked in a closely watched case testing the extent of federal copyright protection for computer software.

The justices divided 4–4 on a bid by Lotus Development Corp. to reinstate a $100–million-plus damage suit against a competitor, Borland International, Inc., for using the command menu of its popular spreadsheet Lotus 1–2–3 software in Borland's rival products.

Although computer programs may be copyrighted, the federal appeals court in Boston had ruled that a command menu—the words displayed on a computer screen to operate a program—cannot be copyrighted. In asking the Court to overturn the decision, Lotus said the ruling would hamper the development of new programs. But attorneys for Borland, backed by briefs from a variety of computer user groups, said copyright protection for command menus would allow the creator of new software to monopolize the market.

The deadlock resulted from Stevens's decision to recuse himself from the case. Stevens gave no reason for not participating. The Court does not announce individual justices' votes in a tie case. Observers who attended the argument said Rehnquist, O'Connor, and Scalia appeared to favor Lotus's side in the case, while Souter, Ginsburg, and Breyer appeared to favor Borland's position.

Maritime Law

Exxon Co., U.S.A. v. Sofec, Inc., decided by a 9–0 vote, June 10, 1996; Thomas wrote the opinion.

The owner of an oil tanker that sank because of navigation errors by the vessel's captain was held completely responsible for the loss despite negligence by the operators of a mooring facility to which the tanker had been tied.

The ruling resolved the issue of how to apply two doctrines from tort law—proximate cause and comparative fault—in a maritime accident. In any damages action, a defendant may be held liable only if its negligent conduct is the "proximate cause" of an injury. Under the comparative fault doctrine, however, damages can be apportioned among several defendants—or between the plaintiff and any defendants—if each of them was guilty of negligence that proximately caused the injury.

The issue arose in the loss of an Exxon tanker after it broke away from a mooring facility off the coast of Hawaii and ran aground on a reef. A federal district court judge ruled the captain's navigational errors were the proximate cause of the accident and refused to apply the doctrine of comparative fault to consider the responsibility of the manufacturers and operators of the mooring facility.

In a unanimous opinion, the Court upheld the ruling. Thomas said the captain's negligence was "the superseding cause" of the accident and cut off any liability for the operators of the mooring facility.

Yamaha Motor Corporation, U.S.A. v. Calhoun, decided by a 9–0 vote, January 9, 1996; Ginsburg wrote the opinion.

State remedies, not federal law, apply in fatal maritime accidents unless the victim is a seaman, longshore worker, or someone engaged in a maritime trade.

The ruling cleared the way for trial of a suit by the parents of a 12–year-old girl killed in a jet ski accident in 1989. The parents brought the suit under Pennsylvania's wrongful-death statute, which provides greater damages than federal maritime law. The manufacturer of the jet ski argued that federal law governed the case, but the Third U.S. Circuit Court of Appeals rejected the argument.

In a unanimous decision, the Court agreed that the parents could sue under Pennsylvania rather than federal law. Ginsburg explained that even though the Court in 1970 recognized a wrongful-death action under federal maritime law, the ruling did not "displace" state law remedies.

The decision did not affect maritime and longshore workers, who are covered under separate federal laws that set stricter standards for liability.

Patents

Markman v. Westview Instruments, Inc., decided by a 9–0 vote, April 23, 1996; Souter wrote the opinion.

Judges, not juries, have exclusive responsibility for construing the terms of a patent claim—the part of a patent that defines the scope of the patentholder's rights.

The decision, significantly narrowing the role of juries in patent cases, came in an infringement claim brought by a Pennsylvania man, Herbert Markman, who held a patent for a dry-cleaning inventory control system. Markman won a jury verdict against the maker of a similar system, Westview Instruments, Inc. But the judge rejected the finding on the ground that Westview's system did not perform the same inventory control functions described in the "claim" in Markman's patent.

Markman then appealed, saying the judge's ruling violated his right to a jury trial under the Seventh Amendment. That amendment provides that "[i]n suits at common law . . . the right of trial by jury shall be preserved. . . ." The Court of Appeals for the Federal Circuit, which hears all patent appeals, rejected his argument and upheld the lower court decision.

In a unanimous ruling, the Court held that the Seventh Amendment does not require a jury finding on the meaning of a patent claim and that judges are "better suited" to perform that role. Souter said the Seventh Amendment did not apply because the legal proceeding for defining a patent claim did not exist when the Constitution was adopted. He then concluded that assigning the responsibility to judges would yield more accurate and more uniform rulings. "The construction of written instruments is one of those things that judges often do and are likely to do better than jurors," Souter wrote.

The ruling was seen as a setback for patentholders because juries, as in Markman's case, may take a broader view of a patent's meaning than do judges. Under the ruling, juries still have responsibility for deciding whether an infringement has occurred, but experts said that in many cases the construction of the patent claim will be the decisive issue.

Taxation

Commissioner of Internal Revenue v. Lundy, decided by a 7–2 vote, January 17, 1996; O'Connor wrote the opinion; Thomas and Stevens dissented.

The Court set a two-year time limit for a taxpayer who fails to file a return and then later seeks a refund in Tax Court.

The ruling came in the case of a Virginia man who failed to file his 1987 tax return and then sought a refund in December 1990 after receiving an erroneous notice from the Internal Revenue Service that he owed money. The Tax Court said the Tax Code allowed a refund only for taxes paid within two years of the date on which his 1987 taxes were due—April 15, 1988. But the Fourth U.S. Circuit Court of Appeals cited a different provision to rule that the so-called "look-back period" was three years.

In a densely statutory ruling, the Court ruled that the correct look-back period for a taxpayer who failed to file a return was two years. O'Connor acknowledged that the taxpayer might be entitled to a longer three-year period if he filed for a refund in federal district court. But she said the problem was for Congress, not the courts, to solve.

Thomas, joined by Stevens, dissented, arguing that the result was a "strange scheme" that Congress probably did not intend to create.

United States v. International Business Machines Corp., decided by a 6–2 vote, June 10, 1996; Thomas wrote the opinion; Kennedy and Ginsburg dissented; Stevens did not participate.

A federal tax on insurance premiums paid to foreign insurers for shipment of exported goods violates the Constitution's ban on taxing exports.

The ruling supported IBM's attempt to get a $1.5 million refund for taxes levied from 1975 through 1984 on premiums paid to foreign insurers for goods shipped to foreign subsidiaries. Congress passed the tax provision in 1942 to eliminate the advantage foreign insurers have from not being subject to federal income tax.

IBM claimed the tax violated the Constitution's Export Clause, which provides, "No Tax or Duty shall be laid on Articles exported from any State." The Federal Court of Claims agreed, rejecting the government's attempt to circumvent a 1915 decision by the Supreme Court using the Export Clause to strike down a similar tax.

In a 6–2 decision, the Court also adhered to the earlier ruling. "A tax on policies insuring exports is not, precisely speaking, the same as a tax on exports," Thomas wrote, "but [the previous decision] held that they were functionally the same under the Export Clause." Thomas said it would be "inappropriate" to re-examine the precedent. He also rejected arguments that the levy was valid because it was a nondiscriminatory tax imposed on all premiums to foreign insurers, not just on insurance for exports.

In a dissent, Kennedy, joined by Ginsburg, argued the tax was valid because it "taxes a service distinct from the actual export of goods, and does not function as a proxy for taking their value."

Courts and Procedure

Abstention

Quackenbush, California Insurance Commissioner v. Allstate Insurance Co., decided by a 9–0 vote, June 3, 1996; O'Connor wrote the opinion.

The abstention doctrine, which permits federal courts to refrain from deciding certain cases to avoid conflict with state judiciaries, cannot be invoked to dismiss a suit for damages.

The ruling sent back to lower federal court a contract dispute originally brought in California state court by the state's insurance commissioner against Allstate Insurance Co. over reinsurance agreements with a defunct insurer. Allstate removed the case to federal court, but the district court judge dismissed the suit under the abstention doctrine and remanded the case to state court. The Ninth U.S. Circuit Court of Appeals reversed the decision, saying the abstention doctrine could be used only in cases seeking equitable or discretionary relief, not in damage suits.

In a unanimous decision, the Court agreed. ". . . [F]ederal courts have the power to dismiss or remand cases based on abstention principles only where the relief sought is equitable or otherwise discretionary," O'Connor wrote. But she left open the possibility that the judge could stay the federal court suit pending state court resolution of any state law issues.

Appeals

Behrens v. Pelletier, decided by a 7–2 vote, February 21, 1996; Scalia wrote the opinion; Breyer and Stevens dissented.

A government official named as a defendant in a federal civil rights suit may be allowed two pretrial appeals on a claim that he is entitled to qualified immunity from the suit.

The ruling stemmed from a suit against a federal regulatory official by a former savings and loan officer who claimed he lost his job because of an unfavorable evaluation by the official. The official moved to dismiss the suit on grounds of qualified immunity, but the motion was denied by the federal district court judge and the federal appeals court. The official then raised the qualified immunity defense in another pretrial motion—a motion for summary judgment, which allows a judge to rule on a case without trial after considering affidavit evidence. After the trial judge rejected the motion, the appeals court refused to consider the official's appeal, on the ground that he was entitled to only one "interlocutory appeal" on the immunity issue.

In a 7–2 decision, the Court disagreed. Scalia said the one-interlocutory-appeal rule was "unsound" because the factors to determine the qualified immunity issue "will be different on summary judgment . . . than on an earlier motion to dismiss."

The dissenting justices argued for applying the normal rule limiting a party to a single interlocutory appeal. "Purpose, precedent, and practicality all argue for one interlocutory qualified immunity appeal per case and no more," Breyer wrote.

Arbitration

Doctor's Associates, Inc. v. Casarotto, decided by an 8–1 vote, May 20, 1996; Ginsburg wrote the opinion; Thomas dissented.

The Court struck down on federal pre-emption grounds a Montana law requiring that contractual arbitration clauses be printed in underlined capital letters and appear on a contract's first page.

The decision cleared the way for arbitration in a franchise dispute between a sandwich shop operator and the company that issued the franchise, Doctor's Associates, Inc. The Montana Supreme Court had blocked arbitration because the arbitration clause in the franchise agreement did not conform to the so-called first-page requirement.

In a nearly unanimous decision, Ginsburg said the state law was "displaced" by the Federal Arbitration Act, which limits states' power to block arbitration. "Courts may not . . . invalidate arbitration agreements under state laws applicable *only* to arbitration," Ginsburg wrote.

Thomas dissented briefly, citing his view from a 1995 decision—*Allied-Bruce Terminix Cos. v. Dobson*—that the Federal Arbitration Act does not apply to state court proceedings.

Judgments

Peacock v. Thomas, decided by an 8–1 vote, February 21, 1996; Thomas wrote the opinion; Stevens dissented.

Federal courts have no jurisdiction over a suit to enforce a judgment won by a litigant in one case against an individual or corporation that is not otherwise liable for the judgment.

The ruling rejected an effort by a South Carolina man, Jack Thomas, to enforce a $187,000 judgment that he won in a federal court suit against his former employer for losses from the company's pension benefits plan. The company transferred most of its assets while the appeal was pending. Thomas then filed a new suit that sought, in legal parlance, to "pierce the corporate veil" in order to collect the money from the company's president and main shareholder.

In an 8–1 decision, the Court said there was no basis for the federal courts to hear the second suit. Justice Thomas said the new suit was not authorized by the federal pension protection law, the Employee Retirement Income Security Act, or by courts' so-called "ancillary" jurisdiction to hear a case related to a separate matter already before the court.

In a lone dissent, Stevens said federal courts should be able to hear a claim that a controlling shareholder "has fraudulently exercised that control to defeat satisfaction of [a] judgment."

Jury Trials

Gasperini v. Center for Humanities, Inc., decided by 6–3 and 5–4 votes, June 24, 1996; Ginsburg wrote the opinion; Stevens disagreed with the result but agreed with the legal holding; Scalia, Rehnquist, and Thomas dissented.

Federal courts hearing damage suits in diversity-of-citizenship cases may apply state law permitting judges to reduce jury awards without violating the Seventh Amendment's protections for jury trials in federal courts.

The ruling allowed the use in federal court of a New York law that requires the state's judges to order a new trial if a jury award "deviates materially from what would be reasonable compensation." The issue arose in a suit brought by photojournalist William Gasperini against the Center for Humanities over the loss of 300 original transparencies he had lent for use in making an educational videotape about wars in Central America. Gasperini, a Californian, brought the suit in federal court in New York under the constitutional provision allowing federal courts to hear cases involving citizens of different states.

A jury awarded Gasperini $450,000. On appeal the Second U.S. Circuit Court of Appeals ruled the verdict excessive under New York's "reasonable compensation" law and gave Gasperini the choice of accepting a $100,000 award or a new trial. Gasperini contended the decision violated the Seventh Amendment, which provides in its so-called Re-examination Clause that "no fact tried by a jury shall be otherwise re-examined in any Court of the United States, than according to the rules of common law."

By a 6–3 majority, the Court ruled that federal courts can apply state damage reduction provisions without violating the Seventh Amendment. ". . . [A]ppellate review for abuse of discretion is reconcilable with the Seventh Amendment as a control necessary and proper to the fair administration of justice," Ginsburg wrote. But she said federal trial-level judges should have "principal responsibility" for applying such laws, and appellate courts should exercise only limited review over those decisions.

The decision returned the case to federal district court for reconsideration of the award. Stevens agreed with the main holding, but found no reason to send the case back for further proceedings.

In a dissent, Scalia, joined by Rehnquist and Thomas, said the ruling amounted to a "nullification of what was long regarded as a core component of the Bill of Rights—the Seventh Amendment's prohibition on reexamination of civil jury awards."

Privileges

Jaffee v. Redmond, decided by a 7–2 vote, June 13, 1996; Stevens wrote the opinion; Scalia and Rehnquist dissented.

Federal courts cannot force psychotherapists or other mental health professionals to disclose patients' statements or records as evidence in judicial proceedings.

The ruling required a new trial in a federal civil rights suit brought by the administrator of the estate of an Illinois woman killed by a police officer during an investigation of a domestic disturbance. After the officer refused to comply with a subpoena for notes of her therapy sessions with a licensed social worker, the judge instructed the jury to presume that the contents would have been unfavorable to her. The jury then returned an award totaling $545,000. The Seventh U.S. Circuit Court of Appeals ordered a new trial, holding that the judge should have recognized a qualified privilege to refuse to turn over the notes.

In a 7–2 decision, the Court held that federal courts ordinarily must recognize a psychotherapist privilege. Stevens said the privilege was needed because compelled disclosure of psychotherapy sessions "may impede development of the confidential relationship necessary for successful treatment." He also said the privilege "serves the public interest by facilitating the provision of appropriate treatment for individuals suffering the effects of a mental or emotional problem."

Stevens said the qualified privilege recognized by the appeals court was inadequate because the possibility of disclosure "would eviscerate the effectiveness of the privilege." But he said in a footnote that the privilege "must give way" if disclosure was required to prevent harm to the patient or to others.

Stevens also agreed with the appeals court in extending the privilege to licensed social workers. "Today, social workers provide a significant amount of mental health treatment," he wrote.

In a dissent, Scalia called the new privilege "new, vast, and ill-defined" and said the issue should have been left to Congress instead of the courts. Scalia also disagreed with the decision to include social workers in the privilege; Rehnquist joined that part of the opinion.

Settlements

Matsushita Electric Industrial Co., Ltd. v. Epstein, decided by 9–0 and 6–3 votes, February 27, 1996; Thomas wrote the opinion; Ginsburg, Stevens, and Souter dissented in part.

Federal courts must recognize a state court's approval of a settlement even if the agreement releases claims that are within the exclusive jurisdiction of federal courts.

The ruling upheld a Delaware court's approval of a settlement in a class action shareholder suit stemming from the 1990 acquisition of the MCA entertainment conglomerate by the Japanese company Matsushita Electric Industrial Co. After the settlement, Matsushita argued the agreement also ended a federal court securities suit over the same transaction, but the Ninth U.S. Circuit Court of Appeals said the state court had no power over federal law claims.

In a mostly unanimous decision, the Court disagreed. Thomas said the federal Full Faith and Credit Act requires federal courts to recognize a state court settlement even if it releases claims "solely within the jurisdiction of the federal courts." Thomas also said that Delaware courts would treat the settlement as precluding further litigation of the federal claims.

Three justices—Stevens, Souter, and Ginsburg—dissented on the second point, arguing that the issue should be addressed first by lower courts. In her opinion, Ginsburg also said that the federal appeals court could still consider whether the plaintiffs in the federal suit could attack the state court settlement on grounds they were not adequately represented in the Delaware courts.

Criminal Law and Procedure

Acquittals

Carlisle v. United States, decided by a 7–2 vote, April 29, 1996; Scalia wrote the opinion; Stevens and Kennedy dissented.

A federal judge cannot consider a defendant's postverdict motion for acquittal filed after the seven-day time limit established by the Federal Rules of Criminal Procedure.

The 7–2 ruling upheld the 1993 federal marijuana conspiracy conviction of a Michigan man whose lawyer missed by one day the seven-day deadline set by the Federal Rules of Criminal Procedure for filing a motion for judgment of acquittal. At sentencing, the judge nonetheless ordered an acquittal, saying there was insufficient evidence of guilt. But the Sixth U.S. Circuit Court of Appeals reinstated the jury verdict.

Writing for the Court, Scalia agreed with the appeals panel that judges have "no authority" to grant a motion for acquittal filed after the prescribed time limit. He said the rules allowed "simply no room" for a judge to act "regardless of whether that motion is accompanied by a claim of legal innocence, is filed before sentencing, or was filed late because of attorney error."

Ginsburg wrote a concurring opinion to say that the defendant could still raise the innocence issue in an appeal or in a postconviction proceeding based on ineffective assistance of counsel. Souter and Breyer joined the opinion.

In a dissenting opinion, Stevens, joined by Kennedy, maintained that the federal rules did not affect a judge's "inherent authority to ensure that a legally innocent defendant is not wrongfully convicted."

Capital Punishment

Loving v. United States, decided by a 9–0 vote, June 3, 1996; Kennedy wrote the opinion.

The Court upheld the military death penalty, rejecting a separation-of-powers challenge to a 1984 presidential directive revising the system to cure constitutional defects.

The decision upheld the death sentence of Army Pvt. Dwight Loving, who was convicted of murder in the 1988 robbery-killings of two taxicab drivers near Fort Hood, Texas. Loving contended that then-president Ronald Reagan had no authority to issue a 1984 regulation that added a list of aggravating factors to be used in imposing the death penalty in courts-martial. The action responded to a ruling by the U.S. Court of Military Appeals that the military's existing death penalty scheme did not comply with Supreme Court precedents on capital punishment. The military appeals court—renamed the U.S. Court of Appeals for the Armed Forces—rejected Loving's challenge.

In a unanimous ruling, the Court agreed that the president's action did not violate separation-of-powers principles. Kennedy said that the Constitution provides for shared responsibility between Congress and the president for prescribing rules and regulations for the armed forces. ". . . [I]t would be contrary to the respect owed the President as Commander in Chief to hold that he may not be given wide discretion and authority," Kennedy wrote.

Although the decision was unanimous, Thomas did not join Kennedy's opinion. He wrote separately to say that he had doubts whether the Court's death penalty rulings applied to the military at all.

In a concurring opinion, Stevens, joined by Souter, Ginsburg, and Breyer, said the ruling left open the question whether the military could impose the death penalty for nonservice connected murders. He said the case did not raise that issue because Loving's victims were an active duty serviceman and a retired serviceman.

Tuggle v. Netherland, Warden, decided by a 9–0 vote, October 30, 1995; *per curiam* (unsigned) opinion.

A Virginia death row inmate was allowed to challenge his death sentence because the state's supreme court failed to correct the effects of a constitutional error in his capital sentencing hearing.

The inmate was convicted of murder and then sentenced to death after prosecutors introduced evidence to show two "aggravating factors"—"vileness" and "future dangerousness." The evidence of dangerousness was later ruled inadmissible because the defendant had not been provided a court-appointed psychiatrist. But the Virginia Supreme Court upheld the death sentence anyway on the ground that the other aggravating factor was sufficient. Federal courts refused to grant habeas corpus relief on the same ground.

In a brief, unsigned opinion, the Court said the Virginia court and the lower federal courts misapplied a previous ruling in rejecting the inmate's plea. The absence of psychiatric evidence in the sentencing hearing, the Court said, "may well have affected the jury's ultimate decision . . . to sentence [the inmate] to death rather than life imprisonment."

Competency

Cooper v. Oklahoma, decided by a 9–0 vote, April 16, 1996; Stevens wrote the opinion.

A defendant seeking to prove that he is incompetent to stand trial cannot be required to make that showing by the heightened standard of "clear and convincing evidence."

The decision ordered a new hearing for an Oklahoma man, Byron Cooper, sentenced to death for the killing of an elderly man during a burglary. Cooper's attorney repeatedly sought to block the trial on grounds that Cooper was mentally incompetent, citing an array of bizarre behavior before and during trial. But the judge ruled that Cooper had failed to show he was incompetent by clear and convincing evidence, as required by Oklahoma law. On appeal, the Oklahoma Supreme Court rejected Cooper's argument that the strict evidentiary standard violated his rights to due process under the Fourteenth Amendment.

In a unanimous opinion, the Court said Oklahoma's law "poses a significant risk of an erroneous determination" on the defendant's competence to stand trial. ". . . [T]he defendant's fundamental right to be tried only while competent outweighs the State's interest in the efficient operation of its criminal justice system," Stevens wrote.

The ruling affected laws in three other states: Connecticut, Pennsylvania, and Rhode Island. Stevens noted that all other states and the federal courts used a "preponderance of the evidence" standard on competency questions in criminal cases.

Criminal Offenses

Bailey v. United States, decided by a 9–0 vote, December 6, 1995; O'Connor wrote the opinion.

A defendant cannot be convicted under a federal law providing at least five years' imprisonment for "using" a firearm in connection with a drug offense unless he actively employed the weapon during the crime.

The decision narrowed the interpretation of a 1988 law that federal prosecutors used to win longer sentences in drug cases. Two Washington, D.C., defendants—Roland Bailey and Candisha Robinson—were convicted and sentenced under the law after they were arrested on drug offenses.

Bailey was charged on the basis of a gun found in the trunk of his car, Robinson on the basis of a pistol found in a locked storage trunk in her bedroom. Both defendants argued the evidence did not show that they had "used" a weapon in connection with the drug offenses. But the federal appeals court for the District of Columbia upheld their convictions under the firearms law as well as for the underlying drug offenses.

In a unanimous ruling, the Court said the appeals court had allowed the law to be applied too broadly. "To sustain a conviction [under the law]," O'Connor wrote, "the Government must show that the defendant actively employed the firearm during and in relation to the predicate crime."

As examples, O'Connor said "use" could include "brandishing, displaying, bartering, striking with, and most obviously, firing or attempting to fire, a firearm." But she said "mere possession" or "placement" near the site of a drug offense would not constitute "use" under the law.

O'Connor said the decision was consistent with a 1993 ruling, *Smith v. United States,* that upheld a conviction under the "use" law against a defendant who traded a weapon for drugs. The Court had split 6–3 in that case; O'Connor wrote the majority opinion.

Montana v. Egelhoff, decided by a 5–4 vote, June 13, 1996; Scalia wrote the plurality opinion; O'Connor, Stevens, Souter, and Breyer dissented.

States may prohibit juries from considering a defendant's intoxication when deciding whether the defendant had the required mental state to be convicted of a crime.

The ruling reinstated the conviction of a Montana man found guilty of the shooting deaths of two companions while he was intoxicated. The Montana Supreme Court overturned the conviction on the ground that a state law prohibiting juries from taking a defendant's intoxication into account violated the Fourteenth Amendment's Due Process Clause.

The Court overturned the state court's ruling in a somewhat fractured decision that divided the justices across normal ideological lines.

Writing for a plurality of four justices, Scalia said the state law did not violate the Due Process Clause because it did not infringe on "a fundamental principle of justice." Scalia said that the common law generally prohibited consideration of a defendant's intoxication in determining his guilt. He discounted the importance of the fact that most states—all but 10—allow the use of such evidence. The new rule, Scalia wrote, "has not received sufficiently uniform and permanent allegiance to qualify as fundamental." Rehnquist, Kennedy, and Thomas concurred in his opinion.

Ginsburg concurred in the judgment on a different ground. She said the law was constitutional because it was not an evidence restriction but a definition of the mental state needed to be convicted of murder. "States enjoy wide latitude in defining the elements of criminal offenses," she said.

Writing for the four dissenters, O'Connor construed the law as an impermissible effort to increase the state's likelihood of convicting a defendant. ". . . [A] state may not first determine the elements of the crime it wishes to punish, and then thwart the accused's defense by categorically disallowing the very evidence that would prove him innocent."

Rutledge v. United States, decided by a 9–0 vote, March 27, 1996; Stevens wrote the opinion.

A defendant convicted of conducting a "continuing criminal enterprise" (CCE) cannot also be convicted of a criminal conspiracy for the same activities.

The decision supported a plea by an Illinois man to overturn his conspiracy conviction and sentence. He was convicted under the conspiracy and CCE statutes in connection with trafficking in cocaine and given concurrent life sentences on the two counts.

In a unanimous opinion, Stevens said that a conspiracy charge is a "lesser included offense" of the CCE charge because both charges require proof of "mutual agreement in a common plan or enterprise."

Discrimination

United States v. Armstrong, decided by an 8–1 vote, May 13, 1996; Rehnquist wrote the opinion; Stevens dissented.

A defendant cannot use pretrial discovery procedures to support a race-based claim of selective prosecution without first presenting some evidence that the government failed in similar cases to prosecute persons of a different race.

The ruling, in a closely watched drug case from Los Angeles, reversed a decision by an en banc panel of the Ninth U.S. Circuit Court of Appeals. The defendants in the case, African Americans charged with conspiracy to possess and distribute crack cocaine, claimed they had been selectively prosecuted in federal court because of their race. The district court judge granted a motion for discovery requiring the government to furnish information regarding prosecution policies in crack cocaine cases. When the government refused to comply, the judge dismissed the case.

A three-judge panel of the Ninth Circuit reversed the decision on grounds the defendants failed to show that "similarly situated individuals" of a different race had not been prosecuted. But an eleven-judge en banc panel disagreed and reinstated the district court's ruling.

The Court reversed the Ninth Circuit's ruling in a decision that was nearly unanimous as to the result but more divided as to the legal reasoning. Rehnquist began by narrowly interpreting the federal pretrial discovery rule—Rule 16 of the Federal Rules of Criminal Procedure—to limit a defendant's right to discovery to support a selective prosecution claim. The rule's provision guaranteeing discovery of information "material to the defendant's defense," Rehnquist said, applies only to claims that "refute the Government's arguments that the defendant committed the crime charged."

Rehnquist continued by rejecting the defendants' argument that they had presented sufficient proof of selective prosecution by introducing statistics that most defendants charged in crack cocaine cases are black. "To establish a discriminatory effect in a race case," Rehnquist said, citing a 1905 precedent, "the claimant must show that similarly situated individuals of a different race were not prosecuted."

Three justices in the majority wrote separately to qualify their support for Rehnquist's opinion. Souter and Ginsburg wrote brief concurring opinions to suggest that defendants could still use Rule 16 to obtain discovery on some affirmative defenses unrelated to the merits of a case. Breyer, concurring in the judgment, described the new limit on discovery as "arbitrary," but agreed that the defendants had failed to make an adequate showing to obtain discovery in this case.

In a lone dissent, Stevens said the defendants had presented "sufficiently disturbing" evidence of racial disparity in prosecution to permit the trial judge to order discovery.

Evidence

Wood, Superintendent, Washington State Penitentiary v. Bartholomew, decided October 10, 1995, by a 5–4 vote; *per curiam* (unsigned) opinion; Stevens, Souter, Ginsburg, and Breyer dissented.

Prosecutors need not disclose to a defendant unfavorable results of a polygraph examination given to a prosecution witness if the information will not help find evidence that would be admissible at trial.

The decision denied a federal habeas corpus petition by a Washington State death row inmate, Dwayne Bartholomew, challenging his conviction and death sentence for a 1981 robbery-murder of a laundromat attendant. His brother, Rodney Bartholomew, testified at trial that he was with Dwayne outside the laundromat and heard Dwayne say he planned to "leave no witnesses." Rodney denied any role himself in planning or carrying out the robbery, but a polygraph examination given before trial indicated he was lying.

In a federal habeas corpus proceeding, Dwayne Bartholomew contended the failure to disclose the polygraph results violated the so-called *Brady* rule requiring prosecutors to turn over information that might be helpful to the defense. Agreeing, the Ninth U.S. Circuit Court of Appeals acknowledged that the polygraph results would not be admissible at trial, but said the information "possibly could have led to some admissible evidence."

In an unsigned decision, the Court disagreed. It said the disclosure of the results "could have had no direct effect on the outcome of the trial" and dismissed as "speculation" the appeals court's suggestion that it might have helped find other evidence.

The Court decided the case without hearing arguments. Four justices noted that they dissented from the summary disposition of the case, but did not write a separate opinion.

Forfeiture

Bennis v. Michigan, decided by a 5–4 vote, March 4, 1996; Rehnquist wrote the opinion; Stevens, Kennedy, Souter, and Breyer dissented.

The government can seize property even if the owner had no knowledge that someone else was using it for criminal activity.

The closely divided decision rejected a Michigan woman's claim that her constitutional rights were violated by the forfeiture of a car she co-owned with her husband after his arrest for having sex with a prostitute in the car. She argued that the Fourteenth Amendment's Due Process Clause required the government to recognize an "innocent owner defense," but the Michigan Supreme Court rejected the argument.

Writing for the Court, Rehnquist also disagreed, citing what he called "well-established authority" dating as far as an 1827 case upholding the seizure of a pirate ship. ". . . [A] long and unbroken line of cases holds that an owner's interest in property may be forfeited by reason of the use to which the property is put even though the owner did not know that it was to be put to such use," he wrote.

Thomas and Ginsburg wrote brief separate concurrences. Thomas said it was up to the states or the "political branches" of the federal government to prevent improper uses of forfeiture. Ginsburg said state courts could also police "exorbitant applications" of forfeiture statutes.

In the main dissent, Stevens said the decision violated "elementary notions of fairness" and would give states "virtually unbridled power to confiscate vast amounts of property." Souter and Breyer joined the dissent. Kennedy wrote a briefer dissent, saying that forfeiture should be allowed only if the owner was guilty of negligence or complicity with regard to the wrongdoing. *(See story, pp. 61–63; excerpts, pp. 145–154.)*

Degen v. United States, decided by a 9–0 vote, June 10, 1996; Kennedy wrote the opinion.

A federal court cannot bar a fugitive criminal defendant from presenting, through an attorney, a defense in a related civil forfeiture proceeding.

The ruling allowed defendant Brian Degen to try to block the forfeiture of $5.5 million worth of real estate. Degen had remained in Switzerland since the government brought a marijuana and money laundering indictment, along with a civil forfeiture proceeding, against him in 1989. When Degen, through his lawyer, presented a defense in the forfeiture proceeding, the federal district court judge refused to consider his pleadings and granted summary judgment against him. The Ninth U.S. Circuit Court of Appeals upheld the ruling.

In a unanimous opinion, Kennedy said the lower courts' decision to strike Degen's filings was "an excessive response." Kennedy said there was "no risk . . . of delay or frustration in determining the merits of the Government's forfeiture claims or in enforcing the resulting judgment."

Libretti v. United States, decided by an 8–1 vote, November 7, 1995; O'Connor wrote the opinion; Stevens dissented.

A federal judge is not required to determine the factual basis for a property forfeiture agreed to by a defendant as part of a guilty plea.

The near-unanimous ruling upheld a plea agreement by a Wyoming accountant, Joseph Libretti, to turn over all of his assets after he admitted running a big marijuana and cocaine operation. Libretti, who also received a reduced twenty-year prison term, later challenged the forfeiture order on grounds it did not comply with two provisions of the Federal Rules of Criminal Procedure: Rule 11(f), requiring a judge to assure that there is a "factual basis" for a guilty plea; and Rule 31(e), establishing a right to jury trial on forfeiture.

The Court rejected both arguments. O'Connor said the guilty-plea rule does not apply to forfeiture. "Forfeiture is an element of the sentence *following* conviction," O'Connor wrote, "and thus falls outside the scope of Rule 11(f)." As to the second point, O'Connor said Libretti gave up his right to a jury determination of the forfeiture when he waived a jury trial.

In separate concurrences, Souter and Ginsburg refused to join the Court's secondary holding. Souter said he would not reach the issue; Ginsburg said the judge made adequate reference to the issue during jury selection to inform the defendant of his right.

In a lone dissent, Stevens argued that a judge has "a legal obligation" to determine the factual basis for any judgment issued after a guilty plea "entirely apart from Rule 11(f)."

United States v. Ursery, decided by an 8–1 vote, June 24, 1996; Rehnquist wrote the opinion; Stevens dissented in part.

The government can both prosecute an individual and seek to seize his or her property by a civil forfeiture proceeding without violating the Constitution's Double Jeopardy Clause.

The ruling backed the government in overturning two federal appeals court decisions that the combined prosecution and forfeiture actions violated the constitutional ban against successive punishments. In one case, the government had moved to seize a home belonging to a Michigan man, Guy Ursery, after state police found marijuana inside. Ursery settled the forfeiture by paying the government $13,250; he was indicted shortly thereafter and eventually convicted and sentenced to sixty-three months in prison. In the second case, *United States v. $405,089.23 in United States Currency,* the government seized real estate and more than $400,000 in cash from two California men—Charles Wesley Arlt and James Wren—who were also being prosecuted on various drug and money-laundering counts.

The Sixth U.S. Circuit Court of Appeals reversed Ursery's criminal conviction, and the Ninth Circuit appeals court invalidated the forfeiture in the Arlt and Wren case. Both appellate panels interpreted the Court's recent precedents to mean that civil forfeiture amounted to punishment under the Double Jeopardy Clause.

In a nearly unanimous decision, the Court said the appeals courts misconstrued its recent rulings. Rehnquist said that civil forfeiture actions had traditionally not been viewed as "punishment" or criminal for purposes of the Double Jeopardy Clause. He also said that forfeitures served "important nonpunitive goals," including deterring people from allowing their property to be used for illegal purposes and preventing people from profiting from illegal acts.

Kennedy joined Rehnquist's opinion, but wrote in a concurring opinion that a civil forfeiture is justified even though it "punishes" an owner because the Double Jeopardy Clause only prohibits a second personal punishment. Scalia, joined by Thomas, concurred in the judgment, repeating his previous view that the Double Jeopardy Clause does not apply to successive punishments, but only to successive prosecutions.

In a partial dissent, Stevens said Ursery's conviction should be set aside on double jeopardy grounds: "There is simply no rational basis for characterizing the seizure of [Ursery's] home as anything other than punishment for his crime." But he said the seizure of the money and property in the Arlt and Wren case was proper. *(See story, pp. 63–65; excerpts, pp. 231–241.)*

Habeas Corpus

Calderon, Warden v. Moore, decided by a 9–0 vote, June 17, 1996; *per curiam* (unsigned) opinion.

The Court summarily rebuked a federal appeals court for dismissing a state's appeal of a habeas corpus ruling granting a new trial to a death row inmate.

In an unsigned opinion issued without hearing argument, the Court said the Ninth U.S. Circuit Court of Appeals was wrong to dismiss the state's appeal as moot once the state had scheduled the inmate's retrial. ". . . [A] decision in the State's favor would release it from the burden of the new trial itself," the Court said.

The inmate, Charles Edward Moore Jr., sought a new trial on the ground that he had been denied the right to represent himself in the original trial.

Felker v. Turpin, Warden, decided by a 9–0 vote, June 28, 1996; Rehnquist wrote the opinion.

The Court upheld part of a new law aimed at limiting death row inmates' ability to challenge their convictions and sentences in federal court, but said inmates can still bring pleas directly to the Court itself.

The decision rejected a challenge to a provision of the Antiterrorism and Effective Death Penalty Act of 1996. The act required inmates to obtain permission from a federal appeals court before filing a second habeas corpus petition before a federal district court. The law also provided that the Supreme Court could not review an appeals court's decision under this so-called "gatekeeper" provision and tightened somewhat the standards for a successful habeas corpus petition. A Georgia death row inmate challenged the law on grounds it violated the constitutional prohibition against "suspending" the writ of habeas corpus and unconstitutionally limited the Court's own jurisdiction.

In a unanimous opinion, Rehnquist rejected both arguments, but only after narrowing the law somewhat. Citing an 1869 precedent, Rehnquist said the provision limiting the Court's review of "gatekeeper" decisions did not abolish the Court's power to hear a habeas corpus petition filed with the Court itself. "This conclusion obviates one of the constitutional challenges raised," he wrote. He also rejected the inmate's argument that the new restrictions were unconstitutional, and he said they would apply to habeas petitions filed directly with the Court.

The ruling, issued less than a month after the case was argued, was an anticlimax of sorts. The Court added the case to the calendar late in the term, over a sharp dissent from four justices—Stevens, Souter, Ginsburg, and Breyer—who complained about the expedited handling. But the anticipated showdown over Congress's power to limit the Court's jurisdiction faded when attorneys for the inmate and the state of Georgia agreed that the Court could still hear an original habeas corpus petition. In concurring opinions, Stevens, Souter, and Breyer said that state inmates also had other ways to present a habeas corpus challenge to the Court.

Gray v. Netherland, Warden, decided by a 5–4 vote, June 20, 1996; Rehnquist wrote the opinion; Ginsburg, Stevens, Souter, and Breyer dissented.

The Court blocked a new trial for a Virginia death row inmate by throwing out a lower court decision that prosecutors surprised him by using evidence at his sentencing hearing linking him to another murder. But the Court left open the possibility that the inmate could win a new trial by showing that prosecutors deliberately misled him.

The inmate, Coleman Gray, was convicted in 1985 of the robbery-murder of a Portsmouth, Virginia, department store manager earlier in the year. After his conviction, prosecutors told Gray's lawyer they would offer testimony linking Gray to a second crime — the heavily publicized slayings of a woman and her three-year-old child. The lawyer sought to exclude the evidence on grounds that he had inadequate time to defend against the evidence and that the prosecutors had earlier said they would introduce Gray's statements about the other crimes but no other evidence.

The judge refused to exclude the additional evidence. The jury sentenced Gray to death, and state courts rejected his appeals. A federal appeals court, however, granted Gray a new trial, ruling that he had been denied due process by the late notice of the additional evidence.

In a 5–4 decision, the Court vacated the appeals court's decision. Rehnquist said the decision violated the Court's precedents against adopting "a new constitutional rule" in a federal habeas corpus proceeding except under limited circumstances. But the Court remanded the case to the appeals court to determine whether Gray could show prosecutors had been guilty of "affirmative misrepresentation."

The dissenting justices said it was "beyond genuine debate" that Gray's due process rights had been violated. "There is nothing 'new' in a rule that capital defendants must be afforded a meaningful opportunity to defend against the State's penalty phase evidence," Ginsburg wrote. Stevens wrote a separate dissent, saying the evidence was too weak to be introduced anyway.

Lonchar v. Thomas, Warden, decided by 9–0 and 5–4 votes, April 1, 1996; Breyer wrote the opinion; Rehnquist, Scalia, Kennedy, and Thomas concurred in the result, but disagreed with one of the legal holdings.

A federal appeals court was wrong to dismiss on "general equitable grounds" a state death row inmate's first federal habeas corpus petition filed on the day of his scheduled execution.

The ruling reinstated a constitutional challenge by a convicted triple-murderer, Larry Lonchar, filed on June 28, 1995, hours before his scheduled execution and nearly eight years after his trial and sentence in a Georgia court. Lonchar took no action to challenge his conviction during the interim, although his brother and sister both sought to file habeas petitions in his behalf. When Lonchar did file his habeas petition, he said he was challenging the state's use of electrocution because he wanted to be executed by lethal injection so that he could donate his organs.

A federal district court judge issued a stay of execution, but it was overturned by a three-judge panel of the Eleventh U.S. Circuit Court of Appeals. The panel based its ruling on what it called "equitable doctrines independent" of the federal habeas corpus rule—Rule 9—governing dismissal of habeas petitions.

The Court ruled the appeals court was wrong in a decision that was unanimous on the result but divided on a significant legal issue. Writing for the majority, Breyer said Rule 9 allows dismissal of a late-filed habeas petition only if the state "has been prejudiced in its ability to respond." He criticized the appeals court for creating "an ad hoc judicial exception" to the rule and stressed that dismissal of a first habeas petition "is a particularly serious matter . . . risking injury to an important interest in human liberty."

On what he called "a preliminary matter," Breyer also limited federal courts' discretion to refuse a stay of execution in habeas cases. He said a district court judge "must issue a stay to prevent the case from becoming moot" unless it can rule on the merits of the petition before the scheduled execution.

In an opinion concurring in the judgment, four justices rejected that part of the decision. Writing for the four, Rehnquist said that federal courts can refuse to block an execution to prevent "last-minute or manipulative uses of the stay power." In his opinion, Breyer responded to the concern by stressing that federal judges can take a variety of steps to expedite proceedings "in order quickly to dispose of meritless first petitions."

Thompson v. Keohane, Warden, decided by a 7–2 vote, November 29, 1995; Ginsburg wrote the opinion; Thomas and Rehnquist dissented.

The Court somewhat strengthened the ability of prison inmates to challenge their convictions by attacking state court rulings permitting the use of statements made during police interrogation.

By a 7–2 vote, the Court held that federal judges must make an independent determination whether an inmate was "in custody" during questioning. Police need not give the so-called *Miranda* warnings to a suspect who is not in custody.

The issue reached the Court in a challenge by an Alaska inmate, Carl Thompson, who confessed to killing his former wife in an interview at Alaska state trooper headquarters. He challenged the conviction on grounds he was not advised of his rights, but Alaska courts ruled that he was not in custody. Two lower federal courts refused to review that determination when Thompson filed a habeas corpus petition.

Writing for the Court, Ginsburg said the custody issue is "a mixed question of law and fact" requiring independent review by federal judges in habeas corpus proceedings.

In a dissent, Thomas, joined by Rehnquist, said state courts were "best situated" to determine the issue.

Jury Trials

Lewis v. United States, decided by 7–2 and 5–4 votes, June 24, 1996; O'Connor wrote the opinion; Kennedy and Breyer concurred in the judgment, but disagreed with the legal holding; Stevens and Ginsburg dissented.

A defendant has no right to a trial by jury for an offense punishable by six months' imprisonment or less even if he faces multiple counts that could carry a longer cumulative sentence.

The ruling upheld an appeals court decision denying a jury trial to a former mail handler on two counts of obstructing the mail by opening letters and pocketing the contents. Each count carried a potential sentence of up to six months—the length of time for a crime the Court previously defined as a "petty" offense not requiring a jury trial. The federal magistrate judge denied the defendant's request for a jury, saying she would not impose more than the six-month sentence. On appeal, the Second U.S. Circuit Court of Appeals ruled more directly that a defendant has no right to a jury trial for multiple petty offenses.

By a 5–4 vote, the Court agreed. Writing for the majority, O'Connor said the sentence prescribed by the legislature for an offense is "the most relevant" criterion for determining whether an offense is "serious" for purposes of the Sixth Amendment right to jury trial. The multiple-count prosecution, she said, "does not revise the legislative judgment as to the gravity of the particular offense, nor does it transform the petty offense into a serious one, to which the jury-trial right would apply."

Kennedy, joined by Breyer, concurred in the judgment on the ground that a defendant is not entitled to a jury trial if a judge announces in advance that he or she will not impose a sentence longer than six months. But Kennedy strongly criticized the legal ruling as "one of the most serious incursions on the right to jury trial in the Court's history."

Stevens, joined by Ginsburg, dissented, endorsing Kennedy's views but voting to apply the jury trial right even if a judge agrees to limit imprisonment to six months.

Prisons and Jails

Lewis, Director, Arizona Department of Corrections v. Casey, decided by 8–1 and 5–4 votes, June 24, 1996; Scalia wrote the opinion; Souter, Ginsburg, and Breyer dissented in part; Stevens dissented.

The Court overturned a federal judge's order requiring Arizona to expand its prison law libraries and made it harder for inmates in future cases to show they have been unconstitutionally denied access to the courts.

The ruling narrowed the Court's 1977 decision, *Bounds v. Smith*, that had required corrections systems to provide inmates access to law libraries and "persons trained in the law." A federal district court judge in Phoenix relied on the precedent in 1992 in issuing an injunction that imposed detailed requirements on prison law libraries, guaranteeing all inmates use of the library at least ten hours per week and establishing standards in such areas as hours of operation and training of prison law librarians. The injunction also required that "lockdown prisoners"—inmates segregated from the general prison population for disciplinary reasons—be allowed access to law libraries unless officials could "document" a threat to security. And it ordered prisons to ensure that illiterate and non-English-speaking inmates be given "direct assistance" from lawyers, paralegals, or "minimally trained prisoner Legal Assistants."

All of the justices agreed the order was too broad. Scalia called the injunction "inordinately—indeed, wildly—intrusive" in a part of the Court's opinion joined by all justices except Stevens. But Scalia led a five-justice majority in going further to establish a stricter standard to govern similar cases in the future.

Scalia said prisons are required only to provide inmates access to materials needed to file "nonfrivolous complaints" either to contest their convictions or to challenge conditions of confinement. He said officials did not need to provide access to other legal materials or help inmates with pretrial discovery or other steps in litigation. "To demand the conferral of such sophisticated legal capabilities upon a mostly uneducated and indeed largely illiterate prison population is effectively to demand permanent provision of counsel, which we do not believe the Constitution requires," he wrote.

In a partial dissent, Souter, joined by Ginsburg and Breyer, disagreed with the new limits. But he said he agreed that the injunction had "not yet been justified by the factual findings of the district court." Stevens dissented separately, but also said the judge's ruling was too broad and the case should be remanded.

Thomas, who joined Scalia's opinion, went even further in a concurring opinion to suggest that the Court overturn the *Bounds* ruling. "I find no basis in the Constitution—and *Bounds* cited none—for the right to have the government finance inmate litigation," he wrote. No justice joined Thomas's opinion.

Search and Seizure

Ornelas v. United States, decided by an 8–1 vote, May 28, 1996; Rehnquist wrote the opinion; Scalia dissented.

Appellate courts should conduct an independent review of lower court decisions on whether police have adequate grounds to make an investigatory stop or warrantless search.

The decision ordered a federal appeals court to reconsider a plea by two California men convicted on drug charges in a federal court in Wisconsin. The men said that local police and federal drug agents had improperly stopped them for questioning. They also contended the officers had no adequate basis for the search of their car that disclosed two kilograms of cocaine.

The trial judge upheld the police actions, saying the officers had "reasonable suspicion" for the stop because the two men were driving a late-model car from California and registration information showed they had both been convicted of drug dealing. The judge also refused to suppress the cocaine, saying that it would have been discovered by drug-sniffing dogs whether or not the search was proper.

On appeal, the Seventh U.S. Circuit Court of Appeals said that lower court rulings on reasonable suspicion for a stop and probable cause for a search should be reviewed "deferentially" and set aside only "for clear error." The Court agreed to hear the case because most federal appeal courts conducted an independent review of such rulings.

In a nearly unanimous decision, the Court held that appellate courts should make independent—or so-called *de novo*—review in such cases. Rehnquist said independent appellate review was consistent with prior decisions and would promote clearer and more uniform rules for police. But he also said appellate courts should defer to lower courts' rulings on "historical facts."

In a lone dissent, Scalia said it was "unwise" to require appellate courts to conduct an independent review because it would have "relatively little benefit." And he said it was "contradictory" for the Court to say that appellate courts should defer to lower courts on some factual issues.

Pennsylvania v. Labron, decided by a 7–2 vote, July 1, 1996; *per curiam* (unsigned) opinion; Ginsburg and Stevens dissented.

The Court summarily overturned two rulings by the Pennsylvania Supreme Court that limited police power to conduct warrantless searches of an automobile after arresting the driver or passengers.

The state court had ruled in a pair of drug cases that police cannot search an automobile without a warrant even if they have probable cause except in "unforeseen circumstances."

In an unsigned opinion issued without hearing argument, the Court said the Pennsylvania justices' decisions "rest on an incorrect reading of the automobile exception to the Fourth Amendment's warrant requirement." "If a car is readily mobile and probable cause exists to believe it contains contraband," the Court said, "the Fourth Amendment . . . permits police to search the vehicle without more."

In a dissent, Stevens, joined by Ginsburg, said the Court should not have reviewed the decision because the Pennsylvania court had based the decision on its interpretation of the state's own constitution.

Whren v. United States, decided by a 9–0 vote, June 10, 1996; Scalia wrote the opinion.

Police may temporarily detain a motorist if they have probable cause to believe a traffic violation has occurred even if they are primarily interested in some other law enforcement purpose, such as looking for drugs.

The ruling—an important victory for law enforcement—upheld the conviction of two men who were stopped by two plainclothes vice officers while patrolling, in an unmarked vehicle, a "high drug area" in Washington, D.C. The officers stopped the car after it drove off at an "unreasonable" speed, and they immediately observed two large plastic bags of crack cocaine on the front seat. The two men challenged use of the evidence on grounds the stop was "pretextual," but a federal district court judge rejected the argument. After their conviction, the U.S. Court of Appeals also upheld the legality of the arrest.

In a unanimous opinion, the Court held that the officers' "subjective intentions" did not affect the legality of the stop. " ... [T]he Fourth Amendment's concern with 'reasonableness' allows certain actions to be taken in certain circumstances, *whatever* the subjective intent," Scalia wrote. He also rejected the argument that traffic enforcement by plainclothes officers in unmarked cars was an "unreasonable" practice under the Fourth Amendment.

Scalia noted that the two defendants, both black, also challenged the stop as racially motivated. But he said issues of selective enforcement must be raised under the Fourteenth Amendment's Equal Protection Clause instead of the Fourth Amendment's search-and-seizure provision.

Sentencing

Koon v. United States, decided by 9–0, 8–1, and 6–3 votes, June 13, 1996; Kennedy wrote the opinion; Stevens dissented in part on one issue; Souter, Ginsburg, and Breyer dissented in part on another issue.

Federal courts of appeals should defer to a lower court judge's decisions to depart from Sentencing Guidelines except in cases of abuse of judicial discretion or legal error.

The ruling rejected most of the government's arguments in seeking to increase the prison sentences imposed on two former Los Angeles police officers, Laurence Powell and Stacey Koon, for the videotaped beating of a black motorist, Rodney King, on March 2, 1991. The two white officers were convicted on federal charges of violating King's constitutional rights after a predominantly white jury had acquitted them of most counts in an earlier state court trial.

Under the Sentencing Guidelines, the normal sentence for the two men would have been seventy months to eighty-seven months. But U.S. District Court Judge John G. Davies in Los Angeles lowered the sentences to thirty months—or two and a half years. On appeal, the Ninth U.S. Circuit Court of Appeals applied a so-called *de novo* review to Davies's decision and ruled that his "downward departure" from the guidelines was not justified. Koon and Powell, who had since completed their prison terms, then appealed to the Court, seeking to bar any increase in the sentences.

In a mostly unanimous ruling, the Court ruled that a federal appeals court should review a trial judge's sentencing decision not on a *de novo* basis but only for an abuse of judicial discretion. "A district court's decision to depart from the Guidelines," Kennedy wrote, "will in most cases be due substantial deference, for it embodies the traditional exercise of discretion by a sentencing court."

Reviewing the judge's decision on that basis, the justices unanimously agreed that Davies was correct in the most important factor for lowering the two men's sentences: King's conduct in provoking the beating. But they were divided in considering the four other factors that the judge used.

Kennedy said that Davies had erred in using two factors to lower the two men's sentences: the potential loss of their jobs and the low likelihood of recidivism. He said the Sentencing Commission had taken each of those factors into account in prescribing the normal sentencing range. But Kennedy said the judge had given proper consideration to two other factors: the likelihood that the two officers would be subject to abuse in prison and the burden of the successive state and federal prosecutions.

Three justices—Souter, Ginsburg, and Breyer—said they would have found Davies was wrong on the prison abuse and successive prosecution issues. Stevens dissented on a separate point, saying he would have upheld the judge's decision to use the officers' potential loss of their jobs as a factor in lowering their sentences.

The ruling ordered the Ninth Circuit to remand the case to Davies for resentencing. "When a reviewing court concludes that a district court based a departure on both valid and invalid factors," Kennedy wrote, "a remand is required unless it determines the district court would have imposed the same sentence absent reliance on the invalid factors." Lawyers on both sides expected the judge not to impose any additional sentence.

Melendez v. United States, decided by a 7–2 vote, June 17, 1996; Thomas wrote the opinion; Breyer and O'Connor dissented in part.

A federal defendant cannot be given a sentence below the statutory minimum in exchange for cooperating with the government unless the prosecution explicitly asks the judge to do so.

The ruling upheld a strict interpretation of procedures under the U.S. Sentencing Guidelines for lowering sentences for defendants who provide "substantial assistance" in the investigation or prosecution of other offenders. After Juan Melendez pleaded guilty to a single cocaine conspiracy count, the government filed a motion acknowledging his cooperation and urging that his sentence be lowered below the level prescribed by the Sentencing Guidelines—135 months to 168 months. The court reduced the sentence, but refused to lower it as Melendez urged below the statutory minimum of ten years.

In a 7–2 decision, the Court held that under the general sentencing statute, federal judges have no authority to reduce a sentence below a statutory minimum unless the government files a specific motion to that effect. Thomas rejected the defendant's argument that a provision in the Sentencing Guidelines allows a court to treat a government motion to make a downward departure from the guidelines as a motion to go below the statutory minimum as well.

In a partial dissent, Breyer, joined by O'Connor, agreed with that argument and urged the case be remanded for resentencing.

Neal v. United States, decided by a 9–0 vote, January 22, 1996; Kennedy wrote the opinion.

Reaffirming a five-year-old precedent, the Court said sentences for defendants in LSD cases must be based on the weight of the material carrying the drug, not the weight of the drug itself.

The ruling effectively nullified a 1993 guideline by the U.S. Sentencing Commission. LSD is ordinarily diffused in blotter paper before distribution. The guideline directed judges to use a per-dose estimate of the weight of the drug in setting sentences in LSD cases, instead of the total weight of the blotter paper.

In a unanimous opinion, the Court said the guideline conflicted with its 1991 ruling, *Chapman v. United States,* that the weight of the blotter paper determined the sentencing range. "Our system demands that we adhere to our prior interpretations of statutes," Kennedy wrote.

The ruling upheld a minimum ten-year sentence for a defendant convicted of distributing LSD-laced blotter paper weighing about 110 grams—well above the ten-gram threshold for triggering the mandatory ten-year term. The weight of the LSD in the paper was estimated at less than five grams. Kennedy said "there may be little logic" in the sentencing scheme, but added: "Congress, not this Court, has the responsibility for revising its statutes."

Election Law

Campaign Finance

Colorado Republican Federal Campaign Committee v. Federal Election Commission, decided by a 7–2 vote, June 26, 1996; Breyer wrote a plurality opinion; Stevens and Ginsburg dissented.

The Court held that political parties may make unlimited independent expenditures in support of congressional candidates, but it stopped short of invalidating all federal campaign contribution limits for parties.

The ruling rejected a Federal Election Commission (FEC) claim that the Colorado Republican Federal Campaign Committee violated federal campaign law by a pre-primary media campaign in connection with the state's 1986 senatorial election. The FEC treated the expenditure as a "coordinated" expenditure that put the party unit over the ceiling set by federal law on political party contributions to candidates for the House or the Senate. A federal district court rejected the FEC's position, but the U.S. Court of Appeals for the Tenth Circuit agreed the expenditure constituted an illegal contribution and rejected the party's constitutional attack on the law.

In a fractured decision, the Court agreed that the party had a First Amendment right to engage in the spending, but the pivotal justices took a narrow approach to the issues. In the plurality opinion, Breyer said the evidence showed the Colorado GOP committee did not coordinate its spending with any of the three contenders for the party's senatorial nomination. On that basis, he said the spending was a constitutionally protected "independent expenditure." He said it was therefore unnecessary to reach broader questions about the constitutionality of limiting political party contributions to candidates. O'Connor and Souter joined his opinion.

Four justices—Rehnquist, Scalia, Kennedy, and Thomas—said, however, that they would go further. Kennedy said he would bar enforcement of the limits against party expenditures coordinated with a candidate. Thomas said he would strike down the contribution limits completely. Rehnquist and Scalia joined both opinions.

In his opinion, Thomas went further and called for nullifying all restrictions on campaign contributions as a violation of the First Amendment. No justice joined that part of Thomas's opinion.

Writing for the dissenters, Stevens argued that the ceiling on political party contributions was justified by preventing corruption and "leveling the electoral playing field." *(See story, pp. 53–57; excerpts, pp. 241–252.)*

Reapportionment and Redistricting

Bush, Governor of Texas v. Vera, decided by a 5–4 vote, June 13, 1996; O'Connor wrote the plurality opinion; Stevens, Souter, Ginsburg, and Breyer dissented.

The Court struck down three majority-minority congressional districts in Texas, saying the district lines were primarily motivated by race and not justified by legitimate state interests. But a majority of the justices said states can deliberately create majority-minority districts in some circumstances.

The ruling threw out a plan approved by the Texas legislature in 1991 that included a majority African-American district in the Dallas area and two interlocking districts in the Houston area with majority African-American and majority Hispanic populations respectively. In a challenge brought by a group of white voters and one Hispanic voter, a three-judge federal court held the three districts were unconstitutional racial gerrymanders under the Court's two prior racial redistricting rulings— *Shaw v. Reno* (1993) and *Miller v. Johnson* (1995)—because race was the predominant motive in drawing the lines. Separate appeals were filed by a group of minority voters, the state of Texas, and the federal government.

Five justices voted to uphold the decision, but there was no majority opinion. Writing for a plurality of three justices, O'Connor agreed with the district court that race was the predominant motive in fashioning each of the districts even though other reasons, including protection of incumbents, were present. She pointed to three findings: the state "neglected traditional districting criteria," was "committed from the outset to creating majority-minority districts," and "manipulated district lines to exploit unprecedentedly detailed racial data." She then said the racial districting could not be justified under "strict scrutiny" on grounds of remedying past discrimination or complying with the federal Voting Rights Act. Rehnquist and Kennedy joined her opinion.

In an unusual procedure, O'Connor wrote a separate concurring opinion to say that states have a "compelling interest" in using race to draw district lines to avoid liability for so-called minority-vote dilution under the Voting Rights Act. But she indicated that rationale would apply only where minority groups are geographically compact and could not justify "bizarrely shaped" districts drawn for "predominantly racial reasons."

In a separate opinion, Thomas, joined by Scalia, said strict scrutiny should apply to any "intentional creation of majority-minority districts." Kennedy, who joined the plurality opinion, wrote a separate concurrence to distance himself from O'Connor's view that strict scrutiny does not necessarily apply in such cases.

In separate dissents, Stevens and Souter criticized the factual and legal bases for the ruling. Stevens argued that because of incumbency protection, the district lines in each case amounted to "a political, not a racial, gerrymander." He also contended the districts were justified by the state's "responsibilities" under the Voting Rights Act. Souter contended the decision showed that the Court's previous rulings had created "inevitable confusion" and shifted responsibility for redistricting from state legislatures to the federal courts. Ginsburg and Breyer joined each of the dissents. *(See story, pp. 28–34; excerpts, pp. 199–224.)*

Shaw v. Hunt, Governor of North Carolina, decided by a 5–4 vote, June 13, 1996; Rehnquist wrote the opinion; Stevens, Souter, Ginsburg, and Breyer dissented.

The Court struck down a majority-black congressional district in North Carolina, saying the plan was racially motivated and failed to serve a "compelling state interest" needed to justify race-based districting.

The ruling—the Court's second in the case—overturned a three-judge district court's decision to uphold the bizarrely shaped district that tied together predominantly black areas in several noncontiguous metropolitan areas. In its first ruling, the Court held that racial redistricting plans are subject to challenge under the Equal Protection Clause. The Court then remanded the case, brought by white voters who lived in the newly drawn Twelfth Congressional District, for further consideration by the three-judge court. (*See* Supreme Court Yearbook, 1992–1993.) On remand, the three-judge court agreed the plan classified voters by race, but said it was justified by the state's interest in eradicating past discrimination and in complying with the federal Voting Rights Act.

Reversing that decision, the Court held that race was the predominant motive in drawing the district and found none of the justifications sufficient to satisfy the "strict scrutiny" applied to racial classifications. Rehnquist began by saying the redistricting plan was drawn mainly to comply with the Voting Rights Act, not to remedy past discrimination. He then said the plan was not needed to satisfy the Voting Rights Act provision requiring "pre-clearance" by the Justice Department because the department was misinterpreting the law to require maximizing the number of majority-black districts. He also said the plan was not required by the Voting Rights Act's "vote dilution" provision because the black population was not geographically compact, one of the criteria previously established for such a claim.

On a separate point, the Court held the plaintiffs had no standing to challenge another majority-black congressional district because none of them lived in it.

In a lengthy dissent, Stevens argued that racial redistricting should not be subject to strict scrutiny, but he said that the plan satisfied that test anyway because of the state's interest in "making it easier for more black leaders" to represent the state in Congress and in avoiding Voting Rights Act challenges by the Justice Department or private litigants. Ginsburg and Breyer joined most of Stevens's opinion. Souter also dissented, pointing to his opinion in the second redistricting case released the same day, *Bush v. Vera;* Ginsburg and Breyer also joined his opinion. (*See above.*)

Voting Rights

Morse v. Republican Party of Virginia, decided by a 5–4 vote, March 27, 1996; Stevens wrote the main opinion; Thomas, Rehnquist, Scalia, and Kennedy dissented.

The Voting Rights Act's requirement for some states to obtain prior Justice Department approval of changes in voting procedures applies to convention rules adopted by major political parties that may limit the ability of voters to participate.

The fractured ruling backed a suit brought by three University of Virginia law students challenging a registration fee imposed by the state Republican Party to participate in the convention that selected its 1994 nominee for the U.S. Senate. The students said the fee—$35 or $45—violated the Voting Rights Act provision, section 5, requiring Virginia and a handful of other states to obtain "preclearance" of "any voting qualification or prerequisite" established after the law took effect.

A three-judge federal district court rejected the suit on the ground that section 5 applies only to party primaries, not to nominating conventions. The court also held that the students had no standing to bring suit under the act's antipoll tax provision, section 10. The court said the section authorized suits only by the attorney general.

The Court reversed both rulings by a 5–4 vote, but with no majority opinion. In the main opinion, Stevens, joined by Ginsburg, argued that the Voting Rights Act applies to nominating conventions for "established" political parties, which he defined as parties given special access to the ballot under state law. He went on to say that the filing fee was covered by the preclearance requirement because it "undercuts [voters'] influence on the field of candidates . . . and thus weakens the 'effectiveness' of their votes cast in the general election itself."

In an opinion concurring only in the result, Breyer said section 5 applied to the Virginia GOP convention because it "resembles a primary about as closely as one could imagine." Citing the history of racially discriminatory voting practices that preceded enactment of the Voting Rights Act in 1965, Breyer said failure to cover party conventions "would have opened a loophole in the statute the size of a mountain." O'Connor and Souter joined the opinion.

In the main dissent, Thomas maintained that the act's preclearance requirement applies only to states or political subdivisions of states. "The Republican Party of Virginia is not an organ of the State," he said, "and the Party has no authority to formulate state law."

Thomas said applying the preclearance provision to political parties also posed "serious constitutional problems." Both Scalia and Kennedy wrote separate dissents that also cited constitutional concerns about the ruling. Scalia and Rehnquist joined all of Thomas's opinion, and Thomas joined Scalia's.

Kennedy did not join the main part of Thomas's opinion, but agreed that Congress intended the act "to reach governmental, not private entities." Rehnquist joined Kennedy's opinion.

The ruling appeared to have only limited immediate impact. Out of the eleven states covered in whole or part by the preclearance requirement, only two—Virginia and Alabama—used conventions to nominate statewide candidates. Nonetheless, Scalia warned that the decision would require political parties to obtain prior approval of "virtually every decision of consequence regarding their internal operations." But Stevens said the ruling applied only to changes "affecting voting" and would not apply to activities such as recruiting party members, conducting campaigns, or writing party platforms.

Environmental Law

Toxic Waste

Meghrig v. KFC Western, Inc., decided by a 9–0 vote, March 19, 1996; O'Connor wrote the opinion.

Owners of contaminated property cannot use the federal Resource and Conservation Recovery Act to recover toxic waste cleanup costs from the previous owners of the property.

The decision rejected an effort by the owner of a fast-food restaurant in Los Angeles to use the 1976 law to recoup about $211,000 in cleanup costs on the site, which had previously been used as a service station. The suit was rejected by a federal district court judge, but reinstated by the Ninth U.S. Circuit Court of Appeals.

In a unanimous opinion, O'Connor said the citizen suit provisions in the 1976 law did not authorize a private cause of action to recover past costs for cleaning up toxic wastes. The ruling did not affect legal remedies under other federal or state laws. O'Connor also noted that the federal government has broader authority to recover cleanup costs under the so-called Superfund Law, the Comprehensive Environmental Response, Compensation, and Liability Act of 1980.

Federal Government

Census

Wisconsin v. City of New York, decided by a 9–0 vote, March 20, 1996; Rehnquist wrote the opinion.

The federal government has no constitutional duty to correct an acknowledged undercounting in the census of African Americans and other minority groups in the nation's cities.

The decision rejected an effort by New York, several other cities, and some civil rights organizations to reverse the decision in 1991 by the Bush administration's secretary of commerce, Robert Mosbacher, not to make a statistical adjustment in the actual population count. The cities contended that the decision was subject to "strict scrutiny," the highest level of constitutional review, because it affected voting rights.

A lower federal court rejected the suit, applying a lower "rational basis" test, but the Second U.S. Circuit Court of Appeals agreed that the higher standard applied. Two states—Wisconsin and Oklahoma—joined the United States in asking the Court to review the ruling.

In a unanimous opinion, Rehnquist said that the government's decision "was not subject to heightened scrutiny" and was "well within the bounds of the Secretary's constitutional discretion." Rehnquist noted that the Census Bureau had acknowledged that minorities are undercounted and had recommended using a statistical estimation method to adjust the figures. But he said that Mosbacher's decision not to adjust the figures "need bear only a reasonable relationship to the accomplishment of an actual enumeration of the population."

The cities wanted to revise the figures to affect the apportionment of seats in the House of Representatives and, more concretely, the allocation of federal aid in programs that use population-based formulas. Although some Democratic politicians criticized the Bush administration's decision during the 1992 presidential campaign, the Clinton administration chose to defend the case in court. But the Census Bureau announced in February that in an effort to save costs, it would use statistical estimation methods in the next census, scheduled for the year 2000.

Federal Regulation

Medtronic, Inc. v. Lohr, decided by 9–0 and 5–4 votes, June 26, 1996; Stevens wrote the main opinion; O'Connor, Rehnquist, Scalia, and Thomas dissented in part.

The federal law regulating medical devices does not completely bar consumers from suing manufacturers in state courts. But the fractured ruling left uncertain whether the act pre-empts some state law claims.

The decision cleared the way for a Florida woman, Lora Lohr, to proceed with state law claims against Medtronic, Inc., a Minneapolis-based manufacturer of heart pacemakers. Lohr filed suit in a Florida court after her pacemaker failed in 1990, requiring emergency surgery to correct the problem. Medtronic—which removed the case to federal court on diversity of citizenship grounds—sought to dismiss the state law claims on grounds they were pre-empted by the Medical Devices Act of 1976.

The act, passed to strengthen federal regulation of medical devices, bars states from enforcing "any requirement" relating to safety or effectiveness "different from, or in addition to" federal requirements. The U.S. Court of Appeals for the Eleventh Circuit ruled that the law blocked Lohr's negligent manufacturing and failure to warn claims, but did not prevent her defective design claim. Medtronic and Lohr both asked the Court to review the case.

The justices unanimously agreed that Lohr's defective design claim was not pre-empted and, by a 5–4 vote, also permitted her to proceed with her other claims. In the main opinion, Stevens said Congress did not intend to deny the states any role in product safety suits involving medical devices. "Nothing [in the law] denies Florida the right to provide a traditional damages remedy for violations of common-law duties when those duties parallel federal requirements," Stevens wrote. He also stressed that the law provided for only limited review of products already sold before the act went into effect or for equivalent products that came on the market later. Kennedy, Souter, and Ginsburg joined Stevens's opinion in full.

Breyer, who provided the fifth vote for permitting all of Lohr's claims, joined most of Stevens's opinion. But he said state law claims would be barred in cases involving more detailed regulations by the Food and Drug Administration, the agency charged with enforcing the law.

In a partial dissent, O'Connor, joined by Rehnquist, Scalia, and Thomas, said Stevens and Breyer were wrong to rely on an FDA regulation barring pre-emption unless the agency had prescribed "specific" regulations. "The statute makes no mention of specificity, and there is no sound basis for determining that such a restriction on 'any requirement' exists," she wrote. But she agreed that the limited review of previously marketed devices meant that Lohr's claim for defective design should be allowed.

Government Contracts

Hercules, Inc. v. United States, decided by a 6–2 vote, March 4, 1996; Rehnquist wrote the opinion; Breyer and O'Connor dissented; Stevens did not participate.

Two chemical companies failed to force the government to pay the costs of litigation brought by Vietnam veterans relating to liability for manufacturing the defoliant Agent Orange used during the Vietnam War.

The companies—Hercules, Inc., and Thompson Co.—had paid $19 million and $3 million, respectively, as their part of a $180 million fund to settle the veterans' class action suit. The suit blamed various diseases on exposure to dioxin, an ingredient used in manufacturing Agent Orange. The two companies then sued the government in U.S. Claims Court to recover the money, along with $9 million in legal fees and expenses. They contended the government made an implied promise to indemnify them when it required them to manufacture the defoliant under the Defense Production Act.

In a 6–2 decision, the Court rejected the argument. Rehnquist said the Defense Production Act does not guarantee indemnification. He also said there was "reason to think" that a government contracting officer "would not agree to the open-ended indemnification agreement" claimed by the two companies.

The dissenting justices argued the case should be returned to the U.S. Claims Court for trial. Breyer added that the ruling could "make it more difficult . . . for courts to interpret Government contracts with an eye towards achieving the fair allocation of risks that the parties likely intended."

United States v. Winstar Corp., decided by a 7–2 vote, July 1, 1996; Souter wrote the plurality opinion; Rehnquist and Ginsburg dissented.

The government may be held liable for billions of dollars of breach of contract damages for tightening accounting rules for savings and loan institutions that took over failing thrifts at the government's behest.

The ruling upheld decisions by two lower federal courts sustaining breach of contract claims filed by three thrift institutions that agreed to so-called supervisory mergers as part of the S&L bailout during the 1980s. To induce healthy thrifts to take over failing S&Ls, the Federal Savings and Loan Insurance Corporation (FSLIC) allowed them to count "supervisory goodwill" as an asset. But in 1989, Congress passed a law prohibiting the accounting gimmick, forcing many thrifts that had agreed to the mergers into financial difficulty or, in some cases, into liquidation.

Some 100 thrifts filed breach of contract claims against the government, which raised as defenses two legal rules—the unmistakability doctrine and the public or general acts doctrine—that limit government liability in contract cases. The first doctrine says contracts will be read to limit the government's sovereign power only if they do so in "unmistakable" terms. The second rule says that the government cannot be held to violate a contract by passing a law of general applicability—a "public or general act." The Court of Federal Claims and the U.S. Court of Appeals for the Federal Circuit rejected the government's defenses.

In a fractured ruling, the Court agreed the government was liable for damages in the three cases brought before it. Writing for a plurality of four justices, Souter said the unmistakability doctrine did not apply because the thrifts were not trying to block the government's regulation, but only to recover damages for violations of the contract. ". . . [W]e must reject the suggestion," Souter wrote, "that the Government may simply shift costs of legislation onto its contractual partners who are adversely affected by the change in the law, when the Government has assumed the risk of such a change."

Souter also rejected the "public acts" defense, saying the doctrine does not apply when the government has a "self-interest" at stake. ". . . [A] governmental act will not be public and general if it has the substantial effect of releasing the Government from its contractual obligations," he wrote.

Stevens and Breyer concurred in Souter's opinion in full; Breyer also wrote a concurring opinion. O'Connor joined all of the opinion except the discussion of the public acts doctrine, but she did not write separately to explain her views.

In an opinion concurring in the result, Scalia, joined by Kennedy and Thomas, took a broader view of the government's liability. He said the government would have been liable for promising to give the thrifts favorable regulatory treatment even if it had not made the additional promise not to change the regulation in the future.

In a dissent, Rehnquist, joined by Ginsburg, said the ruling misapplied the rules limiting the government's liability in contract suits. A general regulatory law, he wrote, "cannot by its enforcement give rise to contractual liability on the part of the Government."

The decision returned the three cases to lower courts to determine damages. In its briefs, the government warned the Court that a ruling in the thrifts' favor could result in damage awards totaling $10 billion. Some industry observers put the potential figure even higher.

First Amendment

Commercial Speech

44 Liquormart, Inc. v. Rhode Island, decided by a 9–0 vote, May 13, 1996; Stevens wrote the main opinion.

The Court struck down a state law banning liquor price advertising in a fractured ruling that nevertheless suggested a substantially stiffened test for upholding laws or regulations affecting commercial speech.

The ruling stemmed from a challenge by two liquor retailers to a 1956 Rhode Island law that prohibited liquor stores from making any reference to prices in their advertising and barred newspapers or other media from publishing any such advertisements. A federal district court judge struck the law down, but the First U.S. Circuit Court of Appeals upheld it on grounds that it promoted the state's interest in temperance. Alternatively, the court held that the Twenty-first Amendment, which repealed prohibition, gave the states authority to regulate liquor advertising without regard to First Amendment protections for commercial speech.

The justices unanimously agreed that the Rhode Island law violated the First Amendment and was not protected from invalidation by the Twenty-first Amendment. In the main opinion, Stevens said state laws that ban "the dissemination of truthful, nonmisleading commercial messages for reasons unrelated to the preservation of a fair bargaining process" are subject to "rigorous review." Applying that test, he said the Rhode Island law failed because the state had presented "no evidence to suggest that its speech prohibition will *significantly* reduce market-wide consumption."

Two justices—Kennedy and Ginsburg—joined in the section of Stevens's opinion establishing the level of review to be used in the case, and they joined, along with Thomas, in the section analyzing the effect of the

Rhode Island law. In a separate opinion, Thomas went further and said he would bar any law designed "to keep legal users of a product or service ignorant in order to manipulate their choices in the marketplace."

In another separate opinion, however, O'Connor said the case could be decided more narrowly by applying a commercial speech test developed in a 1980 case—*Central Hudson Gas & Electric Corp. v. Public Service Commission of New York*. She said the Rhode Island law failed that test because it was "more extensive than necessary" to serve the state's interest. Rehnquist, Souter, and Breyer joined O'Connor's opinion. Scalia wrote a separate opinion agreeing that the law failed the *Central Hudson* test but expressing no opinion on whether a new test was needed. (*See story, pp. 57–61; excerpts, pp. 167–176.*)

Freedom of Speech

O'Hare Truck Service, Inc. v. City of Northlake, decided by a 7–2 vote, June 28, 1996; Kennedy wrote the opinion; Scalia and Thomas dissented.

A government contractor cannot be terminated for refusing to make political contributions.

The ruling backed a free speech claim by John Gratzianna, the operator of a Chicago area towing service, who said he was removed from a list of companies used by the city of Northlake after refusing to contribute to the mayor's re-election campaign. Gratzianna relied on the Court's 1976 decision, *Elrod v. Burns*, limiting patronage-based firing of government employees. But a federal district court and the Seventh U.S. Circuit Court of Appeals both refused to extend the Court's ruling and dismissed the suit.

In a 7–2 decision, the Court reinstated Gratzianna's suit, saying independent contractors and service providers are similarly protected against retaliatory action for exercising political rights. "We cannot accept the proposition," Kennedy wrote, "that those who perform the government's work outside the formal employment relationship are subject to what we conclude is the direct and specific abridgment of First Amendment rights described in the complaint."

In a dissent, Scalia, joined by Thomas, said the ruling—along with a similar decision announced the same day, *Board of County Commissioners, Wabaunsee County, Kansas v. Umbehr (see below)*— upset the time-honored tradition of political patronage. "Favoritism such as this happens all the time in American political life," Scalia wrote, "and no one has ever thought that it violated— of all things— the First Amendment to the Constitution of the United States."

Board of County Commissioners, Wabaunsee County, Kansas v. Umbehr, decided by a 7–2 vote, June 28, 1996; O'Connor wrote the opinion; Scalia and Thomas dissented.

A government contractor cannot be terminated for exercising freedom of speech on a matter of public interest unless the government demonstrates some legitimate interests that outweigh the contractor's First Amendment rights.

The ruling backed a suit brought by Keen Umbehr, the operator of a trash hauling company. Umbehr claimed that officials in Wabaunsee County, Kansas—just west of Topeka—terminated his contract in retaliation for criticizing their handling of the waste disposal operations. A federal district court dismissed the complaint. But the Tenth U.S. Circuit Court of Appeals reinstated the suit, citing the Supreme Court's 1968 decision, *Pickering v. Board of Education of Township High School Dist. 205, Will Cty.*, limiting retaliatory firings of government employees.

In a 7–2 decision, the Court upheld the appeals court's ruling. ". . . [W]e recognize the right of independent government contractors not to be terminated for exercising their First Amendment rights," O'Connor wrote. But she said the government can defend a termination if it shows that its "legitimate interests as contractor . . . outweigh the free speech interests at stake."

Scalia, joined by Thomas, filed a joint dissent in the case and in a second ruling, *O'Hare Truck Service, Inc. v. City of Northlake*, announced the same day. (*See above.*)

Telecommunications

Denver Area Educational Telecommunications Consortium, Inc. v. Federal Communications Commission, decided by 7–2, 6–3, and 5–4 votes, June 28, 1996; Breyer wrote the main opinion; Kennedy and Ginsburg dissented from one part of the decision; Thomas, Rehnquist, and Scalia dissented from two parts of the decision, joined by O'Connor on one part.

The Court struck down provisions of a 1992 law requiring cable system operators to put sexually explicit programming on a restricted-access channel and permitting them to censor such programming on public access channels. But the justices upheld another provision of the law allowing cable operators to block indecent material on commercially leased channels.

The mixed ruling came in a closely watched challenge brought by cable programmers, who said the indecency provisions of the Cable Television Consumer Protection and Competition Act of 1992 violated the First Amendment.

Two of the provisions—sections 10(a) and 10(c)—allowed cable operators to prohibit sexually explicit material on channels leased to independent programmers or set aside for public use respectively. The third provision—section 10(b)—required cable operators that did not prohibit indecent material to "segregate" such programming on a single channel and "block" the channel unless viewers requested access in writing. A three-judge panel of the U.S. Court of Appeals for the District of Columbia initially struck down all three provisions, but the full court reheard the case and voted 7–4 to uphold all three sections.

Breyer wrote the Court's main opinion, striking down two of the provisions but upholding the third. Breyer agreed that all three provisions served the "compelling" government interest of protecting children from "exposure to patently offensive sex-related material," but said that the "segregate and block" requirement and the public-access channel provision violated the First Amendment because they were not "narrowly tailored." The blocking provision, he said, was "more extensive than necessary" because less intrusive means were available — such as individual television lockboxes and the so-called V chip for blocking violent or sexually explicit programs. As for the third provision, he said the government had presented insufficient evidence of indecent programming on public access channels to justify the change.

Stevens and Souter joined Breyer's opinion in full and also wrote brief concurring opinions. O'Connor joined most of Breyer's opinion, but said she would uphold the provision allowing cable operators to censor public-access channels. The other five justices split into two camps that each took an all-or-nothing approach to the law.

Kennedy, joined by Ginsburg, said he would strike down all three provisions. Disagreeing with Breyer, he said both the leased-access and public-access channel provisions were "a classic case of discrimination against speech based on its content" and could not survive strict scrutiny. But the two justices joined the part of Breyer's opinion striking down the "segregate and block" provision.

Thomas, joined by Rehnquist and Scalia, said he would uphold all three provisions. He said the sections permitting cable operators to restrict sexually explicit material on leased or public-access channels protected rather than restricted cable operators' First Amendment rights. And he said the government had presented sufficient proof that the "segregate and block" requirement was a narrowly tailored provision to serve a compelling interest. *(See story, pp. 49–53; excerpts, pp. 275–292.)*

United States v. Chesapeake and Potomac Telephone Company of Virginia, decided by a 9–0 vote, February 27, 1996; *per curiam* (unsigned) opinion.

The Court sidestepped a ruling on the government's power to limit telephone companies from providing cable television service after Congress passed a law lifting the restriction.

Telephone companies had won a series of federal appeals court rulings striking down as unconstitutional federal regulations that generally prohibited telephone companies from offering cable television within their service area. The Court agreed to settle the issue by accepting the government's appeal of a decision by the Fourth U.S. Circuit Court of Appeals in a case brought by the Chesapeake and Potomac Telephone Co. and its parent company, Bell Atlantic.

Several of the justices sharply questioned the constitutionality of the regulation during oral arguments in December. Meanwhile, Congress was working on broad telecommunications reform legislation that repealed the restriction in hopes of fostering increased competition for cable television. Congress gave final approval to the measure on February 1, 1996, and President Clinton signed the bill on February 8. Less than three weeks later, the Court issued a brief, unsigned ruling sending the case back to the appeals court to determine whether the dispute had become moot.

Individual Rights

Abortion

Dalton, Director, Arkansas Department of Human Services v. Little Rock Family Planning Services, decided by a 9–0 vote, March 18, 1996; *per curiam* (unsigned) opinion.

The Court rejected an effort by the state of Arkansas to enforce a state constitutional amendment prohibiting Medicaid-funded abortions in cases of rape or incest.

The ruling stemmed from a conflict between a 1989 voter-approved measure and federal abortion funding provisions, which allowed payment for terminating pregnancies resulting from rape or incest. A group of physicians and clinics providing abortion services challenged the amendment on grounds it was pre-empted by the federal law. A federal district court judge agreed and issued an injunction striking down the amendment "in its entirety."

In a brief, unsigned ruling, the Court said it was "accepting (without deciding)" the lower court's ruling on the pre-emption issue. But the Court narrowed the injunction, saying the state might apply the broader abortion-funding ban in fully state-financed programs.

Leavitt, Governor of Utah v. Jane L., decided by a 5–4 vote, June 17, 1996; *per curiam* (unsigned) opinion; Stevens, Souter, Ginsburg, and Breyer dissented.

The Court cleared the way for the possible reinstatement of part of Utah's 1991 antiabortion statute, ruling that a federal appeals court misconstrued state law in striking down the entire act.

In an unsigned opinion, the Court said that the Tenth U.S. Circuit Court of Appeals was "plainly wrong" when it refused to uphold the law's provisions prohibiting most abortions after twenty weeks' gestation. The appeals court ruled that the law's restrictions on early-term abortions were unconstitutional and that the more stringent restrictions on late-term procedures could not be "severed" from the invalid part.

Without hearing arguments in the case, the Court held that the appeals court was wrong because the law contained an explicit severability clause indicating the legislature's intent to preserve parts of the law if other parts were struck down. The decision sent the case back to the federal appeals court, where plaintiffs said they would continue to challenge the provisions limiting late-term abortions.

Writing for the four dissenters, Stevens said the decision went against the Court's practice of refusing to review federal appeals court decisions solely for the purpose of deciding a state-law question.

Age Discrimination

O'Connor v. Consolidated Coin Caterers Corp., decided by a 9–0 vote, April 1, 1996; Scalia wrote the opinion.

A plaintiff can win an age discrimination suit without proving he was replaced by someone under forty years old, the threshold age for coverage under the federal Age Discrimination in Employment Act.

The ruling reinstated a suit by a North Carolina man, James O'Connor, who was fired from a job as sales manager at the age of fifty-six and replaced by someone who was forty. O'Connor claimed that the company's president had told him that he was "too damn old" for the job. But the Fourth U.S. Circuit Court of Appeals rejected the suit, saying that O'Connor had to show that his replacement was not covered by the age discrimination law.

In a brief and unanimous decision, the Court rejected that requirement. "The fact that one person in the protected class has lost out to another person in the protected class is . . . irrelevant, so long as he has lost out *because of his age*," Scalia wrote.

Disability Rights

Lane v. Peña, Secretary of Transportation, decided by a 7–2 vote, June 20, 1996; O'Connor wrote the opinion; Stevens and Breyer dissented.

The federal government does not have to pay money damages for violating the law that prohibits discrimination against disabled persons in programs run by federal agencies.

The ruling upheld an appeals court decision denying monetary relief to James Griffin Lane for his termination in 1992 from the U.S. Merchant Marine Academy after he was diagnosed with diabetes. A federal district court ordered Lane reinstated after finding the action violated the 1973

Rehabilitation Act provision that bars discrimination on the basis of disability "under any program or activity conducted by any Executive agency." The lower court said he was also entitled to compensatory damages, but the U.S. Court of Appeals for the District of Columbia Circuit disagreed. It said the 1973 law did not waive the federal government's sovereign immunity against monetary damages.

In a 7–2 decision, the Court agreed. O'Connor noted that the Court requires that a waiver of sovereign immunity be "unequivocally expressed in statutory text." After examining the language of the 1973 law, O'Connor concluded, "The clarity of expression necessary to establish a waiver . . . is lacking. . . ." She acknowledged, however, that the government is liable for damages under a separate provision prohibiting discrimination in employment on the basis of disability.

Writing for the dissenters, Stevens called the result "unfortunate." The Court, he said, "relies on an amalgam of judge-made rules to defeat the clear intent of Congress."

Gay Rights

Romer, Governor of Colorado v. Evans, decided by a 6–3 vote, May 20, 1996; Kennedy wrote the opinion; Scalia, Rehnquist, and Thomas dissented.

A Colorado constitutional amendment that prohibited enactment of any state or local law to prevent discrimination against homosexuals was struck down as a violation of equal protection.

The ruling, a major victory for gay rights' groups, struck down an initiative approved by Colorado voters as Amendment 2 in 1992. The amendment repealed existing anti-gay discrimination laws and prohibited enactment of any such laws in the future. The Colorado Supreme Court ruled the measure unconstitutional, saying it denied gays and lesbians a "fundamental right" of participation in the political process.

The Court affirmed the ruling but on a different ground. Writing for a six-justice majority, Kennedy said the law violated the Fourteenth Amendment's Equal Protection Clause because it was a "status-based enactment" that was "born of animosity" toward homosexuals. "Amendment 2 classifies homosexuals not to further a proper legislative end but to make them unequal to everyone else," Kennedy wrote. "This Colorado cannot do."

In a strongly worded dissent that he emphasized by reading from the bench, Scalia said that the amendment was "an entirely reasonable provision" that was "designed to prevent piecemeal deterioration of the sexual morality favored by a majority of Coloradans. . . ." Rehnquist and Thomas joined Scalia in the dissent. *(See story, pp. 34–38; excerpts, pp. 177–188.)*

Sex Discrimination

United States v. Virginia, decided by a 7–1 vote, June 26, 1996; Ginsburg wrote the opinion; Scalia dissented; Thomas did not participate.

The Court ordered the all-male Virginia Military Institute (VMI) to admit women or lose public funding. The decision also appeared to tighten the Court's standards for reviewing laws that treat men and women differently.

The ruling came in a federal government challenge to the men-only admissions policy at the state-funded military college. The suit claimed the policy violated the Fourteenth Amendment's Equal Protection Clause. Virginia responded to a decision by the Fourth U.S. Circuit Court of Appeals sustaining the claim by creating a new military program for women at a private college. A federal district court said the dual programs satisfied constitutional requirements, and the appeals court—in a split decision—agreed.

By a 7–1 vote, the Court rejected the lower courts' rulings and held the plan violated equal protection requirements. "Women seeking and fit for a V.M.I.-quality education cannot be offered anything less under the State's obligation to afford them genuinely equal protection," Ginsburg wrote.

In her opinion, Ginsburg reiterated the so-called intermediate scrutiny test for reviewing gender-based laws or policies: that they must serve "important" government interests and be "substantially related" to those objectives. But she also gave new emphasis to a requirement that the government must demonstrate an "exceedingly persuasive justification" for gender-based policies.

Rehnquist concurred, but did not join Ginsburg's opinion. He said the new women's program was "distinctly inferior to the men's institution." He also faulted VMI for failing to take any steps to cure the inequity until after the lawsuit was brought.

In a lone—and biting—dissent, Scalia said Virginia had a legitimate interest in funding VMI as an all-male institution with a distinctive curriculum and teaching style. He also charged the ruling changed the standard for reviewing gender-based government action and threatened any single-sex college or university that receives government assistance.

Thomas did not participate in the case because his son, Jamal Thomas, attended VMI at the time. *(See story, pp. 38–42; excerpts, pp. 252–275.)*

Labor Law

Antitrust Exemption

Brown v. Pro Football, Inc., dba Washington Redskins, decided by an 8–1 vote, June 20, 1996; Breyer wrote the opinion; Stevens dissented.

A group of employers that has reached an impasse in joint labor negotiations can unilaterally adopt the terms of its last offer without violating federal antitrust laws.

The ruling stemmed from a dispute between the National Football League (NFL) owners and the Players Association, but applied to other industries where joint employers' groups bargain with unions representing workers. The decision nullified a $30 million antitrust damage award against the NFL owners for imposing a salary cap of $1,000 per week on substitute players after the league failed to reach an agreement with the NFL Players Association in 1989. The players, supported by the Clinton administration, brought the case to the Court after a federal appeals court agreed with the owners that the award was improper because of the so-called nonstatutory labor exemption from antitrust laws.

In a nearly unanimous decision, the Court held that the antitrust exemption applies when a multiemployers group adopts its last, best good-faith offer after reaching an impasse in collective bargaining. Breyer said the exemption was needed to protect multiemployer bargaining. "... [T]o permit antitrust liability here threatens to introduce instability and uncertainty into the collective bargaining process," he wrote.

Breyer noted that multiemployer bargaining was common in many industries—including construction, transportation, retail trade, clothing manufacture, and real estate, as well as professional sports. He rejected arguments by the Players Association that professional sports is "special" because individual teams are not independent economic competitors and because players individually negotiate salaries. "... [I]t would be odd to fashion an antitrust exemption that gave additional advantages to professional football players ... that transport workers, coal miners, or meat packers would not enjoy," he wrote.

In a lone dissent, Stevens said the decision extended the antitrust exemption beyond its original purpose. "... [I]t would be most ironic to extend an exemption crafted to protect collective action by employees to protect employers acting jointly to deny employees the opportunity to negotiate their salaries individually in a competitive market," he wrote.

Labor-Management Relations

Auciello Iron Works, Inc. v. National Labor Relations Board, decided by a 9–0 vote, June 3, 1996; Souter wrote the opinion.

An employer cannot disavow a collective bargaining agreement based on doubts about a union's majority status that the employer held prior to formation of the contract.

The ruling upheld a finding by the National Labor Relations Board (NLRB) that a small Massachusetts company committed an unfair labor practice by renouncing a collective bargaining agreement in November

1988, one day after the union accepted the contract to end a strike. The company said it had "good-faith doubts" that the union still enjoyed majority support from the plant's twenty-three workers. The NLRB ruled, however, that an employer cannot disavow an agreement based on doubts that existed before formation of the contract.

In a unanimous opinion, the Court said the NLRB's position was a "reasonable" interpretation of the National Labor Relations Act. Souter said that allowing a "postformation challenge" to a contract "would hardly serve the Act's goal of achieving industrial peace by promoting stable collective-bargaining relationships." He noted that the company could have acted on its doubts before the union accepted its contract offer—for example, by initiating steps to have the union decertified.

Holly Farms Corp. v. National Labor Relations Board, decided by 9–0 and 5–4 votes, April 23, 1996; Ginsburg wrote the opinion; O'Connor, Rehnquist, Scalia, and Thomas dissented in part.

The Court extended federal labor law protection to "chicken-catcher" crews, rejecting a major poultry processor's claim that the workers were agricultural laborers exempt from the federal statute.

The ruling rejected an effort by Holly Farms Corp. to overturn a National Labor Relations Board (NLRB) order recognizing the chicken-catcher crews as a bargaining unit under the National Labor Relations Act. The crews included chicken catchers, forklift operators, and drivers involved in catching, loading, and transporting poultry from farms to the company's processing plant. Holly Farms, which was taken over by Tyson Foods but continued to operate under its prior name, contended all the workers should be classified as exempt agricultural laborers because they performed their work on farms.

The Court unanimously held the drivers were not agricultural workers, but divided 5–4 on the status of the other employees. Writing for the majority, Ginsburg said the NLRB had reached a "reasonable" conclusion that the collection of poultry for slaughter "was an activity serving Holly Farms' processing operations" rather than its "farming operations."

In a partial dissent, O'Connor said the ruling on the chicken catchers and forklift operators "runs contrary to common sense and finds no support in the text of the relevant statute."

National Labor Relations Board v. Town & Country Electric, Inc., decided by a 9–0 vote, November 28, 1995; Breyer wrote the opinion.

Federal labor law protects workers from antiunion discrimination even if a union is paying the worker to help organize the company.

The ruling protected the tactic—called "salting"—of placing union members with nonunion companies to try to organize the company's employees from within. The issue reached the Court after the National

Labor Relations Board found that a nonunion electrical contractor in Wisconsin discriminated against members of the International Brotherhood of Electrical Workers by refusing to hire them or firing them because of their union membership.

In a unanimous opinion, Breyer said the union members were "employees" as defined by "the broad language" of the National Labor Relations Act. He said the interpretation was consistent with the purposes of the act and with prior Court decisions interpreting the law.

Pensions and Benefits

Lockheed Corp. v. Spink, decided by 9–0 and 7–2 votes, June 10, 1996; Thomas wrote the opinion; Breyer and Souter dissented in part.

Employers can require workers to give up any employment-related legal claims in order to receive increased pension benefits under an early buyout plan.

The ruling, an important victory for business groups, backed the aircraft manufacturer Lockheed Corporation in a dispute with a retired military-jet designer, Paul Spink. Spink refused an early retirement buyout in 1990 because the provision required him to give up any potential legal claims against the company. The Ninth U.S. Circuit Court of Appeals ruled that the buyout proviso violated the federal Employee Retirement Income Security Act—known as ERISA—because it amounted to using pension-plan assets to "purchase" legal protection.

Reversing the appeals panel, the Court held that ERISA does not prevent an employer from conditioning the receipt of early retirement benefits upon a waiver of legal claims. In a mostly unanimous opinion, Thomas said that Lockheed and its directors had not violated ERISA because an employer is not subject to special obligations as a "fiduciary" when it revises a pension plan.

Thomas also said that the conditional payment of benefits under the plan did not amount to a "transaction" for which the plan's administrators could be held liable under ERISA. "The payment of benefits pursuant to an amended plan, regardless of what the plan requires of the employee in return for those benefits, does not constitute a prohibited transaction," Thomas wrote.

The ruling also rejected Spink's underlying legal claim that he was entitled to credit under the pension plan for an additional two years of service because of a 1988 federal law that made him eligible for the plan. Thomas said that Spink could not get credit for years worked prior to 1988 because Congress did not intend the law to apply retroactively.

Several business groups filed friend-of-the-court briefs supporting Lockheed, which was merged while the suit was pending into the Lockheed

Martin Corp. The Clinton administration sided with Spink. Breyer, joined by Souter, filed a partial dissent, agreeing with the administration's position that it was unnecessary to rule on the broad question whether a conditional pension-plan payment could ever amount to a prohibited transaction.

Varity Corp. v. Howe, decided by a 6–3 vote, March 19, 1996; Breyer wrote the opinion; Thomas, O'Connor, and Scalia dissented.

Workers may bring individual suits against employers under the federal Employee Retirement Income Security Act (ERISA) for intentionally misleading them about employee health or pension benefits.

The ruling backed a suit by former employees of the Massey-Ferguson Co., a farm implements manufacturer, who said they lost health benefits after agreeing to be transferred to a spinoff company, Varity Corp. Workers were told their benefits would be safe under the new company, but in fact Varity was created to take on Massey-Ferguson's money-losing operations and was financially insolvent.

The workers won a $46 million damage judgment at trial, but the award was eventually reduced by a federal appeals court to $800,000. Varity was also ordered to reinstate the employees' health benefits. Varity asked the Court to review the decision, claiming that the company did not violate ERISA and that the law in any event did not permit the workers' suit.

In a 6–3 decision, the Court backed the workers on both issues. Breyer said the company violated its "fiduciary" obligation as the administrator of the benefits plan. "To participate knowingly and significantly in deceiving a plan's beneficiaries in order to save the employer money at the beneficiaries' expense is not to act 'solely in the interest of the participants and beneficiaries,'" he wrote, quoting the act. He also said the provision authorizing "appropriate equitable relief" for a violation of the act was "broad enough to cover individual relief for breach of a fiduciary obligation."

Writing for the dissenters, Thomas said the ruling was "fundamentally at odds with the statutory scheme enacted by Congress." He also warned that an expansive reading of the decision could result in "heightened liability" for employers and "an eventual reduction in pension benefits."

Plant Closings

United Food and Commercial Workers Union Local 751 v. Brown Group, Inc., dba Brown Shoe Co., decided by a 9–0 vote, May 13, 1996; Souter wrote the opinion.

Labor unions can sue on behalf of their members to enforce a federal law that requires employers to give advance notice of plant closings and provides backpay damages for violations of the act.

The decision backed a United Food and Commercial Workers local in a dispute stemming from the Brown Shoe Company's 1992 closing of a plant in Dixon, Missouri, that resulted in the layoff of 277 workers. The union claimed the company failed to comply with the sixty-days' notice provision of the Worker Adjustment and Retraining and Notification Act. But two federal courts ruled the union had no standing to bring the suit.

In a unanimous opinion, the Court disagreed. Souter said that the law explicitly gives unions the right to sue on behalf of their members and that Congress had power to authorize suits by unions despite a court-made doctrine limiting the ability of associations to sue on behalf of members.

Railroad Employees

Brotherhood of Locomotive Engineers v. Atchison, Topeka & Santa Fe Railroad Co., decided by a 9–0 vote, January 8, 1996; Kennedy wrote the opinion.

Railroad crews are not counted as on duty while waiting for "deadhead transportation" back to a terminal or rest station after having completed their shifts.

The unanimous ruling gave railroads a victory in a disputed interpretation of the Hours of Service Act, a 1907 law limiting the time a train crew can remain on duty. In amending the law in 1969, Congress provided that time spent being transported to a work assignment counts as on-duty time, but time spent "in deadhead transportation from a duty assignment" is classified as "limbo time"—neither on or off duty.

Two federal appeals courts differed on whether to classify the time a crew spends waiting for transportation away from a work assignment as on-duty or limbo time. In settling the issue, the Court ruled that the statutory phrase "can be read to include the time spent waiting" for transportation. In addition, Kennedy said that waiting time after a duty assignment "does not cause the fatigue that implicates [the] safety concerns" underlying the statute.

Norfolk & Western Railway Co. v. Hiles, decided by a 9–0 vote, February 27, 1996; Thomas wrote the opinion.

The Court slightly limited a railroad's liability for injuries to an employee resulting from problems in the operation of the automatic coupling mechanism required on railroad cars since 1893.

The ruling ordered a new state court trial for a Norfolk & Western Railway employee who suffered a back injury in 1990 while trying to correct a misaligned "drawbar," the mechanism that holds the automatic coupling device. Illinois courts ruled that the federal Safety Appliance Act, the 1893 law that required automatic couplers, imposed absolute liability on railroads for any injuries caused by a malfunction in the device.

In a unanimous opinion, Thomas said the ruling extended the railroad's liability too far. Thomas noted that the Court had imposed automatic liability on railroads for having no coupler or a malfunctioning coupler. But he said that a misaligned drawbar was "a part of the normal course of railroad operations" and did not amount to a violation of the 1893 law.

Seaman Suits

Henderson v. United States, decided by a 6–3 vote, May 20, 1996; Ginsburg wrote the opinion; Thomas, Rehnquist, and O'Connor dissented.

The Court loosened the time period for a merchant mariner injured aboard a vessel owned by the United States to have the complaint served on the attorney general or local U.S. attorney.

The ruling resolved a conflict between a provision of the 1920 Suits in Admiralty Act, requiring service of process "forthwith," and recent revisions of the Federal Rules of Civil Procedure, setting a 120-day time period that judges have broad discretion to extend. Two lower federal courts ordered a suit brought by an injured seaman in 1993 dismissed under the 1920 law because of a forty-seven-day delay in serving the complaint on the attorney general.

In a 6–3 decision, the Court held that the general rule on service of process "supersedes" the provision in the 1920 law. Ginsburg rejected the government's argument—adopted by the three dissenting justices—that the requirement for immediate service of process was intended as a condition of the government's agreeing to waive sovereign immunity and permit such suits.

States

Border Disputes

Louisiana v. Mississippi, decided by a 9–0 vote, October 31, 1995; Kennedy wrote the opinion.

The Court sided with Mississippi in a border dispute involving 2,000 acres of land that had gradually shifted from an island in the Mississippi River to adjoin the river's western bank in Louisiana.

In a brief opinion, the Court unanimously upheld findings by the "special master" it appointed to hear the case and ruled that the disputed land should be awarded to Mississippi. The land had moved as the river shifted to the East. But Kennedy explained that a boundary established around an island remains fixed even if the river's main channel shifts to the other side.

The decision came in an original suit filed in the Court by Louisiana. Earlier, the Court in 1992 had refused to rule on the issues in a private lawsuit filed by property owners to settle ownership of the land.

Immunity

Seminole Tribe of Florida v. Florida, decided by a 5–4 vote, March 27, 1996; Rehnquist wrote the opinion; Souter, Stevens, Ginsburg, and Breyer dissented.

A federal law authorizing Native American tribes to sue states to force negotiations over gaming on Indian reservations violates the Eleventh Amendment's restriction on suits against states in federal courts.

The decision—a major ruling on states' rights and federal court jurisdiction—struck down parts of the Indian Gaming Regulatory Act, passed by Congress in 1988. The law required states to negotiate "in good faith" with Indian tribes over gaming issues and gave tribes the right to sue in federal court to enforce the requirement. When the Seminole Tribe took the state of Florida to court over the issue, however, a federal district court and the Eleventh U.S. Circuit Court of Appeals ruled the provision unconstitutional.

In a 5–4 ruling, the Court agreed. In most instances, Rehnquist said, "the Eleventh Amendment prevents congressional authorization of suits by private parties against unconsenting states." He also refused to allow the suit under an alternative doctrine that permits individuals to sue state officials in federal court.

In a ninety-two-page dissent, Souter, joined by Ginsburg and Breyer, argued that the ruling went beyond the text of the Eleventh Amendment and the Court's precedents. In a shorter dissent, Stevens called the ruling an "affront to a coequal branch of our government."

The decision overruled a 1989 ruling, *Pennsylvania v. Union Gas Co.,* that had permitted federal court suits against states to enforce a federal regulatory statute. But it did not affect civil rights suits brought against states under the Fourteenth Amendment's Equal Protection Clause. *(See story, pp. 42–46; excerpts, pp. 154–167.)*

Taxation

Fulton Corp. v. Faulkner, Secretary of Revenue of North Carolina, decided by a 9–0 vote, February 21, 1996; Souter wrote the opinion.

A state may not tax stock owned by state residents in out-of-state corporations while exempting in-state corporate stock from the levy.

The unanimous decision ruled North Carolina's so-called intangibles tax was unconstitutional because it discriminated against interstate commerce. Souter said the law favored in-state corporations over out-of-state companies in raising capital within North Carolina. He also said the tax could not be justified by factors recognized in other rulings as justifying differential treatment of out-of-state companies in limited circumstances.

North Carolina repealed the tax in 1995, but the ruling meant that the state might have to pay refunds. State officials said they had received refund requests totaling $125 million from more than 233,000 individuals and corporations.

Richards v. Jefferson County, Alabama, decided by a 9–0 vote, June 10, 1996; Stevens wrote the opinion.

Alabama courts improperly dismissed a federal law challenge to a county occupation tax brought by taxpayers who had not been parties to a previous unsuccessful state lawsuit against the levy.

The taxpayers filed a class action suit citing state and federal grounds to challenge an occupation tax imposed to help finance construction of the Birmingham–Jefferson County Civic Center. A state court judge and the Alabama Supreme Court ordered the suit dismissed because the levy had previously been upheld in a declaratory judgment action brought by the city of Birmingham and its acting finance director. The state courts cited the doctrine of *res judicata,* which permits a court to dismiss a suit if the issue has already been decided in a previous case.

In a unanimous decision, the Court ruled the state courts had violated the taxpayers' due process rights by misapplying the doctrine. Stevens said that the taxpayers' federal claims could not be dismissed because the taxpayers had not been parties to the first case and had not received notice of the suit or been adequately represented in it.

Torts

Punitive Damages

BMW of North America, Inc. v. Gore, decided by a 5–4 vote, May 20, 1996; Stevens wrote the opinion; Scalia, Rehnquist, Ginsburg, and Thomas dissented.

The Court overturned as "grossly excessive" a $2 million punitive damage award to an Alabama man for an automobile manufacturer's failure to disclose a refinished paint job on a car he purchased as new.

The ruling, an important victory for critics of punitive damage awards, ordered Alabama courts to reconsider the award to Dr. Ira Gore, the Birmingham physician who bought the BMW sedan in 1990. He sued BMW after discovering that the car had been repainted because of damage found after it left the factory. An Alabama jury awarded Gore $4,000 in compensatory damages and $4 million in punitive damages. The Alabama Supreme Court reduced the punitive damage award to $2 million but otherwise upheld the jury's verdict.

In a 5–4 decision, the Court ruled that the $2 million punitive damage award "exceeds the constitutional limit" under the Due Process Clause. Stevens said first that a state "may not impose economic sanctions" in order to punish a defendant's "lawful conduct in other states." He then found the award to Gore excessive for three reasons. First, BMW's conduct was not "particularly reprehensible." Second, the punitive damages award was 500 times the amount of compensatory damages—a "breathtaking" ratio. Third, the award was "substantially greater" than statutory fines for such conduct.

Breyer, joined by O'Connor and Souter, added a concurring opinion that criticized Alabama's standards for punitive damage awards as "vague and open-ended to the point where they risk arbitrary results."

The decision left it to the Alabama Supreme Court to determine whether to reconsider the amount of punitive damages itself or to order a new trial. In separate dissenting opinions, Scalia, joined by Thomas, and Ginsburg, joined by Rehnquist, said the ruling improperly intruded into an area reserved for the states. *(See story, pp. 46–49; excerpts, pp. 188–199.)*

Warsaw Convention

Zicherman v. Korean Air Lines Co., decided by a 9–0 vote, January 16, 1996; Scalia wrote the opinion.

Relatives of passengers killed in an airplane crash over international waters cannot recover damages for loss of companionship.

The decision reduced damage awards won by the mother and sister of one of the victims of the 1983 crash of a Korean Air Lines (KAL) jet that was shot down after it strayed into air space of the Soviet Union. The mother had been awarded $70,000 and the sister $28,000 for "the loss of love, affection, and companionship." But KAL argued on appeal that these so-called "loss of society" damages are not permitted under the Warsaw Convention, the international treaty governing damages for airline crashes involving international carriers.

Writing for a unanimous Court, Scalia said the Warsaw Convention left it up to each country to apply its own law in determining what damages can be recovered. He then said that the crash was covered by the federal Death on the High Seas Act, which expressly limits damage awards to "pecuniary" losses.

The ruling was expected to affect about fifty other suits stemming from the KAL crash. Scalia left open the question whether loss of society damages would be permitted in suits arising from an overland crash, such as the 1988 bombing and crash of Pan Am Flight 103 over Scotland.

4 | *Preview of the 1996–1997 Term*

Out in western Montana, Ravilli County Sheriff Jay Printz oversees a rugged domain twice the size of Rhode Island. Three years ago, when the new Brady act required his small office to run background checks on handgun buyers, the self-described "independent son of a gun" simply refused.

"I've got too much to do, and here they are telling me I have to do federal background checks," Printz said. "I basically felt this was not my job."

In rural southeastern Arizona, Sheriff Richard Mack felt the same way. "I was elected by, for, and of the people of Graham County to do their bidding," Mack remarked. "They're my boss, and the federal government has no right to divert my attention from Graham County matters to serve their agenda."

But gun-control advocate Sarah Brady, who worked for more than eight years on the bill, maintained the federal government had "a responsibility" to enact the law. "When states do not do their own work, there are certain issues that cross state lines," says Brady, whose husband, James, was seriously wounded in the 1981 assassination attempt on President Ronald Reagan. "Gun control is one of those issues."

Printz and Mack took their objections to court, contending that the law violated the states' rights protections contained in the Tenth Amendment of the U.S. Constitution. Federal district court judges in Montana and Arizona agreed. But the government took the case to the Ninth U.S. Circuit Court of Appeals, which upheld the law in a 2–1 ruling in September 1995.

Now the case is before the Supreme Court, which agreed in June to put it on the calendar for the 1996–1997 term. The Court acted after two other federal appeals courts had ruled on suits by local sheriffs contesting the law. The Second Circuit in New York upheld the law, while the New Orleans-based Fifth Circuit struck it down. Mack and Printz both asked the justices to overturn the decision in their case. The Justice Department agreed that the Court should settle the issue, but it urged the justices to uphold the law. "The Brady Act," the Solicitor General's office said in its brief, "is an important federal statute directed at one of the most serious issues of public safety currently facing the nation—the epidemic of gun violence." (*Printz v. United States; Mack v. United States*)

The Brady act case was one of forty-six disputes the justices agreed to carry over to the new term before they left Washington for their summer recess. The other cases included some familiar issues, such as racial redis-

tricting and abortion protests. The Court also agreed to decide an important separation of powers issue: whether President Bill Clinton could delay
until after he left office any proceedings in a civil suit charging him with
sexual harassment.

The number of cases accepted for review at the start of the recess was
appreciably higher than the figure — thirty-three — at the same time in the
previous year. But it was still lower than the comparable figure in the recent
past. The Court began its 1990–1991 term, for example, with seventy cases.
Still, the increase gave some hint that the Court might be moving toward
increasing its overall output of decisions during the term. The number of
signed opinions had fallen for ten consecutive years and reached a forty-
year low of seventy-five in the 1995–1996 term.

In keeping with a new practice of the past several years, the justices in
late September also announced, in advance of the start of the new term,
another seven cases to be added to the calendar for the coming year. The
actions brought to fifty-three the number of disputes before the Court as
the justices prepared to convene on the first Monday in October.

The newly added cases included one of the Court's most important,
and controversial, issues for the coming term: the constitutionality of laws
banning doctor-assisted suicide. A growing "right-to-die" movement had
been contending that someone who is terminally ill has a constitutional
right to seek a doctor's help in ending his or her life. Religious and medical groups strongly opposed the movement, but the public appeared to be
divided and uncertain about the issue. Voters in Oregon approved a ballot
measure to permit doctor-assisted suicide in 1994, but similar initiatives
had gone down to defeat in California and Washington earlier.

The issue reached the Court after federal appeals courts struck down
laws from New York and Washington that made it a crime for a doctor to
assist a patient in committing suicide. The two courts based their rulings on
different rationales. In the Washington case, *Washington v. Glucksberg,* the
Ninth U.S. Circuit Court of Appeals ruled that there was "a liberty interest
in choosing the time and manner of one's death" that outweighed the
state's interest in preventing suicide. In the New York case, *Vacco v. Quill,* the
Second U.S. Circuit Court of Appeals said the ban violated the Fourteenth
Amendment's Equal Protection Clause. The court reasoned that since terminally ill patients have the right to end their lives by refusing life-sustain-
ing treatment, the state had no "rational basis" for preventing others from
seeking a doctor's help in hastening their deaths.

The Court's only ruling in the area had come in 1990, when it held, in
Cruzan v. Missouri Dept. of Health, that a terminally ill patient does have a
constitutional right to refuse life-saving treatment. But that ruling allowed
states to regulate the practice by requiring "clear and convincing evidence"
of the patient's wishes before medical personnel can disconnect life-sup-
port systems.

The justices' decision to review Clinton's presidential immunity claim ensured that any further proceedings in the civil case would be delayed until after the November election. A federal appeals court had ruled that pretrial discovery could proceed, but Clinton, through his personal attorney, and the Justice Department urged the Court to review the decision.

The Court had never before ruled on the issue whether a president could be sued while in office. But the Court in 1982 ruled in a case against President Richard M. Nixon that the chief executive is absolutely immune while serving in the White House and after leaving office from civil suit for any official actions as president.

The abortion protest case gave the Court an opportunity to elaborate on its 1994 decision allowing federal judges to limit antiabortion demonstrations outside clinics. In that case, *Madsen v. Women's Health Center,* the Court had upheld a court order establishing a thirty-six-foot "buffer zone" around a Florida clinic. In the new case, a federal appeals court in New York upheld a lower court's order requiring abortion protesters to keep at least fifteen feet away from women as they entered or left a Buffalo facility.

The racial redistricting case was to be the Court's second look at efforts to draw new congressional districts in Georgia as a result of the 1990 census. In its first ruling, the Court in 1995 struck down a plan drawn by the Georgia legislature, under pressure from the U.S. Justice Department, that contained three majority-black districts. The new case involved a plan drawn by a three-judge federal court that contained only one district with a majority black population. The plan was attacked by the Clinton administration, the state of Georgia, and civil rights groups, but defended by the white voters who challenged the original redistricting scheme.

The Court was also to take a second look at the federal law requiring cable operators to carry local broadcast television stations on their systems. In its first ruling on the "must-carry" provision, the Court in 1994 increased the First Amendment protections for cable systems but, by a 5–4 vote, gave the government another chance to try to justify the law. The cable industry brought the dispute back to the Court again after the three-judge court that had originally upheld the law again sided with the government.

About one-fourth of the cases being carried over to the new term involved criminal law issues. Among the most important was a Kansas case testing the constitutionality of laws permitting sexual offenders to be committed to mental institutions even if they are not diagnosed as mentally ill. Kansas was one of six states to enact such laws, but the state's high court ruled the measure violated the Fourteenth Amendment's Due Process Clause.

The justices also took up a case challenging a restrictive "English-only" constitutional amendment adopted by Arizona in 1988. But procedural difficulties created the possibility that the Court would not rule on the merits of the issue. The Court agreed to review a number of other civil rights cases and Voting Rights Act cases. After a term with a number of important business law rulings, the calendar for the new term seemed to have relatively few such cases.

Legal observers were also closely watching another case that reached the Court over the summer to see whether the justices would add it to the calendar for the term. The government was appealing a ruling that struck down a new law aimed at preventing children from gaining access to sexually explicit material on the Internet or other computer networks.

The Internet case—*Reno v. American Civil Liberties Union*—involved provisions of the Communications Decency Act that prohibited the use of an interactive computer service to knowingly send "patently offensive" material to a minor or to display it in a manner available to a minor. The American Civil Liberties Union led a coalition of First Amendment advocates in bringing a legal challenge to the law in February, on the same day that President Clinton signed the measure. In June, a three-judge court in Philadelphia agreed with the ACLU's claim that the law violated free speech rights protected by the First Amendment. The government filed its appeal of the ruling in late September, and legal observers regarded it as virtually certain that the justices would agree to hear the case.

Brady Act Case

The Brady act case brought a major dispute over states' rights and federalism to the Court for the third year in a row. States' rights advocates had won two victories striking down federal laws. In 1995, the Court threw out a law making it a federal crime to possess a gun near a school zone. The following year, the Court invalidated a provision allowing Indian tribes to sue states in federal courts over gambling issues. "There is a very active interest by a majority of the Court in rethinking the power relationship between Congress and the states," commented Stephen Wermeil, a professor at Georgia State University School of Law in Atlanta who formerly covered the Court for the *Wall Street Journal.*

The Brady act case presented an issue under the Tenth Amendment, added to the Constitution as part of the Bill of Rights in 1791: "The powers not delegated to the United States by the Constitution, nor prohibited by it to the States, are reserved to the States respectively, or to the people." Despite its seemingly broad wording, the amendment lost force over time as Congress took on powers under other constitutional provisions—for example, the power to regulate interstate commerce. From the late 1930s on, the Court upheld congressional enactments against Tenth Amendment challenges. In one case, the Court dismissed the amendment as only "a truism."

In 1992, however, the Court breathed some new life into the amendment. In *New York v. United States,* the Court voted 6–3 to strike down a law aimed at forcing the states to adopt plans to dispose of low-level radioactive wastes from nuclear power plants. The law said that states that failed to deal with the problem would have to take ownership of the privately generated wastes and assume liability for any injuries the waste caused. In an opinion by Justice O'Connor, the Court ruled that Congress had overstepped the bounds of state sovereignty. "The Federal Government may not compel the States to enact or administer a federal regulatory program," O'Connor wrote.

Opponents said the Brady act represented the same kind of congressional overreaching. "The federal government, as a matter of separation of powers and separation of governments, simply cannot control the office of a constitutionally elected sheriff any more than the Wal-Mart manager can tell a K-Mart employee what to do," Sheriff Mack, the Arizona lawman challenging the act, said.

Supporters of the law maintained, however, that the opponents were misreading the New York decision and ignoring other precedents. "The Brady bill does not require states to legislate or to enact public policy," Dennis Henigan, general counsel of the lobbying group Handgun Control, explained. "All it requires is the limited assistance of local officials in carrying out a federal policy. We think that the Tenth Amendment permits the federal government to enlist the help of state and local officials where the federal policy is made more effective through their participation."

Handgun Control had played the pivotal role in winning enactment of the Brady bill over the determined opposition of the National Rifle Association and other gun owners' groups. Sarah Brady, who had worked with the organization for more than a decade, said the bill was designed "to keep guns out of the hands of the wrong people"—for example, convicted felons, persons with a history of mental illness, and young people. The bill established a mandatory five-day waiting period to buy a handgun and required local law enforcement agencies to make a "reasonable effort" to run a background check on the prospective gun purchaser during that time.

The fight over the bill raged through Congress for nearly a decade. First, opponents in both parties bottled it up. Then they diverted it by proposing a study of an alternative system: an instant computerized background check, run by the federal government. Brady bill supporters insisted the "instant check" system would require years to design. The House and the Senate both approved versions of the proposal in 1991, but the measure died in a partisan standoff at the end of the congressional session in 1992.

The next year, however, President Clinton gave the bill his full support, urging the Democratic-controlled Congress to send it to his desk for his signature. To accommodate the critics, the bill was amended to provide that the federal government design an instant-check system and put it into

Former White House press secretary James Brady meets with reporters at the Supreme Court to discuss the constitutional challenge to the Brady act's provision requiring local law enforcement agencies to conduct background checks of prospective handgun purchasers.

operation by 1998. Despite the change, Sarah Brady said she was exhilarated. "That year was wonderful," she said.

Major law enforcement organizations, including the National Sheriffs Association and the International Association of Chiefs of Police, had joined in urging enactment of the bill. Despite that support, Sheriffs Mack and Printz said they always thought the bill would accomplish little in the way of crime control. "It was pretty obvious to me that this was a worthless piece of legislation," said Printz.

In their suits against the law, both sheriffs depicted the bill as a substantial burden on local law enforcement, especially in small rural counties like theirs. "This is not a simple thing," Printz said. "You've got to check for mentally ill people, people who've been discharged from the military, illegal aliens. There are all sorts of people in there that aren't supposed to get these things."

Supporters insisted that the opponents exaggerated the burdens. "The sheriffs have consistently overstated the nature and extent of the mandate," Dennis Henigan said. "They have refused to recognize what is plain from the statute itself: the mandate is a flexible one, giving the sheriffs and other local police great discretion in deciding exactly what background checks to do with regard to each background applicant."

Sheriffs Jay Printz, above, and Richard Mack.

In upholding the law, the Ninth Circuit panel agreed. Writing for the majority, Judge William C. Canby said the law imposed only "minimal obligations" on local law enforcement officials. The law, he said, was not the kind of intrusion on state sovereignty that the Court found unacceptable in the radioactive-waste law.

In a dissent, however, Judge Ferdinand Fernandez called the law objectionable whatever the size of the burden. The act, Fernandez said, "makes every [local law enforcement] office an office of the federal bureaucracy, funded by the states but directed from Washington. The time to stop this journey of a thousand miles is at the first step."

The sheriffs echoed that theme in urging the Court to review the decision. "Sheriffs are not field offices of the [federal] bureaucracy," Printz's attorney, Stephen Halbrook, wrote in his appeal. Mack's attorney, David Hardy, said the law reduced local sheriffs to the status of "messengers and file clerks." But the government responded that the law was "consistent with the long-settled understanding that Congress can impose certain duties on state officers to carry out federal law."

Given the Court's recent states' rights trend, supporters of the law had reason to fear it would be struck down. The six justices who voted to invalidate the radioactive-waste law were all still on the Court. They included the five conservatives who formed the majorities in the two most recent states' rights decisions—Chief Justice Rehnquist and Justices O'Connor, Scalia, Kennedy, and Thomas—as well as Justice Souter, who had voted to uphold the federal laws in the recent cases.

Still, the Brady act's supporters were guardedly optimistic about the outcome. "The plaintiffs are arguing for an absolute prohibition on any kind of federal mandate to state or local officials," Dennis Henigan said. "I do not believe that this Court will take an absolutist view on the power of the federal government to enlist the assistance of state and local officials in implementing federal policy."

Opponents, however, strongly believed that they would prevail. "We're governed by the rule of law, which begins with the Constitution," Stephen Halbrook, who was to argue the case before the justices, said. "It's not within the provisions of the Constitution that Congress can conscript state and local governments as its agent in enforcing federal laws."

Following are some of the other major cases on the Supreme Court calendar as it began its 1996–1997 term:

Business Law

Patents. The justices agreed to re-examine an important court-made rule called the "doctrine of equivalents" that makes it easier for inventors to protect patents. The doctrine allows patent-holders to recover damages for infringement if a competitor markets a process or device that is "substantially equivalent" to the patent-holder's invention even if it is not identical.

The issue arose in a dispute between two chemical companies that independently developed similar processes for removing impurities from food dyes. Hilton-Davis Chemical Co., which patented its process in 1985, won a $3.6 million damage award after a jury agreed the rival process, developed by Warner-Jenkinson Co., infringed its patent. On appeal, the U.S. Court of Appeals for the Federal Circuit upheld the verdict on a 7–5 vote.

In urging the Court to review the case, Warner-Jenkinson contended that the doctrine of equivalents conflicts with the federal patent statute and "leads to obvious uncertainty and complication" for inventors and litigants in patent disputes. But Hilton-Davis, quoting language from a 1950 Supreme Court decision, argued that scrapping the doctrine would "return the patent system to the dark ages when anyone can 'practice a fraud on a patent' simply by making 'unimportant and insubstantial changes.' "

The case attracted more than a dozen friend-of-the-court briefs from companies and industry groups on both sides of the issue. In a brief supporting neither side, the American Intellectual Property Law Association urged the Court to retain the doctrine but give primary responsibility for applying it to judges instead of juries. (*Warner-Jenkinson Co., Inc. v. Hilton-Davis Chemical Co.*)

Savings and loan suits. The government sought to fend off efforts to limit its ability to recover damages from officers and directors of savings and loan institutions that collapsed during the 1980s. The issue arose in a suit by the Federal Deposit Insurance Corporation, acting as receiver for a New Jersey thrift institution that became insolvent because of bad real-estate loans. The former officers and directors contended the 1989 S&L bailout law required the government to prove "gross negligence" rather than ordinary negligence in order to recover. But the government argued the defendants were misreading the law, which it said was designed to strengthen the enforcement powers of federal banking regulators. (*Atherton v. Federal Deposit Insurance Corporation*)

Taxation. The Court agreed to decide whether punitive damage awards are subject to federal income taxation. The husband and children of a Kansas woman who died of toxic shock syndrome were awarded $10 million in punitive damages in a suit against a tampon manufacturer. They argued that the award was exempt from taxation under the federal tax code because it was received "on account of personal injuries." But the government contended the exemption did not apply because punitive damages are intended to punish a wrongdoer rather than compensate an individual for injuries. (*O'Gilvie v. United States*)

Courts and Procedure

Indigent appeals. A Mississippi woman asked the Court to rule that states must guarantee poor people the right to appeal in parental rights cases even if they cannot afford to pay for a transcript of the trial. A state judge in 1993 found the woman physically and mentally unfit and terminated her parental rights to her two young children. The woman sought to appeal, but could not afford the costs, which totaled $2,352, almost all of it for the trial transcript.

Indigent criminal defendants must be provided transcripts at state expense under a 1956 Supreme Court decision, but the Mississippi Supreme Court refused to extend that ruling to civil cases. In urging the justices to review the case, the woman said the ruling "cuts off access to the appellate court for indigents, in a case involving the fundamental right of a parent." But attorneys for the state of Mississippi argued that creating "a new and expansive constitutional right" would result in "potentially huge additional expenses being heaped upon the states." (*M. L. B. v. S. L. G.*)

Criminal Law

Sexual predators. The state of Kansas asked the Court to uphold its law allowing violent sexual offenders to be confined indefinitely even after they have completed their prison sentences. Kansas's Sexually Violent Predators Act permitted the state to commit a sex offender to a mental institution if a jury found the person was suffering from a "mental abnormality" and was likely to commit sexual offenses in the future. The law, similar to recently enacted laws in five other states, was ruled unconstitutional by the Kansas Supreme Court in a 4–3 vote.

The state court's ruling came in the case of a Kansas man, Leroy Hendricks, convicted of a series of child-related sex crimes dating to 1957. Prosecutors invoked the law just as Hendricks was about to be released from prison in 1994, and they won a court order confining him in a mental hospital. But the state high court said it violated Hendricks's due process rights to commit him if he was not suffering from a "mental illness."

In appealing the state court's decision, Kansas's attorney general said the law was needed to protect society from "brutal sex offenders." Hendricks filed a separate petition asking the Court to rule on other issues he had raised in attacking the law. The Court granted both petitions. (*Kansas v. Hendricks; Hendricks v. Kansas*)

Sexual harassment. The government urged the Court to reinstate the federal civil rights conviction of a Tennessee judge for sexually assaulting five women in his chambers during a nearly three-year period. The judge, David Lanier, was charged under the federal statute that prohibits depriving a person of rights protected by the Constitution or federal law. But a federal appeals court voted 9–5 to overturn the conviction, calling the federal prosecution "unprecedented." The government told the justices that the appeals court ruling "would severely impair federal protection of civil rights." But Lanier's attorney argued that the offenses were "common assaults, with no apparent constitutional implications." (*United States v. Lanier*)

Search and seizure. Prosecutors in Ohio and Maryland asked the Court to overturn rulings by their state supreme courts limiting police power to detain motorists and use evidence found during the stop.

The Ohio case stemmed from the arrest of a Dayton man for a half methamphetamine tablet found in his car after he had been stopped for speeding. The man agreed to the search after the officer decided not to write a citation. On appeal, the Ohio Supreme Court ruled police cannot search a car after concluding a traffic stop unless there is some other reason for suspicion. Ohio prosecutors argued the Ohio court's test was too stringent. But defense lawyers said a strict rule was needed to prevent "the widespread practice of officers in Ohio to seek consent to search without any basis during the course of a routine stop." (*Ohio v. Robinette*)

In the Maryland case, the state's attorneys were seeking to reinstate the drug conviction of an automobile passenger who was found with cocaine after police ordered him to get out of the car during a traffic stop. An earlier Court decision allowed police automatically to order a driver out of a car during a traffic stop for safety reasons, but state and federal courts were divided on whether the same rule applied to passengers. The Maryland Court of Special Appeals said it did not. State's attorneys warned the ruling would "endanger the hundreds, if not thousands, of police officers who stop vehicles each day for traffic violations." But defense lawyers said extending the previous ruling would result in "intrusion upon a passenger's Fourth Amendment protection." (*Maryland v. Wilson*)

Election Law

Racial redistricting. The Georgia legislature deadlocked in its efforts to draw new congressional districts after the Court's 1995 ruling that a plan containing three majority-minority districts amounted to racial gerrymandering. Faced with the deadlock, a three-judge court in Georgia drew up a plan that left only one district with a majority black population. The state and the Clinton administration, which had advocated plans calling for two majority-black districts, urged the justices to review the decision.

In its appeal, the Justice Department argued that the lower court violated the Constitution and the federal Voting Rights Act by reducing the opportunities for African-Americans to gain political representation. It also said the court violated general principles in redistricting cases by departing too far from the legislature's own proposal. But the white voters who had challenged the original scheme said the court's plan was correct because African Americans were not sufficiently "compact" to form a second majority-black district under "traditional districting principles." (*Abrams v. Johnson; United States v. Johnson*)

Voting Rights Act. The justices agreed to hear an important case testing the Justice Department's standards for enforcing the 1965 Voting Rights Act provision—section 5—requiring some state and local governments to obtain "preclearance" of any changes in voting procedures. The department refused to approve a redistricting plan for the Bossier Parish, Louisiana, school board that included no majority-black districts. It based the decision on a conclusion that the plan violated the so-called "results test" of the Voting Rights Act—section 2—because it did not promote opportunities for minorities to gain representation on the twelve-member board. But a three-judge federal court in Washington ruled the department could not refuse to approve the plan unless it showed the plan left blacks worse off than before.

In urging the Court to review the case, the Clinton administration said the lower court's ruling "seriously undermines" enforcement of the Voting Rights Act. But the school board defended the decision and criticized what its attorneys called the Justice Department's "unbridled penchant for social engineering." (*Reno v. Bossier Parish School Board; Price v. Bossier Parish School Board*)

Political parties. The state of Minnesota asked the Court to reinstate a law banning a political party from listing a candidate on the ballot who had already been nominated by a different party. The ban on multiple-party nominations was struck down by a federal appeals court, which said it placed "a severe burden" on third parties. The state told the justices that the law served a "compelling interest" in "providing a fair and honest election process." The New Party also urged the Court to take up the case to resolve a conflict with a federal appeals court in Wisconsin, which had upheld a similar law. (*McKenna v. Twin Cities Area New Party*)

Environmental Law

Endangered species. Critics of the Endangered Species Act urged the Court to overturn a ruling preventing them from filing suit under the law to block enforcement actions. A pair of Oregon ranchers and two irrigation districts invoked the powerful environmental law to challenge a move to protect two rare fish species found in a federally operated reservoir that provided their water supply. They said the U.S. Fish and Wildlife Service action threatened their allotments from the water project. But a federal appeals court ordered the suit dismissed, saying the ranchers and irrigation districts did not fall within the "zone of interest" protected by the law.

A host of industry and property rights groups criticized the ruling, saying that opponents of endangered species policies should be able to use the law. In its brief, the government defended the dismissal on a different ground than the appeals court gave. It said the suit should have been brought against the federal Bureau of Reclamation, which operates the reservoir, rather than against the Fish and Wildlife Service. (*Bennett v. Spear*)

Federal Government

Presidential immunity. The suit against President Clinton stemmed from accusations by a former Arkansas state employee, Paula Jones, that he had made an indecent advance toward her in a hotel room while serving as governor of Arkansas in May 1991. Jones filed the suit under federal civil rights law in May 1994. Clinton filed a motion seeking to dismiss the suit on grounds the president is absolutely immune from suit while serving as president or, in the alternative, to delay proceedings in the case until after leaving office. The trial judge in December 1994 rejected the absolute immunity claim, but agreed to the delay in discovery and other proceedings. A federal appeals court, however, rejected both of Clinton's pleas in a divided ruling on January 9, 1996. The court said the president has no protection from civil suit while in office "where only personal, private conduct . . . is at issue."

In asking the justices to bar the suit or delay the proceedings, Clinton's attorneys argued that the appeals court ruling was "inconsistent with the precedents of this Court and with the constitutional tradition of separation of powers." In a supporting brief, the Justice Department urged a delay in the case, saying that legal proceedings would interfere with the "unceasing" demands of the presidency. But Jones's attorneys responded, "No peril would be posed for the presidency by allowing this case to proceed." (*Clinton v. Jones*)

Agricultural marketing orders. The government sought to overturn a ruling that U.S. Department of Agriculture marketing orders requiring farmers to pay for generic advertising programs to promote their crops violated the First Amendment. The federal appeals court ruling came in a case brought by some California fruit growers who complained about the advertising for the state's peaches, nectarines, and plums. The plaintiffs contended that generic advertising had not been proved to be effective and that the ad program approved by the industry marketing committee favored growers of other types of fruit at their expense.

In urging the justices to review the case, the Agriculture Department contended that the generic advertising programs "comport with the First Amendment" because they involved "promoting the purchase of products that [the plaintiffs] have voluntarily chosen to sell." But the growers attacking the programs maintained that they were being "forced to speak, and forced to pay for, messages which do not project what [they] want to say." (*Glickman v. Wileman Bros.*)

First Amendment

Telecommunications. The cable industry again asked the Court to rule that the federal law requiring cable operators to carry local broadcast television stations on their systems violated their First Amendment rights. A three-judge federal court initially upheld the law in 1993, but the Court ordered it to give more careful scrutiny to the government's justification for the law. On remand, the federal court again upheld the law, by the same 2–1 vote.

In their opposing briefs, the industry and the government sharply disagreed on the need for the law and its effects. The industry said the law amounted to a "substantial restriction" on cable operators' freedom of speech, while the government insisted the law had only a "negligible" effect on cable systems. The government also contended the law was needed to protect local broadcasters and prevent anticompetitive conduct by cable operators. But the cable industry insisted the law was not needed to protect broadcasters and was more restrictive than necessary to deal with anticompetitive behavior. (*Turner Broadcasting System, Inc. v. Federal Communications Commission*)

Immigration

Vietnamese boat people. The government asked the Court to uphold its policy of requiring Vietnamese "boat people" to return to Vietnam before U.S. immigration officials acted on their requests for asylum. The government said it adopted the policy as part of an international agreement aimed at discouraging Vietnamese refugees from attempting the dangerous water-crossing to reach Western consular offices in Hong Kong. But the federal appeals court in Washington, D.C., ruled the policy violated an immigration law provision that prohibits discrimination on the basis of nationality.

The government told the justices the ruling would "undermine . . . a major foreign policy initiative" that had helped end "the dangerous, uncontrolled, and clandestine migration of Vietnamese nationals in Southeast Asia." The refugee assistance group that brought the class action suit disagreed. The policy, it said, "unquestionably discriminates against Vietnamese on the basis of their nationality." (*U.S. Dept. of State, Consular Affairs Office v. Legal Assistance for Vietnamese*)

Individual Rights

Abortion protests. The Court agreed to hear an appeal by two antiabortion activists seeking to overturn rulings by federal courts in New York. The rulings limited demonstrations outside women's health clinics in Buffalo and Rochester. Among other tactics, the protesters sought to engage the clinics' clients in what they termed "sidewalk counseling" as they entered the facilities. A federal judge in Buffalo issued an injunction in 1992 that all but barred the tactic. It required demonstrators to stay at least fifteen feet away from a patient if she asked to be left alone. The injunction also set up a fifteen-foot buffer zone around clinic entrances and driveways.

The federal appeals court in New York upheld the order by a 13–2 vote. In an unusual concurring opinion signed by nine other judges, Judge Ralph K. Winter said the injunction was justified to restrict "coercive or obstructionist conduct." In urging the justices to review the decision, however, lawyers for the activists said that the "floating fifteen-foot speech-free zones" restricted "classic forms of peaceful expression in public fora." Lawyers for the clinics countered that the "modest restrictions" imposed by the lower courts were necessary because of what they termed the protesters' "persistent, continuous campaign" to shut down the facilities. (*Schenck v. Pro-Choice Network of Western New York*)

"*Official English.*" The Court took up a challenge to a far-reaching "official English" law in Arizona, but the case was mired in procedural complexity that could prevent a ruling on the controversial issue.

Arizona's voter-approved constitutional amendment—the most extensive of more than twenty English-only statutes passed around the country—required all governmental actions to be conducted in English. A bilingual law student working for the state as a medical malpractice claim analyst challenged the law as a violation of her First Amendment rights. A federal district court agreed. But the student left state employment while the case was on appeal. In addition, Arizona's governor, Rose Mofford, an opponent of the amendment, decided not to appeal the ruling.

Meanwhile, the citizens' group that had sponsored the initiative intervened to appeal the ruling and defend the law. The federal appeals court in California, however, voted 6–5 to uphold the decision striking down the amendment. The citizens' group then asked the Court to review the decision. The justices agreed in March. But the order instructed the parties— the student, the state, and two opposing citizens' groups—to address two procedural questions: whether the student's claim had become moot and whether the citizens' group that sponsored the initiative had standing to defend it in court. (*Arizonans for Official English v. Arizona*)

Job discrimination. The Court agreed to decide whether someone can use the federal civil rights law that prohibits retaliation for making a race discrimination claim to sue his former employer for an unfavorable job reference. A Maryland man who filed an unsuccessful race discrimination claim after being fired as a sales representative for Shell Oil brought the new suit after the company gave an unfavorable job reference to a prospective employer. A federal appeals court ruled, 7–4, that the law did not extend to former employees. The Clinton administration joined the plaintiff in urging the Court to review the decision, which it said would promote "post-employment blacklisting." But Shell contended the job discrimination law "consistently uses 'employee' to refer to current employees." (*Robinson v. Shell Oil Co.*)

In a second job discrimination case, the justices were urged to overturn a federal appeals court decision that broadened the small business exemption in the federal civil rights law for companies using part-time and hourly employees. The law exempts employers with fewer than fifteen workers during at least twenty weeks of the year. The appeals court ruled a Chicago-based encyclopedia distribution company was exempt from the law because it did not have that many employees physically present or on paid leave during twenty weeks of the year. But the Equal Employment Opportunity Commission argued that the exemption should apply only if the number of workers on the company's overall payroll was below the statutory threshold. (*Equal Employment Opportunity Commission v. Metro Educational Enterprises, Inc.; Walters v. Metro Educational Enterprises, Inc.*)

Child support enforcement. The state of Arizona asked the Court to bar a class action suit using federal civil rights law to attack the state's enforcement of child support payment orders. The plaintiffs, custodial parents represented by legal aid lawyers, claimed the state's Department of Economic Security was failing to implement a federally mandated program to help recover child support payments from so-called "deadbeat dads." The suit was based on a Reconstruction-era federal civil rights law normally used in cases of constitutional violations.

A divided federal appeals court allowed the suit to proceed. In asking the justices to review the case, Arizona's lawyers warned that the suit "will not help the custodial parents" and "will impair the program's overall effectiveness." But the legal aid lawyers said the suit was needed "to call state officials to account for their continued failure" to carry out the program. (*Blessing v. Freestone*)

Municipal liability. The Court took up a police brutality case that an Oklahoma county hoped to use to limit municipal government liability for constitutional violations by its officials. The case arose from the 1991 beating of an Oklahoma woman by a part-time Bryan County deputy sheriff who had been hired despite an extensive record of misdemeanor convictions. The woman claimed the county, along with the deputy, should be held liable for the beating. She cited a 1978 Supreme Court decision that allowed municipal governments to be held responsible for actions by their officials that could be tied to an official policy or custom.

A jury awarded the woman $800,000 against the deputy and the county, and the federal appeals court in New Orleans upheld most of the award. In urging the justices to review the decision, the county argued it should not be held liable for hiring the deputy because there was no proof of "a pattern of constitutional deprivations." But lawyers for the woman scoffed at what they called the county's "one tort is not enough" theory. "There is nothing in the Court's [decisions] suggesting that a municipality must be deliberately indifferent at least twice" before it can be held responsible for an official's actions, the lawyers wrote. (*Board of County Commissioners of Bryan County, Okla. v. Brown*)

Labor Law

Overtime pay. A police union asked the Court to broaden supervisory officers' eligibility for overtime pay, but the government urged the justices to reject their argument. The case involved Labor Department regulations issued under the Fair Labor Standards Act defining the overtime exemption for salaried "white-collar" employees. The regulations provided that an employer could not exempt "salaried" employees from the time-and-a-half overtime provision if their pay could be docked for nonsafety disciplinary reasons. A St. Louis police sergeant who was given a two-day suspension without pay for violating the city's residency requirement claimed the disciplinary move made him and other sergeants and lieutenants eligible for overtime pay. The city argued, however, that the suspension was in effect a mistake and that it could still exempt sergeants and lieutenants because it had "disciplinary docking" for those officers.

Two lower federal courts rejected the officers' claim. Lawyers for the International Union of Police Associations urged the justices to review the case to resolve a conflict among lower federal courts. But the Clinton administration sided with the city in defending the ruling. (*Auer v. Robbins*)

States

Sovereign immunity. The Court agreed to hear two cases testing the limits of federal court jurisdiction over private suits brought against state officials and state universities.

The first case arose from a water rights dispute between the state of Idaho and the Coeur d'Alene Tribe. The tribe sued both the state and various state officials in federal court over the issue. A federal appeals court ruled that the suit against the state was barred by the Eleventh Amendment, which generally protects states from private suits in federal court. But the appeals panel invoked a 1908 Supreme Court case called *Ex parte Young* to allow the tribe to continue with the suit for an injunction against the state officials. Lawyers for the tribe argued the suit was a proper way to prevent Idaho officials from interfering with their property rights. But Idaho's lawyers contended the suit would inevitably result in "adjudicating the state's sovereign interests." (*Idaho v. Coeur d'Alene Tribe of Idaho*)

In a second case, the University of California was seeking to block a lawsuit brought by a physicist after the federally financed Lawrence Livermore National Laboratory withdrew an offer of employment. A federal appeals court ruled that the university was not entitled to Eleventh Amendment immunity from federal court suit because it was not an "instrumentality" of the state. Lawyers for the university, backed by higher education groups, contended the decision would create "heavy burdens" for public colleges and universities and "significantly infringe upon state sovereign immunity." But the plaintiff's lawyer argued the ruling would have no impact on the state because the Department of Energy, which operated the laboratory, would reimburse the university for any award. (*Regents of University of California v. Doe*)

Appendix

Opinion Excerpts

Following are excerpts from some of the most important rulings of the Supreme Court's 1995–1996 term. They appear in the order in which they were announced. Footnotes and legal citations are omitted.

No. 94-8729

Tina B. Bennis, Petitioner v. Michigan

On writ of certiorari to the Supreme Court of Michigan

[March 4, 1996]

CHIEF JUSTICE REHNQUIST delivered the opinion of the Court.

Petitioner was a joint owner, with her husband, of an automobile in which her husband engaged in sexual activity with a prostitute. A Michigan court ordered the automobile forfeited as a public nuisance, with no offset for her interest, notwithstanding her lack of knowledge of her husband's activity. We hold that the Michigan court order did not offend the Due Process Clause of the Fourteenth Amendment or the Takings Clause of the Fifth Amendment.

Detroit police arrested John Bennis after observing him engaged in a sexual act with a prostitute in the automobile while it was parked on a Detroit city street. Bennis was convicted of gross indecency. The State then sued both Bennis and his wife, petitioner Tina B. Bennis, to have the car declared a public nuisance and abated as such under §§600.3801 and 600.3825 of Michigan's Compiled Laws.

Petitioner defended against the abatement of her interest in the car on the ground that, when she entrusted her husband to use the car, she did not know that he would use it to violate Michigan's indecency law. The Wayne County Circuit Court rejected this argument, declared the car a public nuisance, and ordered the car's abatement. In reaching this disposition, the trial court judge recognized the remedial discretion he had under Michigan's case law. He took into account the couple's ownership of "another automobile," so they would not be left "without transportation." He also mentioned his authority to order the payment of one-half of the sale proceeds, after the deduction of costs, to "the innocent co-title holder." He declined to order such a division of sale proceeds in this case because of the age and value of the car (an 11-year-old Pontiac sedan recently purchased by John and Tina Bennis for $600); he commented in this regard: "[T]here's practically nothing left minus costs in a situation such as this."

The Michigan Court of Appeals reversed, holding that regardless of the language of Michigan Compiled Law §600.3815(2), Michigan Supreme Court precedent interpreting this section prevented the State from abating petitioner's interest absent proof that she knew to what end the car would be used. Alternatively, the intermediate appellate court ruled that the conduct in question did not qualify as a public nuisance because only one occurrence was shown and there was no evidence of payment for the sexual act. (1993).

The Michigan Supreme Court reversed the Court of Appeals and reinstated the abatement in its entirety. (1994). It concluded as a matter of state law that the episode in the Bennis vehicle was an abatable nuisance. Rejecting the Court of Appeals' interpretation of §600.3815(2), the court then announced that, in order to abate an owner's interest in a vehicle, Michigan does not need to prove that the owner knew or agreed that her vehicle would be used in a manner proscribed by §600.3801 when she entrusted it to another user.

The court next addressed petitioner's federal constitutional challenges to the State's abatement scheme: The court assumed that petitioner did not know of or consent to the misuse of the Bennis car, and concluded in light of our decisions in *Van Oster* v. *Kansas* (1926) and *Calero-Toledo* v. *Pearson Yacht Leasing Co.* (1974) that Michigan's failure to provide an innocent-owner defense was "without constitutional consequence." The Michigan Supreme Court specifically noted that, in its view, an owner's interest may not be abated when "a vehicle is used without the owner's consent." Furthermore, the court confirmed the trial court's description of the nuisance abatement proceeding as an "equitable action," and considered it "critical" that the trial judge so comprehended the statute.

We granted certiorari in order to determine whether Michigan's abatement scheme has deprived petitioner of her interest in the forfeited car without due process, in violation of the Fourteenth Amendment, or has taken her interest for public use without compensation, in violation of the Fifth Amendment as incorporated by the Fourteenth Amendment. (1995). We affirm.

... [The petitioner] claims she was entitled to contest the abatement by showing she did not know her husband would use it to violate Michigan's indecency law. But a long and unbroken line of cases holds that an owner's interest in property may be forfeited by reason of the use to which the property is put even though the owner did not know that it was to be put to such use.

Our earliest opinion to this effect is Justice Story's opinion for the Court in *The Palmyra* (1827). The Palmyra, which had been commissioned as a privateer by the King of Spain and had attacked a United States vessel, was captured by a United States war ship and brought into Charleston, South Carolina, for adjudication. On the Government's appeal from the Circuit Court's acquittal of the vessel, it was contended by the owner that the vessel could not be forfeited until he was convicted for the privateering. The Court rejected this contention, explaining: "The thing is here primarily considered as the offender, or rather the offence is attached primarily to the thing.". . .

In *Dobbins's Distillery* v. *United States* (1878), this Court upheld the forfeiture of property used by a lessee in fraudulently avoiding federal alcohol taxes, observing: "Cases often arise where the property of the owner is forfeited on account of the fraud, neglect, or misconduct of those intrusted with its possession, care, and custody, even when the owner is otherwise without fault . . . and it has always been held . . . that the acts of [the possessors] bind the interest of the owner . . . whether he be innocent or guilty."

In *Van Oster* v. *Kansas* (1926), this Court upheld the forfeiture of a purchaser's interest in a car misused by the seller. Van Oster purchased an automobile from a dealer but agreed that the dealer might retain possession for use in its business. The dealer allowed an associate to use the automobile, and the associate used it for the illegal transportation of intoxicating liquor. The State brought a forfeiture action pursuant to a Kansas statute, and Van Oster defended on the ground that the transportation of the liquor in the car was without her knowledge or authority. This Court rejected Van Oster's claim:

> ". . . It has long been settled that statutory forfeitures of property entrusted by the innocent owner or lienor to another who uses it in violation of the revenue laws of the United States is not a violation of the due process clause of the Fifth Amendment."

The *Van Oster* Court relied on *J. W. Goldsmith, Jr.-Grant Co.* v. *United States* (1921), in which the Court upheld the forfeiture of a seller's interest in a car misused by the purchaser. The automobile was forfeited after the purchaser transported bootleg distilled spirits in it, and the selling dealership lost the title retained as security for unpaid purchase money. The Court discussed the arguments for and against allowing the forfeiture of the interest of an owner who was "without guilt" and concluded that "whether the reason for [the challenged forfeiture scheme] be artificial or real, it is too firmly fixed in the punitive and remedial jurisprudence of the country to be now displaced."

In *Calero-Toledo* v. *Pearson Yacht Leasing Co.* (1974), the most recent decision on point, the Court reviewed the same cases discussed above, and concluded that "the innocence of the owner of property subject to forfeiture has almost uniformly been rejected as a defense." Petitioner is in the same position as the various owners involved in the forfeiture cases beginning with *The Palmyra* in 1827. She did not know that her car would be used in an illegal activity that would subject it to forfeiture. But under these cases the Due Process Clause of the Fourteenth Amendment does not protect her interest against forfeiture by the government.

Petitioner relies on a passage from *Calero-Toledo*, that "it would be difficult to reject the constitutional claim of . . . an owner who proved not only that he was uninvolved in and unaware of the wrongful activity, but also that he had done all that reasonably could be expected to prevent the proscribed use of his property." But she concedes that this comment was *obiter dictum* . . . . The dissent argues that our cases treat contraband differently from instrumentalities used to convey contraband, like cars: Objects in the former class are forfeitable "however blameless or unknowing their owners may be," but with respect to an instrumentality in the latter class, an owner's innocence is no defense only to the "principal use being made of that property." However, this Court's precedent has never made the due process inquiry depend on whether the use for which the instrumentality was forfeited was the principal use. . . .

The dissent also suggests that *The Palmyra* line of cases "would justify the confiscation of an ocean liner just because one of its passengers sinned while on board." None of our cases have held that an ocean liner may be confiscated because of the activities of one passenger. We said in *Goldsmith-Grant*, and we repeat here, that "[w]hen such application shall be made it will be time enough to pronounce upon it."

Notwithstanding this well-established authority rejecting the innocent-owner defense, petitioner argues . . . that our holding in *Austin* v. *United States* (1993) that the Excessive Fines Clause limits the scope of civil forfeiture judgments, "would be difficult to reconcile with any rule allowing truly innocent persons to be punished by civil forfeiture."

In *Austin*, the Court held that because "forfeiture serves, at least in part, to punish the owner," forfeiture proceedings are subject to the limitations of the Eighth Amendment's prohibition against excessive fines. There was no occasion in that case to deal with the validity of the "innocent-owner defense," other than to point out that if a forfeiture statute allows such a defense, the defense is additional evidence that the statute itself is "punitive" in motive. In this case, however, Michigan's Supreme Court emphasized with respect to the forfeiture proceeding at issue: "It is not contested that this is an equitable action," in which the trial judge has discretion to consider "alternatives [to] abating the entire interest in the vehicle."

In any event, . . . forfeiture also serves a deterrent purpose distinct from any punitive purpose. Forfeiture of property prevents illegal uses "both by preventing further illicit use of the [property] and by imposing an economic penalty, thereby rendering illegal behavior unprofitable." This deterrent mechanism is hardly unique to forfeiture. For instance, because Michigan also deters dangerous driving by making a motor vehicle owner liable for the negligent operation of the vehicle by a driver who had the owner's consent to use it, petitioner was also potentially liable for her husband's use of the car in violation of Michigan negligence law. . . .

Petitioner also claims that the forfeiture in this case was a taking of private property for public use in violation of the Takings Clause of the Fifth Amendment, made applicable to the States by the Fourteenth Amendment. But if the forfeiture proceeding here in question did not violate the Fourteenth Amendment, the property in the automobile was transferred by virtue of that proceeding from petitioner to the State. The government may not be required to compensate an owner for property which it has already lawfully acquired under the exercise of governmental authority other than the power of eminent domain.

At bottom, petitioner's claims depend on an argument that the Michigan forfeiture statute is unfair because it relieves prosecutors from the burden of separating co-owners who are complicit in the wrongful use of property from innocent co-owners. This argument, in the abstract, has considerable appeal, as we acknowledged in *Goldsmith-Grant*. Its force is reduced in the instant case, however, by the Michigan Supreme Court's confirmation of the trial court's remedial discretion and petitioner's recognition that Michigan may forfeit her and her husband's car whether or not she is entitled to an offset for her interest in it. We conclude today, as we concluded 75 years ago, that the cases authorizing actions of the kind at issue are "too firmly fixed in the punitive and remedial jurisprudence of the country to be now displaced." *Goldsmith-Grant*. The State here sought to deter illegal activity that contributes to neighborhood deterioration and unsafe streets. The Bennis automobile, it is conceded, facilitated and was used in criminal activity. Both the trial court and the Michigan

Supreme Court followed our longstanding practice, and the judgment of the Supreme Court of Michigan is therefore

Affirmed.

JUSTICE THOMAS, concurring.

I join the opinion of the Court.

. . .This case is ultimately a reminder that the Federal Constitution does not prohibit everything that is intensely undesirable. As detailed in the Court's opinion and the cases cited therein, forfeiture of property without proof of the owner's wrongdoing, merely because it was "used" in or was an "instrumentality" of crime has been permitted in England and this country, both before and after the adoption of the Fifth and Fourteenth Amendments. . . .

The limits on *what* property can be forfeited as a result of what wrongdoing . . . are not clear to me. Those limits, whatever they may be, become especially significant when they are the sole restrictions on the state's ability to take property from those it merely suspects, or does not even suspect, of colluding in crime. It thus seems appropriate, where a constitutional challenge by an innocent owner is concerned, to apply those limits rather strictly, adhering to historical standards for determining whether specific property is an "instrumentality" of crime. . . .

Improperly used, forfeiture could become more like a roulette wheel employed to raise revenue from innocent but hapless owners whose property is unforeseeably misused, or a tool wielded to punish those who associate with criminals, than a component of a system of justice. When the property sought to be forfeited has been entrusted by its owner to one who uses it for crime, however, the Constitution apparently assigns to the States and to the political branches of the Federal Government the primary responsibility for avoiding that result.

JUSTICE GINSBURG, concurring.

I join the opinion of the Court and highlight features of the case key to my judgment.

The dissenting opinions target a law scarcely resembling Michigan's "red light abatement" prescription, as interpreted by the State's courts. First, it bears emphasis that the car in question belonged to John Bennis as much as it did to Tina Bennis. At all times he had her consent to use the car, just as she had his. And it is uncontested that Michigan may forfeit the vehicle itself. The sole question, then, is whether Tina Bennis is entitled not to the car, but to a portion of the proceeds (if any there be after deduction of police, prosecutorial, and court costs) as a matter of constitutional right.

Second, it was "critical" to the judgment of the Michigan Supreme Court that the nuisance abatement proceeding is an "equitable action." That means the State's Supreme Court stands ready to police exorbitant applications of the statute. It shows no respect for Michigan's high court to attribute to its members tolerance of, or insensitivity to, inequitable administration of an "equitable action."

Nor is it fair to charge the trial court with "blatant unfairness" in the case at hand. That court declined to order a division of sale proceeds, as the trial judge took pains to explain, for two practical reasons: the Bennises have "another automobile"; and the age and value of the forfeited car (an 11-year-old Pontiac purchased by John and Tina Bennis for $600) left "practically nothing" to divide after subtraction of costs.

Michigan, in short, has not embarked on an experiment to punish innocent third parties. Nor do we condone any such experiment. Michigan has decided to deter Johns from using cars they own (or co-own) to contribute to neighborhood blight, and that abatement endeavor hardly warrants this Court's disapprobation.

JUSTICE STEVENS, with whom JUSTICE SOUTER and JUSTICE BREYER join, dissenting.

For centuries prostitutes have been plying their trade on other people's property. Assignations have occurred in palaces, luxury hotels, cruise ships, college dormitories, truck stops, back alleys and back seats. A profession of this vintage has provided governments with countless opportunities to use novel weapons to curtail its abuses. As far as I am aware, however, it was not until 1988 that any State decided to experiment with the punishment of innocent third parties by confiscating property in which, or on which, a single transaction with a prostitute has been consummated.

The logic of the Court's analysis would permit the States to exercise virtually unbridled power to confiscate vast amounts of property where professional criminals have engaged in illegal acts. Some airline passengers have marijuana cigarettes in their luggage; some hotel guests are thieves; some spectators at professional sports events carry concealed weapons; and some hitchhikers are prostitutes. The State surely may impose strict obligations on the owners of airlines, hotels, stadiums, and vehicles to exercise a high degree of care to prevent others from making illegal use of their property, but neither logic nor history supports the Court's apparent assumption that their complete innocence imposes no constitutional impediment to the seizure of their property simply because it provided the locus for a criminal transaction.

In order to emphasize the novelty of the Court's holding, I shall first comment on the tenuous connection between the property forfeited here and the illegal act that was intended to be punished, which differentiates this case from the precedent on which the Court relies. I shall then comment on the significance of the complete lack of culpability ascribable to petitioner in this case. Finally, I shall explain why I believe our recent decision in *Austin* v. *United States* (1993) compels reversal.

I

For purposes of analysis it is useful to identify three different categories of property that are subject to seizure: pure contraband; proceeds of criminal activity; and tools of the criminal's trade.

The first category—pure contraband—encompasses items such as adulterated food, sawed-off shotguns, narcotics, and smuggled goods. With respect to such "objects the possession of which, without more, constitutes a crime," the government has an obvious remedial interest in removing the items from private circulation, however blameless or unknowing their owners may be. The

States' broad and well-established power to seize pure contraband is not implicated by this case, for automobiles are not contraband.

The second category — proceeds — traditionally covered only stolen property, whose return to its original owner has a powerful restitutionary justification. Recent federal statutory enactments have dramatically enlarged this category to include the earnings from various illegal transactions. Because those federal statutes include protections for innocent owners, cases arising out of the seizure of proceeds do not address the question whether the Constitution would provide a defense to an innocent owner in certain circumstances if the statute had not done so. The prevalence of protection for innocent owners in such legislation does, however, lend support to the conclusion that elementary notions of fairness require some attention to the impact of a seizure on the rights of innocent parties.

The third category includes tools or instrumentalities that a wrongdoer has used in the commission of a crime, also known as "derivative contraband." Forfeiture is more problematic for this category of property than for the first two, both because of its potentially far broader sweep, and because the government's remedial interest in confiscation is less apparent. Many of our earliest cases arising out of these kinds of seizures involved ships that engaged in piracy on the high seas, in the slave trade, or in the smuggling of cargoes of goods into the United States. These seizures by the sovereign were approved despite the faultlessness of the ship's owner. Because the entire mission of the ship was unlawful, admiralty law treated the vessel itself as if it were the offender. . . .

The early admiralty cases demonstrate that the law may reasonably presume that the owner of valuable property is aware of the principal use being made of that property. . . .

. . . The principal use of the car in this case was not to provide a site for petitioner's husband to carry out forbidden trysts. Indeed, there is no evidence in the record that the car had ever previously been used for a similar purpose. An isolated misuse of a stationary vehicle should not justify the forfeiture of an innocent owner's property on the theory that it constituted an instrumentality of the crime.

This case differs from our historical precedents in a second, crucial way. In those cases, the vehicles or the property actually facilitated the offenses themselves. . . . Here, on the other hand, the forfeited property bore no necessary connection to the offense committed by petitioner's husband. It is true that the act occurred in the car, but it might just as well have occurred in a multitude of other locations. The mobile character of the car played a part only in the negotiation, but not in the consummation of the offense. . . .

The State attempts to characterize this forfeiture as serving exclusively remedial, as opposed to punitive ends, because its goal was to abate what the State termed a "nuisance." Even if the State were correct, that argument would not rebut the excessiveness of the forfeiture, which I have discussed above. But in any event, there is no serious claim that the confiscation in this case was not punitive. . . . At an earlier stage of this litigation, the State unequivocally argued that confiscation of automobiles in the circumstances of this case "is swift and certain 'punishment' of the voluntary vice consumer." Therefore, the idea that this forfeiture did not punish petitioner's husband—and, *a fortiori*, petitioner herself—is simply not sustainable. . . .

II

Apart from the lack of a sufficient nexus between petitioner's car and the offense her husband committed, I would reverse because petitioner is entirely without responsibility for that act. Fundamental fairness prohibits the punishment of innocent people.

The majority insists that it is a settled rule that the owner of property is strictly liable for wrongful uses to which that property is put. Only three Terms ago, however, the Court surveyed the same historical antecedents and held that all of its forfeiture decisions rested "at bottom, on the notion that the owner has been negligent in allowing his property to be misused and that he is properly punished for that negligence." *Austin* v. *United States* [citing other cases]. . . . It is conceded that petitioner was in no way negligent in her use or entrustment of the family car. Thus, no forfeiture should have been permitted. . . .

Even assuming that strict liability applies to "innocent" owners, we have consistently recognized an exception for truly blameless individuals. The Court's opinion in *Calero-Toledo* v. *Pearson Yacht Leasing Co.* established the proposition that the Constitution bars the punitive forfeiture of property when its owner alleges and proves that he took all reasonable steps to prevent its illegal use. Accord *Austin.* The majority dismisses this statement as "*obiter dictum,*" but we have assumed that such a principle existed, or expressly reserved the question, in a line of cases dating back nearly 200 years. . . . In other contexts, we have regarded as axiomatic that persons cannot be punished when they have done no wrong. . . . I would hold now what we have always assumed: that the principle is required by due process.

The unique facts of this case demonstrate that petitioner is entitled to the protection of that rule. The subject of this forfeiture was certainly not contraband. It was not acquired with the proceeds of criminal activity and its principal use was entirely legitimate. It was an ordinary car that petitioner's husband used to commute to the steel mill where he worked. Petitioner testified that they had been married for nine years; that she had acquired her ownership interest in the vehicle by the expenditure of money that she had earned herself; that she had no knowledge of her husband's plans to do anything with the car except "come directly home from work," as he had always done before; and that she even called "Missing Persons" when he failed to return on the night in question. Her testimony is not contradicted and certainly is credible. Without knowledge that he would commit such an act in the family car, or that he had ever done so previously, surely petitioner cannot be accused of failing to take "reasonable steps" to prevent the illicit behavior. She is just as blameless as if a thief, rather than her husband, had used the car in a criminal episode.

While the majority admits that this forfeiture is at least partly punitive in nature, it asserts that Michigan's law also serves a "deterrent purpose distinct from any punitive purpose." But that is no distinction at all; deterrence is itself one of the aims of punishment. Even on a deterrence rationale, moreover, that goal is not fairly served in the case of a person who has taken all reasonable steps to prevent an illegal act.

Forfeiture of an innocent owner's property that plays a central role in a criminal enterprise may be justified on reasoning comparable to the basis for imposing liability on a principal for an agent's torts. . . . [T]he risk of forfeiture encourages owners to exercise care in entrusting their property to others. . . . In this case, petitioner did not "entrust" the car to her husband on the night in question; he was entitled to use it by virtue of their joint ownership. There is no reason to think that the threat of forfeiture will deter an individual from buying a car with her husband — or from marrying him in the first place — if she neither knows nor has reason to know that he plans to use it wrongfully.

The same is true of the second asserted justification for strict liability, that it relieves the State of the difficulty of proving collusion, or disproving the lack thereof, by the alleged innocent owner and the wrongdoer. Whatever validity that interest might have in another kind of case, it has none here. It is patently clear that petitioner did not collude with her husband to carry out this offense.

The absence of any deterrent value reinforces the punitive nature of this forfeiture law. But petitioner has done nothing that warrants punishment. She cannot be accused of negligence or of any other dereliction in allowing her husband to use the car for the wholly legitimate purpose of transporting himself to and from his job. She affirmatively alleged and proved that she is not in any way responsible for the conduct that gave rise to the seizure. If anything, she was a victim of that conduct. In my opinion, these facts establish that the seizure constituted an arbitrary deprivation of property without due process of law.

III

The Court's holding today is dramatically at odds with our holding in *Austin v. United States*. We there established that when a forfeiture constitutes "payment to a sovereign as punishment for some offense"—as it undeniably does in this case — it is subject to the limitations of the Eighth Amendment's Excessive Fines Clause. For both of the reasons I have already discussed, the forfeiture of petitioner's half-interest in her car is surely a form of "excessive" punishment. For an individual who merely let her husband use her car to commute to work, even a modest penalty is out of all proportion to her blameworthiness; and when the assessment is confiscation of the entire car, simply because an illicit act took place once in the driver's seat, the punishment is plainly excessive. This penalty violates the Eighth Amendment for yet another reason. Under the Court's reasoning, the value of the car is irrelevant. A brand-new luxury sedan or a ten-year-old used car would be equally forfeitable. We have held that "dramatic variations" in the value of conveyances subject to forfeiture actions undercut any argument that the latter are reasonably tied to remedial ends.

I believe the Court errs today by assuming that the power to seize property is virtually unlimited and by implying that our opinions in *Calero-Toledo* and *Austin* were misguided. Some 75 years ago, when presented with the argument that the forfeiture scheme we approved had no limit, we insisted that expansive application of the law had not yet come to pass. "When such application shall be made," we said, "it will be time enough to pronounce upon it." *Goldsmith-Grant Co.* That time has arrived when the State forfeits a woman's car because her husband has secretly committed a misdemeanor inside it. While I am not prepared to draw a bright line that will separate the permissible and impermissible forfeitures of the property of innocent owners, I am convinced that the blatant unfairness of this seizure places it on the unconstitutional side of that line. I therefore respectfully dissent.

JUSTICE KENNEDY, dissenting.
... We can assume the continued validity of our admiralty forfeiture cases without in every analogous instance extending them to the automobile, which is a practical necessity in modern life for so many people. At least to this point, it has not been shown that a strong presumption of negligent entrustment or criminal complicity would be insufficient to protect the government's interest where the automobile is involved in a criminal act in the tangential way that it was here. Furthermore, as JUSTICE STEVENS points out, the automobile in this case was not used to transport contraband, and so the seizure here goes beyond the line of cases which sustain the government's use of forfeiture to suppress traffic of that sort.

This forfeiture cannot meet the requirements of due process. Nothing in the rationale of the Michigan Supreme Court indicates that the forfeiture turned on the negligence or complicity of petitioner, or a presumption thereof, and nothing supports the suggestion that the value of her co-ownership is so insignificant as to be beneath the law's protection.

For these reasons, and with all respect, I dissent.

No. 94-12

Seminole Tribe of Florida, Petitioner v. Florida et al.

On writ of certiorari to the United States Court of Appeals
for the Eleventh Circuit

[March 27, 1996]

CHIEF JUSTICE REHNQUIST delivered the opinion of the Court.
The Indian Gaming Regulatory Act provides that an Indian tribe may conduct certain gaming activities only in conformance with a valid compact between the tribe and the State in which the gaming activities are located. 25 U.S.C. §2710(d)(1)(C). The Act, passed by Congress under the Indian Commerce Clause, U. S. Const., Art. I, §10, cl. 3, imposes upon the States a duty to negotiate in good faith with an Indian tribe toward the formation of a compact, §2710(d)(3)(A), and authorizes a tribe to bring suit in federal court against a State in order to compel performance of that duty, §2710(d)(7). We hold that notwithstanding Congress' clear intent to abrogate the States' sovereign immunity, the Indian Commerce Clause does not grant Congress that power, and therefore §2710(d)(7) cannot grant jurisdiction over a State that does not con-

sent to be sued. We further hold that the doctrine of *Ex parte Young* (1908) may not be used to enforce §2710(d)(3) against a state official.

I

Congress passed the Indian Gaming Regulatory Act in 1988 in order to provide a statutory basis for the operation and regulation of gaming by Indian tribes. The Act divides gaming on Indian lands into three classes—I, II, and III—and provides a different regulatory scheme for each class. Class III gaming—the type with which we are here concerned—is defined as "all forms of gaming that are not class I gaming or class II gaming," §2703(8), and includes such things as slot machines, casino games, banking card games, dog racing, and lotteries. It is the most heavily regulated of the three classes. The Act provides that class III gaming is lawful only where it is: (1) authorized by an ordinance or resolution that (a) is adopted by the governing body of the Indian tribe, (b) satisfies certain statutorily prescribed requirements, and (c) is approved by the National Indian Gaming Commission; (2) located in a State that permits such gaming for any purpose by any person, organization, or entity; and (3) "conducted in conformance with a Tribal-State compact entered into by the Indian tribe and the State under paragraph (3) that is in effect."

The "paragraph (3)" to which the last prerequisite ... refers is §2710(d)(3), which describes the permissible scope of a Tribal-State compact and provides that the compact is effective "only when notice of approval by the Secretary [of the Interior] of such compact has been published by the Secretary in the Federal Register." More significant for our purposes, however, is that §2710(d)(3) describes the process by which a State and an Indian tribe begin negotiations toward a Tribal-State compact:

> "(A) Any Indian tribe having jurisdiction over the Indian lands upon which a class III gaming activity is being conducted, or is to be conducted, shall request the State in which such lands are located to enter into negotiations for the purpose of entering into a Tribal-State compact governing the conduct of gaming activities. Upon receiving such a request, the State shall negotiate with the Indian tribe in good faith to enter into such a compact."

The State's obligation to "negotiate with the Indian tribe in good faith," is made judicially enforceable by §§2710(d)(7)(A)(i) and (B)(i):

> "(A) The United States district courts shall have jurisdiction over—
>
> "(i) any cause of action initiated by an Indian tribe arising from the failure of a State to enter into negotiations with the Indian tribe for the purpose of entering into a Tribal-State compact under paragraph (3) or to conduct such negotiations in good faith . . . .
>
> "(B)(i) An Indian tribe may initiate a cause of action described in subparagraph (A)(i) only after the close of the 180-day period beginning on the date on which the Indian tribe requested the State to enter into negotiations under paragraph (3)(A)."

Sections 2710(d)(7)(B)(ii)-(vii) describe an elaborate remedial scheme designed to ensure the formation of a Tribal-State compact. [Details omitted; see section III below.]

In September 1991, the Seminole Tribe of Indians, petitioner, sued the State of Florida and its Governor, Lawton Chiles, respondents. . . . [P]etitioner alleged that respondents had "refused to enter into any negotiation for inclusion of [certain gaming activities] in a tribal-state compact," thereby violating the "requirement of good faith negotiation" contained in §2710(d)(3). Respondents moved to dismiss the complaint, arguing that the suit violated the State's sovereign immunity from suit in federal court. The District Court denied respondents' motion (1992), and the respondents took an interlocutory appeal of that decision.

The Court of Appeals for the Eleventh Circuit reversed the decision of the District Court, holding that the Eleventh Amendment barred petitioner's suit against respondents. (1994). The court agreed with the District Court that Congress in §2710(d)(7) intended to abrogate the States' sovereign immunity, and also agreed that the Act had been passed pursuant to Congress' power under the Indian Commerce Clause. The court disagreed with the District Court, however, that the Indian Commerce Clause grants Congress the power to abrogate a State's Eleventh Amendment immunity from suit, and concluded therefore that it had no jurisdiction over petitioner's suit against Florida. The court further held that *Ex parte Young* does not permit an Indian tribe to force good faith negotiations by suing the Governor of a State. Finding that it lacked subject-matter jurisdiction, the Eleventh Circuit remanded to the District Court with directions to dismiss petitioner's suit.

Petitioner sought our review of the Eleventh Circuit's decision, and we granted certiorari (1995) in order to consider two questions: (1) Does the Eleventh Amendment prevent Congress from authorizing suits by Indian tribes against States for prospective injunctive relief to enforce legislation enacted pursuant to the Indian Commerce Clause?; and (2) Does the doctrine of *Ex parte Young* permit suits against a State's governor for prospective injunctive relief to enforce the good faith bargaining requirement of the Act? We answer the first question in the affirmative, the second in the negative, and we therefore affirm the Eleventh Circuit's dismissal of petitioner's suit.

The Eleventh Amendment provides:

"The Judicial power of the United States shall not be construed to extend to any suit in law or equity, commenced or prosecuted against one of the United States by Citizens of another State, or by Citizens or Subjects of any Foreign State."

Although the text of the Amendment would appear to restrict only the Article III diversity jurisdiction of the federal courts, "we have understood the Eleventh Amendment to stand not so much for what it says, but for the presupposition . . . which it confirms." *Blatchford* v. *Native Village of Noatak* (1991). That presupposition, first observed over a century ago in *Hans* v. *Louisiana* (1890), has two parts: first, that each State is a sovereign entity in our federal system; and second, that " '[i]t is inherent in the nature of sovereignty not to be amenable to the suit of an individual without its consent.' " *Id.*, quoting The Federalist

No. 81. . . . For over a century we have reaffirmed that federal jurisdiction over suits against unconsenting States "was not contemplated by the Constitution when establishing the judicial power of the United States." *Hans.*

Here, petitioner has sued the State of Florida and it is undisputed that Florida has not consented to the suit. Petitioner nevertheless contends that its suit is not barred by state sovereign immunity. First, it argues that Congress through the Act abrogated the States' sovereign immunity. Alternatively, petitioner maintains that its suit against the Governor may go forward under *Ex parte Young.* We consider each of those arguments in turn.

II

Petitioner argues that Congress through the Act abrogated the States' immunity from suit. In order to determine whether Congress has abrogated the States' sovereign immunity, we ask two questions: first, whether Congress has "unequivocally expresse[d] its intent to abrogate the immunity"; and second, whether Congress has acted "pursuant to a valid exercise of power."

A

Congress' intent to abrogate the States' immunity from suit must be obvious from "a clear legislative statement.". . .

Here, we agree with the parties, with the Eleventh Circuit in the decision below, and with virtually every other court that has confronted the question that Congress has in §2710(d)(7) provided an "unmistakably clear" statement of its intent to abrogate. . . . [T]he numerous references to the "State" in the text of §2710(d)(7)(B) make it indubitable that Congress intended through the Act to abrogate the States' sovereign immunity from suit.

B

Having concluded that Congress clearly intended to abrogate the States' sovereign immunity through §2710(d)(7), we turn now to consider whether the Act was passed "pursuant to a valid exercise of power." Before we address that question here, however, we think it necessary first to define the scope of our inquiry.

Petitioner suggests that one consideration weighing in favor of finding the power to abrogate here is that the Act authorizes only prospective injunctive relief rather than retroactive monetary relief. But we have often made it clear that the relief sought by a plaintiff suing a State is irrelevant to the question whether the suit is barred by the Eleventh Amendment. . . . The Eleventh Amendment does not exist solely in order to "preven[t] federal court judgments that must be paid out of a State's treasury"; it also serves to avoid "the indignity of subjecting a State to the coercive process of judicial tribunals at the instance of private parties."

Similarly, petitioner argues that the abrogation power is validly exercised here because the Act grants the States a power that they would not otherwise have, viz., some measure of authority over gaming on Indian lands. . . . [W]e do not see how that consideration is relevant to the question whether Congress may abrogate state sovereign immunity. The Eleventh Amendment immunity may not be lifted by Congress unilaterally deciding that it will be replaced by grant of some other authority. . . .

Thus our inquiry into whether Congress has the power to abrogate unilaterally the States' immunity from suit is narrowly focused on one question: Was the Act in question passed pursuant to a constitutional provision granting Congress the power to abrogate? Previously, in conducting that inquiry, we have found authority to abrogate under only two provisions of the Constitution. In *Fitzpatrick* [v. *Bitzer* (1976)], we recognized that the Fourteenth Amendment, by expanding federal power at the expense of state autonomy, had fundamentally altered the balance of state and federal power struck by the Constitution. We noted that §1 of the Fourteenth Amendment contained prohibitions expressly directed at the States and that §5 of the Amendment expressly provided that "The Congress shall have the power to enforce, by appropriate legislation, the provisions of this article." We held that through the Fourteenth Amendment, federal power extended to intrude upon the province of the Eleventh Amendment and therefore that §5 of the Fourteenth Amendment allowed Congress to abrogate the immunity from suit guaranteed by that Amendment.

In only one other case has congressional abrogation of the States' Eleventh Amendment immunity been upheld. In *Pennsylvania* v. *Union Gas Co.* (1989), a plurality of the Court found that the Interstate Commerce Clause, Art. I, §8, cl. 3, granted Congress the power to abrogate state sovereign immunity, stating that the power to regulate interstate commerce would be "incomplete without the authority to render States liable in damages." Justice White added the fifth vote necessary to the result in that case, but wrote separately in order to express that he "[did] not agree with much of [the plurality's] reasoning."

In arguing that Congress through the Act abrogated the States' sovereign immunity, petitioner does not challenge the Eleventh Circuit's conclusion that the Act was passed pursuant to neither the Fourteenth Amendment nor the Interstate Commerce Clause. Instead, accepting the lower court's conclusion that the Act was passed pursuant to Congress' power under the Indian Commerce Clause, petitioner now asks us to consider whether that clause grants Congress the power to abrogate the States' sovereign immunity.

Petitioner begins with the plurality decision in *Union Gas* and contends that "[t]here is no principled basis for finding that congressional power under the Indian Commerce Clause is less than that conferred by the Interstate Commerce Clause.". . .

. . . If anything, the Indian Commerce Clause accomplishes a greater transfer of power from the States to the Federal Government than does the Interstate Commerce Clause. . . . We agree . . . that the plurality opinion in *Union Gas* allows no principled distinction in favor of the States to be drawn between the Indian Commerce Clause and the Interstate Commerce Clause.

Respondents argue, however, that we need not conclude that the Indian Commerce Clause grants the power to abrogate the States' sovereign immunity. Instead, they contend that if we find the rationale of the *Union Gas* plurality to extend to the Indian Commerce Clause, then "*Union Gas* should be reconsidered and overruled.". . .

The Court in *Union Gas* reached a result without an expressed rationale agreed upon by a majority of the Court. We have already seen that Justice Brennan's opinion received the support of only three other Justices. See *Union Gas* (Marshall, Blackmun, and STEVENS, JJ., joined Justice Brennan). Of the other five, Justice White, who provided the fifth vote for the result, wrote separately in order to indicate his disagreement with the majority's rationale, and four Justices joined together in a dissent that rejected the plurality's rationale. *Id.* (SCALIA, J., dissenting, joined by REHNQUIST, C. J., and O'CONNOR and KENNEDY, JJ.). Since it was issued, *Union Gas* has created confusion among the lower courts that have sought to understand and apply the deeply fractured decision.

The plurality's rationale also deviated sharply from our established federalism jurisprudence and essentially eviscerated our decision in *Hans*. . . .

Never before the decision in *Union Gas* had we suggested that the bounds of Article III could be expanded by Congress operating pursuant to any constitutional provision other than the Fourteenth Amendment. Indeed, it had seemed fundamental that Congress could not expand the jurisdiction of the federal courts beyond the bounds of Article III. The plurality's citation of prior decisions for support was based upon what we believe to be a misreading of precedent. The plurality claimed support for its decision from a case holding the unremarkable, and completely unrelated, proposition that the States may waive their sovereign immunity, and cited as precedent propositions that had been merely assumed for the sake of argument in earlier cases.

The plurality's extended reliance upon our decision in *Fitzpatrick* v. *Bitzer* that Congress could under the Fourteenth Amendment abrogate the States' sovereign immunity was also, we believe, misplaced. *Fitzpatrick* was based upon a rationale wholly inapplicable to the Interstate Commerce Clause, viz., that the Fourteenth Amendment, adopted well after the adoption of the Eleventh Amendment and the ratification of the Constitution, operated to alter the pre-existing balance between state and federal power achieved by Article III and the Eleventh Amendment. . . .

In the five years since it was decided, *Union Gas* has proven to be a solitary departure from established law. Reconsidering the decision in *Union Gas,* we conclude that none of the policies underlying *stare decisis* require our continuing adherence to its holding. The decision has, since its issuance, been of questionable precedential value, largely because a majority of the Court expressly disagreed with the rationale of the plurality. The case involved the interpretation of the Constitution and therefore may be altered only by constitutional amendment or revision by this Court. Finally, both the result in *Union Gas* and the plurality's rationale depart from our established understanding of the Eleventh Amendment and undermine the accepted function of Article III. We feel bound to conclude that *Union Gas* was wrongly decided and that it should be, and now is, overruled. . . .

The dissent . . . disregards our case law in favor of a theory cobbled together from law review articles and its own version of historical events. The dissent cites not a single decision since *Hans* (other than *Union Gas*) that supports its view of state sovereign immunity, instead relying upon the now-discredited decision in *Chisholm* v. *Georgia* (1793). Its undocumented and highly speculative extralegal explanation of the decision in *Hans* is a disservice to the Court's traditional method of adjudication. . . .

In overruling *Union Gas* today, we reconfirm that the background principle of state sovereign immunity embodied in the Eleventh Amendment is not so ephemeral as to dissipate when the subject of the suit is an area, like the regulation of Indian commerce, that is under the exclusive control of the Federal Government. Even when the Constitution vests in Congress complete law-making authority over a particular area, the Eleventh Amendment prevents congressional authorization of suits by private parties against unconsenting States. The Eleventh Amendment restricts the judicial power under Article III, and Article I cannot be used to circumvent the constitutional limitations placed upon federal jurisdiction. Petitioner's suit against the State of Florida must be dismissed for a lack of jurisdiction.

III

Petitioner argues that we may exercise jurisdiction over its suit to enforce §2710(d)(3) against the Governor notwithstanding the jurisdictional bar of the Eleventh Amendment. Petitioner notes that since our decision in *Ex parte Young* (1908), we often have found federal jurisdiction over a suit against a state official when that suit seeks only prospective injunctive relief in order to "end a continuing violation of federal law." The situation presented here, however, is sufficiently different from that giving rise to the traditional *Ex parte Young* action so as to preclude the availability of that doctrine. Here, the "continuing violation of federal law" alleged by petitioner is the Governor's failure to bring the State into compliance with §2710(d)(3). But the duty to negotiate imposed upon the State by that statutory provision does not stand alone. Rather, . . . Congress passed §2710(d)(3) in conjunction with the carefully crafted and intricate remedial scheme set forth in §2710(d)(7).

Where Congress has created a remedial scheme for the enforcement of a particular federal right, we have, in suits against federal officers, refused to supplement that scheme with one created by the judiciary. . . . Here, of course, the question is not whether a remedy should be created, but instead is whether the Eleventh Amendment bar should be lifted, as it was in *Ex parte Young*, in order to allow a suit against a state officer. Nevertheless, we think that the same general principle applies: therefore, where Congress has prescribed a detailed remedial scheme for the enforcement against a State of a statutorily created right, a court should hesitate before casting aside those limitations and permitting an action against a state officer based upon *Ex parte Young*.

Here, Congress intended §2710(d)(3) to be enforced against the State in an action brought under §2710(d)(7); the intricate procedures set forth in that provision show that Congress intended therein not only to define, but also significantly to limit, the duty imposed by §2710(d)(3). For example, where the court finds that the State has failed to negotiate in good faith, the only remedy prescribed is an order directing the State and the Indian tribe to conclude a compact within 60 days. And if the parties disregard the court's order and fail to conclude a compact within the 60-day period, the only sanction is that each party then must submit a proposed compact to a mediator who selects the one which best embodies the terms of the Act. Finally, if the State fails to accept the compact selected by the mediator, the only sanction against it is that the mediator shall notify the Secretary of the Interior who then must prescribe regulations governing Class III gaming on the tribal lands at issue. By contrast with this quite modest set of sanctions, an action brought against a state official under *Ex parte Young* would expose that official to the full remedial powers of a federal court, including, presumably, contempt sanctions. If §2710(d)(3) could be enforced in a suit under *Ex parte Young*, §2710(d)(7) would have been superfluous; it is difficult to see why an Indian tribe would suffer through the intricate scheme of §2710(d)(7) when more complete and more immediate relief would be available under *Ex parte Young*.

Here, of course, we have found that Congress does not have authority under the Constitution to make the State suable in federal court under §2710(d)(7). Nevertheless, the fact that Congress chose to impose upon the State a liability which is significantly more limited than would be the liability imposed upon the state officer under *Ex parte Young* strongly indicates that Congress had no wish to create the latter under §2710(d)(3). Nor are we free to rewrite the statutory scheme in order to approximate what we think Congress might have wanted had it known that §2710(d)(7) was beyond its authority. If that effort is to be made, it should be made by Congress, and not by the federal courts. We hold that *Ex parte Young* is inapplicable to petitioner's suit against the Governor of Florida, and therefore that suit is barred by the Eleventh Amendment and must be dismissed for a lack of jurisdiction.

IV

The Eleventh Amendment prohibits Congress from making the State of Florida capable of being sued in federal court. The narrow exception to the Eleventh Amendment provided by the *Ex parte Young* doctrine cannot be used to enforce §2710(d)(3) because Congress enacted a remedial scheme, §2710(d)(7), specifically designed for the enforcement of that right. The Eleventh Circuit's dismissal of petitioner's suit is hereby affirmed.

It is so ordered.

JUSTICE STEVENS, dissenting.

This case is about power—the power of the Congress of the United States to create a private federal cause of action against a State, or its Governor, for the violation of a federal right. In *Chisholm* v. *Georgia* (1793), the entire Court—including Justice Iredell whose dissent provided the blueprint for the Eleventh Amendment—assumed that Congress had such power. In *Hans* v. *Louisiana* (1890)—a case the Court purports to follow today—the Court again assumed that Congress had such power. In *Fitzpatrick* v. *Bitzer* (1976) and *Pennsylvania* v. *Union Gas Co.* (1989) the Court squarely held that Congress has such power. In a series of cases beginning with *Atascadero State Hospital* v. *Scanlon* (1985), the Court formulated a special "clear statement rule" to determine whether specific Acts of Congress contained an effective exercise of that power. Nevertheless, in a sharp break with the past, today the Court holds that with the narrow and illogical exception of statutes enacted pursuant to the Enforcement Clause of the Fourteenth Amendment, Congress has no such power.

The importance of the majority's decision to overrule the Court's holding in *Pennsylvania* v. *Union Gas Co.* cannot be overstated. The majority's opinion does not simply preclude Congress from establishing the rather curious statutory scheme under which Indian tribes may seek the aid of a federal court to secure a State's good faith negotiations over gaming regulations. Rather, it prevents Congress from providing a federal forum for a broad range of actions against States, from those sounding in copyright and patent law, to those concerning bankruptcy, environmental law, and the regulation of our vast national economy. [Remainder of opinion omitted.]

JUSTICE SOUTER, with whom JUSTICE GINSBURG and JUSTICE BREYER join, dissenting.

In holding the State of Florida immune to suit under the Indian Gaming Regulatory Act, the Court today holds for the first time since the founding of the Republic that Congress has no authority to subject a State to the jurisdiction of a federal court at the behest of an individual asserting a federal right. Although the Court invokes the Eleventh Amendment as authority for this proposition, the only sense in which that amendment might be claimed as pertinent here was tolerantly phrased by Justice Stevens in his concurring opinion in *Pennsylvania* v. *Union Gas* (1989) (STEVENS, J., concurring). There, he explained how it has come about that we have two Eleventh Amendments, the one ratified in 1795, the other (so-called) invented by the Court nearly a century later in *Hans* v. *Louisiana* (1890). JUSTICE STEVENS saw in that second Eleventh Amendment no bar to the exercise of congressional authority under the Commerce Clause in providing for suits on a federal question by individuals against a State, and I can only say that after my own canvass of the matter I believe he was entirely correct in that view, for reasons given below. His position, of course, was also the holding in *Union Gas*, which the Court now overrules and repudiates.

The fault I find with the majority today is not in its decision to reexamine *Union Gas*, for the Court in that case produced no majority for a single rationale supporting congressional authority. Instead, I part company from the Court because I am convinced that its decision is fundamentally mistaken, and for that reason I respectfully dissent.

I

It is useful to separate three questions: (1) whether the States enjoyed sovereign immunity if sued in their own courts in the period prior to ratification of the National Constitution; (2) if so, whether after ratification the States were entitled to claim some such immunity when sued in a federal court exercising jurisdiction either because the suit was between a State and a non-state litigant who was not its citizen, or because the issue in the case raised a federal question; and (3) whether any state sovereign immunity recognized in federal court may be abrogated by Congress.

The answer to the first question is not clear, although some of the Framers assumed that States did enjoy immunity in their own courts. The second question was not debated at the time of ratification, except as to citizen-state diversity jurisdiction; there was no unanimity, but in due course the Court in *Chisholm* v. *Georgia* (1793) answered that a state defendant enjoyed no such immunity. As to federal question jurisdiction, state sovereign immunity seems not to have been debated prior to ratification, the silence probably showing a general understanding at the time that the States would have no immunity in such cases.

The adoption of the Eleventh Amendment soon changed the result in *Chisholm*, not by mentioning sovereign immunity, but by eliminating citizen-state diversity jurisdiction over cases with state defendants. I will explain why the Eleventh Amendment did not affect federal question jurisdiction, a notion that needs to be understood for the light it casts on the soundness of *Hans*'s holding that States did enjoy sovereign immunity in federal question suits. The *Hans* Court erroneously assumed that a State could plead sovereign immunity against a noncitizen suing under federal question jurisdiction, and for that reason held that a State must enjoy the same protection in a suit by one of its citizens. The error of *Hans*'s reasoning is underscored by its clear inconsistency with the Founders' hostility to the implicit reception of common-law doctrine as federal law, and with the Founders' conception of sovereign power as divided between the States and the National Government for the sake of very practical objectives.

The Court's answer today to the third question is likewise at odds with the Founders' view that common law, when it was received into the new American legal systems, was always subject to legislative amendment. In ignoring the reasons for this pervasive understanding at the time of the ratification, and in holding that a nontextual common-law rule limits a clear grant of congressional power under Article I, the Court follows a course that has brought it to grief before in our history, and promises to do so again.

Beyond this third question that elicits today's holding, there is one further issue. To reach the Court's result, it must not only hold the *Hans* doctrine to be outside the reach of Congress, but must also displace the doctrine of *Ex parte Young* (1908) that an officer of the government may be ordered prospectively to follow federal law, in cases in which the government may not itself be sued directly. None of its reasons for displacing *Young*'s jurisdictional doctrine withstand scrutiny.

A

... Whatever the scope of sovereign immunity might have been in the Colonies ... or during the period of Confederation, the proposal to establish a National Government under the Constitution drafted in 1787 presented a prospect unknown to the common law prior to the American experience: the States would become parts of a system in which sovereignty over even domestic matters would be divided or parcelled out between the States and the Nation, the latter to be invested with its own judicial power and the right to prevail against the States whenever their respective substantive laws might be in conflict. ...

The 1787 draft ... said nothing on the subject [of state sovereign immunity], and it was this very silence that occasioned some, though apparently not widespread, dispute among the Framers and others over whether ratification of the Constitution would preclude a State sued in federal court from asserting sovereign immunity as it could have done on any matter of nonfederal law litigated in its own courts. ...

... [T]here was no consensus on the issue. There was, on the contrary, a clear disagreement. ... One other point, however, was also clear: the debate addressed only the question whether ratification of the Constitution would, in diversity cases and without more, abrogate the state sovereign immunity or allow it to have some application. We have no record that anyone argued . . . that the Constitution would affirmatively guarantee state sovereign immunity against any congressional action to the contrary. . . .

B

The argument among the Framers and their friends about sovereign immunity in federal citizen-state diversity cases, in any event, was short lived and ended when this Court, in *Chisholm* v. *Georgia*, chose between the constitutional alternatives of abrogation and recognition of the immunity enjoyed at common law. The 4-to-1 majority adopted the reasonable (although not compelled) interpretation that the first of the two Citizen-State Diversity Clauses abrogated for purposes of federal jurisdiction any immunity the States might have enjoyed in their own courts, and Georgia was accordingly held subject to the judicial power in a common-law assumpsit action by a South Carolina citizen suing to collect a debt. The case also settled, by implication, any question there could possibly have been about recognizing state sovereign immunity in actions depending on the federal question (or "arising under") head of jurisdiction as well. The constitutional text on federal question jurisdiction, after all, was just as devoid of immunity language as it was on citizen-state diversity . . . .

C

The Eleventh Amendment, of course, repudiated *Chisholm* and clearly divested federal courts of some jurisdiction as to cases against state parties:

"The Judicial power of the United States shall not be construed to extend to any suit in law or equity, commenced or prosecuted against one of the United States by Citizens of another State, or by Citizens or Subjects of any Foreign State."

. . . The history and structure of the Eleventh Amendment convincingly show that it reaches only to suits subject to federal jurisdiction exclusively under the Citizen-State Diversity Clauses. . . . If the Framers had meant the Amendment to bar federal question suits as well, they could not only have made their intentions clearer very easily, but could simply have adopted the first post-*Chisholm* proposal, introduced in the House of Representatives by Theodore Sedgwick of Massachusetts on instructions from the Legislature of that Commonwealth. Its provisions would have had exactly that expansive effect [quotation omitted]. . . .

Thus, . . . there is no possible argument that the Eleventh Amendment, by its terms, deprives federal courts of jurisdiction over all citizen lawsuits against the States. Not even the Court advances that proposition, and there would be no textual basis for doing so. Because the plaintiffs in today's case are citizens of the State that they are suing, the Eleventh Amendment simply does not apply to them. We must therefore look elsewhere for the source of that immunity by which the Court says their suit is barred from a federal court.

II

The obvious place to look elsewhere, of course, is *Hans v. Louisiana* (1890), and *Hans* was indeed a leap in the direction of today's holding, even though it does not take the Court all the way. The parties in *Hans* raised, and the Court in that case answered, only what I have called the second question, that is, whether the Constitution, without more, permits a State to plead sovereign immunity to bar the exercise of federal question jurisdiction. Although the Court invoked a principle of sovereign immunity to cure what it took to be the Eleventh Amendment's anomaly of barring only those state suits brought by noncitizen plaintiffs, the *Hans* Court had no occasion to consider whether Congress could abrogate that background immunity by statute. Indeed (except in the special circumstance of Congress's power to enforce the Civil War Amendments), this question never came before our Court until *Union Gas*, and any intimations of an answer in prior cases were mere dicta. In *Union Gas* the Court held that the immunity recognized in *Hans* had no constitutional status and was subject to congressional abrogation. Today the Court overrules *Union Gas* and holds just the opposite. In deciding how to choose between these two positions, the place to begin is with *Hans*'s holding that a principle of sovereign immunity derived from the common law insulates a state from federal question jurisdiction at the suit of its own citizen. A critical examination of that case will show that it was wrongly decided, as virtually every recent commentator has concluded. It follows that the Court's further step today of constitutionalizing *Hans*'s rule against abrogation by Congress compounds and immensely magnifies the century-old mistake of *Hans* itself and takes its place with other historic examples of textually untethered elevations of judicially derived rules to the status of inviolable constitutional law.

A

The Louisiana plaintiff in *Hans* held bonds issued by that State, which, like virtually all of the Southern States, had issued them in substantial amounts during the Reconstruction era to finance public improvements aimed at stimulating industrial development. As Reconstruction governments collapsed, however, the post-Reconstruction regimes sought to repudiate these debts, and the *Hans* litigation arose out of Louisiana's attempt to renege on its bond obligations.

Hans sued the State in federal court, asserting that the State's default amounted to an impairment of the obligation of its contracts in violation of the Contract Clause. This Court affirmed the dismissal of the suit, despite the fact that the case fell within the federal court's "arising under," or federal question, jurisdiction. Justice Bradley's opinion did not purport to hold that the terms either of Article III or of the Eleventh Amendment barred the suit, but that the ancient doctrine of sovereign immunity that had inspired adoption of the Eleventh Amendment applied to cases beyond the Amendment's scope and otherwise within the federal question jurisdiction. . . .

[B omitted]

III

Three critical errors in *Hans* weigh against constitutionalizing its holding as the majority does today. The first we have already seen: the *Hans* Court misread the Eleventh Amendment. It also misunderstood the conditions under which common-law doctrines were received or rejected at the time of the Founding, and it fundamentally mistook the very nature of sovereignty in the young Republic that was supposed to entail a State's immunity to federal question jurisdiction in a federal court. While I would not, as a matter of *stare decisis*, overrule *Hans* today, an understanding of its failings on these points will show how the Court today simply compounds already serious error in taking *Hans* the further step of investing its rule with constitutional inviolability against the considered judgment of Congress to abrogate it.

A

[Souter examined at length what he called the "American reluctance to import English common law into the New World," first in colonial times and then during and after adoption of the Constitution. ". . . (T)he 1787 draft Constitution contained no provision for adopting the common law at all," Souter wrote, and the ratification debates show that "everyone had to know that the new constitution would not draw the common law in its train."]

B

Given the refusal to entertain any wholesale reception of common law, given the failure of the new Constitution to make any provision for adoption of common law as such, and given the protests . . . that no general reception had occurred, the *Hans* Court and the Court today cannot reasonably argue that something like the old immunity doctrine somehow slipped in as a tacit but enforceable background principle. The evidence is even more specific, however, that there was no pervasive understanding that sovereign immunity had limited federal question jurisdiction.

[1 omitted]

2

. . . [T]he adoption of the Constitution made [the states] members of a novel federal system that sought to balance the States' exercise of some sovereign prerogatives delegated from their own people with the principle of a limited but centralizing federal supremacy.

As a matter of political theory, this federal arrangement of dual delegated sovereign powers truly was a more revolutionary turn than the late war had been. . . . The American development of divided sovereign powers . . . was made possible only by a recognition that the ultimate sovereignty rests in the people themselves. . . . The people possessing this plenary bundle of specific powers were free to parcel them out to different governments and different branches of the same government as they saw fit. . . .

. . . [S]overeign immunity as it would have been known to the Framers before ratification thereafter became inapplicable as a matter of logic in a federal suit raising a federal question. . . . [T]he ratification demonstrated that state governments were subject to a superior regime of law in a judicial system established, not by the State, but by the people through a specific delegation of their sovereign power to a National Government that was paramount within its delegated sphere. When individuals sued States to enforce federal rights, the Government that corresponded to the "sovereign" in the traditional common-law sense was not the State but the National Government, and any state immunity from the jurisdiction of the Nation's courts would have required a grant from the true sovereign, the people, in their Constitution, or from the Congress that the Constitution had empowered. . . .

[C omitted]

IV

The Court's holding that the States' *Hans* immunity may not be abrogated by Congress leads to the final question in this case, whether federal question jurisdiction exists to order prospective relief enforcing IGRA [Indian Gaming Regulatory Act] against a state officer, respondent Chiles, who is said to be authorized to take the action required by the federal law. Just as with the issue about authority to order the State as such, this question is entirely jurisdictional, and we need not consider here whether petitioner Seminole Tribe would have a meritorious argument for relief, or how much practical relief the requested order (to bargain in good faith) would actually provide to the Tribe. Nor, of course, does the issue turn in any way on one's views about the scope of the Eleventh Amendment or *Hans* and its doctrine, for we ask whether the state officer is subject to jurisdiction only on the assumption that action directly against the State is barred. The answer to this question is an easy yes, the officer is subject to suit under the rule in *Ex parte Young* (1908), and the case could, and should, readily be decided on this point alone. [Remainder of opinion omitted.]

□ □ □

No. 94-1140

44 Liquormart, Inc. and Peoples Super Liquor Stores, Inc., Petitioners v. Rhode Island and Rhode Island Liquor Stores Association

On writ of certiorari to the United States Court of Appeals for the First Circuit

[May 13, 1996]

JUSTICE STEVENS announced the judgment of the Court and delivered the opinion of the Court with respect to Parts I, II, VII, and VIII, an opinion with respect to Parts III and V, in which JUSTICE KENNEDY, JUSTICE SOUTER, and JUSTICE GINSBURG join, an opinion with respect to Part VI, in which JUSTICE KENNEDY, JUSTICE THOMAS, and JUSTICE GINSBURG join, and an opinion with respect to Part IV, in which JUSTICE KENNEDY and JUSTICE GINSBURG join.

Last Term we held that a federal law abridging a brewer's right to provide the public with accurate information about the alcoholic content of malt beverages is unconstitutional. *Rubin* v. *Coors Brewing Co.* (1995). We now hold that Rhode Island's statutory prohibition against advertisements that provide the public with accurate information about retail prices of alcoholic beverages is also invalid. Our holding rests on the conclusion that such an advertising ban is an abridgment of speech protected by the First Amendment and that it is not shielded from constitutional scrutiny by the Twenty-first Amendment.

I

In 1956, the Rhode Island Legislature enacted two separate prohibitions against advertising the retail price of alcoholic beverages. The first applies to vendors licensed in Rhode Island as well as to out-of-state manufacturers, wholesalers, and shippers. It prohibits them from "advertising in any manner whatsoever" the price of any alcoholic beverage offered for sale in the State; the only exception is for price tags or signs displayed with the merchandise within licensed premises and not visible from the street. The second statute applies to the Rhode Island news media. It contains a categorical prohibition against the publication or broadcast of any advertisements—even those referring to sales in other States—that "make reference to the price of any alcoholic beverages.". . .

II

Petitioners 44 Liquormart, Inc. (44 Liquormart) and Peoples Super Liquor Stores, Inc. (Peoples) are licensed retailers of alcoholic beverages. Petitioner 44 Liquormart operates a store in Rhode Island and petitioner Peoples operates several stores in Massachusetts that are patronized by Rhode Island residents. Peoples uses alcohol price advertising extensively in Massachusetts, where such advertising is permitted, but Rhode Island newspapers and other media outlets have refused to accept such ads.

Complaints from competitors about an advertisement placed by 44 Liquormart in a Rhode Island newspaper in 1991 generated enforcement proceedings that in turn led to the initiation of this litigation. The advertisement did not state the price of any alcoholic beverages. Indeed, it noted that "State law prohibits advertising liquor prices." The ad did, however, state the low prices at which peanuts, potato chips, and Schweppes mixers were being offered, identify various brands of packaged liquor, and include the word "WOW" in large letters next to pictures of vodka and rum bottles. Based on the conclusion that the implied reference to bargain prices for liquor violated the statutory ban on price advertising, the Rhode Island Liquor Control Administrator assessed a $400 fine.

After paying the fine, 44 Liquormart, joined by Peoples, filed this action against the administrator in the Federal District Court seeking a declaratory judgment that the two statutes and the administrator's implementing regulations violate the First Amendment and other provisions of federal law. The Rhode Island Liquor Stores Association was allowed to intervene as a defendant and in due course the State of Rhode Island replaced the administrator as the principal defendant. The parties stipulated that the price advertising ban is vigorously enforced, that Rhode Island permits "all advertising of alcoholic beverages excepting references to price outside the licensed premises," and that petitioners' proposed ads do not concern an illegal activity and presumably would not be false or misleading. The parties disagreed, however, about the impact of the ban on the promotion of temperance in Rhode Island. On that question the District Court heard conflicting expert testimony and reviewed a number of studies.

In his findings of fact [1993], the District Judge first noted that there was a pronounced lack of unanimity among researchers who have studied the impact of advertising on the level of consumption of alcoholic beverages. He referred to a 1985 Federal Trade Commission study that found no evidence that alcohol advertising significantly affects alcohol abuse. Another study indicated that Rhode Island ranks in the upper 30% of States in per capita consumption of alcoholic beverages; alcohol consumption is lower in other States that allow price advertising. After summarizing the testimony of the expert witnesses for both parties, he found "as a fact that Rhode Island's off-premises liquor price advertising ban has no significant impact on levels of alcohol consumption in Rhode Island."

As a matter of law, he concluded that the price advertising ban was unconstitutional because it did not "directly advance" the State's interest in reducing alcohol consumption and was "more extensive than necessary to serve that interest." He reasoned that the party seeking to uphold a restriction on commercial speech carries the burden of justifying it and that the Twenty-first Amendment did not shift or diminish that burden. Acknowledging that it might have been reasonable for the state legislature to "assume a correlation between the price advertising ban and reduced consumption," he held that more than a rational basis was required to justify the speech restriction, and that the State had failed to demonstrate a reasonable " 'fit' " between its policy objectives and its chosen means.

The Court of Appeals reversed [1994]. It found "inherent merit" in the State's submission that competitive price advertising would lower prices and that lower prices would produce more sales. Moreover, it agreed with the reasoning of the Rhode Island Supreme Court that the Twenty-first Amendment gave the statutes an added presumption of validity. Alternatively, it concluded that reversal was compelled by this Court's summary action in *Queensgate Investment Co.* v. *Liquor Control Comm'n of Ohio* (1982). In that case the Court dismissed the appeal from a decision of the Ohio Supreme Court upholding a prohibition against off-premises advertising of the prices of alcoholic beverages sold by the drink.

Queensgate has been both followed and distinguished in subsequent cases reviewing the validity of similar advertising bans. We are now persuaded that the importance of the First Amendment issue, as well [as] the suggested relevance of the Twenty-first Amendment, merits more thorough analysis than it received when we refused to accept jurisdiction of the *Queensgate* appeal. We therefore granted certiorari (1995).

III

Advertising has been a part of our culture throughout our history. Even in colonial days, the public relied on "commercial speech" for vital information about the market. Early newspapers displayed advertisements for goods and services on their front pages, and town criers called out prices in public squares. Indeed, commercial messages played such a central role in public life prior to the Founding that Benjamin Franklin authored his early defense of a free press in support of his decision to print, of all things, an advertisement for voyages to Barbados.

In accord with the role that commercial messages have long played, the law has developed to ensure that advertising provides consumers with accurate information about the availability of goods and services. In the early years, the common law, and later, statutes, served the consumers' interest in the receipt of accurate information in the commercial market by prohibiting fraudulent and misleading advertising. It was not until the 1970's, however, that this Court held that the First Amendment protected the dissemination of truthful and nonmisleading commercial messages about lawful products and services.

In *Bigelow* v. *Virginia* (1975), we held that it was error to assume that commercial speech was entitled to no First Amendment protection or that it was without value in the marketplace of ideas. The following Term in *Virginia Bd. of Pharmacy* v. *Virginia Citizens Consumer Council, Inc.* (1976), we expanded on our holding in *Bigelow* and held that the State's blanket ban on advertising the price of prescription drugs violated the First Amendment.

Virginia Pharmacy Bd. reflected the conclusion that the same interest that supports regulation of potentially misleading advertising, namely the public's interest in receiving accurate commercial information, also supports an interpretation of the First Amendment that provides constitutional protection for the dissemination of accurate and nonmisleading commercial messages. [Excerpt from opinion omitted.] The opinion further explained that a State's paternalistic assumption that the public will use truthful, nonmisleading commercial information unwisely cannot justify a decision to suppress it. [Excerpt from opinion omitted.]

On the basis of these principles, our early cases uniformly struck down several broadly based bans on truthful, nonmisleading commercial speech, each of which served ends unrelated to consumer protection. . . .

At the same time, our early cases recognized that the State may regulate some types of commercial advertising more freely than other forms of protected speech. Specifically, we explained that the State may require commercial messages to "appear in such a form, or include such additional information, warnings, and disclaimers, as are necessary to prevent its being deceptive" and that it may restrict some forms of aggressive sales practices that have the potential to exert "undue influence" over consumers. . . .

In *Central Hudson Gas & Elec. Corp.* v. *Public Serv. Comm'n of N. Y.* (1980), we took stock of our developing commercial speech jurisprudence. In that case, we considered a regulation "completely" banning all promotional advertising by electric utilities. . . .

Five Members of the Court recognized that the state interest in the conservation of energy was substantial, and that there was "an immediate connection between advertising and demand for electricity." Nevertheless, they concluded that the regulation was invalid because the Commission had failed to make a showing that a more limited speech regulation would not have adequately served the State's interest

In reaching its conclusion, the majority explained that although the special nature of commercial speech may require less than strict review of its regulation, special concerns arise from "regulations that entirely suppress commercial speech in order to pursue a nonspeech-related policy." In those circumstances, "a ban on speech could screen from public view the underlying governmental policy." As a result, the Court concluded that "special care" should attend the review of such blanket bans, and it pointedly remarked that "in recent years this Court has not approved a blanket ban on commercial speech unless the speech itself was flawed in some way, either because it was deceptive or related to unlawful activity."

IV

As our review of the case law reveals, Rhode Island errs in concluding that all commercial speech regulations are subject to a similar form of constitutional review simply because they target a similar category of expression. The mere fact that messages propose commercial transactions does not in and of itself dictate the constitutional analysis that should apply to decisions to suppress them.

When a State regulates commercial messages to protect consumers from misleading, deceptive, or aggressive sales practices, or requires the disclosure of beneficial consumer information, the purpose of its regulation is consistent with the reasons for according constitutional protection to commercial speech and therefore justifies less than strict review. However, when a State entirely prohibits the dissemination of truthful, nonmisleading commercial messages for reasons unrelated to the preservation of a fair bargaining process, there is far less reason to depart from the rigorous review that the First Amendment generally demands.

Sound reasons justify reviewing the latter type of commercial speech regulation more carefully. Most obviously, complete speech bans, unlike content-neutral restrictions on the time, place, or manner of expression, are particularly dangerous because they all but foreclose alternative means of disseminating certain information. . . .

V

In this case, there is no question that Rhode Island's price advertising ban constitutes a blanket prohibition against truthful, nonmisleading speech about a lawful product. There is also no question that the ban serves an end unrelated to consumer protection. Accordingly, we must review the price advertising ban with "special care," mindful that speech prohibitions of this type rarely survive constitutional review.

The State argues that the price advertising prohibition should nevertheless be upheld because it directly advances the State's substantial interest in promoting temperance, and because it is no more extensive than necessary. Although there is some confusion as to what Rhode Island means by temperance, we assume that the State asserts an interest in reducing alcohol consumption.

In evaluating the ban's effectiveness in advancing the State's interest, we note that a commercial speech regulation "may not be sustained if it provides only ineffective or remote support for the government's purpose.". . . Accordingly, we must determine whether the State has shown that the price advertising ban will significantly reduce alcohol consumption.

We can agree that common sense supports the conclusion that a prohibition against price advertising, like a collusive agreement among competitors to refrain from such advertising, will tend to mitigate competition and maintain prices at a higher level than would prevail in a completely free market. Despite the absence of proof on the point, we can even agree with the State's contention that it is reasonable to assume that demand, and hence consumption throughout the market, is somewhat lower whenever a higher, noncompetitive price level prevails. However, without any findings of fact, or indeed any evidentiary support whatsoever, we cannot agree with the assertion that the price advertising ban will *significantly* advance the State's interest in promoting temperance.

Although the record suggests that the price advertising ban may have some impact on the purchasing patterns of temperate drinkers of modest means, the State has presented no evidence to suggest that its speech prohibition will significantly reduce marketwide consumption. Indeed, the District Court's considered and uncontradicted finding on this point is directly to the contrary. Moreover, the evidence suggests that the abusive drinker will probably not be deterred by a marginal price increase, and that the true alcoholic may simply reduce his purchases of other necessities. . . .

The State also cannot satisfy the requirement that its restriction on speech be no more extensive than necessary. It is perfectly obvious that alternative forms of regulation that would not involve any restriction on speech would be more likely to achieve the State's goal of promoting temperance. As the State's own expert conceded, higher prices can be maintained either by direct regulation or by increased taxation. Per capita purchases could be limited as is the case with prescription drugs. Even educational campaigns focused on the problems of excessive, or even moderate, drinking might prove to be more effective.

As a result, even under the less than strict standard that generally applies in commercial speech cases, the State has failed to establish a "reasonable fit" between its abridgment of speech and its temperance goal. . . . It necessarily follows that the price advertising ban cannot survive the more stringent constitutional review that *Central Hudson* itself concluded was appropriate for the complete suppression of truthful, nonmisleading commercial speech.

VI

The State responds by arguing that it merely exercised appropriate "legislative judgment" in determining that a price advertising ban would best promote temperance. Relying on the *Central Hudson* analysis set forth in *Posadas de Puerto Rico Associates* v. *Tourism Co. of P. R.* (1986) and *United States* v. *Edge Broadcasting Co.* (1993), Rhode Island first argues that, because expert opinions as to the effectiveness of the price advertising ban "go both ways," the Court of Appeals correctly concluded that the ban constituted a "reasonable choice" by the legislature. The State next contends that precedent requires us to give particular deference to that legislative choice because the State could, if it chose, ban the sale of alcoholic beverages outright. Finally, the State argues that deference is appropriate because alcoholic beverages are so-called "vice" products. We consider each of these contentions in turn.

The State's first argument fails to justify the speech prohibition at issue. Our commercial speech cases recognize some room for the exercise of legislative judgment. However, Rhode Island errs in concluding that *Edge* and *Posadas* establish the degree of deference that its decision to impose a price advertising ban warrants.

In *Edge*, we upheld a federal statute that permitted only those broadcasters located in States that had legalized lotteries to air lottery advertising. The statute was designed to regulate advertising about an activity that had been deemed illegal in the jurisdiction in which the broadcaster was located. Here, by contrast, the commercial speech ban targets information about entirely lawful behavior.

Posadas is more directly relevant. There, a five-Member majority held that, under the *Central Hudson* test, it was "up to the legislature" to choose to reduce gambling by suppressing in-state casino advertising rather than engaging in educational speech. Rhode Island argues that this logic demonstrates the constitutionality of its own decision to ban price advertising in lieu of raising taxes or employing some other less speech-restrictive means of promoting temperance.

The reasoning in *Posadas* does support the State's argument, but, on reflection, we are now persuaded that *Posadas* erroneously performed the First Amendment analysis. . . .

. . . *Posadas* clearly erred in concluding that it was "up to the legislature" to choose suppression over a less speech-restrictive policy. The *Posadas* majority's conclusion on that point cannot be reconciled with the unbroken line of prior cases striking down similarly broad regulations on truthful, nonmisleading advertising when non-speech-related alternatives were available. . . .

Because the 5-to-4 decision in *Posadas* marked such a sharp break from our prior precedent, and because it concerned a constitutional question about which this Court is the final arbiter, we decline to give force to its highly deferential approach. Instead, in keeping with our prior holdings, we conclude that a state legislature does not have the broad discretion to suppress truthful, nonmisleading information for paternalistic purposes that the *Posadas* majority was willing to tolerate. . . .

We also cannot accept the State's second contention, which is premised entirely on the "greater-includes-the-lesser" reasoning endorsed toward the end of the majority's opinion in *Posadas*. There, the majority stated that "the greater power to completely ban casino gambling necessarily includes the lesser power to ban advertising of casino gambling.". . .

. . . Contrary to the assumption made in *Posadas*, we think . . . banning speech may sometimes prove far more intrusive than banning conduct. . . .

Finally, we find unpersuasive the State's contention that, under *Posadas* and *Edge*, the price advertising ban should be upheld because it targets commercial speech that pertains to a "vice" activity. The appellees premise their request for a so-called "vice" exception to our commercial speech doctrine on language in *Edge* which characterized gambling as a "vice." The respondents misread our precedent. Our decision last Term [*Rubin*] striking down an alcohol-related advertising restriction effectively rejected the very contention respondents now make.

Moreover, the scope of any "vice" exception to the protection afforded by the First Amendment would be difficult, if not impossible, to define. Almost any product that poses some threat to public health or public morals might reasonably be characterized by a state legislature as relating to "vice activity.". . .

VII

From 1919 until 1933, the Eighteenth Amendment to the Constitution totally prohibited "the manufacture, sale, or transportation of intoxicating liquors" in the United States and its territories. Section 1 of the Twenty-first Amendment repealed that prohibition, and §2 delegated to the several States the power to prohibit commerce in, or the use of, alcoholic beverages. . . .

. . . [T]he text of the Twenty-first Amendment supports the view that, while it grants the States authority over commerce that might otherwise be reserved to the Federal Government, it places no limit whatsoever on other constitutional provisions. Nevertheless, Rhode Island argues, and the Court of Appeals agreed, that in this case the Twenty-first Amendment tilts the First Amendment analysis in the State's favor.

In reaching its conclusion, the Court of Appeals relied on our decision in *California* v. *LaRue* (1972). In *LaRue*, five Members of the Court relied on the Twenty-first Amendment to buttress the conclusion that the First Amendment did not invalidate California's prohibition of certain grossly sexual exhibitions in premises licensed to serve alcoholic beverages. . . . We are now persuaded that the Court's analysis in *LaRue* would have led to precisely the same result if it had placed no reliance on the Twenty-first Amendment.

Without questioning the holding in *LaRue*, we now disavow its reasoning insofar as it relied on the Twenty-first Amendment. . . . Accordingly, we now hold that the Twenty-first Amendment does not qualify the constitutional prohibition against laws abridging the freedom of speech embodied in the First Amendment. The Twenty-first Amendment, therefore, cannot save Rhode Island's ban on liquor price advertising.

VIII

Because Rhode Island has failed to carry its heavy burden of justifying its complete ban on price advertising, we conclude that R. I. Gen. Laws §§3-8-7 and 3-8-8.1, as well as Regulation 32 of the Rhode Island Liquor Control Administration, abridge speech in violation of the First Amendment as made applicable to the States by the Due Process Clause of the Fourteenth Amendment. The judgment of the Court of Appeals is therefore reversed.

It is so ordered.

JUSTICE SCALIA, concurring in part and concurring in the judgment.

I share JUSTICE THOMAS' discomfort with the *Central Hudson* test, which seems to me to have nothing more than policy intuition to support it. I also share JUSTICE STEVENS' aversion towards paternalistic governmental policies that prevent men and women from hearing facts that might not be good for them. On the other hand, it would also be paternalism for us to prevent the people of the States from enacting laws that we consider paternalistic, unless we have good reason to believe that the Constitution itself forbids them. I will take my guidance as to what the Constitution forbids, with regard to a text as indeterminate as the First Amendment's preservation of "the freedom of speech," and where the core offense of suppressing particular political ideas is not at issue, from the long accepted practices of the American people.

The briefs and arguments of the parties in the present case provide no illumination on that point; understandably so, since both sides accepted *Central Hudson.* . . .

Since I do not believe we have before us the wherewithal to declare *Central Hudson* wrong — or at least the wherewithal to say what ought to replace it — I must resolve this case in accord with our existing jurisprudence, which all except JUSTICE THOMAS agree would prohibit the challenged regulation. I am not disposed to develop new law, or reinforce old, on this issue, and accordingly I merely concur in the judgment of the Court. I believe, however, that JUSTICE STEVENS' treatment of the application of the Twenty-First Amendment to this case is correct, and accordingly join Parts I, II, VII, and VIII of JUSTICE STEVENS' opinion.

JUSTICE THOMAS, concurring in Parts I, II, VI, and VII, and concurring in the judgment.

In cases such as this, in which the government's asserted interest is to keep legal users of a product or service ignorant in order to manipulate their choices in the marketplace, the balancing test adopted in *Central Hudson Gas & Elec. Corp.* v. *Public Serv. Comm'n of N. Y.* (1980) should not be applied, in my view. Rather, such an "interest" is *per se* illegitimate and can no more justify regulation of "commercial" speech than it can justify regulation of "noncommercial" speech. [Remainder of opinion omitted.]

JUSTICE O'CONNOR, with whom The CHIEF JUSTICE, JUSTICE SOUTER, and JUSTICE BREYER join, concurring in the judgment.

. . . I agree with the Court that Rhode Island's price-advertising ban is invalid. I would resolve this case more narrowly, however, by applying our established *Central Hudson* test to determine whether this commercial-speech regulation survives First Amendment scrutiny.

Under that test, we first determine whether the speech at issue concerns lawful activity and is not misleading, and whether the asserted governmental interest is substantial. If both these conditions are met, we must decide whether the regulation "directly advances the governmental interest asserted, and whether it is not more extensive than is necessary to serve that interest." *Central Hudson Gas & Elec. Corp.* v. *Public Serv. Comm'n of N. Y.* (1980).

Given the means by which this regulation purportedly serves the State's interest, our conclusion is plain: Rhode Island's regulation fails First Amendment scrutiny. . . .

Rhode Island offers one, and only one, justification for its ban on price advertising. Rhode Island says that the ban is intended to keep alcohol prices high as a way to keep consumption low. By preventing sellers from informing customers of prices, the regulation prevents competition from driving prices down and requires consumers to spend more time to find the best price for alcohol. The higher cost of obtaining alcohol, Rhode Island argues, will lead to reduced consumption.

The fit between Rhode Island's method and this particular goal is not reasonable. If the target is simply higher prices generally to discourage consumption, the regulation imposes too great, and unnecessary, a prohibition on speech in order to achieve it. The State has other methods at its disposal—methods that would more directly accomplish this stated goal without intruding on sellers' ability to provide truthful, nonmisleading information to customers. Indeed, Rhode Island's own expert conceded that " 'the objective of lowering consumption of alcohol by banning price advertising could be accomplished by establishing minimum prices and/or by increasing sales taxes on alcoholic beverages.' " A tax, for example, is not normally very difficult to administer and would have a far more certain and direct effect on prices, without any restriction on speech. The principal opinion suggests further alternatives, such as limiting per capita purchases or conducting an educational campaign about the dangers of alcohol consumption. The ready availability of such alternatives—at least some of which would far more effectively achieve Rhode Island's only professed goal, at comparatively small additional administrative cost—demonstrates that the fit between ends and means is not narrowly tailored. Too, this regulation prevents sellers of alcohol from communicating price information anywhere but at the point of purchase. No channels exist at all to permit them to publicize the price of their products. . . .

Because Rhode Island's regulation fails even the less stringent standard set out in *Central Hudson*, nothing here requires adoption of a new analysis for the evaluation of commercial speech regulation. The principal opinion acknowledges that "even under the less than strict standard that generally applies in commercial speech cases, the State has failed to establish a reasonable fit between its abridgement of speech and its temperance goal." Because we need go no further, I would not here undertake the question whether the test we have employed since *Central Hudson* should be displaced. . . .

No. 94-1039

Roy Romer, Governor of Colorado, et al., Petitioners v. Richard G. Evans et al.

On writ of certiorari to the Supreme Court of Colorado

[May 20, 1996]

JUSTICE KENNEDY delivered the opinion of the Court.

One century ago, the first Justice Harlan admonished this Court that the Constitution "neither knows nor tolerates classes among citizens." *Plessy* v. *Ferguson* (1896) (dissenting opinion). Unheeded then, those words now are understood to state a commitment to the law's neutrality where the rights of persons are at stake. The Equal Protection Clause enforces this principle and today requires us to hold invalid a provision of Colorado's Constitution.

I

The enactment challenged in this case is an amendment to the Constitution of the State of Colorado, adopted in a 1992 statewide referendum. The parties and the state courts refer to it as "Amendment 2," its designation when submitted to the voters. The impetus for the amendment and the contentious campaign that preceded its adoption came in large part from ordinances that had been passed in various Colorado municipalities. For example, the cities of Aspen and Boulder and the City and County of Denver each had enacted ordinances which banned discrimination in many transactions and activities, including housing, employment, education, public accommodations, and health and welfare services. What gave rise to the statewide controversy was the protection the ordinances afforded to persons discriminated against by reason of their sexual orientation. Amendment 2 repeals these ordinances to the extent they prohibit discrimination on the basis of "homosexual, lesbian or bisexual orientation, conduct, practices or relationships."

Yet Amendment 2, in explicit terms, does more than repeal or rescind these provisions. It prohibits all legislative, executive or judicial action at any level of state or local government designed to protect the named class, a class we shall refer to as homosexual persons or gays and lesbians. The amendment reads:

> "No Protected Status Based on Homosexual, Lesbian, or Bisexual Orientation. Neither the State of Colorado, through any of its branches or departments, nor any of its agencies, political subdivisions, municipalities or school districts, shall enact, adopt or enforce any statute, regulation, ordinance or policy whereby homosexual, lesbian or bisexual orientation, conduct, practices or relationships shall constitute or otherwise be the basis of or entitle any person or class of persons to have or claim any minority status, quota preferences, protected status or claim of discrimination. This Section of the Constitution shall be in all respects self-executing."

Soon after Amendment 2 was adopted, this litigation to declare its invalidity and enjoin its enforcement was commenced in the District Court for the

City and County of Denver. Among the plaintiffs (respondents here) were homosexual persons, some of them government employees. They alleged that enforcement of Amendment 2 would subject them to immediate and substantial risk of discrimination on the basis of their sexual orientation. Other plaintiffs (also respondents here) included the three municipalities whose ordinances we have cited and certain other governmental entities which had acted earlier to protect homosexuals from discrimination but would be prevented by Amendment 2 from continuing to do so. Although Governor Romer had been on record opposing the adoption of Amendment 2, he was named in his official capacity as a defendant, together with the Colorado Attorney General and the State of Colorado.

The trial court granted a preliminary injunction to stay enforcement of Amendment 2, and an appeal was taken to the Supreme Court of Colorado. Sustaining the interim injunction and remanding the case for further proceedings, the State Supreme Court held that Amendment 2 was subject to strict scrutiny under the Fourteenth Amendment because it infringed the fundamental right of gays and lesbians to participate in the political process. *Evans* v. *Romer* (1993) (*Evans I*). To reach this conclusion, the state court relied on our voting rights cases and on our precedents involving discriminatory restructuring of governmental decisionmaking. On remand, the State advanced various arguments in an effort to show that Amendment 2 was narrowly tailored to serve compelling interests, but the trial court found none sufficient. It enjoined enforcement of Amendment 2, and the Supreme Court of Colorado, in a second opinion, affirmed the ruling. *Evans* v. *Romer* (1994) (*Evans II*). We granted certiorari and now affirm the judgment, but on a rationale different from that adopted by the State Supreme Court.

II

The State's principal argument in defense of Amendment 2 is that it puts gays and lesbians in the same position as all other persons. So, the State says, the measure does no more than deny homosexuals special rights. This reading of the amendment's language is implausible. We rely not upon our own interpretation of the amendment but upon the authoritative construction of Colorado's Supreme Court. The state court, deeming it unnecessary to determine the full extent of the amendment's reach, found it invalid even on a modest reading of its implications. The critical discussion of the amendment, set out in *Evans I*, is as follows:

> "The immediate objective of Amendment 2 is, at a minimum, to repeal existing statutes, regulations, ordinances, and policies of state and local entities that barred discrimination based on sexual orientation. *See* Aspen, Colo., Mun. Code §13-98 (1977) (prohibiting discrimination in employment, housing and public accommodations on the basis of sexual orientation); Boulder, Colo., Rev. Code §§12-1-2 to -4 (1987) (same); Denver, Colo., Rev. Mun. Code art. IV, §§28-91 to -116 (1991) (same); Executive Order No. D0035 (December 10, 1990) (prohibiting employment discrimination for 'all state employees, classified and exempt' on the basis of sexual orientation); Colorado Insurance Code, §10-3-1104, 4A C. R. S. (1992 Supp.) (forbidding health insurance providers from

determining insurability and premiums based on an applicant's, a bene-
ficiary's, or an insured's sexual orientation); and various provisions prohibiting discrimination based on sexual orientation at state colleges.
[Footnote omitted.]

"The 'ultimate effect' of Amendment 2 is to prohibit any governmental
entity from adopting similar, or more protective statutes, regulations,
ordinances, or policies in the future unless the state constitution is first
amended to permit such measures."

Sweeping and comprehensive is the change in legal status effected by this
law. So much is evident from the ordinances that the Colorado Supreme Court
declared would be void by operation of Amendment 2. Homosexuals, by state
decree, are put in a solitary class with respect to transactions and relations in
both the private and governmental spheres. The amendment withdraws from
homosexuals, but no others, specific legal protection from the injuries caused
by discrimination, and it forbids reinstatement of these laws and policies. The
change that Amendment 2 works in the legal status of gays and lesbians in the
private sphere is far-reaching, both on its own terms and when considered in
light of the structure and operation of modern anti-discrimination laws. . . .

Colorado's state and municipal laws typify this emerging tradition of statutory protection and follow a consistent pattern. The laws first enumerate the
persons or entities subject to a duty not to discriminate. The list goes well
beyond the entities covered by the common law. The Boulder ordinance, for
example, has a comprehensive definition of entities deemed places of "public
accommodation." They include "any place of business engaged in any sales to
the general public and any place that offers services, facilities, privileges, or
advantages to the general public or that receives financial support through
solicitation of the general public or through governmental subsidy of any kind."
The Denver ordinance is of similar breadth, applying, for example, to hotels,
restaurants, hospitals, dental clinics, theaters, banks, common carriers, travel
and insurance agencies, and "shops and stores dealing with goods or services of
any kind."

These statutes and ordinances also depart from the common law by enu-
merating the groups or persons within their ambit of protection. Enumeration
is the essential device used to make the duty not to discriminate concrete and
to provide guidance for those who must comply. In following this approach,
Colorado's state and local governments have not limited anti-discrimination
laws to groups that have so far been given the protection of heightened equal
protection scrutiny under our cases. See, *e.g., J. E. B.* v. *Alabama ex rel. T. B.*
(1994) (sex); *Lalli* v. *Lalli* (1978) (illegitimacy); *McLaughlin* v. *Florida* (1964)
(race); *Oyama* v. *California* (1948) (ancestry). Rather, they set forth an extensive
catalogue of traits which cannot be the basis for discrimination, including age,
military status, marital status, pregnancy, parenthood, custody of a minor child,
political affiliation, physical or mental disability of an individual or of his or her
associates—and, in recent times, sexual orientation.

Amendment 2 bars homosexuals from securing protection against the
injuries that these public-accommodations laws address. That in itself is a
severe consequence, but there is more. Amendment 2, in addition, nullifies spe-

cific legal protections for this targeted class in all transactions in housing, sale of real estate, insurance, health and welfare services, private education, and employment.

Not confined to the private sphere, Amendment 2 also operates to repeal and forbid all laws or policies providing specific protection for gays or lesbians from discrimination by every level of Colorado government. The State Supreme Court cited two examples of protections in the governmental sphere that are now rescinded and may not be reintroduced. The first is Colorado Executive Order D0035 (1990), which forbids employment discrimination against " 'all state employees, classified and exempt' on the basis of sexual orientation." Also repealed, and now forbidden, are "various provisions prohibiting discrimination based on sexual orientation at state colleges." The repeal of these measures and the prohibition against their future reenactment demonstrates that Amendment 2 has the same force and effect in Colorado's governmental sector as it does elsewhere and that it applies to policies as well as ordinary legislation.

Amendment 2's reach may not be limited to specific laws passed for the benefit of gays and lesbians. It is a fair, if not necessary, inference from the broad language of the amendment that it deprives gays and lesbians even of the protection of general laws and policies that prohibit arbitrary discrimination in governmental and private settings. . . .

If this consequence follows from Amendment 2, as its broad language suggests, it would compound the constitutional difficulties the law creates. The state court did not decide whether the amendment has this effect, however, and neither need we. . . . [E]ven if, as we doubt, homosexuals could find some safe harbor in laws of general application, we cannot accept the view that Amendment 2's prohibition on specific legal protections does no more than deprive homosexuals of special rights. To the contrary, the amendment imposes a special disability upon those persons alone. Homosexuals are forbidden the safeguards that others enjoy or may seek without constraint. They can obtain specific protection against discrimination only by enlisting the citizenry of Colorado to amend the state constitution or perhaps, on the State's view, by trying to pass helpful laws of general applicability. This is so no matter how local or discrete the harm, no matter how public and widespread the injury. We find nothing special in the protections Amendment 2 withholds. These are protections taken for granted by most people either because they already have them or do not need them; these are protections against exclusion from an almost limitless number of transactions and endeavors that constitute ordinary civic life in a free society.

III

The Fourteenth Amendment's promise that no person shall be denied the equal protection of the laws must co-exist with the practical necessity that most legislation classifies for one purpose or another, with resulting disadvantage to various groups or persons. We have attempted to reconcile the principle with the reality by stating that, if a law neither burdens a fundamental right nor targets a suspect class, we will uphold the legislative classification so long as it bears a rational relation to some legitimate end.

Amendment 2 fails, indeed defies, even this conventional inquiry. First, the amendment has the peculiar property of imposing a broad and undifferentiated disability on a single named group, an exceptional and, as we shall explain, invalid form of legislation. Second, its sheer breadth is so discontinuous with the reasons offered for it that the amendment seems inexplicable by anything but animus toward the class that it affects; it lacks a rational relationship to legitimate state interests.

Taking the first point, even in the ordinary equal protection case calling for the most deferential of standards, we insist on knowing the relation between the classification adopted and the object to be attained. The search for the link between classification and objective gives substance to the Equal Protection Clause; it provides guidance and discipline for the legislature, which is entitled to know what sorts of laws it can pass; and it marks the limits of our own authority. In the ordinary case, a law will be sustained if it can be said to advance a legitimate government interest, even if the law seems unwise or works to the disadvantage of a particular group, or if the rationale for it seems tenuous. . . . .

Amendment 2 confounds this normal process of judicial review. It is at once too narrow and too broad. It identifies persons by a single trait and then denies them protection across the board. The resulting disqualification of a class of persons from the right to seek specific protection from the law is unprecedented in our jurisprudence. . . .

It is not within our constitutional tradition to enact laws of this sort. Central both to the idea of the rule of law and to our own Constitution's guarantee of equal protection is the principle that government and each of its parts remain open on impartial terms to all who seek its assistance. . . . Respect for this principle explains why laws singling out a certain class of citizens for disfavored legal status or general hardships are rare. A law declaring that in general it shall be more difficult for one group of citizens than for all others to seek aid from the government is itself a denial of equal protection of the laws in the most literal sense. . . .

Davis v. *Beason* (1890), not cited by the parties but relied upon by the dissent, is not evidence that Amendment 2 is within our constitutional tradition, and any reliance upon it as authority for sustaining the amendment is misplaced. In *Davis*, the Court approved an Idaho territorial statute denying Mormons, polygamists, and advocates of polygamy the right to vote and to hold office because, as the Court construed the statute, it "simply excludes from the privilege of voting, or of holding any office of honor, trust or profit, those who have been convicted of certain offences, and those who advocate a practical resistance to the laws of the Territory and justify and approve the commission of crimes forbidden by it." To the extent *Davis* held that persons advocating a certain practice may be denied the right to vote, it is no longer good law. *Brandenburg* v. *Ohio* (1969). To the extent it held that the groups designated in the statute may be deprived of the right to vote because of their status, its ruling could not stand without surviving strict scrutiny, a most doubtful outcome. *Dunn* v. *Blumstein* (1972). To the extent *Davis* held that a convicted felon may be denied the right to vote, its holding is not implicated by our decision and is unexceptionable.

A second and related point is that laws of the kind now before us raise the inevitable inference that the disadvantage imposed is born of animosity toward the class of persons affected. . . . Even laws enacted for broad and ambitious purposes often can be explained by reference to legitimate public policies which justify the incidental disadvantages they impose on certain persons. Amendment 2, however, in making a general announcement that gays and lesbians shall not have any particular protections from the law, inflicts on them immediate, continuing, and real injuries that outrun and belie any legitimate justifications that may be claimed for it. We conclude that, in addition to the far-reaching deficiencies of Amendment 2 that we have noted, the principles it offends, in another sense, are conventional and venerable; a law must bear a rational relationship to a legitimate governmental purpose, and Amendment 2 does not.

The primary rationale the State offers for Amendment 2 is respect for other citizens' freedom of association, and in particular the liberties of landlords or employers who have personal or religious objections to homosexuality. Colorado also cites its interest in conserving resources to fight discrimination against other groups. The breadth of the Amendment is so far removed from these particular justifications that we find it impossible to credit them. We cannot say that Amendment 2 is directed to any identifiable legitimate purpose or discrete objective. It is a status-based enactment divorced from any factual context from which we could discern a relationship to legitimate state interests; it is a classification of persons undertaken for its own sake, something the Equal Protection Clause does not permit. "[C]lass legislation . . . [is] obnoxious to the prohibitions of the Fourteenth Amendment. . . ." *Civil Rights Cases.*

We must conclude that Amendment 2 classifies homosexuals not to further a proper legislative end but to make them unequal to everyone else. This Colorado cannot do. A State cannot so deem a class of persons a stranger to its laws. Amendment 2 violates the Equal Protection Clause, and the judgment of the Supreme Court of Colorado is affirmed.

It is so ordered.

JUSTICE SCALIA, with whom THE CHIEF JUSTICE and JUSTICE THOMAS join, dissenting.

The Court has mistaken a Kulturkampf for a fit of spite. The constitutional amendment before us here is not the manifestation of a " 'bare . . . desire to harm' " homosexuals, but is rather a modest attempt by seemingly tolerant Coloradans to preserve traditional sexual mores against the efforts of a politically powerful minority to revise those mores through use of the laws. That objective, and the means chosen to achieve it, are not only unimpeachable under any constitutional doctrine hitherto pronounced (hence the opinion's heavy reliance upon principles of righteousness rather than judicial holdings); they have been specifically approved by the Congress of the United States and by this Court.

In holding that homosexuality cannot be singled out for disfavorable treatment, the Court contradicts a decision, unchallenged here, pronounced only 10 years ago, see *Bowers* v. *Hardwick* (1986), and places the prestige of this institution behind the proposition that opposition to homosexuality is as reprehensible as racial or religious bias. Whether it is or not is precisely the cultural debate that gave rise to the Colorado constitutional amendment (and to the preferential laws against which the amendment was directed). Since the Constitution of the United States says nothing about this subject, it is left to be resolved by normal democratic means, including the democratic adoption of provisions in state constitutions. This Court has no business imposing upon all Americans the resolution favored by the elite class from which the Members of this institution are selected, pronouncing that "animosity" toward homosexuality is evil. I vigorously dissent.

I

Let me first discuss Part II of the Court's opinion, its longest section, which is devoted to rejecting the State's arguments that Amendment 2 "puts gays and lesbians in the same position as all other persons," and "does no more than deny homosexuals special rights." The Court concludes that this reading of Amendment 2's language is "implausible" under the "authoritative construction" given Amendment 2 by the Supreme Court of Colorado.

In reaching this conclusion, the Court considers it unnecessary to decide the validity of the State's argument that Amendment 2 does not deprive homosexuals of the "protection [afforded by] general laws and policies that prohibit arbitrary discrimination in governmental and private settings." I agree that we need not resolve that dispute, because the Supreme Court of Colorado has resolved it for us. In *Evans* v. *Romer* (1994), the Colorado court stated:

> "[I]t is significant to note that Colorado law currently proscribes discrimination against persons who are not suspect classes, including discrimination based on age; marital or family status; veterans' status; and for any legal, off-duty conduct such as smoking tobacco. *Of course Amendment 2 is not intended to have any effect on this legislation, but seeks only to prevent the adoption of anti-discrimination laws intended to protect gays, lesbians, and bisexuals.*" (emphasis added).

The Court utterly fails to distinguish this portion of the Colorado court's opinion. Colorado Rev. Stat. §24-34-402.5, which this passage authoritatively declares not to be affected by Amendment 2, was respondents' primary example of a generally applicable law whose protections would be unavailable to homosexuals under Amendment 2. The clear import of the Colorado court's conclusion that it is not affected is that "general laws and policies that prohibit arbitrary discrimination" would continue to prohibit discrimination on the basis of homosexual conduct as well. This analysis . . . lays to rest such horribles, raised in the course of oral argument, as the prospect that assaults upon homosexuals could not be prosecuted. The amendment prohibits special treatment of homosexuals, and nothing more. . . .

Despite all of its hand-wringing about the potential effect of Amendment 2 on general antidiscrimination laws, the Court's opinion ultimately does not dispute all this, but assumes it to be true. The only denial of equal treatment it contends homosexuals have suffered is this: They may not obtain preferential treatment without amending the state constitution. . . .

The central thesis of the Court's reasoning is that any group is denied equal protection when, to obtain advantage (or, presumably, to avoid disadvantage), it must have recourse to a more general and hence more difficult level of political decisionmaking than others. The world has never heard of such a principle, which is why the Court's opinion is so long on emotive utterance and so short on relevant legal citation. And it seems to me most unlikely that any multilevel democracy can function under such a principle. For whenever a disadvantage is imposed, or conferral of a benefit is prohibited, at one of the higher levels of democratic decisionmaking (i.e., by the state legislature rather than local government, or by the people at large in the state constitution rather than the legislature), the affected group has (under this theory) been denied equal protection. . . . It is ridiculous to consider this a denial of equal protection, which is why the Court's theory is unheard-of. . . .

II

I turn next to whether there was a legitimate rational basis for the substance of the constitutional amendment—for the prohibition of special protection for homosexuals. It is unsurprising that the Court avoids discussion of this question, since the answer is so obviously yes. The case most relevant to the issue before us today is not even mentioned in the Court's opinion: In *Bowers* v. *Hardwick* [1986], we held that the Constitution does not prohibit what virtually all States had done from the founding of the Republic until very recent years—making homosexual conduct a crime. That holding is unassailable, except by those who think that the Constitution changes to suit current fashions. But in any event it is a given in the present case: Respondents' briefs did not urge overruling *Bowers*, and at oral argument respondents' counsel expressly disavowed any intent to seek such overruling. If it is constitutionally permissible for a State to make homosexual conduct criminal, surely it is constitutionally permissible for a State to enact other laws merely disfavoring homosexual conduct. . . . And *a fortiori* it is constitutionally permissible for a State to adopt a provision not even disfavoring homosexual conduct, but merely prohibiting all levels of state government from bestowing special protections upon homosexual conduct. . . .

III

The foregoing suffices to establish what the Court's failure to cite any case remotely in point would lead one to suspect: No principle set forth in the Constitution, nor even any imagined by this Court in the past 200 years, prohibits what Colorado has done here. But the case for Colorado is much stronger than that. What it has done is not only unprohibited, but eminently reasonable, with close, congressionally approved precedent in earlier constitutional practice.

First, as to its eminent reasonableness. The Court's opinion contains grim, disapproving hints that Coloradans have been guilty of "animus" or "animosity" toward homosexuality, as though that has been established as Unamerican. Of course it is our moral heritage that one should not hate any human being or class of human beings. But I had thought that one could consider certain conduct reprehensible—murder, for example, or polygamy, or cruelty to animals—and could exhibit even "animus" toward such conduct. Surely that is the only sort of "animus" at issue here: moral disapproval of homosexual conduct, the same sort of moral disapproval that produced the centuries-old criminal laws that we held constitutional in *Bowers*. . . .

But though Coloradans are, as I say, entitled to be hostile toward homosexual conduct, the fact is that the degree of hostility reflected by Amendment 2 is the smallest conceivable. The Court's portrayal of Coloradans as a society fallen victim to pointless, hate-filled "gay-bashing" is so false as to be comical. Colorado not only is one of the 25 States that have repealed their antisodomy laws, but was among the first to do so. But the society that eliminates criminal punishment for homosexual acts does not necessarily abandon the view that homosexuality is morally wrong and socially harmful; often, abolition simply reflects the view that enforcement of such criminal laws involves unseemly intrusion into the intimate lives of citizens. . . .

There is a problem, however, which arises when criminal sanction of homosexuality is eliminated but moral and social disapprobation of homosexuality is meant to be retained. The Court cannot be unaware of that problem; it is evident in many cities of the country, and occasionally bubbles to the surface of the news, in heated political disputes over such matters as the introduction into local schools of books teaching that homosexuality is an optional and fully acceptable "alternate life style." The problem . . . is that, because those who engage in homosexual conduct tend to reside in disproportionate numbers in certain communities, and of course care about homosexual-rights issues much more ardently than the public at large, they possess political power much greater than their numbers, both locally and statewide. Quite understandably, they devote this political power to achieving not merely a grudging social toleration, but full social acceptance, of homosexuality. . . .

By the time Coloradans were asked to vote on Amendment 2, their exposure to homosexuals' quest for social endorsement was not limited to newspaper accounts of happenings in places such as New York, Los Angeles, San Francisco, and Key West. Three Colorado cities—Aspen, Boulder, and Denver— had enacted ordinances that listed "sexual orientation" as an impermissible ground for discrimination, equating the moral disapproval of homosexual conduct with racial and religious bigotry. The phenomenon had even appeared statewide: the Governor of Colorado had signed an executive order pronouncing that "in the State of Colorado we recognize the diversity in our pluralistic society and strive to bring an end to discrimination in any form," and directing state agency-heads to "ensure non-discrimination" in hiring and promotion based on, among other things, "sexual orientation." I do not mean to be critical of these legislative successes; homosexuals are as entitled to use the legal system for reinforcement of their moral sentiments as are the rest of society. But they are subject to being countered by lawful, democratic countermeasures as well.

That is where Amendment 2 came in. It sought to counter both the geographic concentration and the disproportionate political power of homosexuals by resolving the controversy at the statewide level, and making the election a single-issue contest for both sides. It put directly, to all the citizens of the State, the question: Should homosexuality be given special protection? They answered no. The Court today asserts that this most democratic of procedures is unconstitutional. Lacking any cases to establish that facially absurd proposition, it simply asserts that it must be unconstitutional, because it has never happened before.

"[Amendment 2] identifies persons by a single trait and then denies them protection across the board. The resulting disqualification of a class of persons from the right to seek specific protection from the law is unprecedented in our jurisprudence. The absence of precedent for Amendment 2 is itself instructive. . . .

"It is not within our constitutional tradition to enact laws of this sort. Central both to the idea of the rule of law and to our own Constitution's guarantee of equal protection is the principle that government and each of its parts remain open on impartial terms to all who seek its assistance."

. . . [T]his is proved false every time a state law prohibiting or disfavoring certain conduct is passed, because such a law prevents the adversely affected group—whether drug addicts, or smokers, or gun owners, or motorcyclists—from changing the policy thus established in "each of [the] parts" of the State. What the Court says is even demonstrably false at the constitutional level. The Eighteenth Amendment to the Federal Constitution, for example, deprived those who drank alcohol not only of the power to alter the policy of prohibition *locally* or through *state legislation*, but even of the power to alter it through *state constitutional amendment* or *federal legislation*. The Establishment Clause of the First Amendment prevents theocrats from having their way by converting their fellow citizens at the local, state, or federal statutory level; as does the Republican Form of Government Clause prevent monarchists.

But there is a much closer analogy, one that involves precisely the effort by the majority of citizens to preserve its view of sexual morality statewide, against the efforts of a geographically concentrated and politically powerful minority to undermine it. The constitutions of the States of Arizona, Idaho, New Mexico, Oklahoma, and Utah *to this day* contain provisions stating that polygamy is "forever prohibited." Polygamists, and those who have a polygamous "orientation," have been "singled out" by these provisions for much more severe treatment than merely denial of favored status; and that treatment can only be changed by achieving amendment of the state constitutions. The Court's disposition today suggests that these provisions are unconstitutional, and that polygamy must be permitted in these States on a state-legislated, or perhaps even local-option, basis—unless, of course, polygamists for some reason have fewer constitutional rights than homosexuals. . . .

I cannot say that this Court has explicitly approved any of these state constitutional provisions; but it has approved a territorial statutory provision that went even further, depriving polygamists of the ability even to achieve a constitutional amendment, by depriving them of the power to vote. [Excerpt from *Davis* v. *Beason* (1890) omitted.] To the extent, if any, that this opinion permits the imposition of adverse consequences upon mere abstract advocacy of polygamy, it has of course been overruled by later cases. But the proposition that polygamy can be criminalized, and those engaging in that crime deprived of the vote, remains good law. . . .

IV

. . . The Court today . . . employs a constitutional theory heretofore unknown to frustrate Colorado's reasonable effort to preserve traditional

American moral values. The Court's stern disapproval of "animosity" towards homosexuality might be compared with what an earlier Court . . . said in *Murphy* v. *Ramsey* (1885), rejecting a constitutional challenge to a United States statute that denied the franchise in federal territories to those who engaged in polygamous cohabitation:

> "[C]ertainly no legislation can be supposed more wholesome and necessary in the founding of a free, self-governing commonwealth, fit to take rank as one of the co-ordinate States of the Union, than that which seeks to establish it on the basis of the idea of the family, as consisting in and springing from the union for life of one man and one woman in the holy estate of matrimony; the sure foundation of all that is stable and noble in our civilization; the best guaranty of that reverent morality which is the source of all beneficent progress in social and political improvement."

I would not myself indulge in such official praise for heterosexual monogamy, because I think it no business of the courts . . . to take sides in this culture war.

But the Court today has done so, not only by inventing a novel and extravagant constitutional doctrine to take the victory away from traditional forces, but even by verbally disparaging as bigotry adherence to traditional attitudes. To suggest, for example, that this constitutional amendment springs from nothing more than " 'a bare . . . desire to harm a politically unpopular group' " is nothing short of insulting. (It is also nothing short of preposterous to call "politically unpopular" a group which enjoys enormous influence in American media and politics, and which, as the trial court here noted, though composing no more than 4% of the population had the support of 46% of the voters on Amendment 2.)

When the Court takes sides in the culture wars, it tends to be with the knights rather than the villeins—and more specifically with the Templars, reflecting the views and values of the lawyer class from which the Court's Members are drawn. How that class feels about homosexuality will be evident to anyone who wishes to interview job applicants at virtually any of the Nation's law schools. The interviewer may refuse to offer a job because the applicant is a Republican; because he is an adulterer; because he went to the wrong prep school or belongs to the wrong country club; because he eats snails; because he is a womanizer; because she wears real-animal fur; or even because he hates the Chicago Cubs. But if the interviewer should wish not to be an associate or partner of an applicant because he disapproves of the applicant's homosexuality, then he will have violated the pledge which the Association of American Law Schools requires all its member-schools to exact from job interviewers: "assurance of the employer's willingness" to hire homosexuals. This law-school view of what "prejudices" must be stamped out may be contrasted with the more plebeian attitudes that apparently still prevail in the United States Congress, which has been unresponsive to repeated attempts to extend to homosexuals the protections of federal civil rights laws and which took the pains to exclude them specifically from the Americans With Disabilities Act of 1990.

* * *

Today's opinion has no foundation in American constitutional law, and barely pretends to. The people of Colorado have adopted an entirely reasonable provision which does not even disfavor homosexuals in any substantive sense, but merely denies them preferential treatment. Amendment 2 is designed to prevent piecemeal deterioration of the sexual morality favored by a majority of Coloradans, and is not only an appropriate means to that legitimate end, but a means that Americans have employed before. Striking it down is an act, not of judicial judgment, but of political will. I dissent.

□ □ □

No. 94-896

BMW of North America, Inc., Petitioner v. Ira Gore, Jr.

On writ of certiorari to the Supreme Court of Alabama

[May 20, 1996]

JUSTICE STEVENS delivered the opinion of the Court.

The Due Process Clause of the Fourteenth Amendment prohibits a State from imposing a "'grossly excessive'" punishment on a tortfeasor. *TXO Production Corp.* v. *Alliance Resources Corp.* (1993). The wrongdoing involved in this case was the decision by a national distributor of automobiles not to advise its dealers, and hence their customers, of predelivery damage to new cars when the cost of repair amounted to less than 3 percent of the car's suggested retail price. The question presented is whether a $2 million punitive damages award to the purchaser of one of these cars exceeds the constitutional limit.

I

In January 1990, Dr. Ira Gore, Jr. (respondent), purchased a black BMW sports sedan for $40,750.88 from an authorized BMW dealer in Birmingham, Alabama. After driving the car for approximately nine months, and without noticing any flaws in its appearance, Dr. Gore took the car to "Slick Finish," an independent detailer, to make it look "'snazzier than it normally would appear.'" Mr. Slick, the proprietor, detected evidence that the car had been repainted. Convinced that he had been cheated, Dr. Gore brought suit against petitioner BMW of North America (BMW), the American distributor of BMW automobiles. Dr. Gore alleged, *inter alia*, that the failure to disclose that the car had been repainted constituted suppression of a material fact. The complaint prayed for $500,000 in compensatory and punitive damages, and costs.

At trial, BMW acknowledged that it had adopted a nationwide policy in 1983 concerning cars that were damaged in the course of manufacture or transportation. If the cost of repairing the damage exceeded 3 percent of the car's suggested retail price, the car was placed in company service for a period of time and then sold as used. If the repair cost did not exceed 3 percent of the suggested retail price, however, the car was sold as new without advising the dealer that any repairs had been made. Because the $601.37 cost of repainting Dr. Gore's car was only about 1.5 percent of its suggested retail price, BMW did not disclose the damage or repair to the Birmingham dealer.

Dr. Gore asserted that his repainted car was worth less than a car that had not been refinished. To prove his actual damages of $4,000, he relied on the testimony of a former BMW dealer, who estimated that the value of a repainted BMW was approximately 10 percent less than the value of a new car that had not been damaged and repaired. To support his claim for punitive damages, Dr. Gore introduced evidence that since 1983 BMW had sold 983 refinished cars as new, including 14 in Alabama, without disclosing that the cars had been repainted before sale at a cost of more than $300 per vehicle. Using the actual damage estimate of $4,000 per vehicle, Dr. Gore argued that a punitive award of $4 million would provide an appropriate penalty for selling approximately 1,000 cars for more than they were worth.

. . . BMW argued that it was under no obligation to disclose repairs of minor damage to new cars and that Dr. Gore's car was as good as a car with the original factory finish. It disputed Dr. Gore's assertion that the value of the car was impaired by the repainting and argued that this good-faith belief made a punitive award inappropriate. BMW also maintained that transactions in jurisdictions other than Alabama had no relevance to Dr. Gore's claim.

The jury returned a verdict finding BMW liable for compensatory damages of $4,000. In addition, the jury assessed $4 million in punitive damages, based on a determination that the nondisclosure policy constituted "gross, oppressive or malicious" fraud.

BMW filed a post-trial motion to set aside the punitive damages award. The company introduced evidence to establish that its nondisclosure policy was consistent with the laws of roughly 25 States . . . . The most stringent of these statutes required disclosure of repairs costing more than 3 percent of the suggested retail price; none mandated disclosure of less costly repairs. . . . BMW contended that its conduct was lawful in these States and therefore could not provide the basis for an award of punitive damages.

BMW also drew the court's attention to the fact that its nondisclosure policy had never been adjudged unlawful before this action was filed. Just months before Dr. Gore's case went to trial, the jury in a similar lawsuit filed by another Alabama BMW purchaser found that BMW's failure to disclose paint repair constituted fraud. Before the judgment in this case, BMW changed its policy by taking steps to avoid the sale of any refinished vehicles in Alabama and two other States. When the $4 million verdict was returned in this case, BMW promptly instituted a nationwide policy of full disclosure of all repairs, no matter how minor.

In response to BMW's arguments, Dr. Gore asserted that the policy change demonstrated the efficacy of the punitive damages award. He noted that while no jury had held the policy unlawful, BMW had received a number of customer complaints relating to undisclosed repairs and had settled some lawsuits. Finally, he maintained that the disclosure statutes of other States were irrelevant because

BMW had failed to offer any evidence that the disclosure statutes supplanted, rather than supplemented, existing causes of action for common-law fraud.

The trial judge denied BMW's post-trial motion, holding, *inter alia*, that the award was not excessive. On appeal, the Alabama Supreme Court also rejected BMW's claim that the award exceeded the constitutionally permissible amount. (1994). The court's excessiveness inquiry applied the factors articulated in *Green Oil Co.* v. *Hornsby* (Ala. 1989) and approved [by the U.S. Supreme Court] in *Pacific Mut. Life Ins. Co.* v. *Haslip* (1991). Based on its analysis, the court concluded that BMW's conduct was "reprehensible"; the nondisclosure was profitable for the company; the judgment "would not have a substantial impact upon [BMW's] financial position"; the litigation had been expensive; no criminal sanctions had been imposed on BMW for the same conduct; the award of no punitive damages in [the prior Alabama case] reflected "the inherent uncertainty of the trial process"; and the punitive award bore a "reasonable relationship" to "the harm that was likely to occur from [BMW's] conduct as well as . . . the harm that actually occurred."

The Alabama Supreme Court did, however, rule in BMW's favor on one critical point: The court found that the jury improperly computed the amount of punitive damages by multiplying Dr. Gore's compensatory damages by the number of similar sales in other jurisdictions. Having found the verdict tainted, the court held that "a constitutionally reasonable punitive damages award in this case is $2,000,000" and therefore ordered a remittitur in that amount. The court's discussion of the amount of its remitted award expressly disclaimed any reliance on "acts that occurred in other jurisdictions"; instead, the court explained that it had used a "comparative analysis" that considered Alabama cases, "along with cases from other jurisdictions, involving the sale of an automobile where the seller misrepresented the condition of the vehicle and the jury awarded punitive damages to the purchaser."

Because we believed that a review of this case would help to illuminate "the character of the standard that will identify constitutionally excessive awards" of punitive damages, see *Honda Motor Co.* v. *Oberg* (1994), we granted certiorari (1995).

II

Punitive damages may properly be imposed to further a State's legitimate interests in punishing unlawful conduct and deterring its repetition. In our federal system, States necessarily have considerable flexibility in determining the level of punitive damages that they will allow in different classes of cases and in any particular case. Most States that authorize exemplary damages afford the jury similar latitude, requiring only that the damages awarded be reasonably necessary to vindicate the State's legitimate interests in punishment and deterrence. Only when an award can fairly be categorized as "grossly excessive" in relation to these interests does it enter the zone of arbitrariness that violates the Due Process Clause of the Fourteenth Amendment. For that reason, the federal excessiveness inquiry appropriately begins with an identification of the state interests that a punitive award is designed to serve. We therefore focus our attention first on the scope of Alabama's legitimate interests in punishing BMW and deterring it from future misconduct.

No one doubts that a State may protect its citizens by prohibiting deceptive trade practices and by requiring automobile distributors to disclose presale repairs that affect the value of a new car. But the States need not, and in fact do not, provide such protection in a uniform manner. . . .

We may assume, *arguendo*, that it would be wise for every State to adopt Dr. Gore's preferred rule, requiring full disclosure of every presale repair to a car, no matter how trivial and regardless of its actual impact on the value of the car. But while we do not doubt that Congress has ample authority to enact such a policy for the entire Nation, it is clear that no single State could do so, or even impose its own policy choice on neighboring States. Similarly, one State's power to impose burdens on the interstate market for automobiles is not only subordinate to the federal power over interstate commerce, but is also constrained by the need to respect the interests of other States.

We think it follows from these principles of state sovereignty and comity that a State may not impose economic sanctions on violators of its laws with the intent of changing the tortfeasors' lawful conduct in other States. Before this Court Dr. Gore argued that the large punitive damages award was necessary to induce BMW to change the nationwide policy that it adopted in 1983. But by attempting to alter BMW's nationwide policy, Alabama would be infringing on the policy choices of other States. Alabama may insist that BMW adhere to a particular disclosure policy in that State. Alabama does not have the power, however, to punish BMW for conduct that was lawful where it occurred and that had no impact on Alabama or its residents. Nor may Alabama impose sanctions on BMW in order to deter conduct that is lawful in other jurisdictions.

In this case, we accept the Alabama Supreme Court's interpretation of the jury verdict as reflecting a computation of the amount of punitive damages "based in large part on conduct that happened in other jurisdictions." As the Alabama Supreme Court noted, neither the jury nor the trial court was presented with evidence that any of BMW's out-of-state conduct was unlawful. . . . The Alabama Supreme Court therefore properly eschewed reliance on BMW's out-of-state conduct and based its remitted award solely on conduct that occurred within Alabama. The award must be analyzed in the light of the same conduct, with consideration given only to the interests of Alabama consumers, rather than those of the entire Nation. When the scope of the interest in punishment and deterrence that an Alabama court may appropriately consider is properly limited, it is apparent — for reasons that we shall now address — that this award is grossly excessive.

III

. . . Three guideposts, each of which indicates that BMW did not receive adequate notice of the magnitude of the sanction that Alabama might impose for adhering to the nondisclosure policy adopted in 1983, lead us to the conclusion that the $2 million award against BMW is grossly excessive: the degree of reprehensibility of the nondisclosure; the disparity between the harm or potential harm suffered by Dr. Gore and his punitive damages award; and the difference between this remedy and the civil penalties authorized or imposed in comparable cases. We discuss these considerations in turn.

Degree of Reprehensibility

Perhaps the most important indicium of the reasonableness of a punitive damages award is the degree of reprehensibility of the defendant's conduct. . . . This principle reflects the accepted view that some wrongs are more blameworthy than others. . . .

In this case, none of the aggravating factors associated with particularly reprehensible conduct is present. The harm BMW inflicted on Dr. Gore was purely economic in nature. The presale refinishing of the car had no effect on its performance or safety features, or even its appearance for at least nine months after his purchase. BMW's conduct evinced no indifference to or reckless disregard for the health and safety of others. To be sure, infliction of economic injury, especially when done intentionally through affirmative acts of misconduct or when the target is financially vulnerable, can warrant a substantial penalty. But this observation does not convert all acts that cause economic harm into torts that are sufficiently reprehensible to justify a significant sanction in addition to compensatory damages.

Dr. Gore contends that BMW's conduct was particularly reprehensible because nondisclosure of the repairs to his car formed part of a nationwide pattern of tortious conduct. Certainly, evidence that a defendant has repeatedly engaged in prohibited conduct while knowing or suspecting that it was unlawful would provide relevant support for an argument that strong medicine is required to cure the defendant's disrespect for the law. . . .

In support of his thesis, Dr. Gore advances two arguments. First, he asserts that the state disclosure statutes supplement, rather than supplant, existing remedies for breach of contract and common-law fraud. Thus, according to Dr. Gore, the statutes may not properly be viewed as immunizing from liability the nondisclosure of repairs costing less than the applicable statutory threshold. Second, Dr. Gore maintains that BMW should have anticipated that its failure to disclose similar repair work could expose it to liability for fraud.

We recognize, of course, that only state courts may authoritatively construe state statutes. . . . A review of the text of the statutes, however, persuades us that in the absence of a state-court determination to the contrary, a corporate executive could reasonably interpret the disclosure requirements as establishing safe harbors. . . .

Dr. Gore's second argument for treating BMW as a recidivist is that the company should have anticipated that its actions would be considered fraudulent in some, if not all, jurisdictions. . . . There is no evidence that BMW acted in bad faith when it sought to establish the appropriate line between presumptively minor damage and damage requiring disclosure to purchasers. . . .

Finally, the record in this case discloses no deliberate false statements, acts of affirmative misconduct, or concealment of evidence of improper motive, such as were present in *Haslip* and *TXO*. We accept, of course, the jury's finding that BMW suppressed a material fact which Alabama law obligated it to communicate to prospective purchasers of repainted cars in that State. But the omission of a material fact may be less reprehensible than a deliberate false statement, particularly when there is a good-faith basis for believing that no duty to disclose exists.

... Because this case exhibits none of the circumstances ordinarily associated with egregiously improper conduct, we are persuaded that BMW's conduct was not sufficiently reprehensible to warrant imposition of a $2 million exemplary damages award.

Ratio

The second and perhaps most commonly cited indicium of an unreasonable or excessive punitive damages award is its ratio to the actual harm inflicted on the plaintiff. ... Our decisions in both *Haslip* and *TXO* endorsed the proposition that a comparison between the compensatory award and the punitive award is significant.

In *Haslip* we concluded that even though a punitive damages award of "more than 4 times the amount of compensatory damages" might be "close to the line," it did not "cross the line into the area of constitutional impropriety." *TXO*, following dicta in *Haslip*, refined this analysis by confirming that the proper inquiry is " 'whether there is a reasonable relationship between the punitive damages award and *the harm likely to result* from the defendant's conduct as well as the harm that actually has occurred.' " Thus, in upholding the $10 million award in *TXO*, we relied on the difference between that figure and the harm to the victim that would have ensued if the tortious plan had succeeded. That difference suggested that the relevant ratio was not more than 10 to 1.

The $2 million in punitive damages awarded to Dr. Gore by the Alabama Supreme Court is 500 times the amount of his actual harm as determined by the jury. Moreover, there is no suggestion that Dr. Gore or any other BMW purchaser was threatened with any additional potential harm by BMW's nondisclosure policy. The disparity in this case is thus dramatically greater than those considered in *Haslip* and *TXO*.

Of course, we have consistently rejected the notion that the constitutional line is marked by a simple mathematical formula, even one that compares actual and potential damages to the punitive award. Indeed, low awards of compensatory damages may properly support a higher ratio than high compensatory awards, if, for example, a particularly egregious act has resulted in only a small amount of economic damages. A higher ratio may also be justified in cases in which the injury is hard to detect or the monetary value of noneconomic harm might have been difficult to determine. It is appropriate, therefore, to reiterate our rejection of a categorical approach. Once again, "we return to what we said ... in *Haslip*: 'We need not, and indeed we cannot, draw a mathematical bright line between the constitutionally acceptable and the constitutionally unacceptable that would fit every case. We can say, however, that [a] general concer[n] of reasonableness ... properly enter[s] into the constitutional calculus.' " *TXO*. In most cases, the ratio will be within a constitutionally acceptable range, and remittitur will not be justified on this basis. When the ratio is a breathtaking 500 to 1, however, the award must surely "raise a suspicious judicial eyebrow." *TXO* (O'CONNOR, J., dissenting).

Sanctions for Comparable Misconduct

Comparing the punitive damages award and the civil or criminal penalties that could be imposed for comparable misconduct provides a third indicium of excessiveness. . . . In this case the $2 million economic sanction imposed on BMW is substantially greater than the statutory fines available in Alabama and elsewhere for similar malfeasance.

The maximum civil penalty authorized by the Alabama Legislature for a violation of its Deceptive Trade Practices Act is $2,000; other States authorize more severe sanctions, with the maxima ranging from $5,000 to $10,000. Significantly, some statutes draw a distinction between first offenders and recidivists; thus, in New York the penalty is $50 for a first offense and $250 for subsequent offenses. None of these statutes would provide an out-of-state distributor with fair notice that the first violation — or, indeed the first 14 violations — of its provisions might subject an offender to a multimillion dollar penalty. Moreover, at the time BMW's policy was first challenged, there does not appear to have been any judicial decision in Alabama or elsewhere indicating that application of that policy might give rise to such severe punishment.

The sanction imposed in this case cannot be justified on the ground that it was necessary to deter future misconduct without considering whether less drastic remedies could be expected to achieve that goal. The fact that a multimillion dollar penalty prompted a change in policy sheds no light on the question whether a lesser deterrent would have adequately protected the interests of Alabama consumers. In the absence of a history of noncompliance with known statutory requirements, there is no basis for assuming that a more modest sanction would not have been sufficient to motivate full compliance with the disclosure requirement imposed by the Alabama Supreme Court in this case.

IV

We assume, as the juries in this case and in the [prior Alabama] case found, that the undisclosed damage to the new BMW's affected their actual value. . . . [W]e also assume that [BMW] knew, or should have known, that as time passed the repainted cars would lose their attractive appearance more rapidly than other BMW's. Moreover, we of course accept the Alabama courts' view that the state interest in protecting its citizens from deceptive trade practices justifies a sanction in addition to the recovery of compensatory damages. We cannot, however, accept the conclusion of the Alabama Supreme Court that BMW's conduct was sufficiently egregious to justify a punitive sanction that is tantamount to a severe criminal penalty.

The fact that BMW is a large corporation rather than an impecunious individual does not diminish its entitlement to fair notice of the demands that the several States impose on the conduct of its business. Indeed, its status as an active participant in the national economy implicates the federal interest in preventing individual States from imposing undue burdens on interstate commerce. While each State has ample power to protect its own consumers, none may use the punitive damages deterrent as a means of imposing its regulatory policies on the entire Nation.

As in *Haslip*, we are not prepared to draw a bright line marking the limits of a constitutionally acceptable punitive damages award. Unlike that case, however, we are fully convinced that the grossly excessive award imposed in this case transcends the constitutional limit. Whether the appropriate remedy requires a new trial or merely an independent determination by the Alabama Supreme Court of the award necessary to vindicate the economic interests of Alabama consumers is a matter that should be addressed by the state court in the first instance. The judgment is reversed, and the case is remanded for further proceedings not inconsistent with this opinion.

It is so ordered.

JUSTICE BREYER, with whom JUSTICE O'CONNOR and JUSTICE SOUTER join, concurring.

. . . The Court's opinion, which I join, explains why we have concluded that this award, in this case, was "grossly excessive" in relation to legitimate punitive damages objectives, and hence an arbitrary deprivation of life, liberty, or property in violation of the Due Process Clause. Members of this Court have generally thought, however, that if "fair procedures were followed, a judgment that is a product of that process is entitled to a strong presumption of validity." And the Court also has found that punitive damages procedures very similar to those followed here were not, by themselves, fundamentally unfair. Thus, I believe it important to explain why this presumption of validity is overcome in this instance.

. . . The standards the Alabama courts applied here are vague and open-ended to the point where they risk arbitrary results. In my view, although the vagueness of those standards does not, by itself, violate due process, it does invite the kind of scrutiny the Court has given the particular verdict before us. . . . This is because the standards, as the Alabama Supreme Court authoritatively interpreted them here, provided no significant constraints or protection against arbitrary results.

First, the Alabama statute that permits punitive damages does not itself contain a standard that readily distinguishes between conduct warranting very small, and conduct warranting very large, punitive damages awards. That statute permits punitive damages in cases of "oppression, fraud, wantonness, or malice." But the statute goes on to define those terms broadly, to encompass far more than the egregious conduct that those terms, at first reading, might seem to imply. An intentional misrepresentation, made through a statement or silence, can easily amount to "fraud" sufficient to warrant punitive damages. . . . The statute thereby authorizes punitive damages for the most serious kinds of misrepresentations, say, tricking the elderly out of their life savings, for much less serious conduct, such as the failure to disclose repainting a car, at issue here, and for a vast range of conduct in between.

Second, the Alabama courts, in this case, have applied the "factors" intended to constrain punitive damages awards, in a way that belies that purpose. *Green Oil Co.* v. *Hornsby* (1989) sets forth seven factors that appellate courts use to determine whether or not a jury award was "grossly excessive" and which, in principle, might make up for the lack of significant constraint in the statute. But, as the Alabama courts have authoritatively interpreted them, and as their application in this case illustrates, they impose little actual constraint. [Detailed discussion of factors omitted.]

Third, the state courts neither referred to, nor made any effort to find, nor enunciated any other standard, that either directly, or indirectly as background, might have supplied the constraining legal force that the statute and *Green Oil* standards (as interpreted here) lack. Dr. Gore did argue to the jury an economic theory based on the need to offset the totality of the harm that the defendant's conduct caused. Some theory of that general kind might have provided a significant constraint on arbitrary awards . . . .

The record before us, however, contains nothing suggesting that the Alabama Supreme Court, when determining the allowable award, applied any "economic" theory that might explain the $2 million recovery. . . .

Fourth, I cannot find any community understanding or historic practice that this award might exemplify and which, therefore, would provide background standards constraining arbitrary behavior and excessive awards. A punitive damages award of $2 million for intentional misrepresentation causing $56,000 of harm is extraordinary by historical standards, and, as far as I am aware, finds no analogue until relatively recent times. . . .

Fifth, there are no other legislative enactments here that classify awards and impose quantitative limits that would significantly cabin the fairly unbounded discretion created by the absence of constraining legal standards.

The upshot is that the rules that purport to channel discretion in this kind of case, here did not do so in fact. That means that the award in this case was both (a) the product of a system of standards that did not significantly constrain a court's, and hence a jury's, discretion in making that award; and (b) was grossly excessive in light of the State's legitimate punitive damages objectives. . . .

JUSTICE SCALIA, with whom JUSTICE THOMAS joins, dissenting.

Today we see the latest manifestation of this Court's recent and increasingly insistent "concern about punitive damages that 'run wild.' " *Pacific Mut. Life Ins. Co. v. Haslip* (1991). Since the Constitution does not make that concern any of our business, the Court's activities in this area are an unjustified incursion into the province of state governments. . . .

I

The most significant aspects of today's decision — the identification of a "substantive due process" right against a "grossly excessive" award, and the concomitant assumption of ultimate authority to decide anew a matter of "reasonableness" resolved in lower court proceedings — are of course not new. *Haslip* and *TXO* revived the notion, moribund since its appearance in the first years of this century, that the measure of civil punishment poses a question of constitutional dimension to be answered by this Court. Neither of those cases, however, nor any of the precedents upon which they relied, actually took the step of declaring a punitive award unconstitutional simply because it was "too big.". . .

There is no precedential warrant for giving our judgment priority over the judgment of state courts and juries on this matter. The only support for the Court's position is to be found in a handful of errant federal cases, bunched within a few years of one other, which invented the notion that an unfairly severe civil sanction amounts to a violation of constitutional liberties. These were the decisions upon which the *TXO* plurality relied in pronouncing that the Due Process Clause "imposes substantive limits 'beyond which penalties may not go.' " Although they are our precedents, they are themselves too shallowly rooted to justify the Court's recent undertaking. . . .

II

One might understand the Court's eagerness to enter this field, rather than leave it with the state legislatures, if it had something useful to say. In fact, however, its opinion provides virtually no guidance to legislatures, and to state and federal courts, as to what a "constitutionally proper" level of punitive damages might be.

We are instructed at the outset of Part II of the Court's opinion — the beginning of its substantive analysis — that "the federal excessiveness inquiry . . . begins with an identification of the state interests that a punitive award is designed to serve.". . .

. . . As Part II of the Court's opinion unfolds, it turns out to be directed, not to the question "How much punishment is too much?" but rather to the question "Which acts can be punished?" "Alabama does not have the power," the Court says, "to punish BMW for conduct that was lawful where it occurred and that had no impact on Alabama or its residents." That may be true, though only in the narrow sense that a person cannot be *held liable to be punished* on the basis of a lawful act. But if a person has been held subject to punishment because he committed an *un*lawful act, the *degree* of his punishment assuredly *can* be increased on the basis of any other conduct of his that displays his wickedness, unlawful or not. . . . Why could the Supreme Court of Alabama not consider lawful (but disreputable) conduct, both inside and outside Alabama, for the purpose of assessing just how bad an actor BMW was?

The Court follows up its statement that "Alabama does not have the power . . . to punish BMW for conduct that was lawful where it occurred" with the statement: "Nor may Alabama impose sanctions on BMW in order to deter conduct that is lawful in other jurisdictions." The Court provides us no citation of authority to support this proposition — other than the barely analogous cases cited earlier in the opinion — and I know of none. . . .

III

In Part III of its opinion, the Court identifies "[t]hree guideposts" that lead it to the conclusion that the award in this case is excessive: degree of reprehensibility, ratio between punitive award and plaintiff's actual harm, and legislative sanctions provided for comparable misconduct.

The legal significance of these "guideposts" is nowhere explored, but their necessary effect is to establish federal standards governing the hitherto exclusively state law of damages. Apparently . . . all three federal "guideposts" can be overridden if "necessary to deter future misconduct" — a loophole that will encourage state reviewing courts to uphold awards as necessary for the "adequat[e] protect[ion]" of state consumers. By effectively requiring state reviewing courts to concoct rationalizations — whether within the "guideposts" or through the loophole — to justify the intuitive punitive reactions of state juries, the Court accords neither category of institution the respect it deserves.

Of course it will not be easy for the States to comply with this new federal law of damages, no matter how willing they are to do so. In truth, the "guideposts" mark a road to nowhere; they provide no real guidance at all. As to "degree of reprehensibility" of the defendant's conduct, we learn that " 'nonviolent crimes are less serious than crimes marked by violence or the threat of violence,' " and that " 'trickery and deceit' " are "more reprehensible than negligence." As to the ratio of punitive to compensatory damages, we are told that a " 'general concer[n] of reasonableness . . . enter[s] into the constitutional calculus,' "—though even "a breathtaking 500 to 1" will not necessarily do anything more than " 'raise a suspicious judicial eyebrow.' " . . . And as to legislative sanctions provided for comparable misconduct, they should be accorded " 'substantial deference.' " One expects the Court to conclude: "To thine own self be true."

These criss-crossing platitudes yield no real answers in no real cases. And it must be noted that the Court nowhere says that these three "guideposts" are the only guideposts; indeed, it makes very clear that they are not. . . . In other words, even these utter platitudes . . . may be overridden by other unnamed considerations. The Court has constructed a framework that does not genuinely constrain, that does not inform state legislatures and lower courts — that does nothing at all except confer an artificial air of doctrinal analysis upon its essentially ad hoc determination that this particular award of punitive damages was not "fair.". . .

For the foregoing reasons, I respectfully dissent.

JUSTICE GINSBURG, with whom THE CHIEF JUSTICE joins, dissenting.

The Court, I am convinced, unnecessarily and unwisely ventures into territory traditionally within the States' domain, and does so in the face of reform measures recently adopted or currently under consideration in legislative arenas. The Alabama Supreme Court, in this case, endeavored to follow this Court's prior instructions; and, more recently, Alabama's highest court has installed further controls on awards of punitive damages. I would therefore leave the state court's judgment undisturbed, and resist unnecessary intrusion into an area dominantly of state concern.

[I omitted]

II

A

Alabama's Supreme Court reports that it "thoroughly and painstakingly" reviewed the jury's award, according to principles set out in its own pathmarking decisions and in this Court's opinions in *TXO* and *Pacific Mut. Life Ins. Co. v. Haslip* (1991). The Alabama court said it gave weight to several factors, including BMW's deliberate ("reprehensible") presentation of refinished cars as new and undamaged, without disclosing that the value of those cars had been reduced by an estimated 10%, the financial position of the defendant, and the costs of litigation. These standards, we previously held, "impos[e] a sufficiently definite and meaningful constraint on the discretion of Alabama factfinders in awarding punitive damages." Alabama's highest court could have displayed its labor pains more visibly, but its judgment is nonetheless entitled to a presumption of legitimacy.

We accept, of course, that Alabama's Supreme Court applied the State's own law correctly. Under that law, the State's objectives —"punishment and deterrence" —guide punitive damages awards. Nor should we be quick to find a constitutional infirmity when the highest state court endeavored a corrective for one counsel's slip and the other's oversight —counsel for plaintiff's excess in summation, unobjected to by counsel for defendant —and when the state court did so intending to follow the process approved in our *Haslip* and *TXO* decisions.

B

The Court finds Alabama's $2 million award not simply excessive, but grossly so, and therefore unconstitutional. The decision leads us further into territory traditionally within the States' domain, and commits the Court, now and again, to correct "misapplication of a properly stated rule of law.".... The Court is not well equipped for this mission. Tellingly, the Court repeats that it brings to the task no "mathematical formula," no "categorical approach," no "bright line." It has only a vague concept of substantive due process, a "raised eyebrow" test, as its ultimate guide.

In contrast to habeas corpus review . . . , the Court will work at this business alone. It will not be aided by the federal district courts and courts of appeals. It will be the only federal court policing the area. The Court's readiness to superintend state court punitive damages awards is all the more puzzling in view of the Court's longstanding reluctance to countenance review, even by courts of appeals, of the size of verdicts returned by juries in federal district court proceedings. And the reexamination prominent in state courts and in legislative arenas serves to underscore why the Court's enterprise is undue.

For the reasons stated, I dissent from this Court's disturbance of the judgment the Alabama Supreme Court has made.

□ □ □

Nos. 94-805, 94-806 and 94-988

George W. Bush, Governor of Texas, et al., Appellants v. Al Vera et al.

William Lawson, et al., Appellants v. Al Vera et al.

United States, Appellant v. Al Vera et al.

On appeals from the United States District Court
for the Southern District of Texas

[June 13, 1996]

JUSTICE O'CONNOR announced the judgment of the Court and delivered an opinion, in which the CHIEF JUSTICE and JUSTICE KENNEDY join.

This is the latest in a series of appeals involving racial gerrymandering challenges to state redistricting efforts in the wake of the 1990 census. See *Shaw* v. *Hunt* (*Shaw II*); *United States* v. *Hays* (1995); *Miller* v. *Johnson* (1995); *Shaw* v. *Reno* (1993) (*Shaw I*). That census revealed a population increase, largely in urban minority populations, that entitled Texas to three additional congressional seats. In response, and with a view to complying with the Voting Rights Act of 1965 (VRA), as amended, 42 U.S.C. §1973 *et seq.*, the Texas Legislature promulgated a redistricting plan that, among other things: created District 30, a new majority-African-American district in Dallas County; created District 29, a new majority-Hispanic district in and around Houston in Harris County; and reconfigured District 18, which is adjacent to District 29, to make it a majority-African-American district. The Department of Justice precleared that plan under VRA §5 in 1991, and it was used in the 1992 congressional elections.

The plaintiffs, six Texas voters, challenged the plan, alleging that 24 of Texas' 30 congressional districts constitute racial gerrymanders in violation of the Fourteenth Amendment. The three-judge United States District Court for the Southern District of Texas held Districts 18, 29, and 30 unconstitutional. (1994). The Governor of Texas, private intervenors, and the United States (as intervenor) now appeal. Finding that, under this Court's decisions in *Shaw I* and *Miller*, the district lines at issue are subject to strict scrutiny, and that they are not narrowly tailored to serve a compelling state interest, we affirm.

[I omitted]

II

We must . . . determine whether those districts are subject to strict scrutiny. Our precedents have used a variety of formulations to describe the threshold for the application of strict scrutiny. Strict scrutiny applies where "redistricting legislation . . . is so extremely irregular on its face that it rationally can be viewed only as an effort to segregate the races for purposes of voting, without regard for traditional districting principles," *Shaw I*, or where "race for its own sake, and not other districting principles, was the legislature's dominant and controlling rationale in drawing its district lines," *Miller*, and "the legislature subordinated traditional race-neutral districting principles . . . to racial considerations," *id*. See also *id*. (O'CONNOR, J., concurring) (strict scrutiny only applies where "the State has relied on race in substantial disregard of customary and traditional districting practices").

Strict scrutiny does not apply merely because redistricting is performed with consciousness of race. Nor does it apply to all cases of intentional creation of majority-minority districts. See *DeWitt* v. *Wilson* (ED Cal. 1994) (strict scrutiny did not apply to an intentionally created compact majority-minority district), summarily aff'd, (1995); *cf. Shaw I* (reserving this question). Electoral district lines are "facially race neutral," so a more searching inquiry is necessary before strict scrutiny can be found applicable in redistricting cases than in cases of "classifications based explicitly on race." For strict scrutiny to apply, the plaintiffs must prove that other, legitimate districting principles were "subordinated" to race. By that, we mean that race must be "the predominant factor motivating the legislature's [redistricting] decision." We thus differ from JUSTICE

THOMAS, who would apparently hold that it suffices that racial considerations be a motivation for the drawing of a majority-minority district.

The present case is a mixed motive case. The appellants concede that one of Texas' goals in creating the three districts at issue was to produce majority-minority districts, but they also cite evidence that other goals, particularly incumbency protection (including protection of "functional incumbents," i.e., sitting members of the Texas Legislature who had declared an intention to run for open congressional seats), also played a role in the drawing of the district lines. . . . [R]eview of the District Court's findings of primary fact and the record convinces us that the District Court's determination that race was the "predominant factor" in the drawing of each of the districts must be sustained.

We begin with general findings and evidence regarding the redistricting plan's respect for traditional districting principles, the legislators' expressed motivations, and the methods used in the redistricting process. . . . The court . . . found that "generally, Texas has not intentionally disregarded traditional districting criteria," and that only one pre-1991 congressional district in Texas was comparable in its irregularity and noncompactness to the three challenged districts. . . .

The District Court also found substantial direct evidence of the legislature's racial motivations. The State's submission to the Department of Justice for preclearance under VRA §5 reports a consensus within the legislature that the three new congressional districts

> " 'should be configured in such a way as to allow members of racial, ethnic, and language minorities to elect Congressional representatives.' "
> [Remainder of excerpt omitted.]

The appellants also conceded in this litigation that the three districts at issue "were created for the purpose of enhancing the opportunity of minority voters to elect minority representatives to Congress." And testimony of individual state officials confirmed that the decision to create the districts now challenged as majority-minority districts was made at the outset of the process and never seriously questioned.

The means that Texas used to make its redistricting decisions provides further evidence of the importance of race. The primary tool used in drawing district lines was a computer program called "REDAPPL." REDAPPL permitted redistricters to manipulate district lines on computer maps, on which racial and other socioeconomic data were superimposed. At each change in configuration of the district lines being drafted, REDAPPL displayed updated racial composition statistics for the district as drawn. REDAPPL contained racial data at the block-by-block level, whereas other data, such as party registration and past voting statistics, were only available at the level of voter tabulation districts (which approximate election precincts). The availability and use of block-by-block racial data was unprecedented; before the 1990 census, data were not broken down beyond the census tract level. By providing uniquely detailed racial data, REDAPPL enabled districters to make more intricate refinements on the basis of race than on the basis of other demographic information. The District Court found that the districters availed themselves fully of that opportunity. . . .

These findings—that the State substantially neglected traditional district-ing criteria such as compactness, that it was committed from the outset to cre-ating majority-minority districts, and that it manipulated district lines to exploit unprecedentedly detailed racial data—together weigh in favor of the applica-tion of strict scrutiny. We do not hold that any one of these factors is indepen-dently sufficient to require strict scrutiny. The Constitution does not mandate regularity of district shape, and the neglect of traditional districting criteria is merely necessary, not sufficient. For strict scrutiny to apply, traditional district-ing criteria must be *subordinated to race.* Nor, as we have emphasized, is the deci-sion to create a majority-minority district objectionable in and of itself. The direct evidence of that decision is not, as JUSTICE STEVENS suggests, "the real key" to our decision; it is merely one of several essential ingredients. Nor do we "condemn state legislation merely because it was based on accurate informa-tion." The use of sophisticated technology and detailed information in the drawing of majority-minority districts is no more objectionable than it is in the drawing of majority-majority districts. But, as the District Court explained, the direct evidence of racial considerations, coupled with the fact that the comput-er program used was significantly *more* sophisticated with respect to race than with respect to other demographic data, provides substantial evidence that it was race that led to the neglect of traditional districting criteria here. We must therefore consider what role other factors played in order to determine whether race predominated.

Several factors other than race were at work in the drawing of the districts. Traditional districting criteria were not *entirely* neglected: Districts 18 and 29 maintain the integrity of county lines; each of the three districts takes its char-acter from a principal city and the surrounding urban area; and none of the dis-tricts is as widely dispersed as the North Carolina district held unconstitutional in *Shaw II.* . . . More significantly, the District Court found that incumbency pro-tection influenced the redistricting plan to an unprecedented extent. . . .

Strict scrutiny would not be appropriate if race-neutral, traditional dis-tricting considerations predominated over racial ones. We have not subjected political gerrymandering to strict scrutiny. See *Davis* v. *Bandemer* (1986). And we have recognized incumbency protection, at least in the limited form of "avoid-ing contests between incumbent[s]," as a legitimate state goal. [Citations omit-ted.] Because it is clear that race was not the only factor that motivated the leg-islature to draw irregular district lines, we must scrutinize each challenged dis-trict to determine whether the District Court's conclusion that race predomi-nated over legitimate districting considerations, including incumbency, can be sustained.

A

The population of District 30 is 50% African-American and 17.1% His-panic. Fifty percent of the district's population is located in a compact, albeit irregularly shaped, core in south Dallas, which is 69% African-American. But the remainder of the district consists of narrow and bizarrely shaped tenta-cles—the State identifies seven "segments"—extending primarily to the north and west. Over 98% of the district's population is within Dallas County, but it crosses two county lines at its western and northern extremities. Its western excursion into Tarrant County grabs a small community that is 61.9% African-American; its northern excursion into Collin County occupies a hook-like shape mapping exactly onto the only area in the southern half of that county with a combined African-American and Hispanic percentage population in excess of 50%. . . .

Appellants do not deny that District 30 shows substantial disregard for the traditional districting principles of compactness and regularity, or that the redistricters pursued unwaveringly the objective of creating a majority-African-American district. But they argue that its bizarre shape is explained by efforts to unite communities of interest in a single district and, especially, to protect incumbents.

Appellants highlight the facts that the district has a consistently urban character and has common media sources throughout, and that its tentacles include several major transportation lines into the city of Dallas. These factors, which implicate traditional districting principles, do correlate to some extent with the district's layout. But we see no basis in the record for displacing the District Court's conclusion that race predominated over them . . . .

Appellants present a more substantial case for their claim that incumbency protection rivaled race in determining the district's shape. [State Senator] Johnson was the principal architect of District 30, which was designed in part to create a safe Democratic seat for her. At an early stage in the redistricting process, Johnson submitted to the state legislature a plan for Dallas County with a relatively compact 44% African-American district that did not violate the integrity of any voter tabulation district or county lines. The District Court found that "[w]hile minority voters did not object" to it, "[t]hat plan drew much opposition from incumbents and was quickly abandoned. . . . [F]ive other congressmen would have been thrown into districts other than the ones they currently represent." Appellants also point to testimony from Johnson and others to the effect that the incumbents of the adjacent Democratic Districts 5 and 24 exerted strong and partly successful efforts to retain predominantly African-American Democratic voters in their districts. . . .

In some circumstances, incumbency protection might explain as well as, or better than, race a State's decision to depart from other traditional districting principles, such as compactness, in the drawing of bizarre district lines. And the fact that, "[a]s it happens, . . . many of the voters being fought over [by the neighboring Democratic incumbents] were African-American," would not, in and of itself, convert a political gerrymander into a racial gerrymander, no matter how conscious redistricters were of the correlation between race and party affiliation. . . .

If the State's goal is otherwise constitutional political gerrymandering, it is free to use the kind of political data on which JUSTICE STEVENS focuses—precinct general election voting patterns, precinct primary voting patterns, and legislators' experience—to achieve that goal regardless of its awareness of its racial implications and regardless of the fact that it does so in the context of a majority-minority district. To the extent that the District Court suggested the contrary, it erred. But to the extent that race is used as a proxy for political characteristics, a racial stereotype requiring strict scrutiny is in operation. . . .

Here, the District Court had ample bases on which to conclude both that racially motivated gerrymandering had a qualitatively greater influence on the drawing of district lines than politically motivated gerrymandering, and that political gerrymandering was accomplished in large part by the use of race as a proxy. . . .

B

In Harris County, centered on the city of Houston, Districts 18 and 29 interlock "like a jigsaw puzzle . . . in which it might be impossible to get the pieces apart." [Quoting *The Almanac of American Politics* (1996).] . . . According to the leading statistical study of relative district compactness and regularity, they are two of the three least regular districts in the country.

District 18's population is 51% African-American and 15% Hispanic. It "has some of the most irregular boundaries of any congressional district in the country[,] . . . boundaries that squiggle north toward Intercontinental Airport and northwest out radial highways, then spurt south on one side toward the port and on the other toward the Astrodome."[*Almanac of American Politics.*] Its "many narrow corridors, wings, or fingers . . . reach out to enclose black voters, while excluding nearby Hispanic residents."[Quoting law review article.]

District 29 has a 61% Hispanic and 10% African-American population. It resembles

> "a sacred Mayan bird, with its body running eastward along the Ship Channel from downtown Houston until the tail terminates in Baytown. Spindly legs reach south to Hobby Airport, while the plumed head rises northward almost to Intercontinental. In the western extremity of the district, an open beak appears to be searching for worms in Spring Branch. Here and there, ruffled feathers jut out at odd angles."[*Almanac of American Politics.*]

Not only are the shapes of the districts bizarre; they also exhibit utter disregard of city limits, local election precincts, and voter tabulation district lines. This caused a severe disruption of traditional forms of political activity. Campaigners seeking to visit their constituents "had to carry a map to identify the district lines, because so often the borders would move from block to block"; voters "did not know the candidates running for office" because they did not know which district they lived in. In light of Texas' requirement that voting be arranged by precinct, with each precinct representing a community which shares local, state, and federal representatives, it also created administrative headaches for local election officials . . . .

As with District 30, appellants adduced evidence that incumbency protection played a role in determining the bizarre district lines. The District Court found that one constraint on the shape of District 29 was the rival ambitions of its two "functional incumbents," who distorted its boundaries in an effort to include larger areas of their existing state legislative constituencies. But the District Court's findings amply demonstrate that such influences were overwhelmed in the determination of the districts' bizarre shapes by the State's efforts to maximize racial divisions. The State's VRA §5 submission explains that the bizarre configuration of Districts 18 and 29 "result[s] in the maximization of minority voting strength" in Harris County, corroborating the District Court's finding that "[i]n the earliest stages of the Congressional redistricting process, state Democratic and Republican leaders rallied behind the idea of creating a new Hispanic safe seat in Harris County while preserving the safe African-American seat in District 18.". . . And, even more than in District 30, the intricacy of the lines drawn, separating Hispanic voters from African-American voters on a block-by-block basis, betrays the critical impact of the block-by-block racial data available on the REDAPPL program. The District Court's conclusion is, therefore, inescapable: "Because Districts 18 and 29 are formed in utter disregard for traditional redistricting criteria and because their shapes are ultimately unexplainable on grounds other than the racial quotas established for those districts, they are the product of [presumptively] unconstitutional racial gerrymandering."

III

Having concluded that strict scrutiny applies, we must determine whether the racial classifications embodied in any of the three districts are narrowly tailored to further a compelling state interest. Appellants point to three compelling interests: the interest in avoiding liability under the "results" test of VRA §2(b), the interest in remedying past and present racial discrimination, and the "nonretrogression" principle of VRA §5 (for District 18 only). We consider them in turn.

A

Section 2(a) of the VRA prohibits the imposition of any electoral practice or procedure that "results in a denial or abridgement of the right of any citizen . . . to vote on account of race or color." In 1982, Congress amended the VRA by changing the language of §2(a) and adding §2(b), which provides a "results" test for violation of §2(a). A violation exists if,

> "based on the totality of circumstances, it is shown that the political processes leading to nomination or election in the State or political subdivision are not equally open to participation by members of a class of citizens protected by subsection (a) of this section in that its members have less opportunity than other members of the electorate to participate in the political process and to elect representatives of their choice." 42 U.S.C. §1973(b).

Appellants contend that creation of each of the three majority-minority districts at issue was justified by Texas' compelling state interest in complying with this results test.

As we have done in each of our previous cases in which this argument has been raised as a defense to charges of racial gerrymandering, we assume without deciding that compliance with the results test, as interpreted by our precedents, can be a compelling state interest. We also reaffirm that the "narrow tailoring" requirement of strict scrutiny allows the States a limited degree of leeway in furthering such interests. If the State has a "strong basis in evidence," *Shaw I,* for concluding that creation of a majority-minority district is reasonably necessary to comply with §2, and the districting that is based on race "substantially addresses the §2 violation," *Shaw II*, it satisfies strict scrutiny. We thus reject, as impossibly stringent, the District Court's view of the narrow tailoring requirement, that "a district must have the least possible amount of irregularity in shape, making allowances for traditional districting criteria."

A §2 district that is *reasonably* compact and regular, taking into account traditional districting principles such as maintaining communities of interest and traditional boundaries, may pass strict scrutiny without having to defeat rival compact districts designed by plaintiffs' experts in endless "beauty contests." The dissenters misread us when they make the leap from our disagreement about the facts of this case to the conclusion that we are creating a "stalemate" by requiring the States to "get things just right" or to draw "the precise compact district that a court would impose in a successful §2 challenge.". . . [N]othing that we say today should be read as limiting "a State's discretion to apply traditional districting principles" in majority-minority, as in other, districts. The constitutional problem arises only from the subordination of those principles to race.

Strict scrutiny remains, nonetheless, strict. The State must have a "strong basis in evidence" for finding that the threshold conditions for §2 liability are present:

> "first, 'that [the minority group] is sufficiently large and *geographically compact* to constitute a majority in a single member district'; second, 'that it is politically cohesive'; and third, 'that the white majority votes sufficiently as a bloc to enable it . . . usually to defeat the minority's preferred candidate.' " *Growe* [*v. Emison* (1993)], (emphasis added) (quoting *Thornburg* v. *Gingles* (1986)).

And, as we have noted above, the district drawn in order to satisfy §2 must not subordinate traditional districting principles to race substantially more than is "reasonably necessary" to avoid §2 liability. Districts 18, 29, and 30 fail to meet these requirements.

We assume, without deciding, that the State had a "strong basis in evidence" for finding the second and third threshold conditions for §2 liability to be present. We have, however, already found that all three districts are bizarrely shaped and far from compact, and that those characteristics are predominantly attributable to gerrymandering that was racially motivated and/or achieved by the use of race as a proxy. . . .

These characteristics defeat any claim that the districts are narrowly tailored to serve the State's interest in avoiding liability under §2, because §2 does not require a State to create, on predominantly racial lines, a district that is not "reasonably compact." If, because of the dispersion of the minority population, a reasonably compact majority-minority district cannot be created, §2 does not require a majority-minority district; if a reasonably compact district can be created, nothing in §2 requires the race-based creation of a district that is far from compact. Appellants argue that bizarre shaping and noncompactness do not raise narrow tailoring concerns. Appellants Lawson et al. claim that under *Shaw I* and *Miller*, "[s]hape is relevant only as evidence of an improper motive.". . . The United States takes a more moderate position, accepting that in the context of narrow tailoring, "consideration must be given to the extent to which the districts drawn by a State substantially depart from its customary redistricting practices," but asserting that insofar as bizarreness and noncompactness are necessary to achieve the State's compelling interest in compliance with §2 "while simultaneously achieving other legitimate redistricting goals," such as incumbency protection, the narrowly tailoring requirement is satisfied. . . .

These arguments cannot save the districts before us. The Lawson appellants misinterpret *Miller*: district shape is not irrelevant to the narrow tailoring inquiry. Our discussion in *Miller* served only to emphasize that the ultimate constitutional values at stake involve the harms caused by the use of unjustified racial classifications, and that bizarreness is not necessary to trigger strict scrutiny. Significant deviations from traditional districting principles, such as the bizarre shape and noncompactness demonstrated by the districts here, cause constitutional harm insofar as they convey the message that political identity is, or should be, predominantly racial. For example, the bizarre shaping of Districts 18 and 29, cutting across pre-existing precinct lines and other natural or traditional divisions, is not merely evidentially significant; it is part of the constitutional problem insofar as it disrupts nonracial bases of political identity and thus intensifies the emphasis on race.

Nor is the United States' argument availing here. In determining that strict scrutiny applies here, we agreed with the District Court that in fact the bizarre shaping and noncompactness of these districts were predominantly attributable to racial, not political, manipulation. The United States' argument, and that of the dissent, address[es] the case of an otherwise compact majority-minority district that is misshapen by predominantly nonracial, political manipulation. We disagree with the factual premise of JUSTICE STEVENS' dissent, that these districts were drawn using "racial considerations only in a way reasonably designed" to avoid a §2 violation. The districts before us exhibit a level of racial manipulation that exceeds what §2 could justify.

B

The United States and the State next contend that the district lines at issue are justified by the State's compelling interest in "ameliorating the effects of racially polarized voting attributable to past and present racial discrimination." In support of that contention, they cite Texas' long history of discrimination against minorities in electoral processes, stretching from the Reconstruction to modern times, including violations of the Constitution and of the VRA. [Citations omitted.] Appellants attempt to link that history to evidence that in recent elections in majority-minority districts, "Anglos usually bloc voted against" Hispanic and African-American candidates. [Quoting district court opinion.]

A State's interest in remedying discrimination is compelling when two conditions are satisfied. First, the discrimination that the State seeks to remedy must be specific, "identified discrimination"; second, the State "must have had a 'strong basis in evidence' to conclude that remedial action was necessary, 'before it embarks on an affirmative action program.' " *Shaw II*. Here, the only current problem that appellants cite as in need of remediation is alleged vote dilution as a consequence of racial bloc voting, the same concern that underlies their VRA §2 compliance defense, which we have assumed to be valid for purposes of this opinion. We have indicated that such problems will not justify race-based districting unless "the State employ[s] sound districting principles, and . . . the affected racial group's residential patterns afford the opportunity of creating districts in which they will be in the majority." *Shaw I.* Once that standard is applied, our agreement with the District Court's finding that these districts are not narrowly tailored to comply with §2 forecloses this line of defense.

C

The final contention offered by the State and private appellants is that creation of District 18 (only) was justified by a compelling state interest in complying with VRA §5. We have made clear that §5 has a limited substantive goal: " 'to insure that no voting-procedure changes would be made that would lead to a retrogression in the position of racial minorities with respect to their effective exercise of the electoral franchise.' " *Miller* (quoting *Beer* v. *United States* (1976)). Appellants contend that this "nonretrogression" principle is implicated because Harris County had, for two decades, contained a congressional district in which African-American voters had succeeded in selecting representatives of their choice, all of whom were African-Americans.

The problem with the State's argument is that it seeks to justify not maintenance, but substantial augmentation, of the African-American population percentage in District 18. At the previous redistricting, in 1980, District 18's population was 40.8% African-American. As a result of Hispanic population increases and African-American emigration from the district, its population had reached 35.1% African-American and 42.2% Hispanic at the time of the 1990 census. The State has shown no basis for concluding that the *increase* to a 50.9% African-American population in 1991 was necessary to insure nonretrogression. Nonretrogression is not a license for the State to do whatever it deems necessary to insure continued electoral *success;* it merely mandates that the minority's *opportunity* to elect representatives of its choice not be diminished, directly or indirectly, by the State's actions. . . . Applying that principle, it is clear that District 18 is not narrowly tailored to the avoidance of §5 liability.

IV

The dissents make several further arguments against today's decision, none of which address the specifics of this case. We have responded to these points previously. JUSTICE SOUTER, for example, reiterates his contention from *Shaw I* that because districts created with a view to satisfying §2 do not involve "racial subjugation," and may in a sense be " 'benign[ly]' " motivated, strict scrutiny should not apply to them. We rejected that argument in *Shaw I,* and we reject it now. As we explained then, we subject racial classifications to strict scrutiny precisely because that scrutiny is necessary to determine whether they are benign . . . or whether they misuse race and foster harmful and divisive stereotypes without a compelling justification. We see no need to revisit our prior debates.

Both dissents contend that the recognition of the *Shaw I* cause of action threatens public respect for, and the independence of, the federal judiciary by inserting the courts deep into the districting process. We believe that the dissents both exaggerate the dangers involved, and fail to recognize the implications of their suggested retreat from *Shaw I.* As to the dangers of judicial entanglement, the principal dissent makes much of cases stemming from State districting plans originally drawn up before *Shaw I*, in which problems have arisen from the uncertainty in the law prior to and during its gradual clarification in *Shaw I*, *Miller*, and today's cases. We are aware of the difficulties faced by the States, and by the district courts, in confronting new constitutional precedents, and we also know that the nature of the expressive harms with which we are dealing, and the complexity of the districting process, are such that bright-line rules are not available. But we believe that today's decisions, which both illustrate the defects that offend the principles of *Shaw I* and reemphasize the importance of the States' discretion in the redistricting process, will serve to clarify the States' responsibilities. The States have traditionally guarded their sovereign districting prerogatives jealously, and we are confident that they can fulfill that requirement, leaving the courts to their customary and appropriate backstop role.

This Court has now rendered decisions after plenary consideration in five cases applying the *Shaw I* doctrine (*Shaw I*, *Miller*, *Hays*, *Shaw II*, and this case). The dissenters would have us abandon those precedents, suggesting that fundamental concerns relating to the judicial role are at stake. While we agree that those concerns are implicated here, we believe they point the other way. Our legitimacy requires, above all, that we adhere to *stare decisis*, especially in such sensitive political contexts as the present, where partisan controversy abounds. Legislators and district courts nationwide have modified their practices — or, rather, reembraced the traditional districting practices that were almost universally followed before the 1990 census — in response to *Shaw I*. Those practices and our precedents, which acknowledge voters as more than mere racial statistics, play an important role in defining the political identity of the American voter. Our Fourteenth Amendment jurisprudence evinces a commitment to eliminate unnecessary and excessive governmental use and reinforcement of racial stereotypes. [Citations omitted.] We decline to retreat from that commitment today.

* * *

The judgment of the District Court is

Affirmed.

JUSTICE O'CONNOR, concurring.

I write separately to express my view on two points. First, compliance with the results test of §2 of the Voting Rights Act (VRA) is a compelling state interest. Second, that test can co-exist in principle and in practice with *Shaw v. Reno* (1993), and its progeny, as elaborated in today's opinions.

I

As stated in the plurality opinion, this Court has thus far assumed without deciding that compliance with the results test of VRA §2(b) is a compelling state interest. Although that assumption is not determinative of the Court's decisions today, I believe that States and lower courts are entitled to more definite guidance as they toil with the twin demands of the Fourteenth Amendment and the Voting Rights Act. [Quotation of §2(b) omitted; see plurality opinion, section III (A), above.]

In the 14 years since the enactment of §2(b), we have interpreted and enforced the obligations that it places on States in a succession of cases, assuming but never directly addressing its constitutionality. [Citation of cases omitted.] Meanwhile, lower courts have unanimously affirmed its constitutionality. [Citation of cases omitted.] . . .

In my view, therefore, the States have a compelling interest in complying with the results test as this Court has interpreted it.

II

Although I agree with the dissenters about §2's role as part of our national commitment to racial equality, I differ from them in my belief that that commitment can and must be reconciled with the complementary commitment of our Fourteenth Amendment jurisprudence to eliminate the unjustified use of racial stereotypes. At the same time that we combat the symptoms of racial polarization in politics, we must strive to eliminate unnecessary race-based state action that appears to endorse the disease.

Today's decisions, in conjunction with the recognition of the compelling state interest in compliance with the reasonably perceived requirements of §2, present a workable framework for the achievement of these twin goals. I would summarize that framework, and the rules governing the States' consideration of race in the districting process, as follows.

First, so long as they do not subordinate traditional districting criteria to the use of race for its own sake or as a proxy, States may intentionally create majority-minority districts, and may otherwise take race into consideration, without coming under strict scrutiny. Only if traditional districting criteria are neglected and that neglect is predominantly due to the misuse of race does strict scrutiny apply.

Second, where voting is racially polarized, §2 prohibits States from adopting districting schemes that would have the effect that minority voters "have less opportunity than other members of the electorate to . . . elect representatives of their choice." §2(b). That principle may require a State to create a majority-minority district where the three *Gingles* factors are present—viz., (i) the minority group "is sufficiently large and geographically compact to constitute a majority in a single-member district," (ii) "it is politically cohesive," and (iii) "the white majority votes sufficiently as a bloc to enable it . . . usually to defeat the minority's preferred candidate," *Thornburg* v. *Gingles* [1986].

Third, the state interest in avoiding liability under VRA §2 is compelling. If a State has a strong basis in evidence for concluding that the *Gingles* factors are present, it may create a majority-minority district without awaiting judicial findings. Its "strong basis in evidence" need not take any particular form, although it cannot simply rely on generalized assumptions about the prevalence of racial bloc voting.

Fourth, if a State pursues that compelling interest by creating a district that "substantially addresses" the potential liability and does not deviate substantially from a hypothetical court-drawn §2 district for predominantly racial reasons, its districting plan will be deemed narrowly tailored.

Finally, however, districts that are bizarrely shaped and non-compact, and that otherwise neglect traditional districting principles and deviate substantially from the hypothetical court-drawn district, *for predominantly racial reasons,* are unconstitutional. . . .

. . . [T]he application of the principles that I have outlined sometimes requires difficult exercises of judgment. That difficulty is inevitable. The Voting Rights Act requires the States and the courts to take action to remedy the reality of racial inequality in our political system, sometimes necessitating race-based action, while the Fourteenth Amendment requires us to look with suspicion on the excessive use of racial considerations by the government. But I believe that the States, playing a primary role, and the courts, in their secondary role, are capable of distinguishing the appropriate and reasonably necessary uses of race from its unjustified and excessive uses.

JUSTICE KENNEDY, concurring.

I join the plurality opinion, but the statements in Part II of the opinion that strict scrutiny would not apply to all cases of intentional creation of majority-minority districts require comment. Those statements are unnecessary to our decision, for strict scrutiny applies here. I do not consider these dicta to commit me to any position on the question whether race is predominant whenever a State, in redistricting, foreordains that one race be the majority in a certain number of districts or in a certain part of the State. In my view, we would no doubt apply strict scrutiny if a State decreed that certain districts had to be at least 50 percent white, and our analysis should be no different if the State so favors minority races. . . .

JUSTICE THOMAS, with whom JUSTICE SCALIA joins, concurring in the judgment.

In my view, application of strict scrutiny in this case was never a close question. I cannot agree with JUSTICE O'CONNOR's assertion that strict scrutiny is not invoked by the intentional creation of majority-minority districts. . . .

Strict scrutiny applies to all governmental classifications based on race, and we have expressly held that there is no exception for race-based redistricting. While we have recognized the evidentiary difficulty of proving that a redistricting plan is, in fact, a racial gerrymander, we have never suggested that a racial gerrymander is subject to anything less than strict scrutiny. . . .

We have said that impermissible racial classifications do not follow inevitably from a legislature's mere awareness of racial demographics. But the intentional creation of a majority-minority district certainly means more than mere awareness that application of traditional, race-neutral districting principles will result in the creation of a district in which a majority of the district's residents are members of a particular minority group. In my view, it means that the legislature affirmatively undertakes to create a majority-minority district that would not have existed but for the express use of racial classifications—in other words, that a majority-minority district is created "because of," and not merely "in spite of," racial demographics. When that occurs, traditional race-neutral districting principles are necessarily subordinated (and race necessarily predominates), and the legislature has classified persons on the basis of race. The resulting redistricting must be viewed as a racial gerrymander. . . .

JUSTICE STEVENS, with whom JUSTICE GINSBURG and JUSTICE BREYER join, dissenting.

The 1990 census revealed that Texas' population had grown, over the past decade, almost twice as fast as the population of the country as a whole. As a result, Texas was entitled to elect three additional Representatives to the United States Congress, enlarging its delegation from 27 to 30. Because Texas' growth was concentrated in South Texas and the cities of Dallas and Houston, the state legislature concluded that the new congressional districts should be carved out of existing districts in those areas. The consequences of the political battle that produced the new map are some of the most oddly shaped congressional districts in the United States.

Today, the Court strikes down three of Texas' majority-minority districts, concluding, *inter alia*, that their odd shapes reveal that the State impermissibly relied on predominantly racial reasons when it drew the districts as it did. For two reasons, I believe that the Court errs in striking down those districts.

First, I believe that the Court has misapplied its own tests for racial gerrymandering, both by applying strict scrutiny to all three of these districts, and then by concluding that none can meet that scrutiny. . . . [T]he Court improperly ignores the "complex interplay" of political and geographical considerations that went into the creation of Texas' new congressional districts and focuses exclusively on the role that race played in the State's decisions to adjust the shape of its districts. A quick comparison of the unconstitutional majority-minority districts with three equally bizarre majority-Anglo districts [Districts 3, 6, and 25] demonstrates that race was not necessarily the predominant factor contorting the district lines. [Appendix with maps of districts omitted.] I would follow the fair implications of the District Court's findings and conclude that Texas' entire map is a political, not a racial, gerrymander.

Even if strict scrutiny applies, I would find these districts constitutional, for each considers race only to the extent necessary to comply with the State's responsibilities under the Voting Rights Act while achieving other race-neutral political and geographical requirements. The plurality's finding to the contrary unnecessarily restricts the ability of States to conform their behavior to the Voting Rights Act while simultaneously complying with other race-neutral goals.

Second, even if I concluded that these districts failed an appropriate application of this still-developing law to appropriately read facts, I would not uphold the District Court decision. The decisions issued today serve merely to reinforce my conviction that the Court has, with its "analytically distinct" jurisprudence of racial gerrymandering, *Shaw* v. *Reno* (*Shaw I*) (1993), struck out into a jurisprudential wilderness that lacks a definable constitutional core and threatens to create harms more significant than any suffered by the individual plaintiffs challenging these districts.

I

The factors motivating Texas' redistricting plan are clearly revealed in the results of the 1992 elections. Both before and immediately after the 1990 census, the Democratic Party was in control of the Texas Legislature. Under the new map in 1992, more than two-thirds of the Districts—including each of the new ones—elected Democrats, even though Texas voters are arguably more likely to vote Republican than Democrat. Incumbents of both parties were just as successful: 26 of the 27 incumbents were reelected, while each of the three new districts elected a state legislator who had essentially acted as an incumbent in the districting process, giving "incumbents" a 97 percent success rate.

It was not easy for the State to achieve these results while simultaneously guaranteeing that each district enclosed the residence of its incumbent, contained the same number of people, and complied with other federal and state districting requirements. . . .

It is clear that race also played a role in Texas' redistricting decisions. . . . Given the omnipresence of §2 of the Voting Rights Act, 42 U.S.C. §1973, the demographics of the two communities, and the pressure from leaders of the minority communities in those cities, it was not unreasonable—and certainly not invidious discrimination of any sort—for the State to accede to calls for the creation of majority-minority districts in both cities. . . .

II

We have traditionally applied strict scrutiny to state action that discriminates on the basis of race. Prior to *Shaw I*, however, we did so only in cases in which that discrimination harmed an individual or set of individuals because of their race. In contrast, the harm identified in *Shaw I* and its progeny is much more diffuse. Racial gerrymandering of the sort being addressed in these cases is "discrimination" only in the sense that the lines are drawn based on race, not in the sense that harm is imposed on specific persons on account of their race.

Aware of this distinction, a majority of this Court has endorsed a position crucial to a proper evaluation of Texas' congressional districts: neither the Equal Protection Clause nor any other provision of the Constitution was offended merely because the legislature considered race when it deliberately created three majority-minority districts. . . .

III

While the Court has agreed that race can, to a point, govern the drawing of district lines, it nonetheless suggests that at a certain point, when the State uses race "too much," illegitimate racial stereotypes threaten to overrun and contaminate an otherwise legitimate redistricting process. In *Miller* [*v. Johnson* (1995)], the Court concluded that this point was reached when "race for its own sake, and not other districting principles, was the . . . dominant and controlling rationale" behind the shape of the district. For strict scrutiny to apply, therefore, the plaintiff must demonstrate that "the legislature subordinated traditional race-neutral districting principles, including but not limited to compactness, contiguity, [and] respect for political subdivisions . . . to racial considerations."

Of course, determining the "predominant" motive of the Texas Legislature is not a simple matter. The members of that body faced many unrelenting pressures when they negotiated the creation of the contested districts. They had to ensure that there was no deviation in population from district to district. They reasonably believed that they had to create districts that would comply with the Voting Rights Act. If the redistricting legislation was to be enacted, they had to secure the support of incumbent Congressmen of both parties by drawing districts that would ensure their election. And all of these desires had to be achieved within a single contiguous district. Every time a district line was shifted from one place to another, each of these considerations was implicated, and additional, compensating shifts were necessary to ensure that all competing goals were simultaneously accomplished. In such a constrained environment, there will rarely be one "dominant and controlling" influence. Nowhere is this better illustrated than in Dallas' District 30 where, at the very least, it is clear that race was not such an overriding factor.

IV

The Court lists several considerations which, when taken in combination, lead it to conclude that race, and no other cause, was the predominant factor influencing District 30's configuration. First, there is the shape itself. Second, there is evidence that the districts were intentionally drawn with consciousness of race in an effort to comply with the Voting Rights Act. Third, the Court dismisses two race-neutral considerations (communities of interest and incumbency protection) that petitioners advanced as race-neutral considerations that led to the odd shape of the districts. Finally, the plurality concludes that race was impermissibly used as a proxy for political affiliation during the course of redistricting. In my opinion, an appropriate reading of the record demonstrates that none of these factors—either singly or in combination—suggests that racial considerations "subordinated" race-neutral districting principles. I discuss each in turn.

Bizarre Shape

As noted, Texas' Legislature concluded that it would add a new district to Dallas County that would incorporate the rapidly growing minority communities in South Dallas. To do so, the new district would have to fit into the existing districts: Before redistricting, most of southern Dallas County (including the African-American communities in South Dallas) was divided between Districts 5 and 24, represented by Democratic Representatives Bryant and Frost, respectively. The middle of the northern section of the county was divided between Districts 3 and 26, both represented by Republicans.

Then-State Senator Johnson began the redistricting process by proposing a compact, Democratic, majority-minority district encompassing all of South Dallas. Representatives Bryant and Frost objected, however, because the proposed district included not only Johnson's residence, but their own homes. . . . Furthermore, Johnson's plan transferred many of Frost and Bryant's most reliable Democratic supporters into the proposed district. Rather than acquiesce to the creation of this compact majority-minority district, Frost and Bryant insisted that the new district avoid both their own homes and many of the communities that had been loyal to them. . . .

To accommodate the incumbents' desires, District 30 required geographical adjustments that had telling effects on its shape. First, two notches carefully avoiding the residences of and neighborhoods surrounding Frost and Bryant were carved out of District 30's side. Furthermore, Frost and Bryant retained several communities—many majority-black—along the southern and eastern sides of the proposed district.

Had these communities been retained by District 30, it would have been much more compact. By giving up these voters to Frost and Bryant, however, District 30 was forced to seek out population and Democratic voters elsewhere. The Democratic incumbents had blocked its way to the south and east; north (and, to a lesser extent, west) was the only way it could go. . . .

Intent

Perhaps conscious that noncompact congressional districts are the rule rather than the exception in Texas, the plurality suggests that the real key is the direct evidence, particularly in the form of Texas' §5 Voting Rights Act submissions and the person of then-State Senator Johnson, that the State expressed an intent to create these districts with a given "minimum percentage of the favored minority.". . . [T]his information does little more than confirm that the State believed it necessary to comply with the Voting Rights Act. Given its reasonable understanding of its legal responsibilities, the legislature acted to ensure that its goal of creating a majority-black district in Dallas County was not undermined by the changes made to accommodate District 30 to other, race-neutral districting principles. . . .

Nonracial Factors: Community

In an effort to provide a definitive explanation for the odd shape of the district, the State emphasized two factors: The presence of communities of interest tying together the populations of the district, and the role of incumbency protection. The District Court and the plurality improperly dismissed these considerations as ultimately irrelevant to the shape of the districts.

First, the appellants presented testimony that the districts were drawn to align with certain communities of interest, such as land use, family demographics, and transportation corridors. Although the District Court recognized that these community characteristics amounted to accurate descriptions of District 30, it dismissed them as irrelevant to the districting process, concluding that there was no evidence that "the Legislature had these particular 'communities of interest' in mind when drawing the boundaries of District 30.". . .

I do not understand why we should require such evidence ever to exist. It is entirely reasonable for the legislature to rely on the experience of its members when drawing particular boundaries rather than on clearly identifiable "evidence" presented by demographers and political scientists. . . . Unless the Court intends to interfere in state political processes even more than it has already expressed an intent to do, I presume that it does not intend to require States to create a comprehensive administrative record in support of their redistricting process. . . . To the extent that the presence of obvious communities of interest among members of a district explicitly or implicitly guided the shape of District 30, it amounts to an entirely legitimate non-racial consideration.

Nonracial Factors: Incumbency

The plurality admits that the appellants "present a . . . substantial case for their claim that incumbency protection rivalled race in determining the district's shape." Every individual who participated in the redistricting process knew that incumbency protection was a critical factor in producing the bizarre lines. . . . Despite this overwhelming evidence that incumbency protection was the critical motivating factor in the creation of the bizarre Texas districts, the District Court reached the stunning conclusion that because the process was so "different in degree" from the "generalized, and legitimate, goal of incumbent and seniority protection" that this Court has previously recognized, it could not serve as a legitimate explanation for the bizarre boundaries of the congressional districts. . . .

It is difficult to know where to begin to attack the misperceptions reflected in these conclusions. . . .

. . . We have . . . affirmed that a State has an interest in incumbency protection, and also assured States that the Constitution does not require compactness, contiguity, or respect for political borders. While egregious political gerrymandering may not be particularly praiseworthy, it may nonetheless provide the race-neutral explanation necessary for a State to avoid strict scrutiny of the district lines where gerrymandering is the "dominant and controlling" explanation for the odd district shapes. . . .

Race as a Proxy

. . . [T]he plurality ultimately makes little effort to contradict appellants' assertions that incumbency protection was far more important in the placement of District 30's lines than race. Instead, it adopts a fall-back position. . . . [T]he Court suggests that even if the predominant reason for the bizarre features of the majority-minority districts was incumbency protection, the State impermissibly used race as a proxy for determining the likely political affiliation of blocks of voters. . . .

[T]o the extent that race served as a proxy at all, it did so merely as a means of "fine tuning" borders that were already in particular locations for primarily political reasons. This "fine tuning" through the use of race is, of course, little different from the kind of fine tuning that could have legitimately occurred around the edges of a compact majority-minority district. I perceive no reason why a legitimate process—choosing minority voters for inclusion in a majority-minority district—should become suspect once nonracial considerations force district lines away from its core.

Finally, I note that in most contexts racial classifications are invidious because they are irrational. . . . It is neither irrational, nor invidious, however, to assume that a black resident of a particular community is a Democrat if reliable statistical evidence discloses that 97% of the blacks in that community vote in Democratic primary elections. For that reason, the fact that the architects of the Texas plan sometimes appear to have used racial data as a proxy for making political judgments seems to me to be no more "unjustified," and to have no more constitutional significance, than an assumption that wealthy suburbanites, whether black or white, are more likely to be Republicans than communists. . . .

Despite all the efforts by the plurality and the District Court, then, the evidence demonstrates that race was not, in all likelihood, the "predominant" goal leading to the creation of District 30. The most reasonable interpretation of the record evidence instead demonstrates that political considerations were. In accord with the presumption against interference with a legislature's consideration of complex and competing factors, I would conclude that the configuration of District 30 does not require strict scrutiny.

V

The Houston districts present a closer question on the application of strict scrutiny. There is evidence that many of the same race-neutral factors motivating the zigzags of District 30 were present at the creation (or recreation) of Districts 29 and 18. In contrast to District 30, however, there is also evidence that the interlocking shapes of the Houston districts were specifically, and almost exclusively, the result of an effort to create, out of largely integrated communities, both a majority-black and a majority-Hispanic district. For purposes of this opinion, then, I am willing to accept *arguendo* the Court's conclusion that the Houston districts should be examined with strict scrutiny. Even so, the Court errs by concluding that these districts would fail that test.

The plurality begins with the perfectly obvious assumptions that a State has a compelling interest in complying with §2 of the Voting Rights Act and that Texas had a strong basis for believing that it would have violated that Act in 1991 if it did not create three new majority-minority districts. The plurality goes on to conclude, however, that because the final shape of these districts is not coextensive with the community that would form the core of a §2 violation, these districts would not be "narrowly tailored" to further that state interest. I respectfully disagree.

Neither evidence nor insinuation suggests that the State in the redistricting process considered race for any reason other than as a means of accomplishing its compelling interest of creating majority-minority districts in accord with the Voting Rights Act. The goal was, by all accounts, achieved, for these districts would certainly avoid liability under §2 of the Voting Rights Act. For reasons that continue to escape me, however, the Court simply insists that the lack of compactness in the districts prevent[s] them from being "narrowly tailored" solutions to the State's interests. The Court uses two premises to reach its conclusion that compactness is required to meet the "narrow tailoring" requirement: (i) §2 would not have been violated unless a reasonably compact majority-minority district could have been created; and, (ii) nothing in §2 requires the creation of a noncompact district. I have no quarrel with either proposition, but each falls far short of mandating the conclusion that the Court draws from it. While a State can be liable for a §2 violation only if it could have drawn a compact district and failed to do so, it does not follow that creating such a district is the only way to avoid a §2 violation. The plurality admits that a State retains "a limited degree of leeway" in drawing a district to alleviate fears of §2 liability, but if there is no independent constitutional duty to create compact districts in the first place, and the Court suggests none, there is no reason why noncompact districts should not be a permissible method of avoiding violations of law. The fact that they might be unacceptable judicial remedies does not speak to the question whether they may be acceptable when adopted by a state legislature. Because these districts satisfy the State's compelling interest and do so in a manner that uses racial considerations only in a way reasonably designed to ensure such a satisfaction, I conclude that the Districts are narrowly tailored.

[VI omitted]

VII

The history of race relations in Texas and throughout the South demonstrates overt evidence of discriminatory voting practices lasting through the 1970's. Even in recent years, Texans have elected only two black candidates to statewide office; majority-white Texas districts have never elected a minority to either the State Senate or the United States Congress. One recent study suggests that majority-white districts throughout the South remain suspiciously unlikely to elect black representatives. And nationwide, fewer than 15 of the hundreds of legislators that have passed through Congress since 1950 have been black legislators elected from majority-white districts. In 1994, for example, 36 of the Nation's 39 black Representatives were elected from majority-minority districts, while only three were elected from majority-white districts.

Perhaps the state of race relations in Texas and, for that matter, the Nation, is more optimistic than might be expected in light of these facts. If so, it may be that the plurality's exercise in redistricting will be successful. Perhaps minority candidates, forced to run in majority-white districts, will be able to overcome the long history of stereotyping and discrimination that has heretofore led the vast majority of majority-white districts to reject minority candidacies. Perhaps not. I am certain only that bodies of elected federal and state officials are in a far better position than anyone on this Court to assess whether the Nation's long history of discrimination has been overcome, and that nothing in the Constitution requires this unnecessary intrusion into the ability of States to negotiate solutions to political differences while providing long-excluded groups the opportunity to participate effectively in the democratic process. I respectfully dissent.

JUSTICE SOUTER, with whom JUSTICE GINSBURG and JUSTICE BREYER join, dissenting.

When the Court devises a new cause of action to enforce a constitutional provision, it ought to identify an injury distinguishable from the consequences of concededly constitutional conduct, and it should describe the elements necessary and sufficient to make out such a claim. . . . Those principles of justification, fair notice, and guidance, have never been satisfied in the instance of the action announced three Terms ago in *Shaw* v. *Reno* (1993) (*Shaw I*), when a majority of this Court decided that a State violates the Fourteenth Amendment's Equal Protection Clause by excessive consideration of race in drawing the boundaries of voting districts, even when the resulting plan does not dilute the voting strength of any voters and so would not otherwise give rise to liability under the Fourteenth or Fifteenth Amendments, or under the Voting Rights Act.

. . . *Shaw I* addressed a putative harm subject to complaint by any voter objecting to an untoward consideration of race in the political process. Although the Court has repeatedly disclaimed any intent to go as far as to outlaw all conscious consideration of race in districting, after three rounds of appellate litigation seeking to describe the elements and define the contours of the *Shaw* cause of action, a helpful statement of a *Shaw* claim still eludes this Court. This is so for reasons that go to the conceptual bone.

The result of this failure to provide a practical standard for distinguishing between the lawful and unlawful use of race has not only been inevitable confusion in state houses and courthouses, but a consequent shift in responsibility for setting district boundaries from the state legislatures, which are invested with front-line authority by Article I of the Constitution, to the courts, and truly to this Court, which is left to superintend the drawing of every legislative district in the land.

Today's opinions do little to solve *Shaw*'s puzzles or return districting responsibility to the States. To say this is not to denigrate the importance of JUSTICE O'CONNOR's position in her separate opinion, that compliance with §2 of the Voting Rights Act is a compelling state interest; her statement takes a very significant step toward alleviating apprehension that *Shaw* is at odds with the Voting Rights Act. It is still true, however, that the combined plurality, minority, and Court opinions do not ultimately leave the law dealing with a *Shaw* claim appreciably clearer or more manageable than *Shaw I* itself did. And to the extent that some clarity follows from the knowledge that race may be considered when reasonably necessary to conform to the Voting Rights Act, today's opinions raise the specter that this ostensible progress may come with a heavy constitutional price. The price of *Shaw I*, indeed, may turn out to be the practical elimination of a State's discretion to apply traditional districting principles, widely accepted in States without racial districting issues as well as in States confronting them.

As the flaws of *Shaw I* persist, and as the burdens placed on the States and the courts by *Shaw* litigation loom larger with the approach of a new census and a new round of redistricting, the Court has to recognize that *Shaw*'s problems result from a basic misconception about the relation between race and districting principles, a mistake that no amount of case-by-case tinkering can eliminate. There is, therefore, no reason for confidence that the Court will eventually bring much order out of the confusion created by *Shaw I*, and because it has not, in any case, done so yet, I respectfully dissent.

I

... Article I of the Constitution places responsibility for drawing voting districts on the States in the first instance. The Court has nonetheless recognized limits on state districting autonomy when it could discern a strong constitutional justification and a reasonably definite standard for doing so, as, for example, in announcing the numerical requirement of one person, one vote, *Reynolds* v. *Sims* (1964). But the Court has never ignored the Constitution's commitment of districting responsibility to the political branches of the States and has accordingly assumed over the years that traditional districting principles widely accepted among States represented an informal baseline of acceptable districting practices. We have thus accorded substantial respect to such traditional principles (as those, for example, meant to preserve the integrity of neighborhood communities, to protect incumbents, to follow existing political boundaries, to recognize communities of interest, and to achieve compactness and contiguity); we have seen these objectives as entirely consistent with the Fourteenth and Fifteenth Amendments' demands. [Citation of cases omitted.] . . .

A

. . . [B]efore *Shaw I*, the Court required evidence of substantial harm to an identifiable group of voters to justify any judicial displacement of these traditional districting principles. . . .

Before *Shaw I*, we not only thus limited judicial interference with state districting efforts to cases of readily demonstrable harm to an identifiable class of voters, but we also confined our concern with districting to cases in which we were capable of providing a manageable standard for courts to apply and for legislators to follow. Within two years of holding in *Baker* v. *Carr* (1962) that malapportionment was a justiciable issue, "the Court recognized that its general equal protection jurisprudence was insufficient for the task and announced an increasingly rigid, simple to apply, voting-specific mandate of equipopulousity." [Quoting law review article.] Likewise, although it is quite true that the common definition of a racial vote-dilution injury ("less opportunity . . . to participate in the political process and to elect representatives . . . ," 42 U.S.C. §1973(b)) is no model of concrete description, the Court has identified categories of readily comprehensible evidence bearing on the likelihood of such an injury, including facts about size of minority population, quantifiable indications of political cohesiveness and bloc voting, historical patterns of success or failure of favored candidates, and so on. See, *e.g., Thornburg* v. *Gingles* (1986); *White* v. *Regester* [1973]. The particularity of this evidence goes far to separate victims of political "inequality" from those who just happened to support losing candidates.

B

Shaw I, however, broke abruptly with these standards, including the very understanding of equal protection as a practical guarantee against harm to some class singled out for disparate treatment. Whereas malapportionment measurably reduces the influence of voters in more populous districts, and vote dilution predestines members of a racial minority to perpetual frustration as political losers, what *Shaw I* spoke of as harm is not confined to any identifiable class singled out for disadvantage. . . .

Just as the logic of traditional equal protection analysis is at odds with *Shaw*'s concept of injury, so the Court's rhetoric of racially motivated injury is inapposite to describe the consideration of race that it thinks unreasonable. Although the Court used the metaphor of "political apartheid" as if to refer to the segregation of a minority group to eliminate its association with a majority that opposed integration, talk of this sort of racial separation is not on point here. The *de jure* segregation that the term "political apartheid" brings to mind is unconstitutional because it emphatically implies the inferiority of one race. . . . *Shaw I*, in contrast, vindicated the complaint of a white voter who objected not to segregation but to the particular racial proportions of the district. . . . Whatever this district may have symbolized, it was not "apartheid." Nor did the proportion of its racial mixture reflect any purpose of racial subjugation. . . . In light of a majority-minority district's purpose to allow previously submerged members of racial minorities into the active political process, this use of race cannot plausibly be said to affect any individual or group in any sense comparable to the injury inflicted by *de jure* segregation. . . .

Added to the anomalies of *Shaw I*'s idea of equal protection injury and the rhetoric of its descriptions, there is a further conceptual inadequacy in *Shaw I*. . . . When voting is . . . racially polarized, it is just because of this polarization that majority-minority districts provide the only practical means of avoiding dilution or remedying the dilution injury that has occurred already. *Shaw I* has thus placed those who choose to avoid the long-recognized constitutional harm of vote dilution at risk by casting doubt on the legitimacy of its classic remedy. . . .

C

The Court's failure to devise a concept of *Shaw* harm that distinguishes those who are injured from those who are not, or to differentiate violation from remedy, is matched by its inability to provide any manageable standard to distinguish forbidden districting conduct from the application of traditional state districting principles and the plans that they produce. This failure, while regrettable, need not have occurred, for when the Court spoke in *Shaw I* of a district shape so "bizarre" as to be an unequivocal indication that race had influenced the districting decision to an unreasonable degree, *Shaw I* could have been pointing to some workable criterion of shape translatable into objective standards. . . .

The Court, however, rejected this opportunity last Term in *Miller* v. *Johnson* [1995] when it declined to contain *Shaw* by any standard sufficiently quantifiable to guide the decisions of state legislators or to inform and limit review of districting decisions by the courts. The Court rejected shape as a sufficient condition for finding a *Shaw* violation, or even a necessary one. . . . Instead, it recharacterized the cause of action in terms devised in other cases addressing essentially different problems, by proscribing the consideration of race when it is the "predominant factor motivating the legislatur[e]," or when the use of race is "in substantial disregard of customary and traditional districting practices."

As a standard addressed to the untidy world of politics, neither "predominant factor" nor "substantial disregard" inspires much hope. . . .

. . . It is not merely that the very nature of districting decisions makes it difficult to identify whether any particular consideration, racial or otherwise, was the "predominant motive," though that is certainly true. . . .

The reason that use of the predominant motive standard in reviewing a districting decision is bound to fail is more fundamental than that: in the political environment in which race can affect election results, many of these traditional districting principles cannot be applied without taking race into account and are thus, as a practical matter, inseparable from the supposedly illegitimate racial considerations. . . .

If, for example, a legislature may draw district lines to preserve the integrity of a given community, leaving it intact so that all of its members are served by one representative, this objective is inseparable from preserving the community's racial identity when the community is characterized, or even self-defined, by the race of the majority of those who live there. This is an old truth, having been recognized every time the political process produced an Irish or Italian or Polish ward. . . .

Or take the traditional principle of providing protection for incumbents. The plurality seems to assume that incumbents may always be protected by drawing lines on the basis of data about political parties. But what if the incumbent has drawn support largely for racial reasons? What, indeed, if the incumbent was elected in a majority-minority district created to remedy vote dilution that resulted from racial bloc voting? It would be sheer fantasy to assume that consideration of race in these circumstances is somehow separable from application of the traditional principle of incumbency protection, and sheer incoherence to think that the consideration of race that is constitutionally required to remedy Fourteenth and Fifteenth Amendment vote dilution somehow becomes unconstitutional when aimed at protecting the incumbent the next time the census requires redistricting. . . .

[II omitted]

III

Although today's cases do not address the uncertainties that stem from *Shaw*'s underlying incoherence, they do aim to mitigate its inscrutability with some specific rules.

A

In each of today's cases, the Court expressly assumes that avoiding a violation of the Voting Rights Act qualifies as a sufficiently compelling government interest to satisfy the requirements of strict scrutiny. . . . While the Court's decision to assume this important point *arguendo* is no holding, the assumption itself is encouraging because it confirms the view that the intentional creation of majority-minority districts is not necessarily a violation of *Shaw I*, and it indicates that the Court does not intend to bring the *Shaw* cause of action to what would be the cruelly ironic point of finding in the Voting Rights Act of 1965 (as amended) a violation of the Fourteenth Amendment's equal protection guarantee. . . . JUSTICE O'CONNOR's separate opinion bears on each of these points all the more emphatically, for her view that compliance with §2 is . . . a compelling state interest and her statement of that position virtually insulate the Voting Rights Act from jeopardy under *Shaw* as such.

B

The second point of reference to come out of today's cases is the rule that if a State begins its map-drawing efforts with a compact majority-minority district required by *Gingles*, the State may not rely too heavily on racial data in adjusting that district to serve traditional districting principles. While this rule may indeed provide useful guidance to state legislatures, its inherent weakness is clear from what was said above: it is in theory and in fact impossible to apply "traditional districting principles" in areas with substantial minority populations without considering race. . . .

C

The third point of reference attributable to today's cases is as yet only a possibility; a suggestion in the discussions of the narrow tailoring test that States seeking to avoid violating §2 of the Voting Rights Act may draw the district that the Voting Rights Act compels, and this district alone. . . .

If the Court ultimately were to reach such a conclusion, it would in one respect be taking a step back toward *Shaw I* and its suggestion that a district's shape might play an important, if not determinative role in establishing a cause of action. Such a step would, however, do much more than return to *Shaw I*, which suggested that a compact district would be a safe haven, but not that the district hypothesized under *Gingles* was the only haven. . . . I refer to this step as a "possibility" deliberately. The Court in *Shaw II* does not go beyond an intimation to this effect, and *Bush* raises doubt that the Court would go so far. . . . Indeed, *Bush* leaves open the possibility that a State could create a majority-minority district that does not coincide with the *Gingles* shape so long as racial data is not overused, and it does not suggest that a *Shaw* claim could be premised solely on a deviation from a *Gingles* district. . . .

D

In sum, the three steps the Court takes today toward a more definite cause of action either fail to answer the objections to *Shaw I* or prompt objections of their own. Recognition of a State's interest in complying with the Voting Rights Act does not address the practical impossibility courts will encounter in identifying a predominant use of race, as distinguished from some lesser, reasonable consideration of it, when a State applies its customary districting principles. The limitation on the use of racial data is unlikely to make much difference in practice except to jeopardize minority incumbency protection. And the possibility that the Court will require *Gingles* districts (or districts substantially close to them) when compliance with §2 of the Voting Rights Act is an object of districting would render a State's districting obligation more definite only by eliminating its ability to apply the very districting principles traditionally considered to be important enough to furnish a theoretical baseline of reasonable districting practices.

IV

. . . [T]here is presently no good reason that the Court's withdrawal from the presently untenable state of the law should not be complete. While I take the commands of *stare decisis* very seriously, the problems with *Shaw* and its progeny are themselves very serious. The Court has been unable to provide workable standards, the chronic uncertainty has begotten no discernible reliance, and the costs of persisting doubt about the limits of state discretion and state responsibility are high.

There is, indeed, an added reason to admit *Shaw*'s failure in providing a manageable constitutional standard and to allow for some faith in the political process. That process not only evolved the very traditional districting principles that the Court has pledged to preserve, but has applied them in the past to deal with ethnicity in a way that should influence our thinking about the prospects for race. It is difficult to see how the consideration of race that *Shaw* condemns (but cannot avoid) is essentially different from the consideration of ethnicity that entered American politics from the moment that immigration began to temper regional homogeneity. Recognition of the ethnic character of neighborhoods and incumbents, through the application of just those districting principles we now view as traditional, allowed ethnically identified voters and their preferred candidates to enter the mainstream of American politics and to attain a level of political power in American democracy. The result has been not a state regime of ethnic apartheid, but ethnic participation and even a moderation of ethnicity's divisive effect in political practice. For although consciousness of ethnicity has not disappeared from the American electorate, its talismanic force does appear to have cooled over time. It took Boston Irish voters, for example, to elect Thomas Menino mayor in 1993.

There is, then, some reason to hope that if vote dilution is attacked at the same time that race is given the recognition that ethnicity has historically received in American politics, the force of race in politics will also moderate in time. There are even signs that such hope may be vindicated, even if the evidence is necessarily tentative as yet. . . . This possibility that racial politics, too, may grow wiser so long as minority votes are rescued from submergence should be considered in determining how far the Fourteenth and Fifteenth Amendments require us to devise constitutional common law to supplant the democratic process with litigation in federal courts. It counsels against accepting the profession that *Shaw* has yet evolved into a manageable constitutional standard, and from that case's invocation again today I respectfully dissent.

Nos. 94-923 and 94-924

Ruth O. Shaw, et al., Appellants v. James B. Hunt, Jr., Governor of North Carolina, et al.

James Arthur Pope, et al., Appellants v. James B. Hunt, Jr., Governor of North Carolina, et al.

On appeals from the United States District Court
for the Eastern District of North Carolina

[June 13, 1996]

CHIEF JUSTICE REHNQUIST delivered the opinion of the Court.

This case is here for a second time. In *Shaw v. Reno* (1993) (*Shaw I*), we held that plaintiffs whose complaint alleged that the deliberate segregation of voters into separate and bizarre-looking districts on the basis of race stated a claim for relief under the Equal Protection Clause of the Fourteenth Amendment. We remanded the case for further consideration by the District Court. That court held that the North Carolina redistricting plan did classify voters by race, but that the classification survived strict scrutiny and therefore did not offend the Constitution. We now hold that the North Carolina plan does violate the Equal Protection Clause because the State's reapportionment scheme is not narrowly tailored to serve a compelling state interest.

The facts are set out in detail in our prior opinion, and we shall only summarize them here. After the 1990 census, North Carolina's congressional delegation increased from 11 to 12 members. The State General Assembly adopted a reapportionment plan, Chapter 601, that included one majority-black district, District 1, located in the northeastern region of the State. The legislature then submitted the plan to the Attorney General of the United States for preclearance under §5 of the Voting Rights Act of 1965, as amended, 42 U.S.C. §1973c. The Assistant Attorney General for Civil Rights, acting on the Attorney General's behalf, objected to the proposed plan because it failed "to give effect to black and Native American voting strength" in "the south-central to southeastern part of the state" and opined that the State's reasons for not creating a second majority-minority district appeared "to be pretextual." Duly chastened, the legislature revised its districting scheme to include a second majority-black district. The new plan, Chapter 7, located the minority district, District 12, in the north-central or Piedmont region, not in the south-central or south-eastern region identified in the Justice Department's objection letter. The Attorney General nonetheless precleared the revised plan.

By anyone's measure, the boundary lines of Districts 1 and 12 are unconventional. . . . [O]ur prior opinion describes them as follows [description of District 1 omitted]:

> "The second majority-black district, District 12, is . . . approximately 160 miles long and, for much of its length, no wider than the [Interstate]-85 corridor. It winds in snakelike fashion through tobacco country, financial centers, and manufacturing areas 'until it gobbles in enough enclaves of black neighborhoods.' "

Five North Carolinians commenced the present action in the United States District Court for the Eastern District of North Carolina against various state officials. Following our reversal of the District Court's dismissal of their complaint in *Shaw I*, the District Court allowed a number of individuals to intervene, 11 on behalf of the plaintiffs and 22 for the defendants. After a 6-day trial, the District Court unanimously found "that the Plan's lines were deliberately drawn to produce one or more districts of a certain racial composition." (1994). A majority of the court held that the plan was constitutional, nonetheless, because it was narrowly tailored to further the State's compelling interests in complying with §§2 and 5 of the Voting Rights Act. The dissenting judge disagreed with that portion of the judgment. We noted probable jurisdiction. (1995).

As a preliminary matter, appellees challenge appellants' standing to continue this lawsuit. [Rehnquist concluded that none of the plaintiffs had standing to challenge District 1, but that two who resided within District 12 did have standing to challenge the drawing of that district.]

We explained in *Miller* v. *Johnson* [1995] that a racially gerrymandered districting scheme, like all laws that classify citizens on the basis of race, is constitutionally suspect. This is true whether or not the reason for the racial classification is benign or the purpose remedial. Applying traditional equal protection principles in the voting-rights context is "a most delicate task," however, because a legislature may be conscious of the voters' races without using race as a basis for assigning voters to districts. *Shaw I*; *Miller*. The constitutional wrong occurs when race becomes the "dominant and controlling" consideration.

The plaintiff bears the burden of proving the race-based motive and may do so either through "circumstantial evidence of a district's shape and demographics" or through "more direct evidence going to legislative purpose." After a detailed account of the process that led to enactment of the challenged plan, the District Court found that the General Assembly of North Carolina "deliberately drew" District 12 so that it would have an effective voting majority of black citizens.

Appellees urge upon us their view that this finding is not phrased in the same language that we used in our opinion in *Miller* v. *Johnson*, where we said that a plaintiff must show "that race was the predominant factor motivating the legislature's decision to place a significant number of voters within or without a particular district."

The District Court, of course, did not have the benefit of our opinion in *Miller* at the time it wrote its opinion. . . . [W]e think that the District Court's findings, read in the light of the evidence that it had before it, comport with the *Miller* standard.

First, the District Court had evidence of the district's shape and demographics. . . . The District Court also had direct evidence of the legislature's objective. The State's submission for preclearance expressly acknowledged that the Chapter 7's "*overriding* purpose was to comply with the dictates of the Attorney General's December 18, 1991 letter and to create two congressional districts with effective black voting majorities." (Emphasis added). . . .

In his dissent, JUSTICE STEVENS argues that strict scrutiny does not apply where a State "respects" or "compl[ies]" with traditional districting principles.". . . We do not quarrel with the dissent's claims that, in shaping District 12, the State effectuated its interest in creating one rural and one urban district, and that partisan politicking was actively at work in the districting process. That the legislature addressed these interests does not in any way refute the fact that race was the legislature's predominant consideration. . . .

Racial classifications are antithetical to the Fourteenth Amendment. . . . While appreciating that a racial classification causes "fundamental injury" to the "individual rights of a person," we have recognized that, under certain circumstances, drawing racial distinctions is permissible where a governmental body is pursuing a "compelling state interest." A State, however, is constrained in how it may pursue that end. . . . North Carolina . . . must show not only that its redistricting plan was in pursuit of a compelling state interest, but also that "its districting legislation is narrowly tailored to achieve [that] compelling interest." [Citing *Miller.*]

Appellees point to three separate compelling interests to sustain District 12: to eradicate the effects of past and present discrimination; to comply with

§5 of the Voting Rights Act; and to comply with §2 of that Act. We address each in turn.

A State's interest in remedying the effects of past or present racial discrimination may in the proper case justify a government's use of racial distinctions. [*Richmond* v. *J. A.*] *Croson* [*Co.* (1989)]. For that interest to rise to the level of a compelling state interest, it must satisfy two conditions. First, the discrimination must be " 'identified discrimination.' " . . . A generalized assertion of past discrimination in a particular industry or region is not adequate. . . . Accordingly, an effort to alleviate the effects of societal discrimination is not a compelling interest. Second, the institution that makes the racial distinction must have had a "strong basis in evidence" to conclude that remedial action was necessary, "*before* it embarks on an affirmative-action program." (Emphasis added).

In this case, the District Court found that an interest in ameliorating past discrimination did not actually precipitate the use of race in the redistricting plan. While some legislators invoked the State's history of discrimination as an argument for creating a second majority-black district, the court found that these members did not have enough voting power to have caused the creation of the second district on that basis alone. . . .

Appellees devote most of their efforts to arguing that the race-based redistricting was constitutionally justified by the State's duty to comply with the Voting Rights Act. The District Court agreed and held that compliance with §§2 and 5 of the Act could be, and in this case was, a compelling state interest. In *Miller*, we expressly left open the question whether under the proper circumstances compliance with the Voting Rights Act, on its own, could be a compelling interest. . . . Here once again we do not reach that question because we find that creating an additional majority-black district was not required under a correct reading of §5 and that District 12, as drawn, is not a remedy narrowly tailored to the State's professed interest in avoiding §2 liability.

With respect to §5 of the Voting Rights Act, we believe our decision in *Miller* forecloses the argument, adopted by the District Court, that failure to engage in the race-based districting would have violated that section. In *Miller*, we considered an equal protection challenge to Georgia's Eleventh Congressional District. As appellees do here, Georgia contended that its redistricting plan was necessary to meet the Justice Department's preclearance demands. The Justice Department had interposed an objection to a prior plan that created only two majority-minority districts. We held that the challenged congressional plan was not required by a correct reading of §5 and therefore compliance with that law could not justify race-based districting. . . .

We believe the same conclusion must be drawn here. . . .

It appears that the Justice Department was pursuing in North Carolina the same policy of maximizing the number of majority-black districts that it pursued in Georgia. . . . We explained in *Miller* that this maximization policy is not properly grounded in §5 and the Department's authority thereunder. . . . We again reject the Department's expansive interpretation of §5. . . .

With respect to §2, appellees contend, and the District Court found, that failure to enact a plan with a second majority-black district would have left the State vulnerable to a lawsuit under this section. Our precedent establishes that a plaintiff may allege a §2 violation in a single-member district if the manipulation of districting lines fragments politically cohesive minority voters among several districts or packs them into one district or a small number of districts, and thereby dilutes the voting strength of members of the minority population. To prevail on such a claim, a plaintiff must prove that the minority group "is sufficiently large and geographically compact to constitute a majority in a single-member district"; that the minority group "is politically cohesive"; and that "the white majority votes sufficiently as a bloc to enable it . . . usually to defeat the minority's preferred candidate." *Thornburg* v. *Gingles* (1986). . . . A court must also consider all other relevant circumstances and must ultimately find based on the totality of those circumstances that members of a protected class "have less opportunity than other members of the electorate to participate in the political process and to elect representatives of their choice."

We assume, *arguendo,* for the purpose of resolving this case, that compliance with §2 could be a compelling interest, and we likewise assume, *arguendo,* that the General Assembly believed a second majority-minority district was needed in order not to violate §2, and that the legislature at the time it acted had a strong basis in evidence to support that conclusion. We hold that even with the benefit of these assumptions, the North Carolina plan does not survive strict scrutiny because the remedy—the creation of District 12—is not narrowly tailored to the asserted end. . . .

District 12 could not remedy any potential §2 violation. As discussed above, a plaintiff must show that the minority group is "geographically compact" to establish §2 liability. No one looking at District 12 could reasonably suggest that the district contains a "geographically compact" population of any race. Therefore where that district sits, "there neither has been a wrong nor can be a remedy." *Growe* [v. *Emison* (1993)].

Appellees do not defend District 12 by arguing that the district is geographically compact, however. Rather they contend, and a majority of the District Court agreed, that once a legislature has a strong basis in evidence for concluding that a §2 violation exists in the State, it may draw a majority-minority district anywhere, even if the district is in no way coincident with the compact *Gingles* district, as long as racially polarized voting exists where the district is ultimately drawn.

We find this position singularly unpersuasive. We do not see how a district so drawn would avoid §2 liability. If a §2 violation is proven for a particular area, it flows from the fact that individuals in this area "have less opportunity than other members of the electorate to participate in the political process and to elect representatives of their choice." The vote dilution injuries suffered by these persons are not remedied by creating a safe majority-black district somewhere else in the State. . . .

Arguing, as appellees do and the District Court did, that the State may draw the district anywhere derives from a misconception of the vote-dilution claim. To accept that the district may be placed anywhere implies that the claim, and hence the coordinate right to an undiluted vote (to cast a ballot equal among voters), belongs to the minority as a group and not to its individual members. It does not. . . .

The United States submits that District 12 does, in fact, incorporate a "substantial portio[n]" of the concentration of minority voters that would have given rise to a §2 claim. Specifically, the Government claims that "District 12 . . . contains the heavy concentration of African Americans in Mecklenburg County, the same urban component included in the second minority opportunity district in some of the alternative plans." The portion of District 12 that lies in Mecklenburg County covers not more than 20% of the district. We do not think that this degree of incorporation could mean that District 12 substantially addresses the §2 violation. We hold, therefore, that District 12 is not narrowly tailored to the State's asserted interest in complying with §2 of the Voting Rights Act.

For the foregoing reasons, the judgment of the District Court is

Reversed.

JUSTICE STEVENS, with whom JUSTICE GINSBURG and JUSTICE BREYER join as to Parts II–V, dissenting.

. . . I am convinced that the Court's aggressive supervision of state action designed to accommodate the political concerns of historically disadvantaged minority groups is seriously misguided. A majority's attempt to enable the minority to participate more effectively in the process of democratic government should not be viewed with the same hostility that is appropriate for oppressive and exclusionary abuses of political power. [Citations omitted.] But even if we accept the Court's refusal to recognize any distinction between two vastly different kinds of situations, we should affirm the judgment of the District Court in this case.

As the Court analyzes the case, it raises three distinct questions: (1) Should North Carolina's decision to create two congressional districts in which a majority of the voters are African-American be subject to strict constitutional scrutiny?; (2) If so, did North Carolina have a compelling interest in creating such districts?; and (3) If so, was the creation of those districts "narrowly tailored" to further the asserted compelling interest? The Court inadequately explains its answer to the first question, and it avoids answering the second because it concludes that its answer to the third disposes of the case. In my estimation, the Court's disposition of all three questions is most unsatisfactory. . . .

[I omitted]

II

. . . North Carolina's admission reveals that it intended to create a second majority-minority district. That says nothing about whether it subordinated traditional districting principles in drawing District 12. . . .

District 12's noncompact appearance also fails to show that North Carolina engaged in suspect race-based districting. There is no federal statutory or constitutional requirement that state electoral boundaries conform to any particular ideal of geographic compactness. . . .

. . . [N]o evidence suggests that race played any role in the legislature's decision to choose the winding contours of District 12 over the more cartographically pleasant boundaries proposed by the Attorney General. Rather, the record reveals that two race-neutral, traditional districting criteria determined District 12's shape: the interest in ensuring that incumbents would remain residents of the districts they have previously represented; and the interest in placing predominantly rural voters in one district and predominantly urban voters in another. . . .

III

. . . [E]ven if I were to assume that strict scrutiny applies, . . . I would not share the majority's hesitancy in concluding that North Carolina had a "compelling interest" in drawing District 12. In my view, the record identifies not merely one, but at least three acceptable reasons that may have motivated legislators to favor the creation of two such districts. . . .

First, some legislators felt that the sorry history of race relations in North Carolina in past decades was a sufficient reason for making it easier for more black leaders to participate in the legislative process and to represent the State in the Congress of the United States. . . .

Second, regardless of whether §5 of the Act was actually violated, I believe the State's interest in avoiding the litigation that would have been necessary to overcome the Attorney General's objection to the original plan provides an acceptable reason for creating a second majority-minority district. . . .

Third, regardless of the possible outcome of litigation alleging that §2 of the Voting Rights Act would be violated by a plan that ensured the election of white legislators in 11 of the State's 12 congressional districts, the interest in avoiding the expense and unpleasantness of such litigation was certainly legitimate and substantial. . . .

IV

Although the Court assumes that North Carolina had a compelling interest in "avoiding liability" under §2, it avoids conclusively resolving that question because it holds that District 12 was not a "narrowly tailored" means of achieving that end. The majority reaches this conclusion by determining that District 12 did not "remedy" any potential violation of §2 that may have occurred.

In my judgment, if a State's new plan successfully avoids the potential litigation entirely, there is no reason why it must also take the form of a "remedy" for an unproven violation. . . .

. . . [T]he "narrow tailoring" requirement that the Court has fashioned is a pure judicial invention that unfairly deprives the legislature of a sovereign state of its traditional discretion in determining the boundaries of its electoral districts. The Court's analysis gives rise to the unfortunate suggestion that a State which fears a §2 lawsuit must draw the precise district that it believes a federal court would have the power to impose. Such a proposition confounds basic principles of federalism, and forces States to imagine the legally "correct" outcome of a lawsuit that has not even been filed. . . .

V

It is, of course, irrelevant whether we, as judges, deem it wise policy to create majority-minority districts as a means of assuring fair and effective representation to minority voters. We have a duty to respect Congress' considered judgment that such a policy may serve to effectuate the ends of the constitutional Amendment that it is charged with enforcing. We should also respect North Carolina's conscientious effort to conform to that congressional determination. Absent some demonstration that voters are being denied fair and effective representation as a result of their race, I find no basis for this Court's intervention into a process by which federal and state actors, both black and white, are jointly attempting to resolve difficult questions of politics and race that have long plagued North Carolina. Nor do I see how our constitutional tradition can countenance the suggestion that a State may draw unsightly lines to favor farmers or city dwellers, but not to create districts that benefit the very group whose history inspired the Amendment that the Voting Rights Act was designed to implement.

Because I have no hesitation in concluding that North Carolina's decision to adopt a plan in which white voters were in the majority in only 10 of the State's 12 districts did not violate the Equal Protection Clause, I respectfully dissent.

JUSTICE SOUTER, with whom JUSTICE GINSBURG and JUSTICE BREYER join, dissenting.

My views on this case are substantially expressed in my dissent to *Bush* v. *Vera*. [See above.]

Nos. 95-345 and 95-346

United States, Petitioner v. Guy Jerome Ursery

On writ of certiorari to the United States Court of Appeals for the Sixth Circuit

United States, Petitioner
v. $405,089.23 in United States Currency et al.

On writ of certiorari to the United States Court of Appeals
for the Ninth Circuit

[June 24, 1996]

CHIEF JUSTICE REHNQUIST delivered the opinion of the Court.

In separate cases, the United States Court of Appeals for the Sixth Circuit and the United States Court of Appeals for the Ninth Circuit held that the Double Jeopardy Clause prohibits the Government from both punishing a defendant for a criminal offense and forfeiting his property for that same offense in a separate civil proceeding. We consolidated those cases for our review, and now reverse. These civil forfeitures (and civil forfeitures generally), we hold, do not constitute "punishment" for purposes of the Double Jeopardy Clause.

I

No. 95-345: Michigan police found marijuana growing adjacent to respondent Guy Ursery's house, and discovered marijuana seeds, stems, stalks, and a growlight within the house. The United States instituted civil forfeiture proceedings against the house, alleging that the property was subject to forfeiture under 21 U.S.C. §881(a)(7) because it had been used for several years to facilitate the unlawful processing and distribution of a controlled substance. Ursery ultimately paid the United States $13,250 to settle the forfeiture claim in full. Shortly before the settlement was consummated, Ursery was indicted for manufacturing marijuana. A jury found him guilty, and he was sentenced to 63 months in prison.

The Court of Appeals for the Sixth Circuit by a divided vote reversed Ursery's criminal conviction, holding that the conviction violated the Double Jeopardy Clause of the Fifth Amendment of the United States Constitution. (1995). The court based its conclusion in part upon its belief that our decisions in *United States* v. *Halper* (1989) and *Austin* v. *United States* (1993) meant that any civil forfeiture under §881(a)(7) constitutes punishment for purposes of the Double Jeopardy Clause. Ursery, in the court's view, had therefore been "punished" in the forfeiture proceeding against his property, and could not be subsequently criminally tried for violation of 21 U.S.C. §841(a)(1).

No. 95-346: Following a jury trial, Charles Wesley Arlt and James Wren were convicted of: conspiracy to aid and abet the manufacture of methamphetamine; conspiracy to launder monetary instruments; and numerous counts of money laundering. The District Court sentenced Arlt to life in prison and a 10-year term of supervised release, and imposed a fine of $250,000. Wren was sentenced to life imprisonment and a 5-year term of supervised release.

Before the criminal trial had started, the United States had filed a civil *in rem* complaint against various property seized from, or titled to, Arlt and Wren, or Payback Mines, a corporation controlled by Arlt. The complaint alleged that each piece of property was subject to forfeiture both under 18 U.S.C. §981(a)(1)(A), which provides that "[a]ny property . . . involved in a transaction or attempted transaction in violation of" the money-laundering statute "is subject to forfeiture to the United States"; and under 21 U.S.C. §881(a)(6), which provides for the forfeiture of (i) "[a]ll . . . things of value furnished or intended to be furnished by any person in exchange for" illegal drugs, (ii) "all proceeds traceable to such an exchange," and (iii) "all moneys, negotiable instruments, and securities used or intended to be used to facilitate" a federal drug felony. The parties agreed to defer litigation of the forfeiture action during the criminal prosecution. More than a year after the conclusion of the criminal trial, the District Court granted the Government's motion for summary judgment in the civil forfeiture proceeding.

Arlt and Wren appealed the decision in the forfeiture action, and the Court of Appeals for the Ninth Circuit reversed, holding that the forfeiture violated the Double Jeopardy Clause. (1994). The court's decision was based in part upon the same view as that expressed by the Court of Appeals for the Sixth Circuit in Ursery's case — that our decisions in *Halper* and *Austin* meant that, as a categorical matter, forfeitures under §981(a)(1)(A) and §881(a)(6) always constitute "punishment."

We granted the Government's petition for certiorari in each of the two cases, and we now reverse.

II

The Double Jeopardy Clause provides: "[N]or shall any person be subject for the same offence to be twice put in jeopardy of life or limb." The Clause serves the function of preventing both "successive punishments and . . . successive prosecutions." The protection against multiple punishments prohibits the Government from " 'punishing twice, or attempting a second time to punish criminally for the same offense.' " *Witte* v. *United States* (1995) (emphasis omitted), quoting *Helvering* v. *Mitchell* (1938).

In the decisions that we review, the Courts of Appeals held that the civil forfeitures constituted "punishment," making them subject to the prohibitions of the Double Jeopardy Clause. The Government challenges that characterization of the forfeitures, arguing that the courts were wrong to conclude that civil forfeitures are punitive for double jeopardy purposes.

A

Since the earliest years of this Nation, Congress has authorized the Government to seek parallel *in rem* civil forfeiture actions and criminal prosecutions based upon the same underlying events. . . . And, in a long line of cases, this Court has considered the application of the Double Jeopardy Clause to civil forfeitures, consistently concluding that the Clause does not apply to such actions because they do not impose punishment.

One of the first cases to consider the relationship between the Double Jeopardy Clause and civil forfeiture was *Various Items of Personal Property* v. *United States* (1931). In *Various Items,* the Waterloo Distilling Corporation had been ordered to forfeit a distillery, warehouse, and denaturing plant, on the ground that the corporation had conducted its distilling business in violation of federal law. The Government conceded that the corporation had been convicted of criminal violations prior to the initiation of the forfeiture proceeding, and admitted that the criminal conviction had been based upon "the transactions set forth . . . as a basis for the forfeiture." Considering the corporation's argument that the forfeiture action violated the Double Jeopardy Clause, this Court unanimously held that the Clause was inapplicable to civil forfeiture actions. [Excerpt from opinion omitted.]

In reaching its conclusion, the Court drew a sharp distinction between *in rem* civil *forfeitures* and *in personam* civil *penalties* such as fines: Though the latter could, in some circumstances, be punitive, the former could not. . . .

Following its decision in *Various Items,* the Court did not consider another double jeopardy case involving a civil forfeiture for 40 years. Then, in *One Lot Emerald Cut Stones* v. *United States* (1972), the Court's brief opinion reaffirmed the rule of *Various Items.* . . .

In our most recent decision considering whether a civil forfeiture constitutes punishment under the Double Jeopardy Clause, we again affirmed the rule of *Various Items.* In *United States* v. *One Assortment of 89 Firearms* (1984), the owner of the defendant weapons was acquitted of charges of dealing firearms without a license. The Government then brought a forfeiture action against the firearms under 18 U.S.C. §924(d), alleging that they were used or were intended to be used in violation of federal law. In another unanimous decision, we held that the forfeiture was not barred by the prior criminal proceeding. We began our analysis by stating the rule for our decision:

> "Unless the forfeiture sanction was intended as punishment, so that the proceeding is essentially criminal in character, the Double Jeopardy Clause is not applicable. The question, then, is whether a §924(d) forfeiture proceeding is intended to be, or by its nature necessarily is, criminal and punitive, or civil and remedial." *89 Firearms*.

Our inquiry proceeded in two stages. In the first stage, we looked to Congress' intent, and concluded that "Congress designed forfeiture under §924(d) as a remedial civil sanction." This conclusion was based upon several findings. First, noting that the forfeiture proceeding was *in rem*, we found it significant that "actions *in rem* have traditionally been viewed as civil proceedings, with jurisdiction dependent upon the seizure of a physical object." Second, we found that the forfeiture provision, because it reached both weapons used in violation of federal law and those "intended to be used" in such a manner, reached a broader range of conduct than its criminal analogue. Third, we concluded that the civil forfeiture "further[ed] broad remedial aims," including both "discouraging unregulated commerce in firearms," and "removing from circulation firearms that have been used or intended for use outside regulated channels of commerce."

In the second stage of our analysis, we looked to " 'whether the statutory scheme was so punitive either in purpose or effect as to negate' Congress' intention to establish a civil remedial mechanism." Considering several factors that we had used previously in order to determine whether a civil proceeding was so punitive as to require application of the full panoply of constitutional protections required in a criminal trial, we found only one of those factors to be present in the §924(d) forfeiture. By itself, however, the fact that the behavior proscribed by the forfeiture was already a crime proved insufficient to turn the forfeiture into a punishment subject to the Double Jeopardy Clause. Hence, we found that the petitioner had "failed to establish by the 'clearest proof' that Congress has provided a sanction so punitive as to 'transfor[m] what was clearly intended as a civil remedy into a criminal penalty.' " We concluded our decision by restating that civil forfeiture is "not an additional penalty for the commission of a criminal act, but rather is a separate civil sanction, remedial in nature."

B

Our cases reviewing civil forfeitures under the Double Jeopardy Clause adhere to a remarkably consistent theme. Though the two-part analytical construct employed in *89 Firearms* was more refined, perhaps, than that we had used over 50 years earlier in *Various Items*, the conclusion was the same in each case: *in rem* civil forfeiture is a remedial civil sanction, distinct from potentially punitive *in personam* civil penalties such as fines, and does not constitute a punishment under the Double Jeopardy Clause. . . .

In the case that we currently review, the Court of Appeals for the Ninth Circuit recognized as much, concluding that after *89 Firearms*, "the law was clear that civil forfeitures did not constitute 'punishment' for double jeopardy purposes." Nevertheless, that court read three of our decisions to have "abandoned" *89 Firearms* and the oft-affirmed rule of *Various Items*. According to the Court of Appeals for the Ninth Circuit, through our decisions in *United States* v. *Halper* (1989), *Austin* v. *United States* (1993), and *Department of Revenue of Mont.* v. *Kurth Ranch* (1994), we "changed [our] collective mind," and "adopted a new test for determining whether a nominally civil sanction constitutes 'punishment' for double jeopardy purposes." The Court of Appeals for the Sixth Circuit shared the view of the Ninth Circuit, though it did not directly rely upon *Kurth Ranch*. We turn now to consider whether *Halper, Austin,* and *Kurth Ranch* accomplished the radical jurisprudential shift perceived by the Courts of Appeals.

[Rehnquist detailed the factual and legal backgrounds of the three cases. In *Halper*, the defendant was first convicted of violating the false-claims statute by filing inflated Medicare claims and then ordered in a separate proceeding to pay civil penalties totaling $130,000. The Court ruled that the penalty was "sufficiently disproportionate" to the government's actual damages that it constituted "a second punishment in violation of double jeopardy." In *Austin*, the government initiated a civil forfeiture proceeding against a mobile home and auto body shop belonging to a defendant in a drug case, contending the property had been "used" or was "intended for use" in the commission of a drug offense. The Court held that forfeiture under the drug statute was "subject to the limitations of the Eighth Amendment's Excessive Fines Clause" because it amounted to "payment to a sovereign as punishment for some offense." Finally, in *Kurth Ranch*, the Court cited the Double Jeopardy Clause in striking down a state tax imposed on marijuana when the taxpayer had already been criminally convicted of owning the marijuana that was taxed.]

We think that the Court of Appeals for the Sixth Circuit and the Court of Appeals for the Ninth Circuit misread *Halper, Austin,* and *Kurth Ranch*. None of those decisions purported to overrule the well-established teaching of *Various Items, Emerald Cut Stones,* and *89 Firearms*. *Halper* involved not a civil forfeiture, but a civil penalty. That its rule was limited to the latter context is clear from the decision itself, from the historical distinction that we have drawn between civil forfeiture and civil penalties, and from the practical difficulty of applying *Halper* to a civil forfeiture. . . .

. . . Civil penalties are designed as a rough form of "liquidated damages" for the harms suffered by the Government as a result of a defendant's conduct. . . . Civil forfeitures, in contrast to civil penalties, are designed to do more than simply compensate the Government. Forfeitures serve a variety of purposes, but are designed primarily to confiscate property used in violation of the law, and to require disgorgement of the fruits of illegal conduct. Though it may be possible to quantify the value of the property forfeited, it is virtually impossible to quantify, even approximately, the nonpunitive purposes served by a particular civil forfeiture. Hence, it is practically difficult to determine whether a particular forfeiture bears no rational relationship to the nonpunitive purposes of that forfeiture. Quite simply, the case-by-case balancing test set forth in

Halper, in which a court must compare the harm suffered by the Government against the size of the penalty imposed, is inapplicable to civil forfeiture. . . .

In the cases that we review, the Courts of Appeals did not find *Halper* difficult to apply to civil forfeiture because they concluded that its case-by-case balancing approach had been supplanted in *Austin* by a categorical approach that found a civil sanction to be punitive if it could not "fairly be said solely to serve a remedial purpose." But *Austin,* it must be remembered, did not involve the Double Jeopardy Clause at all. *Austin* was decided solely under the Excessive Fines Clause of the Eighth Amendment, a constitutional provision which we never have understood as parallel to, or even related to, the Double Jeopardy Clause of the Fifth Amendment. The only discussion of the Double Jeopardy Clause contained in *Austin* appears in a footnote that acknowledges our decisions holding that "[t]he Double Jeopardy Clause has been held not to apply in civil forfeiture proceedings . . . where the forfeiture could properly be characterized as remedial." And in *Austin* we expressly recognized and approved our decisions in *One Lot Emerald Cut Stones* v. *United States* and *United States* v. *One Assortment of 89 Firearms.*

. . . Forfeitures effected under 21 U.S.C. §§881(a)(4) and (a)(7) are subject to review for excessiveness under the Eighth Amendment after *Austin;* this does not mean, however, that those forfeitures are so punitive as to constitute punishment for the purposes of double jeopardy. The holding of *Austin* was limited to the Excessive Fines Clause of the Eighth Amendment, and we decline to import the analysis of *Austin* into our double jeopardy jurisprudence. . . .

In sum, nothing in *Halper, Kurth Ranch,* or *Austin,* purported to replace our traditional understanding that civil forfeiture does not constitute punishment for the purpose of the Double Jeopardy Clause. . . . *Halper* dealt with *in personam* civil penalties under the Double Jeopardy Clause; *Kurth Ranch* with a tax proceeding under the Double Jeopardy Clause; and *Austin* with civil forfeitures under the Excessive Fines Clause. None of those cases dealt with the subject of this case: *in rem* civil forfeitures for purposes of the Double Jeopardy Clause.

C

We turn now to consider the forfeitures in these cases under the teaching of *Various Items, Emerald Cut Stones,* and *89 Firearms.* Because it provides a useful analytical tool, we conduct our inquiry within the framework of the two-part test used in *89 Firearms.* First, we ask whether Congress intended proceedings under 21 U.S.C. §881, and 18 U.S.C. §981, to be criminal or civil. Second, we turn to consider whether the proceedings are so punitive in fact as to "persuade us that the forfeiture proceeding[s] may not legitimately be viewed as civil in nature," despite Congress' intent. *89 Firearms.*

There is little doubt that Congress intended these forfeitures to be civil proceedings. As was the case in *89 Firearms,* "Congress' intent in this regard is most clearly demonstrated by the procedural mechanisms it established for enforcing forfeitures under the statute[s]." Both 21 U.S.C. §881 and 18 U.S.C. §981, which is entitled "Civil forfeiture," provide that the laws "relating to the seizure, summary and judicial forfeiture, and condemnation of property for violation of the customs laws . . . shall apply to seizures and forfeitures incurred" under §881 and §981. Because forfeiture proceedings under the customs laws are *in rem*, it is clear that Congress intended that a forfeiture under §881 or §981, like the forfeiture reviewed in *89 Firearms*, would be a proceeding *in rem*. Congress specifically structured these forfeitures to be impersonal by targeting the property itself. . . .

Other procedural mechanisms governing forfeitures under §981 and §881 also indicate that Congress intended such proceedings to be civil. Forfeitures under either statute are governed by 19 U.S.C. §1607, which provides that actual notice of the impending forfeiture is unnecessary when the Government cannot identify any party with an interest in the seized article, and by §1609, which provides that seized property is subject to forfeiture through a summary administrative procedure if no party files a claim to the property. And 19 U.S.C. §1615, which governs the burden of proof in forfeiture proceedings under §881 and §981, provides that once the Government has shown probable cause that the property is subject to forfeiture, then "the burden of proof shall lie upon [the] claimant." In sum, "[b]y creating such distinctly civil procedures for forfeitures under [§881 and §981], Congress has 'indicate[d] clearly that it intended a civil, not a criminal sanction.' " *89 Firearms*, quoting *Helvering* v. *Mitchell* [1938].

Moving to the second stage of our analysis, we find that there is little evidence, much less the " 'clearest proof' " that we require, suggesting that forfeiture proceedings under 21 U.S.C. §§881(a)(6) and (a)(7), and 19 U.S.C. §981(a)(1)(A), are so punitive in form and effect as to render them criminal despite Congress' intent to the contrary. . . .

Most significant is that §981(a)(1)(A), and §§881(a)(6) and (a)(7), while perhaps having certain punitive aspects, serve important nonpunitive goals. Title 21 U.S.C. §881(a)(7), under which Ursery's property was forfeited, provides for the forfeiture of "all real property . . . which is used or intended to be used, in any manner or part, to commit, or to facilitate the commission of" a federal drug felony. Requiring the forfeiture of property used to commit federal narcotics violations encourages property owners to take care in managing their property and ensures that they will not permit that property to be used for illegal purposes. . . . In many circumstances, the forfeiture may abate a nuisance.

The forfeiture of the property claimed by Arlt and Wren took place pursuant to 18 U.S.C. §981(a)(1)(A), and 21 U.S.C. §881(a)(6). Section 981(a)(1)(A) provides for the forfeiture of "any property" involved in illegal money-laundering transactions. Section 881(a)(6) provides for the forfeiture of "[a]ll . . . things of value furnished or intended to be furnished by any person in exchange for" illegal drugs; "all proceeds traceable to such an exchange"; and "all moneys, negotiable instruments, and securities used or intended to be used to facilitate" a federal drug felony. The same remedial purposes served by §881(a)(7) are served by §881(a)(6) and §981(a)(1)(A). Only one point merits separate discussion. To the extent that §881(a)(6) applies to "proceeds" of illegal drug activity, it serves the additional nonpunitive goal of ensuring that persons do not profit from their illegal acts.

Other considerations that we have found relevant to the question whether a proceeding is criminal also tend to support a conclusion that §981(a)(1)(A) and §§881 (a)(6) and (a)(7) are civil proceedings. First, in light of our decisions in *Various Items*, *Emerald Cut Stones*, and *89 Firearms*, and the long tradition of federal statutes providing for a forfeiture proceeding following a criminal prosecution, it is absolutely clear that *in rem* civil forfeiture has not historically been regarded as punishment, as we have understood that term under the Double Jeopardy Clause. Second, there is no requirement in the statutes that we currently review that the Government demonstrate *scienter* in order to establish that the property is subject to forfeiture; indeed, the property may be subject to forfeiture even if no party files a claim to it and the Government never shows any connection between the property and a particular person. Though both §881(a) and §981(a) contain an "innocent owner" exception, we do not think that such a provision, without more indication of an intent to punish, is relevant to the question whether a statute is punitive under the Double Jeopardy Clause. Third, though both statutes may fairly be said to serve the purpose of deterrence, we long have held that this purpose may serve civil as well as criminal goals. We recently reaffirmed this conclusion in *Bennis* v. *Michigan* [1996], where we held that "forfeiture . . . serves a deterrent purpose distinct from any punitive purpose." Finally, though both statutes are tied to criminal activity, as was the case in *89 Firearms*, this fact is insufficient to render the statutes punitive. It is well settled that "Congress may impose both a criminal and a civil sanction in respect to the same act or omission." *Helvering* [1938]. By itself, the fact that a forfeiture statute has some connection to a criminal violation is far from the "clearest proof" necessary to show that a proceeding is criminal.

We hold that these *in rem* civil forfeitures are neither "punishment" nor criminal for purposes of the Double Jeopardy Clause. The judgments of the Court of Appeals for the Sixth Circuit, in No. 95-345, and of the Court of Appeals for the Ninth Circuit, in No. 95-346, are accordingly reversed.

It is so ordered.

JUSTICE KENNEDY, concurring.

I join the Court's opinion and add these further observations. . . .

Forfeiture . . . punishes an owner by taking property involved in a crime, and it may happen that the owner is also the wrongdoer charged with a criminal offense. But the forfeiture is not a second *in personam* punishment for the offense, which is all the Double Jeopardy Clause prohibits. . . .

Distinguishing between *in rem* and *in personam* punishments does not depend upon, or revive, the fiction alive in *Various Items* [*of Personal Property* v. *United States* (1931)], but condemned in *Austin* [v. *United States* (1993)], that the property is punished as if it were a sentient being capable of moral choice. It is the owner who feels the pain and receives the stigma of the forfeiture, not the property. The distinction simply recognizes that Congress, in order to quiet title to forfeitable property in one proceeding, has structured the forfeiture action as a proceeding against the property, not against a particular defendant. Indeed, the Government will often file a forfeiture complaint without any knowledge of who the owner is. True, the forfeiture statutes require proof of a violation of a drug trafficking or other offense, but the purpose of this predicate showing is just to establish that the property was used in a crime. In contrast to criminal forfeiture, civil *in rem* forfeiture actions do not require a showing that the owner who stands to lose his property interest has committed a criminal offense. The offenses committed by Ursery, Arlt, and Wren were proffered as evidence that the property was used in a crime, but this does not make forfeiture a punishment for those offenses. . . .

JUSTICE SCALIA, with whom JUSTICE THOMAS joins, concurring in the judgment.

In my view, the Double Jeopardy Clause prohibits successive prosecution, not successive punishment. See *Department of Revenue of Mont. v. Kurth Ranch* (1994) (SCALIA, J., dissenting). Civil forfeiture proceedings of the sort at issue here are not criminal prosecutions. . . .

JUSTICE STEVENS, concurring in the judgment in part and dissenting in part.

The question the Court poses is whether civil forfeitures constitute "punishment" for purposes of the Double Jeopardy Clause. Because the numerous federal statutes authorizing forfeitures cover such a wide variety of situations, it is quite wrong to assume that there is only one answer to that question. For purposes of analysis it is useful to identify three different categories of property that are subject to seizure: proceeds, contraband, and property that has played a part in the commission of a crime. The facts of these two cases illustrate the point.

[Stevens explained that he concurred in upholding the forfeiture of the $405,089.23 in currency in No. 95-346 because the funds were "the proceeds of unlawful activity." He also said that the government had the right to seize as "contraband" marijuana seeds, stems, stalks, and a growlight found in Ursery's house.]

The critical question presented in No. 95-345 arose, not out of the seizure of contraband by the Michigan police, but rather out of the decision by the United States Attorney to take respondent's home. There is no evidence that the house had been purchased with the proceeds of unlawful activity and the house itself was surely not contraband. Nonetheless, 21 U.S.C. §881(a)(7) authorized the Government to seek forfeiture of respondent's residence because it had been used to facilitate the manufacture and distribution of marijuana. Respondent was then himself prosecuted for and convicted of manufacturing marijuana. In my opinion none of the reasons supporting the forfeiture of proceeds or contraband provides a sufficient basis for concluding that the confiscation of respondent's home was not punitive. . . .

I

In recent years, both Congress and the state legislatures have armed their law enforcement authorities with new powers to forfeit property that vastly exceed their traditional tools. In response, this Court has reaffirmed the fundamental proposition that all forfeitures must be accomplished within the constraints set by the Constitution. See, *e.g., Austin* v. *United States* (1993); *United States* v. *James Daniel Good Real Property* (1993). This Term the Court has begun dismantling the protections it so recently erected. In *Bennis* v. *Michigan* (1996), the Court held that officials may confiscate an innocent person's automobile. And today, for the first time it upholds the forfeiture of a person's home. On the way to its surprising conclusion that the owner is not punished by the loss of his residence, the Court repeatedly professes its adherence to tradition and time-honored practice. As I discuss below, however, the decision shows a stunning disregard not only for modern precedents but for our older ones as well. . . .

More important, neither of those cases endorsed the asserted categorical rule that civil forfeitures never give rise to double jeopardy rights. Instead, each carefully considered the nature of the particular forfeiture at issue, classifying it as either "punitive" or "remedial," before deciding whether it implicated double jeopardy. . . .

The majority, surprisingly, claims that *Austin* v. *United States* (1993) "expressly recognized and approved" those decisions. But the Court creates the appearance that we endorsed its interpretation of *89 Firearms* and *Emerald Cut Stones* by quoting selectively from *Austin*. We actually stated the following:

> "The Double Jeopardy Clause has been held not to apply in civil forfeiture proceedings, but only in cases where the forfeiture could properly be characterized as remedial. . . ."

In reality, both cases rejected the monolithic view that all *in rem* civil forfeitures should be treated the same, and recognized the possibility that other types of forfeitures that could not "properly be characterized as remedial" might constitute "an additional penalty for the commission of a criminal act.". . .

Read properly, therefore, *89 Firearms* and *Emerald Cut Stones* are not inconsistent with, but set the stage for the modern understanding of how the Double Jeopardy Clause applies in nominally civil proceedings. That understanding has been developed in a trio of recent decisions: *United States* v. *Halper* (1989), *Austin* v. *United States* (1993), and *Department of Revenue of Mont.* v. *Kurth Ranch* (1994). The court of appeals found that the combined effect of two of those decisions—*Halper* and *Austin*—established the proposition that forfeitures under 21 U.S.C. §881(a)(7) implicated double jeopardy. This Court rejects that conclusion, asserting that none of these cases changed the "oft-affirmed rule" of *Various Items.*

It is the majority, however, that has "misread" *Halper, Austin,* and *Kurth Ranch* by artificially cabining each to a separate sphere and treating the three as if they concerned unrelated subjects. In fact, all three were devoted to the common enterprise of giving meaning to the idea of "punishment," a concept that plays a central role in the jurisprudence of both the Excessive Fines Clause and the Double Jeopardy Clause. . . .

The recurrent theme of the Court's opinion is that there is some mystical difference between *in rem* and *in personam* proceedings, such that only the latter can give rise to double jeopardy concerns. The Court claims that "[s]ince at least *Various Items,*" we have drawn this distinction for purposes of applying relevant constitutional provisions. That statement, however, is incorrect. We have repeatedly rejected the idea that the nature of the court's jurisdiction has any bearing on the constitutional protections that apply at a proceeding before it. . . .

The pedantic distinction between *in rem* and *in personam* actions is ultimately only a cover for the real basis for the Court's decision: the idea that the property, not the owner, is being "punished" for offenses of which it is "guilty." Although the Court prefers not to rely on this notorious fiction too blatantly, its repeated citations to *Various Items* make clear that the Court believes respondent's home was "guilty" of the drug offenses with which he was charged. On that rationale, of course, the case is easy. The owner of the property is not being punished when the Government confiscates it, just the property. The same sleight-of-hand would have worked in *Austin*, too: The owner of the property is not being excessively fined, just the property itself. Despite the Government's heavy reliance on that fiction in *Austin*, we did not allow it to stand in the way of our holding that the seizure of property may punish the owner.

Even if the point had not been settled by prior decisions, common sense would dictate the result in this case. There is simply no rational basis for characterizing the seizure of this respondent's home as anything other than punishment for his crime. The house was neither proceeds nor contraband and its value had no relation to the Government's authority to seize it. Under the controlling statute an essential predicate for the forfeiture was proof that respondent had used the property in connection with the commission of a crime. The forfeiture of this property was unquestionably "a penalty that had absolutely no correlation to any damages sustained by society or to the cost of enforcing the law." *United States* v. *Ward* [1980]. As we unanimously recognized in *Halper*, formalistic distinctions that obscure the obvious practical consequences of governmental action deserve the " 'humane interests' " protected by the Double Jeopardy Clause. Fidelity to both reason and precedent dictates the conclusion that this forfeiture was "punishment" for purposes of the Double Jeopardy Clause. [Remainder of opinion omitted.]

□ □ □

No. 95-489

Colorado Republican Federal Campaign Committee and Douglas Jones, Treasurer, Petitioners v. Federal Election Commission

On writ of certiorari to the United States Court of Appeals for the Tenth Circuit

[June 26, 1996]

JUSTICE BREYER announced the judgment of the Court and delivered an opinion, in which JUSTICE O'CONNOR and JUSTICE SOUTER join.

In April 1986, before the Colorado Republican Party had selected its senatorial candidate for the fall's election, that Party's Federal Campaign Committee bought radio advertisements attacking Timothy Wirth, the Democratic Party's likely candidate. The Federal Election Commission (FEC) charged that this "expenditure" exceeded the dollar limits that a provision of the Federal

Election Campaign Act of 1971 (FECA) imposes upon political party "expenditure[s] in connection with" a "general election campaign" for congressional office. 2 U.S.C. §441a(d)(3). This case focuses upon the constitutionality of those limits as applied to this case. We conclude that the First Amendment prohibits the application of this provision to the kind of expenditure at issue here—an expenditure that the political party has made independently, without coordination with any candidate.

I

To understand the issues and our holding, one must begin with FECA as it emerged from Congress in 1974. That Act sought both to remedy the appearance of a "corrupt" political process (one in which large contributions seem to buy legislative votes) and to level the electoral playing field by reducing campaign costs. See *Buckley* v. *Valeo* (1976). It consequently imposed limits upon the amounts that individuals, corporations, "political committees" (such as political action committees, or PAC's), and political parties could *contribute* to candidates for federal office, and it also imposed limits upon the amounts that candidates, corporations, labor unions, political committees, and political parties could *spend,* even on their own, to help a candidate win election.

This Court subsequently examined several of the Act's provisions in light of the First Amendment's free speech and association protections. [Citation of cases omitted.] In these cases, the Court essentially weighed the First Amendment interest in permitting candidates (and their supporters) to spend money to advance their political views, against a "compelling" governmental interest in assuring the electoral system's legitimacy, protecting it from the appearance and reality of corruption. After doing so, the Court found that the First Amendment prohibited some of FECA's provisions, but permitted others.

Most of the provisions this Court found unconstitutional imposed *expenditure* limits. Those provisions limited candidates' rights to spend their own money, limited a candidate's campaign expenditures, limited the right of individuals to make "independent" expenditures (not coordinated with the candidate or candidate's campaign), and similarly limited the right of political committees to make "independent" expenditures. The provisions that the Court found constitutional mostly imposed *contribution* limits—limits that apply both when an individual or political committee contributes money directly to a candidate and also when they indirectly contribute by making expenditures that they coordinate with the candidate. Consequently, for present purposes, the Act now prohibits individuals and political committees from making direct, or indirect, contributions that exceed the following limits:

> (a) For any "person": $1,000 to a candidate "with respect to any election"; $5,000 to any political committee in any year; $20,000 to the national committees of a political party in any year; but all within an overall limit (for any individual in any year) of $25,000. 2 U.S.C. §§441a(a)(1), (3).
>
> (b) For any "multicandidate political committee": $5,000 to a candidate "with respect to any election"; $5,000 to any political committee in any year; and $15,000 to the national committees of a political party in any year. §441a(a)(2).

FECA also has a special provision, directly at issue in this case, that governs contributions and expenditures by political parties. §441a(d). This special provision creates, in part, an *exception* to the above contribution limits. That is, without special treatment, political parties ordinarily would be subject to the general limitation on contributions by a "multicandidate political committee" just described. . . .

However, FECA's special provision, which we shall call the "Party Expenditure Provision," creates a *general exception* from this contribution limitation, and from any other limitation on expenditures. It says:

> "Notwithstanding any other provision of law with respect to *limitations on expenditures* or *limitations on contributions*, . . . political party [committees] . . . may make *expenditures* in connection with the general election campaign of candidates for Federal office. . . . " §441a(d)(1) (emphasis added).

After exempting political parties from the general contribution and expenditure limitations of the statute, the Party Expenditure Provision then imposes a *substitute limitation* upon party "expenditures" in a senatorial campaign equal to the greater of $20,000 or "2 cents multiplied by the voting age population of the State," §441a(d)(3)(A)(i), adjusted for inflation since 1974, §441a(c). The Provision permitted a political party in Colorado in 1986 to spend about $103,000 in connection with the general election campaign of a candidate for the United ed States Senate. . . .

In January 1986, Timothy Wirth, then a Democratic Congressman, announced that he would run for an open Senate seat in November. In April, before either the Democratic primary or the Republican convention, the Colorado Republican Federal Campaign Committee (Colorado Party), the petitioner here, bought radio advertisements attacking Congressman Wirth. The State Democratic Party complained to the Federal Election Commission. It pointed out that the Colorado Party had previously assigned its $103,000 general election allotment to the National Republican Senatorial Committee, leaving it without any permissible spending balance. . . . It argued that the purchase of radio time was an "expenditure in connection with the general election campaign of a candidate for Federal office," which, consequently, exceeded the Party Expenditure Provision limits.

The FEC agreed with the Democratic Party. It brought a complaint against the Colorado Republican Party, charging a violation. The Colorado Party defended in part by claiming that the Party Expenditure Provision's expenditure limitations violated the First Amendment—a charge that it repeated in a counterclaim that said the Colorado Party intended to make other "expenditures directly in connection with" senatorial elections and attacked the constitutionality of the entire Party Expenditure Provision. The Federal District Court interpreted the Provision's words " 'in connection with' the general election campaign of a candidate" narrowly, as meaning only expenditures for advertising using " 'express words of advocacy of election or defeat.' " [Quoting *Buckley* v. *Valeo.*] As so interpreted, the court held, the provision did not cover the expenditures here. The court entered summary judgment for the Colorado Party and dismissed its counterclaim as moot. [1993]

Both sides appealed. The Government, for the FEC, argued for a somewhat broader interpretation of the statute—applying the limits to advertisements containing an "electioneering message" about a "clearly identified candidate"—which, it said, both covered the expenditure and satisfied the Constitution. The Court of Appeals agreed. It found the Party Expenditure Provision applicable, held it constitutional, and ordered judgment in the FEC's favor. (1995).

We granted certiorari primarily to consider the Colorado Party's argument that the Party Expenditure Provision violates the First Amendment "either facially or as applied." For reasons we shall discuss in Part IV below, we consider only the latter question—whether the Party Expenditure Provision as applied here violates the First Amendment. We conclude that it does.

II

The summary judgment record indicates that the expenditure in question is what this Court in *Buckley* called an "independent" expenditure, not a "coordinated" expenditure that other provisions of FECA treat as a kind of campaign "contribution." The record describes how the expenditure was made. In a deposition, the Colorado Party's Chairman, Howard Callaway, pointed out that, at the time of the expenditure, the Party had not yet selected a senatorial nominee from among the three individuals vying for the nomination. He added that he arranged for the development of the script at his own initiative, that he, and no one else, approved it, that the only other politically relevant individuals who might have read it were the party's executive director and political director, and that all relevant discussions took place at meetings attended only by party staff.

Notwithstanding the above testimony, the Government argued in District Court—and reiterates in passing in its brief to this Court—that the deposition showed that the Party had coordinated the advertisement with its candidates. . . . We can find no "genuine" issue of fact in this respect. And we therefore treat the expenditure, for constitutional purposes, as an "independent" expenditure, not an indirect campaign contribution.

So treated, the expenditure falls within the scope of the Court's precedents that extend First Amendment protection to independent expenditures. . . .

. . . A political party's independent expression not only reflects its members' views about the philosophical and governmental matters that bind them together, it also seeks to convince others to join those members in a practical democratic task, the task of creating a government that voters can instruct and hold responsible for subsequent success or failure. The independent expression of a political party's views is "core" First Amendment activity no less than is the independent expression of individuals, candidates, or other political committees.

We are not aware of any special dangers of corruption associated with political parties that tip the constitutional balance in a different direction. . . .

We recognize that FECA permits individuals to contribute more money ($20,000) to a party than to a candidate ($1,000) or to other political committees ($5,000). We also recognize that FECA permits unregulated "soft money" contributions to a party for certain activities, such as electing candidates for state office or for voter registration and "get out the vote" drives. But the opportunity for corruption posed by these greater opportunities for contributions is, at best, attenuated. Unregulated "soft money" contributions may not be used to influence a federal campaign, except when used in the limited, party-building activities specifically designated in the statute. Any contribution to a party that is earmarked for a particular campaign is considered a contribution to the candidate and is subject to the contribution limitations. A party may not simply channel unlimited amounts of even undesignated contributions to a candidate, since such direct transfers are also considered contributions and are subject to the contribution limits on a "multicandidate political committee." The greatest danger of corruption, therefore, appears to be from the ability of donors to give sums up to $20,000 to a party which may be used for independent party expenditures for the benefit of a particular candidate. We could understand how Congress, were it to conclude that the potential for evasion of the individual contribution limits was a serious matter, might decide to change the statute's limitations on contributions to political parties. . . . But we do not believe that the risk of corruption present here could justify the "markedly greater burden on basic freedoms caused by" the statute's limitations on expenditures. . . .

The Government does not point to record evidence or legislative findings suggesting any special corruption problem in respect to independent party expenditures. . . . To the contrary, this Court's opinions suggest that Congress wrote the Party Expenditure Provision not so much because of a special concern about the potentially "corrupting" effect of party expenditures, but rather for the constitutionally insufficient purpose of reducing what it saw as wasteful and excessive campaign spending. In fact, rather than indicating a special fear of the corruptive influence of political parties, the legislative history demonstrates Congress' general desire to enhance what was seen as an important and legitimate role for political parties in American elections. . . .

We therefore believe that this Court's prior case law controls the outcome here. We do not see how a Constitution that grants to individuals, candidates, and ordinary political committees the right to make unlimited independent expenditures could deny the same right to political parties. . . .

III

The Government does not deny the force of the precedent we have discussed. Rather, it argued below, and the lower courts accepted, that the expenditure in this case should be treated under those precedents, not as an "independent expenditure," but rather as a "coordinated expenditure," which those cases have treated as "contributions," and which those cases have held Congress may constitutionally regulate.

While the District Court found that the expenditure in this case was "coordinated," it did not do so based on any factual finding that the Party had consulted with any candidate in the making or planning of the advertising campaign in question. Instead, the District Court accepted the Government's argument that all party expenditures should be treated as if they had been coordinated *as a matter of law,* "[b]ased on Supreme Court precedent and the Commission's interpretation of the statute." The Court of Appeals agreed with this legal conclusion. . . . The question . . . is whether the Court of Appeals erred as a legal matter in accepting the Government's conclusive presumption that all party expenditures are "coordinated." We believe it did.

In support of its argument, the Government points to a set of legal materials, based on FEC interpretations, that seem to say or imply that all party expenditures are "coordinated.". . .

The Government argues, on the basis of these materials, that the FEC has made an "empirical judgment that party officials will as a matter of course consult with the party's candidates before funding communications intended to influence the outcome of a federal election." The FEC materials, however, do not make this empirical judgment. For the most part those materials use the word "coordinated" as a description that does not necessarily deny the possibility that a party could also make independent expenditures. . . . In these circumstances, we cannot take the cited materials as an empirical, or experience-based, determination that, as a factual matter, all party expenditures are coordinated with a candidate. That being so, we need not hold, on the basis of these materials, that the expenditures here were "coordinated.". . .

Finally, the Government and supporting *amici* argue that the expenditure is "coordinated" because a party and its candidate are identical, i.e., the party, in a sense, "is" its candidates. We cannot assume, however, that this is so. . . . Congress chose to treat candidates and their parties quite differently under the Act, for example, by regulating contributions from one to the other. And we are not certain whether a metaphysical identity would help the Government, for in that case one might argue that the absolute identity of views and interests eliminates any potential for corruption, as would seem to be the case in the relationship between candidates and their campaign committees. . . .

IV

The Colorado Party and supporting *amici* have argued a broader question than we have decided, for they have claimed that, in the special case of political parties, the First Amendment forbids congressional efforts to limit coordinated expenditures as well as independent expenditures. Because the expenditure before us is an independent expenditure we have not reached this broader question in deciding the Party's "as applied" challenge.

We recognize that the Party filed a counterclaim in which it sought to raise a facial challenge to the Party Expenditure Provision as a whole. But that counterclaim did not focus specifically upon coordinated expenditures. . . .

More importantly, the opinions of the lower courts, and the parties' briefs in this case, did not squarely isolate, and address, party expenditures that in fact are coordinated, nor did they examine, in that context, relevant similarities or differences with similar expenditures made by individuals or other political groups. . . .

But the focus of this litigation, and the lower court opinions, has not been on such issues, but rather on whether the Government may conclusively deem independent party expenditures to be coordinated. . . .

Finally, we note that neither the parties nor the lower courts have considered whether or not Congress would have wanted the Party Expenditure Provisions limitations to stand were they to apply only to coordinated, and not to independent, expenditures. This non-constitutional ground for exempting party coordinated expenditures from FECA limitations should be briefed and considered before addressing the constitutionality of such regulation.

JUSTICE THOMAS disagrees and would reach the broader constitutional question notwithstanding the above prudential considerations. In fact, he would reach a great number of issues neither addressed below, nor presented by the facts of this case, nor raised by the parties, for he believes it appropriate here to overrule *sua sponte* this Court's entire campaign finance jurisprudence, developed in numerous cases over the last 20 years. Doing so seems inconsistent with this Court's view that it is ordinarily "inappropriate for us to reexamine" prior precedent "without the benefit of the parties' briefing," since the "principles that animate our policy of *stare decisis* caution against overruling a longstanding precedent on a theory not argued by the parties." In our view, given the important competing interests involved in campaign finance issues, we should proceed cautiously, consistent with this precedent, and remand for further proceedings.

For these reasons, the judgment of the Court of Appeals is vacated, and the case is remanded for further proceedings.

It is so ordered.

JUSTICE KENNEDY, with whom THE CHIEF JUSTICE and JUSTICE SCALIA join, concurring in the judgment and dissenting in part.

In agreement with JUSTICE THOMAS, I would hold that the Colorado Republican Party, in its pleadings in the District Court and throughout this litigation, has preserved its claim that the constraints imposed by the Federal Election Campaign Act of 1971 (FECA), both on its face and as interpreted by the Federal Election Commission (FEC), violate the First Amendment. . . .

The central holding in *Buckley* v. *Valeo* (1976) is that spending money on one's own speech must be permitted, and this is what political parties do when they make the expenditures FECA restricts. FECA calls spending of this nature a "contribution," and it is true that contributions can be restricted consistent with *Buckley*. As the plurality acknowledges, however, and as our cases hold, we cannot allow the Government's suggested labels to control our First Amendment analysis. . . .

We had no occasion in *Buckley* to consider possible First Amendment objections to limitations on spending by parties. While our cases uphold contribution limitations on individuals and associations, political party spending "in cooperation, consultation, or concert with" a candidate does not fit within our description of "contributions" in *Buckley*. In my view, we should not transplant the reasoning of cases upholding ordinary contribution limitations to a case involving FECA's restrictions on political party spending.

The First Amendment embodies a "profound national commitment to the principle that debate on public issues should be uninhibited, robust, and wide-open." Political parties have a unique role in serving this principle; they exist to advance their members' shared political beliefs. . . . Having identified its members, however, a party can give effect to their views only by selecting and supporting candidates. A political party has its own traditions and principles that transcend the interests of individual candidates and campaigns; but in the context of particular elections, candidates are necessary to make the party's message known and effective, and vice versa.

It makes no sense, therefore, to ask, as FECA does, whether a party's spending is made "in cooperation, consultation, or concert with" its candidate. The answer in most cases will be yes, but that provides more, not less, justification for holding unconstitutional the statute's attempt to control this type of party spending, which bears little resemblance to the contributions discussed in *Buckley*. Party spending "in cooperation, consultation, or concert with" its candidates of necessity "communicate[s] the underlying basis for the support," *i. e.,* the hope that he or she will be elected and will work to further the party's political agenda. . . .

We have a constitutional tradition of political parties and their candidates engaging in joint First Amendment activity; we also have a practical identity of interests between the two entities during an election. Party spending "in cooperation, consultation, or concert with" a candidate therefore is indistinguishable in substance from expenditures by the candidate or his campaign committee. We held in *Buckley* that the First Amendment does not permit regulation of the latter, and it should not permit this regulation of the former. . . .

I would resolve the Party's First Amendment claim in accord with these principles rather than remit the Party to further protracted proceedings. Because the plurality would do otherwise, I concur only in the judgment.

JUSTICE THOMAS, concurring in the judgment and dissenting in part, with whom THE CHIEF JUSTICE and JUSTICE SCALIA join in Parts I and III.

I agree that petitioners' rights under the First Amendment have been violated, but I think we should reach the facial challenge in this case in order to make clear the circumstances under which political parties may engage in political speech without running afoul of 2 U.S.C. §441a(d)(3). In resolving that challenge, I would reject the framework established by *Buckley* v. *Valeo* (1976) for analyzing the constitutionality of campaign finance laws and hold that §441a(d)(3)'s limits on independent and coordinated expenditures fail strict scrutiny. But even under *Buckley*, §441a(d)(3) cannot stand, because the anti-corruption rationale that we have relied upon in sustaining other campaign finance laws is inapplicable where political parties are the subject of such regulation.

I

As an initial matter, I write to make clear that we should decide the Party's facial challenge to §441a(d)(3) and thus address the constitutionality of limits on coordinated expenditures by political parties. JUSTICE BREYER's reasons for not reaching the facial constitutionality of the statute are unpersuasive. In addition, concerns for the chilling of First Amendment expression counsel in favor of resolving that question. . . .

II

A

Critical to JUSTICE BREYER's reasoning is the distinction between contributions and independent expenditures that we first drew in *Buckley* v. *Valeo*. . . .

In my view, the distinction lacks constitutional significance, and I would not adhere to it. . . . Contributions and expenditures both involve core First Amendment expression because they further the "[d]iscussion of public issues and debate on the qualifications of candidates . . . integral to the operation of the system of government established by our Constitution." [*Buckley*]. . .

Giving and spending in the electoral process also involve basic associational rights under the First Amendment. . . . Political associations allow citizens to pool their resources and make their advocacy more effective, and such efforts are fully protected by the First Amendment. If an individual is limited in the amount of resources he can contribute to the pool, he is most certainly limited in his ability to associate for purposes of effective advocacy. And if an individual cannot be subject to such limits, neither can political associations be limited in their ability to give as a means of furthering their members' viewpoints. . . .

Turning from similarities to differences, I can discern only one potentially meaningful distinction between contributions and expenditures. In the former case, the funds pass through an intermediary—some individual or entity responsible for organizing and facilitating the dissemination of the message—whereas in the latter case they may not necessarily do so. But the practical judgment by a citizen that another person or an organization can more effectively deploy funds for the good of a common cause than he can ought not deprive that citizen of his First Amendment rights. Whether an individual donates money to a candidate or group who will use it to promote the candidate or whether the individual spends the money to promote the candidate himself, the individual seeks to engage in political expression and to associate with likeminded persons. A contribution is simply an indirect expenditure; though contributions and expenditures may thus differ in form, they do not differ in substance. . . .

The other justification in *Buckley* for the proposition that contribution caps only marginally restrict speech—that is, that a contribution signals only general support for the candidate but indicates nothing about the reasons for that support—is similarly unsatisfying. Assuming the assertion is descriptively accurate . . . , it still cannot mean that giving is less important than spending in terms of the First Amendment. A campaign poster that reads simply "We support candidate Smith" does not seem to me any less deserving of constitutional protection than one that reads "We support candidate Smith because we like his position on agriculture subsidies." Both express a political opinion. Even a pure message of support, unadorned with reasons, is valuable to the democratic process.

In sum, unlike the *Buckley* Court, I believe that contribution limits infringe as directly and as seriously upon freedom of political expression and association as do expenditure limits. . . . [P]eople and groups give money to candidates and other groups for the same reason that they spend money in support of those candidates and groups: because they share social, economic, and political beliefs and seek to have those beliefs affect governmental policy. I think that the *Buckley* framework for analyzing the constitutionality of campaign finance laws is deeply flawed. Accordingly, I would not employ it, as JUSTICE BREYER and JUSTICE KENNEDY do.

B

Instead, I begin with the premise that there is no constitutionally significant difference between campaign contributions and expenditures: both forms of speech are central to the First Amendment. Curbs on protected speech, we have repeatedly said, must be strictly scrutinized. I am convinced that under traditional strict scrutiny, broad prophylactic caps on both spending and giving in the political process, like §441a(d)(3), are unconstitutional.

The formula for strict scrutiny is, of course, well-established. It requires both a compelling governmental interest and legislative means narrowly tailored to serve that interest. In the context of campaign finance reform, the only governmental interest that we have accepted as compelling is the prevention of corruption or the appearance of corruption, and we have narrowly defined "corruption" as a "financial quid pro quo: dollars for political favors." As for the means-ends fit under strict scrutiny, we have specified that "[w]here at all possible, government must curtail speech only to the degree necessary to meet the particular problem at hand, and must avoid infringing on speech that does not pose the danger that has prompted regulation."

In *Buckley*, we expressly stated that the means adopted must be "closely drawn to avoid unnecessary abridgment" of First Amendment rights. But the *Buckley* Court summarily rejected the argument that, because less restrictive means of preventing corruption existed—for instance, bribery laws and disclosure requirements—FECA's contribution provisions were invalid. . . .

In my opinion, FECA's monetary caps fail the narrow tailoring test. . . . Broad prophylactic bans on campaign expenditures and contributions are not designed with the precision required by the First Amendment because they sweep protected speech within their prohibitions.

Section 441a(d)(3), in particular, suffers from this infirmity. It flatly bans all expenditures by all national and state party committees in excess of certain dollar limits without any evidence that covered committees who exceed those limits are in fact engaging, or likely to engage, in bribery or anything resembling it. . . . Thus, the statute indiscriminately covers the many conceivable instances in which a party committee could exceed the spending limits without any intent to extract an unlawful commitment from a candidate. . . .

In contrast, federal bribery laws are designed to punish and deter the corrupt conduct the Government seeks to prevent under FECA, and disclosure laws work to make donors and donees accountable to the public for any questionable financial dealings in which they may engage. . . . In light of these alternatives, wholesale limitations that cover contributions having nothing to do with bribery—but with speech central to the First Amendment—are not narrowly tailored. . . .

III

Were I convinced that the *Buckley* framework rested on a principled distinction between contributions and expenditures, which I am not, I would nevertheless conclude that §441a(d)(3)'s limits on political parties violate the First Amendment. Under *Buckley* and its progeny, a substantial threat of corruption must exist before a law purportedly aimed at the prevention of corruption will be sustained against First Amendment attack. Just as some of the monetary limits in the *Buckley* line of cases were held to be invalid because the government interest in stemming corruption was inadequate under the circumstances to justify the restrictions on speech, so too is §441a(d)(3) invalid.

The Government asserts that the purpose of §441a(d)(3) is to prevent the corruption of candidates and elected representatives by party officials. . . .

As applied in the specific context of campaign funding by political parties, the anti-corruption rationale loses its force. What could it mean for a party to "corrupt" its candidate or to exercise "coercive" influence over him? . . . For instance, if the Democratic Party spends large sums of money in support of a candidate who wins, takes office, and then implements the Party's platform, that is not corruption; that is successful advocacy of ideas in the political marketplace and representative government in a party system. . . .

In sum, there is only a minimal threat of "corruption" . . . when a political party spends to support its candidate or to oppose his competitor, whether or not that expenditure is made in concert with the candidate. Parties and candidates have traditionally worked together to achieve their common goals, and when they engage in that work, there is no risk to the Republic. To the contrary, the danger to the Republic lies in Government suppression of such activity. Under *Buckley* and our subsequent cases, §441a(d)(3)'s heavy burden on First Amendment rights is not justified by the threat of corruption at which it is assertedly aimed.

* * *

To conclude, I would find §441a(d)(3) unconstitutional not just as applied to petitioners, but also on its face. Accordingly, I concur only in the Court's judgment.

JUSTICE STEVENS, with whom JUSTICE GINSBURG joins, dissenting.

In my opinion, all money spent by a political party to secure the election of its candidate for the office of United States Senator should be considered a "contribution" to his or her campaign. I therefore disagree with the conclusion reached in Part III of the Court's opinion.

I am persuaded that three interests provide a constitutionally sufficient predicate for federal limits on spending by political parties. First, such limits serve the interest in avoiding both the appearance and the reality of a corrupt political process. A party shares a unique relationship with the candidate it sponsors because their political fates are inextricably linked. That interdependency creates a special danger that the party—or the persons who control the party—will abuse the influence it has over the candidate by virtue of its power to spend. The provisions at issue are appropriately aimed at reducing that threat. . . .

Second, these restrictions supplement other spending limitations embodied in the Act, which are likewise designed to prevent corruption. Individuals and certain organizations are permitted to contribute up to $1,000 to a candidate. Since the same donors can give up to $5,000 to party committees, if there were no limits on party spending, their contributions could be spent to benefit the candidate and thereby circumvent the $1,000 cap. We have recognized the legitimate interest in blocking similar attempts to undermine the policies of the

Act. See *California Medical Assn.* v. *Federal Election Comm'n* (1981) (approving ceiling on contributions to political action committees to prevent circumvention of limitations on individual contributions to candidates); *Buckley* v. *Valeo* (1976) (approving limitation on total contributions by an individual in connection with an election on same rationale).

Finally, I believe the Government has an important interest in leveling the electoral playing field by constraining the cost of federal campaigns. . . . It is quite wrong to assume that the net effect of limits on contributions and expenditures—which tend to protect equal access to the political arena, to free candidates and their staffs from the interminable burden of fund-raising, and to diminish the importance of repetitive 30-second commercials—will be adverse to the interest in informed debate protected by the First Amendment.

Congress surely has both wisdom and experience in these matters that is far superior to ours. I would therefore accord special deference to its judgment on questions related to the extent and nature of limits on campaign spending. Accordingly, I would affirm the judgment of the Court of Appeals.

□ □ □

Nos. 94-1941 and 94-2107

United States, Petitioner v. Virginia et al.

Virginia, et al., Petitioners v. United States

On writs of certiorari to the United States Court of Appeals
for the Fourth Circuit

[June 26, 1996]

JUSTICE GINSBURG delivered the opinion of the Court.

Virginia's public institutions of higher learning include an incomparable military college, Virginia Military Institute (VMI). The United States maintains that the Constitution's equal protection guarantee precludes Virginia from reserving exclusively to men the unique educational opportunities VMI affords. We agree.

I

Founded in 1839, VMI is today the sole single-sex school among Virginia's 15 public institutions of higher learning. VMI's distinctive mission is to produce "citizen-soldiers," men prepared for leadership in civilian life and in military service. VMI pursues this mission through pervasive training of a kind not available anywhere else in Virginia. Assigning prime place to character development, VMI uses an "adversative method" modeled on English public schools and once characteristic of military instruction. VMI constantly endeavors to instill physical and mental discipline in its cadets and impart to them a strong moral code. The school's graduates leave VMI with heightened comprehension of their capacity to deal with duress and stress, and a large sense of accomplishment for completing the hazardous course.

VMI has notably succeeded in its mission to produce leaders; among its alumni are military generals, Members of Congress, and business executives. The school's alumni overwhelmingly perceive that their VMI training helped them to realize their personal goals. VMI's endowment reflects the loyalty of its graduates; VMI has the largest per-student endowment of all [public] undergraduate institutions in the Nation.

Neither the goal of producing citizen-soldiers nor VMI's implementing methodology is inherently unsuitable to women. And the school's impressive record in producing leaders has made admission desirable to some women. Nevertheless, Virginia has elected to preserve exclusively for men the advantages and opportunities a VMI education affords.

II

A

From its establishment in 1839 as one of the Nation's first state military colleges, VMI has remained financially supported by Virginia and "subject to the control of the [Virginia] General Assembly.". . .

VMI today enrolls about 1,300 men as cadets. Its academic offerings in the liberal arts, sciences, and engineering are also available at other public colleges and universities in Virginia. But VMI's mission is special. It is the mission of the school

> " 'to produce educated and honorable men, prepared for the varied work of civil life, imbued with love of learning, confident in the functions and attitudes of leadership, possessing a high sense of public service, advocates of the American democracy and free enterprise system, and ready as citizen-soldiers to defend their country in time of national peril.' " [Excerpt from the 1991 district court opinion, quoting Mission Study Committee of the VMI Board of Visitors, Report, May 16, 1986.]

In contrast to the federal service academies, institutions maintained "to prepare cadets for career service in the armed forces," VMI's program "is directed at preparation for both military and civilian life"; "[o]nly about 15% of VMI cadets enter career military service."

VMI produces its "citizen-soldiers" through "an adversarial, or doubting, model of education" which features "[p]hysical rigor, mental stress, absolute equality of treatment, absence of privacy, minute regulation of behavior, and indoctrination in desirable values.". . .

VMI cadets live in spartan barracks where surveillance is constant and privacy nonexistent; they wear uniforms, eat together in the mess hall, and regularly participate in drills. Entering students are incessantly exposed to the rat line, "an extreme form of the adversarial model," comparable in intensity to Marine Corps boot camp. Tormenting and punishing, the rat line bonds new cadets to their fellow sufferers and, when they have completed the 7-month experience, to their former tormentors.

VMI's "adversative model" is further characterized by a hierarchical "class system" of privileges and responsibilities, a "dyke system" for assigning a senior class mentor to each entering class "rat," and a stringently enforced "honor code," which prescribes that a cadet " 'does not lie, cheat, steal nor tolerate those who do.' "

VMI attracts some applicants because of its reputation as an extraordinarily challenging military school, and "because its alumni are exceptionally close to the school." "[W]omen have no opportunity anywhere to gain the benefits of [the system of education at VMI]."

B

In 1990, prompted by a complaint filed with the Attorney General by a female high-school student seeking admission to VMI, the United States sued the Commonwealth of Virginia and VMI, alleging that VMI's exclusively male admission policy violated the Equal Protection Clause of the Fourteenth Amendment. Trial of the action consumed six days and involved an array of expert witnesses on each side.

In the two years preceding the lawsuit, the District Court noted, VMI had received inquiries from 347 women, but had responded to none of them. "[S]ome women, at least," the court said, "would want to attend the school if they had the opportunity." The court further recognized that, with recruitment, VMI could "achieve at least 10% female enrollment"—"a sufficient 'critical mass' to provide the female cadets with a positive educational experience." And it was also established that "some women are capable of all of the individual activities required of VMI cadets." In addition, experts agreed that if VMI admitted women, "the VMI ROTC experience would become a better training program from the perspective of the armed forces, because it would provide training in dealing with a mixed-gender army."

The District Court ruled in favor of VMI, however, and rejected the equal protection challenge pressed by the United States. That court correctly recognized that *Mississippi Univ. for Women* v. *Hogan* (1982) was the closest guide. There, this Court underscored that a party seeking to uphold government action based on sex must establish an "exceedingly persuasive justification" for the classification. To succeed, the defender of the challenged action must show "at least that the classification serves important governmental objectives and that the discriminatory means employed are substantially related to the achievement of those objectives."

The District Court reasoned that education in "a single-gender environment, be it male or female," yields substantial benefits. VMI's school for men brought diversity to an otherwise coeducational Virginia system, and that diversity was "enhanced by VMI's unique method of instruction.". . .

"Women are [indeed] denied a unique educational opportunity that is available only at VMI," the District Court acknowledged. But "[VMI's] single-sex status would be lost, and some aspects of the [school's] distinctive method would be altered" if women were admitted: "Allowance for personal privacy would have to be made"; "[p]hysical education requirements would have to be altered"; the adversative environment could not survive unmodified. Thus, "sufficient constitutional justification" had been shown, the District Court held, "for continuing [VMI's] single-sex policy."

The Court of Appeals for the Fourth Circuit disagreed and vacated the District Court's judgment. The appellate court held: "The Commonwealth of Virginia has not . . . advanced any state policy by which it can justify its determination, under an announced policy of diversity, to afford VMI's unique type of program to men and not to women." (1992).

The appeals court greeted with skepticism Virginia's assertion that it offers single-sex education at VMI as a facet of the State's overarching and undisputed policy to advance "autonomy and diversity.". . . [T]he court concluded, "[a] policy of diversity which aims to provide an array of educational opportunities, including single-gender institutions, must do more than favor one gender."

. . . The Court of Appeals, however, accepted the District Court's finding that "at least these three aspects of VMI's program—physical training, the absence of privacy, and the adversative approach—would be materially affected by coeducation." Remanding the case, the appeals court assigned to Virginia, in the first instance, responsibility for selecting a remedial course. The court suggested these options for the State: Admit women to VMI; establish parallel institutions or programs; or abandon state support, leaving VMI free to pursue its policies as a private institution. . . .

C

In response to the Fourth Circuit's ruling, Virginia proposed a parallel program for women: Virginia Women's Institute for Leadership (VWIL). The 4-year, state-sponsored undergraduate program would be located at Mary Baldwin College, a private liberal arts school for women, and would be open, initially, to about 25 to 30 students. Although VWIL would share VMI's mission—to produce "citizen-soldiers"—the VWIL program would differ . . . from VMI in academic offerings, methods of education, and financial resources. [Referencing 1994 district court opinion.]. . .

Experts in educating women at the college level composed the Task Force charged with designing the VWIL program; Task Force members were drawn from Mary Baldwin's own faculty and staff. Training its attention on methods of instruction appropriate for "most women," the Task Force determined that a military model would be "wholly inappropriate" for VWIL.

. . . Virginia represented that it will provide equal financial support for in-state VWIL students and VMI cadets, and the VMI Foundation agreed to supply a $5.4625 million endowment for the VWIL program. Mary Baldwin's own endowment is about $19 million; VMI's is $131 million. Mary Baldwin will add $35 million to its endowment based on future commitments; VMI will add $220 million. The VMI Alumni Association has developed a network of employers interested in hiring VMI graduates. The Association has agreed to open its network to VWIL graduates, but those graduates will not have the advantage afforded by a VMI degree.

D

Virginia returned to the District Court seeking approval of its proposed remedial plan, and the court decided the plan met the requirements of the

Equal Protection Clause. . . . The court anticipated that the two schools would "achieve substantially similar outcomes.". . .

A divided Court of Appeals affirmed the District Court's judgment. (1995). This time, the appellate court determined to give "greater scrutiny to the selection of means than to the [State's] proffered objective." The official objective or purpose, the court said, should be reviewed deferentially. Respect for the "legislative will," the court reasoned, meant that the judiciary should take a "cautious approach," inquiring into the "legitima[cy]" of the governmental objective and refusing approval for any purpose revealed to be "pernicious."

"[P]roviding the option of a single-gender college education may be considered a legitimate and important aspect of a public system of higher education," the appeals court observed; that objective, the court added, is "not pernicious." Moreover, the court continued, the adversative method vital to a VMI education "has never been tolerated in a sexually heterogeneous environment.". . . [W]omen could not be accommodated in the VMI program, the court believed, for female participation in VMI's adversative training "would destroy . . . any sense of decency that still permeates the relationship between the sexes."

Having determined, deferentially, the legitimacy of Virginia's purpose, the court considered the question of means. Exclusion of "men at Mary Baldwin College and women at VMI," the court said, was essential to Virginia's purpose, for without such exclusion, the State could not "accomplish [its] objective of providing single-gender education."

. . . The court . . . added another inquiry, a decisive test it called "substantive comparability." The key question, the court said, was whether men at VMI and women at VWIL would obtain "substantively comparable benefits at their institution or through other means offered by the [S]tate." Although the appeals court recognized that the VWIL degree "lacks the historical benefit and prestige" of a VMI degree, it nevertheless found the educational opportunities at the two schools "sufficiently comparable."

Senior Circuit Judge Phillips dissented. The court, in his judgment, had not held Virginia to the burden of showing an " 'exceedingly persuasive [justification]' " for the State's action. . . .

Judge Phillips suggested that the State would satisfy the Constitution's equal protection requirement if it "simultaneously opened single-gender undergraduate institutions having substantially comparable curricular and extra-curricular programs, funding, physical plant, administration and support services, and faculty and library resources." But he thought it evident that the proposed VWIL program, in comparison to VMI, fell "far short . . . from providing substantially equal tangible and intangible educational benefits to men and women."

The Fourth Circuit denied rehearing en banc. (1995). Judge Motz, joined by Circuit Judges Hall, Murnaghan, and Michael, filed a dissenting opinion. Judge Motz agreed with Judge Phillips that Virginia had not shown an " 'exceedingly persuasive justification' " for the disparate opportunities the State supported. . . .

III

The cross-petitions in this case present two ultimate issues. First, does Virginia's exclusion of women from the educational opportunities provided by VMI—extraordinary opportunities for military training and civilian leadership development—deny to women "capable of all of the individual activities required of VMI cadets," the equal protection of the laws guaranteed by the Fourteenth Amendment? Second, if VMI's "unique" situation—as Virginia's sole single-sex public institution of higher education—offends the Constitution's equal protection principle, what is the remedial requirement?

IV

We note, once again, the core instruction of this Court's pathmarking decisions in *J. E. B.* v. *Alabama ex rel. T. B.* (1994) and *Mississippi Univ. for Women*: Parties who seek to defend gender-based government action must demonstrate an "exceedingly persuasive justification" for that action.

Today's skeptical scrutiny of official action denying rights or opportunities based on sex responds to volumes of history. As a plurality of this Court acknowledged a generation ago, "our Nation has had a long and unfortunate history of sex discrimination." *Frontiero* v. *Richardson* (1973). Through a century plus three decades and more of that history, women did not count among voters composing "We the People"; not until 1920 did women gain a constitutional right to the franchise. And for a half century thereafter, it remained the prevailing doctrine that government, both federal and state, could withhold from women opportunities accorded men so long as any "basis in reason" could be conceived for the discrimination. . . .

In 1971, for the first time in our Nation's history, this Court ruled in favor of a woman who complained that her State had denied her the equal protection of its laws. *Reed* v. *Reed* (holding unconstitutional Idaho Code prescription that, among " 'several persons claiming and equally entitled to administer [a decedent's estate], males must be preferred to females' "). Since *Reed*, the Court has repeatedly recognized that neither federal nor state government acts compatibly with the equal protection principle when a law or official policy denies to women, simply because they are women, full citizenship stature— equal opportunity to aspire, achieve, participate in and contribute to society based on their individual talents and capacities. [Citation of cases omitted.]

Without equating gender classifications, for all purposes, to classifications based on race or national origin, the Court, in post-*Reed* decisions, has carefully inspected official action that closes a door or denies opportunity to women (or to men). . . . To summarize the Court's current directions for cases of official classification based on gender: Focusing on the differential treatment or denial of opportunity for which relief is sought, the reviewing court must determine whether the proffered justification is "exceedingly persuasive." The burden of justification is demanding and it rests entirely on the State. The State must show "at least that the [challenged] classification serves 'important governmental objectives and that the discriminatory means employed' are 'substantially related to the achievement of those objectives.'" The justification must be genuine, not hypothesized or invented *post hoc* in response to litigation. And it must not rely on overbroad generalizations about the different talents, capacities, or preferences of males and females.

The heightened review standard our precedent establishes does not make sex a proscribed classification. . . .

"Inherent differences" between men and women, we have come to appreciate, remain cause for celebration, but not for denigration of the members of either sex or for artificial constraints on an individual's opportunity. Sex classifications may be used to compensate women "for particular economic disabilities [they have] suffered," *Califano* v. *Webster* (1977), to "promot[e] equal employment opportunity," *California Federal Sav. & Loan Assn.* v. *Guerra* (1987), to advance full development of the talent and capacities of our Nation's people. But such classifications may not be used, as they once were, to create or perpetuate the legal, social, and economic inferiority of women.

Measuring the record in this case against the review standard just described, we conclude that Virginia has shown no "exceedingly persuasive justification" for excluding all women from the citizen-soldier training afforded by VMI. We therefore affirm the Fourth Circuit's initial judgment, which held that Virginia had violated the Fourteenth Amendment's Equal Protection Clause. Because the remedy proffered by Virginia—the Mary Baldwin VWIL program—does not cure the constitutional violation, *i.e.*, it does not provide equal opportunity, we reverse the Fourth Circuit's final judgment in this case.

V

The Fourth Circuit initially held that Virginia had advanced no state policy by which it could justify, under equal protection principles, its determination "to afford VMI's unique type of program to men and not to women." Virginia challenges that "liability" ruling and asserts two justifications in defense of VMI's exclusion of women. First, the Commonwealth contends, "single-sex education provides important educational benefits," and the option of single-sex education contributes to "diversity in educational approaches." Second, the Commonwealth argues, "the unique VMI method of character development and leadership training," the school's adversative approach, would have to be modified were VMI to admit women. We consider these two justifications in turn.

A

Single-sex education affords pedagogical benefits to at least some students, Virginia emphasizes, and that reality is uncontested in this litigation. Similarly, it is not disputed that diversity among public educational institutions can serve the public good. But Virginia has not shown that VMI was established, or has been maintained, with a view to diversifying, by its categorical exclusion of women, educational opportunities within the State. . . .

Neither recent nor distant history bears out Virginia's alleged pursuit of diversity through single-sex educational options. [Ginsburg noted that at the time of VMI's establishment, Virginia offered no public higher education opportunities for women. The University of Virginia, founded in 1819, did not admit women until 1972. Several women's seminaries and colleges were established between 1884 and 1910, she said; all have since become coeducational.]

Our 1982 decision in *Mississippi Univ. for Women* prompted VMI to reexamine its male-only admission policy. Virginia relies on that reexamination as a legitimate basis for maintaining VMI's single-sex character. A Mission Study Committee, appointed by the VMI Board of Visitors, studied the problem from October 1983 until May 1986, and in that month counseled against "change of VMI status as a single-sex college." Whatever internal purpose the Mission Study Committee served—and however well-meaning the framers of the report—we can hardly extract from that effort any state policy evenhandedly to advance diverse educational options. As the District Court observed, the Committee's analysis "primarily focuse[d] on anticipated difficulties in attracting females to VMI," and the report, overall, supplied "very little indication of how th[e] conclusion was reached."

In sum, we find no persuasive evidence in this record that VMI's male-only admission policy "is in furtherance of a state policy of 'diversity.' " No such policy, the Fourth Circuit observed, can be discerned from the movement of all other public colleges and universities in Virginia away from single-sex education. That court also questioned "how one institution with autonomy, but with no authority over any other state institution, can give effect to a state policy of diversity among institutions." A purpose genuinely to advance an array of educational options, as the Court of Appeals recognized, is not served by VMI's historic and constant plan—a plan to "affor[d] a unique educational benefit only to males." However "liberally" this plan serves the State's sons, it makes no provision whatever for her daughters. That is not *equal* protection.

B

Virginia next argues that VMI's adversative method of training provides educational benefits that cannot be made available, unmodified, to women. Alterations to accommodate women would necessarily be "radical," so "drastic," Virginia asserts, as to transform, indeed "destroy," VMI's program. Neither sex would be favored by the transformation, Virginia maintains: Men would be deprived of the unique opportunity currently available to them; women would not gain that opportunity because their participation would "eliminat[e] the very aspects of [the] program that distinguish [VMI] from . . . other institutions of higher education in Virginia."

The District Court forecast from expert witness testimony, and the Court of Appeals accepted, that coeducation would materially affect "at least these three aspects of VMI's program—physical training, the absence of privacy, and the adversative approach." And it is uncontested that women's admission would require accommodations, primarily in arranging housing assignments and physical training programs for female cadets. It is also undisputed, however, that "the VMI methodology could be used to educate women.". . . The parties, furthermore, agree that "*some* women can meet the physical standards [VMI] now impose[s] on men." In sum, as the Court of Appeals stated, "neither the goal of producing citizen soldiers," VMI's *raison d'être*, "nor VMI's implementing methodology is inherently unsuitable to women."

In support of its initial judgment for Virginia, . . . the District Court made "findings" on "gender-based developmental differences." These "findings" restate the opinions of Virginia's expert witnesses, opinions about typically male or typically female "tendencies." For example, "[m]ales tend to need an atmosphere of adversativeness," while "[f]emales tend to thrive in a cooperative atmosphere.". . .

It may be assumed, for purposes of this decision, that most women would not choose VMI's adversative method. As Fourth Circuit Judge Motz observed, however, in her dissent from the Court of Appeals' denial of rehearing en banc, it is also probable that "many men would not want to be educated in such an environment.". . . The issue, however, is not whether "women—or men—should be forced to attend VMI"; rather, the question is whether the State can constitutionally deny to women who have the will and capacity, the training and attendant opportunities that VMI uniquely affords. The notion that admission of women would downgrade VMI's stature, destroy the adversative system and, with it, even the school, is a judgment hardly proved, a prediction hardly different from other "self-fulfilling prophec[ies]," once routinely used to deny rights or opportunities. . . .

Women's successful entry into the federal military academies, and their participation in the Nation's military forces, indicate that Virginia's fears for the future of VMI may not be solidly grounded. The State's justification for excluding all women from "citizen-soldier" training for which some are qualified, in any event, cannot rank as "exceedingly persuasive," as we have explained and applied that standard.

Virginia and VMI trained their argument on "means" rather than "end," and thus misperceived our precedent. Single-sex education at VMI serves an "important governmental objective," they maintained, and exclusion of women is not only "substantially related," it is essential to that objective. By this notably circular argument, the "straightforward" test *Mississippi Univ. for Women* described, was bent and bowed.

The State's misunderstanding and, in turn, the District Court's, is apparent from VMI's mission: to produce "citizen-soldiers," individuals

> " 'imbued with love of learning, confident in the functions and attitudes of leadership, possessing a high sense of public service, advocates of the American democracy and free enterprise system, and ready . . . to defend their country in time of national peril.' " (quoting Mission Study Committee of the VMI Board of Visitors, Report, May 16, 1986).

Surely that goal is great enough to accommodate women, who today count as citizens in our American democracy equal in stature to men. Just as surely, the State's great goal is not substantially advanced by women's categorical exclusion, in total disregard of their individual merit, from the State's premier "citizen-soldier" corps. Virginia, in sum, "has fallen far short of establishing the 'exceedingly persuasive justification' " that must be the solid base for any gender-defined classification.

VI

In the second phase of the litigation, Virginia presented its remedial plan—maintain VMI as a male-only college and create VWIL as a separate program for women. The plan met District Court approval. The Fourth Circuit, in turn, deferentially reviewed the State's proposal and decided that the two single-sex programs directly served Virginia's reasserted purposes: single-gender education, and "achieving the results of an adversative method in a military environment." Inspecting the VMI and VWIL educational programs to determine whether they "afford[ed] to both genders benefits comparable in substance, [if] not in form and detail," the Court of Appeals concluded that Virginia had arranged for men and women opportunities "sufficiently comparable" to survive equal protection evaluation. The United States challenges this "remedial" ruling as pervasively misguided.

A

A remedial decree, this Court has said, must closely fit the constitutional violation; it must be shaped to place persons unconstitutionally denied an opportunity or advantage in "the position they would have occupied in the absence of [discrimination]." The constitutional violation in this case is the categorical exclusion of women from an extraordinary educational opportunity afforded men. A proper remedy for an unconstitutional exclusion, we have explained, aims to "eliminate [so far as possible] the discriminatory effects of the past" and to "bar like discrimination in the future."

Virginia chose not to eliminate, but to leave untouched, VMI's exclusionary policy. For women only, however, Virginia proposed a separate program, different in kind from VMI and unequal in tangible and intangible facilities. Having violated the Constitution's equal protection requirement, Virginia was obliged to show that its remedial proposal "directly address[ed] and relate[d] to" the violation, *i.e.,* the equal protection denied to women ready, willing, and able to benefit from educational opportunities of the kind VMI offers. . . .

VWIL affords women no opportunity to experience the rigorous military training for which VMI is famed. . . . Instead, the VWIL program "deemphasize[s]" military education and uses a "cooperative method" of education "which reinforces self-esteem."

VWIL students participate in ROTC and a "largely ceremonial" Virginia Corps of Cadets, but Virginia deliberately did not make VWIL a military institute. The VWIL House is not a military-style residence and VWIL students need not live together throughout the 4-year program, eat meals together, or wear uniforms during the school day. . . . "[T]he most important aspects of the VMI educational experience occur in the barracks," the District Court found, yet Virginia deemed that core experience nonessential, indeed inappropriate, for training its female citizen-soldiers.

VWIL students receive their "leadership training" in seminars, externships, and speaker series, episodes and encounters lacking the "[p]hysical rigor, mental stress, . . . minute regulation of behavior, and indoctrination in desirable values" made hallmarks of VMI's citizen-soldier training. Kept away from the pressures, hazards, and psychological bonding characteristic of VMI's adversative training, VWIL students will not know the "feeling of tremendous accomplishment" commonly experienced by VMI's successful cadets.

Virginia maintains that these methodological differences are "justified pedagogically," based on "important differences between men and women in learning and developmental needs," "psychological and sociological differences" Virginia describes as "real" and "not stereotypes.". . .

. . . [G]eneralizations about "the way women are," estimates of what is appropriate for most women, no longer justify denying opportunity to women whose talent and capacity place them outside the average description. . . .

In contrast to the generalizations about women on which Virginia rests, we note again these dispositive realties: VMI's "implementing methodology" is not "inherently unsuitable to women"; "some women . . . do well under [the] adversative model;" "some women, at least, would want to attend [VMI] if they had the opportunity;" "some women are capable of all of the individual activities required of VMI cadets" and "can meet the physical standards [VMI] now impose[s] on men." It is on behalf of these women that the United States has instituted this suit, and it is for them that a remedy must be crafted, a remedy that will end their exclusion from a state-supplied educational opportunity for which they are fit, a decree that will "bar like discrimination in the future."

B

In myriad respects other than military training, VWIL does not qualify as VMI's equal. VWIL's student body, faculty, course offerings, and facilities hardly match VMI's. Nor can the VWIL graduate anticipate the benefits associated with VMI's 157-year history, the school's prestige, and its influential alumni network.

Mary Baldwin College, whose degree VWIL students will gain, enrolls first-year women with an average combined SAT score about 100 points lower than the average score for VMI freshmen. The Mary Baldwin faculty holds "significantly fewer Ph.D.'s" and receives substantially lower salaries than the faculty at VMI.

Mary Baldwin does not offer a VWIL student the range of curricular choices available to a VMI cadet. VMI awards baccalaureate degrees in liberal arts, biology, chemistry, civil engineering, electrical and computer engineering, and mechanical engineering. VWIL students attend a school that "does not have a math and science focus"; they cannot take at Mary Baldwin any courses in engineering or the advanced math and physics courses VMI offers.

For physical training, Mary Baldwin has "two multipurpose fields" and "[o]ne gymnasium." VMI has "an NCAA competition level indoor track and field facility; a number of multi-purpose fields; baseball, soccer and lacrosse fields; an obstacle course; large boxing, wrestling and martial arts facilities; an 11-laps-to-the-mile indoor running course; an indoor pool; indoor and outdoor rifle ranges; and a football stadium that also contains a practice field and outdoor track."

Although Virginia has represented that it will provide equal financial support for in-state VWIL students and VMI cadets, and the VMI Foundation has agreed to endow VWIL with $5.4625 million, the difference between the two schools' financial reserves is pronounced. Mary Baldwin's endowment, currently about $19 million, will gain an additional $35 million based on future commitments; VMI's current endowment, $131 million . . . will gain $220 million.

The VWIL student does not graduate with the advantage of a VMI degree. Her diploma does not unite her with the legions of VMI "graduates [who] have distinguished themselves" in military and civilian life. . . . A VWIL graduate cannot assume that the "network of business owners, corporations, VMI graduates and non-graduate employers . . . interested in hiring VMI graduates" will be equally responsive to her search for employment. . . .

Virginia, in sum, while maintaining VMI for men only, has failed to provide any "comparable single-gender women's institution." Instead, the Commonwealth has created a VWIL program fairly appraised as a "pale shadow" of VMI in terms of the range of curricular choices and faculty stature, funding, prestige, alumni support and influence. . . .

. . . [W]e rule here that Virginia has not shown substantial equality in the separate educational opportunities the State supports at VWIL and VMI.

C

When Virginia tendered its VWIL plan, the Fourth Circuit did not inquire whether the proposed remedy . . . placed women denied the VMI advantage in "the position they would have occupied in the absence of [discrimination]." Instead, the Court of Appeals considered whether the State could provide, with fidelity to the equal protection principle, separate and unequal educational programs for men and women. . . .

The Fourth Circuit plainly erred in exposing Virginia's VWIL plan to a deferential analysis, for "all gender-based classifications today" warrant "heightened scrutiny." Valuable as VWIL may prove for students who seek the program offered, Virginia's remedy affords no cure at all for the opportunities and advantages withheld from women who want a VMI education and can make the grade. In sum, Virginia's remedy does not match the constitutional violation; the State has shown no "exceedingly persuasive justification" for withholding from women qualified for the experience premier training of the kind VMI affords.

VII

. . . VMI . . . offers an educational opportunity no other Virginia institution provides, and the school's "prestige"—associated with its success in developing "citizen-soldiers"—is unequaled. Virginia has closed this facility to its daughters and, instead, has devised for them a "parallel program," with a faculty less impressively credentialed and less well paid, more limited course offerings, fewer opportunities for military training and for scientific specialization. VMI, beyond question, "possesses to a far greater degree" than the VWIL program "those qualities which are incapable of objective measurement but which make for greatness in a . . . school," including "position and influence of the alumni, standing in the community, traditions and prestige." [*Sweatt v. Painter* (1950).] Women seeking and fit for a VMI-quality education cannot be offered anything less, under the State's obligation to afford them genuinely equal protection.

A prime part of the history of our Constitution, historian Richard Morris recounted, is the story of the extension of constitutional rights and protections to people once ignored or excluded. VMI's story continued as our comprehension of "We the People" expanded. There is no reason to believe that the admission of women capable of all the activities required of VMI cadets would destroy the Institute rather than enhance its capacity to serve the "more perfect Union."

* * *

For the reasons stated, the initial judgment of the Court of Appeals (1992) is affirmed, the final judgment of the Court of Appeals (1995) is reversed, and the case is remanded for further proceedings consistent with this opinion.

It is so ordered.

JUSTICE THOMAS took no part in the consideration or decision of this case.

CHIEF JUSTICE REHNQUIST, concurring in judgment.

The Court holds first that Virginia violates the Equal Protection Clause by maintaining the Virginia Military Institute's (VMI's) all-male admissions policy, and second that establishing the Virginia Women's Institute for Leadership (VWIL) program does not remedy that violation. While I agree with these conclusions, I disagree with the Court's analysis and so I write separately.

I

Two decades ago in *Craig* v. *Boren* (1976), we announced that "[t]o withstand constitutional challenge, . . . classifications by gender must serve important governmental objectives and must be substantially related to achievement of those objectives." We have adhered to that standard of scrutiny ever since. [Citation of cases omitted.] While the majority adheres to this test today, it also says that the State must demonstrate an " 'exceedingly persuasive justification' " to support a gender-based classification. It is unfortunate that the Court thereby introduces an element of uncertainty respecting the appropriate test.

While terms like "important governmental objective" and "substantially related" are hardly models of precision, they have more content and specificity than does the phrase "exceedingly persuasive justification." That phrase is best confined, as it was first used, as an observation on the difficulty of meeting the applicable test, not as a formulation of the test itself. . . . To avoid introducing potential confusion, I would have adhered more closely to our traditional, "firmly established" standard that a gender-based classification "must bear a close and substantial relationship to important governmental objectives."

Our cases dealing with gender discrimination also require that the proffered purpose for the challenged law be the actual purpose. It is on this ground that the Court rejects the first of two justifications Virginia offers for VMI's single-sex admissions policy, namely, the goal of diversity among its public educational institutions. While I ultimately agree that the State has not carried the day with this justification, I disagree with the Court's method of analyzing the issue.

VMI was founded in 1839, and . . . admission was limited to men because under the then-prevailing view men, not women, were destined for higher education. However misguided this point of view may be by present-day standards, it surely was not unconstitutional in 1839. The adoption of the Fourteenth

Amendment, with its Equal Protection Clause, was nearly 30 years in the future. The interpretation of the Equal Protection Clause to require heightened scrutiny for gender discrimination was yet another century away.

Long after the adoption of the Fourteenth Amendment, and well into this century, legal distinctions between men and women were thought to raise no question under the Equal Protection Clause. . . .

Then, in 1971, we decided *Reed* v. *Reed*, which the Court correctly refers to as a seminal case. But its facts have nothing to do with admissions to any sort of educational institution. . . .

Even at the time of our decision in *Reed* v. *Reed*, therefore, Virginia and VMI were scarcely on notice that its holding would be extended across the constitutional board. They were entitled to believe that "one swallow doesn't make a summer" and await further developments. Those developments were 11 years in coming. In *Mississippi Univ. for Women* v. *Hogan* (1982), a case actually involving a single-sex admissions policy in higher education, the Court held that the exclusion of men from a nursing program violated the Equal Protection Clause. This holding did place Virginia on notice that VMI's men-only admissions policy was open to serious question.

The VMI Board of Visitors, in response, appointed a Mission Study Committee to examine "the legality and wisdom of VMI's single-sex policy in light of" *Hogan*. But the committee ended up cryptically recommending against changing VMI's status as a single-sex college. . . . The reasons given in the report for not changing the policy were the changes that admission of women to VMI would require, and the likely effect of those changes on the institution. That VMI would have to change is simply not helpful in addressing the constitutionality of the status after *Hogan*.

Before this Court, Virginia has sought to justify VMI's single-sex admissions policy primarily on the basis that diversity in education is desirable, and that while most of the public institutions of higher learning in the State are coeducational, there should also be room for single-sex institutions. I agree with the Court that there is scant evidence in the record that this was the real reason that Virginia decided to maintain VMI as men only. But, unlike the majority, I would consider only evidence that postdates our decision in *Hogan*, and would draw no negative inferences from the State's actions before that time. I think that after *Hogan*, the State was entitled to reconsider its policy with respect to VMI, and to not have earlier justifications, or lack thereof, held against it.

Even if diversity in educational opportunity were the State's actual objective, the State's position would still be problematic. The difficulty with its position is that the diversity benefited only one sex; there was single-sex public education available for men at VMI, but no corresponding single-sex public education available for women. When *Hogan* placed Virginia on notice that VMI's admissions policy possibly was unconstitutional, VMI could have dealt with the problem by admitting women; but its governing body felt strongly that the admission of women would have seriously harmed the institution's educational approach. Was there something else the State could have done to avoid an equal protection violation? Since the State did nothing, we do not have to definitively answer that question.

I do not think, however, that the State's options were as limited as the majority may imply. The Court cites, without expressly approving it, a statement from the opinion of the dissenting judge in the Court of Appeals, to the effect that the State could have "simultaneously opened single-gender undergraduate institutions having substantially comparable curricular and extra-curricular programs, funding, physical plant, administration and support services, and faculty and library resources." If this statement is thought to exclude other possibilities, it is too stringent a requirement. VMI had been in operation for over a century and a half, and had an established, successful and devoted group of alumni. No legislative wand could instantly call into existence a similar institution for women; and it would be a tremendous loss to scrap VMI's history and tradition. . . . Had Virginia made a genuine effort to devote comparable public resources to a facility for women, and followed through on such a plan, it might well have avoided an equal protection violation. I do not believe the State was faced with the stark choice of either admitting women to VMI, on the one hand, or abandoning VMI and starting from scratch for both men and women, on the other.

But . . . neither the governing board of VMI nor the State took any action after 1982. If diversity in the form of single-sex, as well as coeducational, institutions of higher learning were to be available to Virginians, that diversity had to be available to women as well as to men. . . .

Virginia offers a second justification for the single-sex admissions policy: maintenance of the adversative method. I agree with the Court that this justification does not serve an important governmental objective. A State does not have substantial interest in the adversative methodology unless it is pedagogically beneficial. While considerable evidence shows that a single-sex education is pedagogically beneficial for some students, and hence a State may have a valid interest in promoting that methodology, there is no similar evidence in the record that an adversative method is pedagogically beneficial or is any more likely to produce character traits than other methodologies.

II

The Court defines the constitutional violation in this case as "the categorical exclusion of women from an extraordinary educational opportunity afforded to men." By defining the violation in this way, and by emphasizing that a remedy for a constitutional violation must place the victims of discrimination in "the position they would have occupied in the absence of [discrimination]," the Court necessarily implies that the only adequate remedy would be the admission of women to the all-male institution. . . . I would not define the violation in this way; it is not the "exclusion of women" that violates the Equal Protection Clause, but the maintenance of an all-men school without providing any — much less a comparable — institution for women.

Accordingly, the remedy should not necessarily require either the admission of women to VMI, or the creation of a VMI clone for women. An adequate remedy in my opinion might be a demonstration by Virginia that its interest in educating men in a single-sex environment is matched by its interest in educating women in a single-sex institution. To demonstrate such, the State does not need to create two institutions with the same number of faculty PhD's, similar SAT scores, or comparable athletic fields. Nor would it necessarily require that the women's institution offer the same curriculum as the men's; one could be strong in computer science, the other could be strong in liberal arts. It would be a sufficient remedy, I think, if the two institutions offered the same quality of education and were of the same overall calibre.

If a state decides to create single-sex programs, the state would, I expect, consider the public's interest and demand in designing curricula. And rightfully so. But the state should avoid assuming demand based on stereotypes; it must not assume *a priori*, without evidence, that there would be no interest in a women's school of civil engineering, or in a men's school of nursing.

In the end, the women's institution Virginia proposes, VWIL, fails as a remedy, because it is distinctly inferior to the existing men's institution and will continue to be for the foreseeable future. VWIL simply is not, in any sense, the institution that VMI is. In particular, VWIL is a program appended to a private college, not a self-standing institution; and VWIL is substantially underfunded as compared to VMI. I therefore ultimately agree with the Court that Virginia has not provided an adequate remedy.

JUSTICE SCALIA, dissenting.

Today the Court shuts down an institution that has served the people of the Commonwealth of Virginia with pride and distinction for over a century and a half. To achieve that desired result, it rejects (contrary to our established practice) the factual findings of two courts below, sweeps aside the precedents of this Court, and ignores the history of our people. As to facts: it explicitly rejects the finding that there exist "gender-based developmental differences" supporting Virginia's restriction of the "adversative" method to only a men's institution, and the finding that the all-male composition of the Virginia Military Institute (VMI) is essential to that institution's character. As to precedent: it drastically revises our established standards for reviewing sex-based classifications. And as to history: it counts for nothing the long tradition, enduring down to the present, of men's military colleges supported by both States and the Federal Government.

Much of the Court's opinion is devoted to deprecating the closed-mindedness of our forebears with regard to women's education, and even with regard to the treatment of women in areas that have nothing to do with education. Closed-minded they were — as every age is, including our own, with regard to matters it cannot guess, because it simply does not consider them debatable. The virtue of a democratic system with a First Amendment is that it readily enables the people, over time, to be persuaded that what they took for granted is not so, and to change their laws accordingly. That system is destroyed if the smug assurances of each age are removed from the democratic process and written into the Constitution. So to counterbalance the Court's criticism of our ancestors, let me say a word in their praise: they left us free to change. The same cannot be said of this most illiberal Court, which has embarked on a course of inscribing one after another of the current preferences of the society (and in some cases only the counter-majoritarian preferences of the society's law-trained elite) into our Basic Law. Today it enshrines the notion that no substantial educational value is to be served by an all-men's military academy—so that the decision by the people of Virginia to maintain such an institution denies equal protection to women who cannot attend that institution but can attend others. Since it is entirely clear that the Constitution of the United States—the old one—takes no sides in this educational debate, I dissent.

I

I shall devote most of my analysis to evaluating the Court's opinion on the basis of our current equal-protection jurisprudence, which regards this Court as free to evaluate everything under the sun by applying one of three tests: "rational basis" scrutiny, intermediate scrutiny, or strict scrutiny. . . .

I have no problem with a system of abstract tests such as rational-basis, intermediate, and strict scrutiny. . . . But . . . it is my view that, whatever abstract tests we may choose to devise, they cannot supersede—and indeed ought to be crafted so as to reflect—those constant and unbroken national traditions that embody the people's understanding of ambiguous constitutional texts. . . .

The all-male constitution of VMI comes squarely within such a governing tradition. Founded by the Commonwealth of Virginia in 1839 and continuously maintained by it since, VMI has always admitted only men. And in that regard it has not been unusual. For almost all of VMI's more than a century and a half of existence, its single-sex status reflected the uniform practice for government-supported military colleges. Another famous Southern institution, The Citadel, has existed as a state-funded school of South Carolina since 1842. And all the federal military colleges—West Point, the Naval Academy at Annapolis, and even the Air Force Academy, which was not established until 1954—admitted only males for most of their history. Their admission of women in 1976 (upon which the Court today relies) came not by court decree, but because the people, through their elected representatives, decreed a change. In other words, the tradition of having government-funded military schools for men is as well rooted in the traditions of this country as the tradition of sending only men into military combat. The people may decide to change the one tradition, like the other, through democratic processes; but the assertion that either tradition has been unconstitutional through the centuries is not law, but politics-smuggled-into-law.

And the same applies, more broadly, to single-sex education in general, which, as I shall discuss, is threatened by today's decision with the cut-off of all state and federal support. Government-run nonmilitary educational institutions for the two sexes have until very recently also been part of our national tradition. . . . These traditions may of course be changed by the democratic decisions of the people, as they largely have been.

Today, however, change is forced upon Virginia, and reversion to single-sex education is prohibited nationwide, not by democratic processes but by order of this Court. Even while bemoaning the sorry, bygone days of "fixed notions" concerning women's education, the Court favors current notions so fixedly that it is willing to write them into the Constitution of the United States by application of custom-built "tests." This is not the interpretation of a Constitution, but the creation of one.

II

To reject the Court's disposition today, however, it is not necessary to accept my view that the Court's made-up tests cannot displace longstanding national traditions as the primary determinant of what the Constitution means. It is only necessary to apply honestly the test the Court has been applying to sex-based classifications for the past two decades. It is well settled, as JUSTICE O'CONNOR stated some time ago for a unanimous Court, that we evaluate a statutory classification based on sex under a standard that lies "[b]etween th[e] extremes of rational basis review and strict scrutiny." *Clark* v. *Jeter* [1988]. We have denominated this standard "intermediate scrutiny" and under it have inquired whether the statutory classification is "substantially related to an important governmental objective." [Citation of cases omitted.]

Before I proceed to apply this standard to VMI, I must comment upon the manner in which the Court avoids doing so. Notwithstanding our above-described precedents and their " 'firmly established principles,' " the United States urged us to hold in this case "that strict scrutiny is the correct constitutional standard for evaluating classifications that deny opportunities to individuals based on their sex.". . . The Court, while making no reference to the Government's argument, effectively accepts it.

Although the Court in two places recites the test as stated in [*Mississippi Univ. for Women* v.] *Hogan* [1982], which asks whether the State has demonstrated "that the classification serves important governmental objectives and that the discriminatory means employed are substantially related to the achievement of those objectives," the Court never answers the question presented in anything resembling that form. When it engages in analysis, the Court instead prefers the phrase "exceedingly persuasive justification" from *Hogan*. The Court's nine invocations of that phrase and even its fanciful description of that imponderable as "the core instruction" of the Court's decisions in *J. E. B.* v. *Alabama ex rel. T. B.* (1994) and *Hogan* would be unobjectionable if the Court acknowledged that *whether* a "justification" is "exceedingly persuasive" must be assessed by asking "[whether] the classification serves important governmental objectives and [whether] the discriminatory means employed are substantially related to the achievement of those objectives." Instead, however, the Court proceeds to interpret "exceedingly persuasive justification" in a fashion that contradicts the reasoning of *Hogan* and our other precedents. . . .

Only the amorphous "exceedingly persuasive justification" phrase, and not the standard elaboration of intermediate scrutiny, can be made to yield [the] conclusion that VMI's single-sex composition is unconstitutional because there exist several women (or, one would have to conclude under the Court's reasoning, a single woman) willing and able to undertake VMI's program. Intermediate scrutiny has never required a least-restrictive-means analysis, but only a "substantial relation" between the classification and the state interests that it serves. [Discussion of cases omitted.] There is simply no support in our cases for the notion that a sex-based classification is invalid unless it relates to characteristics that hold true in every instance. . . .

III

. . . I now proceed to describe how the analysis should have been conducted. The question to be answered, I repeat, is whether the exclusion of women from VMI is "substantially related to an important governmental objective."

A

It is beyond question that Virginia has an important state interest in providing effective college education for its citizens. That single-sex instruction is an approach substantially related to that interest should be evident enough from the long and continuing history in this country of men's and women's colleges. But beyond that, as the Court of Appeals here stated: "That single-gender education at the college level is beneficial to both sexes is *a fact established in this case.*" (1995) (emphasis added).

The evidence establishing that fact was overwhelming—indeed, "virtually uncontradicted" in the words of the court that received the evidence [citing 1991 district court opinion]. . . . This finding alone, which even this Court cannot dispute, should be sufficient to demonstrate the constitutionality of VMI's all-male composition.

But besides its single-sex constitution, VMI is different from other colleges in another way. It employs a "distinctive educational method," sometimes referred to as the "adversative, or doubting, model of education.". . . [A] State's decision to maintain within its system one school that provides the adversative method is "substantially related" to its goal of good education. Moreover, it was uncontested that "if the state were to establish a women's VMI-type [*i.e.,* adversative] program, the program would attract an insufficient number of participants to make the program work"; and it was found by the District Court that if Virginia were to include women in VMI, the school "would eventually find it necessary to drop the adversative system altogether." Thus, Virginia's options were an adversative method that excludes women or no adversative method at all. . . .

. . . In these circumstances, Virginia's election to fund one public all-male institution and one on the adversative model—and to concentrate its resources in a single entity that serves both these interests in diversity—is substantially related to the State's important educational interests.

B

The Court today has no adequate response to this clear demonstration of the conclusion produced by application of intermediate scrutiny. Rather, it relies on a series of contentions that are irrelevant or erroneous as a matter of law, foreclosed by the record in this case, or both.

1. I have already pointed out the Court's most fundamental error, which is its reasoning that VMI's all-male composition is unconstitutional because "some women are capable of all of the individual activities required of VMI cadets" and would prefer military training on the adversative model. This unacknowledged adoption of what amounts to (at least) strict scrutiny is without antecedent in our sex-discrimination cases and by itself discredits the Court's decision.

2. The Court suggests that Virginia's claimed purpose in maintaining VMI as an all-male institution—its asserted interest in promoting diversity of educational options—is not "genuin[e]," but is a pretext for discriminating against women. To support this charge, the Court would have to impute that base motive to VMI's Mission Study Committee, which conducted a 3-year study from 1983 to 1986 and recommended to VMI's Board of Visitors that the school remain all-male. . . . The relevance of the Mission Study Committee is that its very creation, its sober 3-year study, and the analysis it produced, utterly refute the claim that VMI has elected to maintain its all-male student-body composition for some misogynistic reason. . . .

Finally, the Court unreasonably suggests that there is some pretext in Virginia's reliance upon decentralized decisionmaking to achieve diversity—its granting of substantial autonomy to each institution with regard to student-body composition and other matters. . . . Each Virginia institution . . . has a natural incentive to make itself distinctive in order to attract a particular segment of student applicants. And of course none of the institutions is entirely autonomous; if and when the legislature decides that a particular school is not well serving the interest of diversity—if it decides, for example, that a men's school is not much needed—funding will cease.

3. In addition to disparaging Virginia's claim that VMI's single-sex status serves a state interest in diversity, the Court finds fault with Virginia's failure to offer education based on the adversative training method to women. It dismisses the District Court's "'findings' on 'gender-based developmental differences'" on the ground that "[t]hese 'findings' restate the opinions of Virginia's expert witnesses, opinions about typically male or typically female 'tendencies.'" How remarkable to criticize the District Court on the ground that its findings rest on the evidence (*i.e.,* the testimony of Virginia's witnesses)! That is what findings are supposed to do. It is indefensible to tell the Commonwealth that "[t]he burden of justification is demanding and it rests entirely on [you]," and then to ignore the District Court's findings because they rest on the evidence put forward by the Commonwealth—particularly when, as the District Court said, "[t]he evidence in the case . . . is *virtually uncontradicted*" (emphasis added). . . .

4. The Court contends that Virginia, and the District Court, erred, and "misperceived our precedent," by "train[ing] their argument on 'means' rather than 'end.'" The Court focuses on "VMI's mission," which is to produce individuals "imbued with love of learning, confident in the functions and attitudes of leadership, possessing a high sense of public service, advocates of the American democracy and free enterprise system, and ready . . . to defend their country in time of national peril." [Excerpt from 1991 district court opinion, quoting Mission Study Committee of the VMI Board of Visitors, Report, May 16, 1986.] "Surely," the Court says, "that goal is great enough to accommodate women."

This is law-making by indirection. What the Court describes as "VMI's mission" is no less the mission of *all* Virginia colleges. . . . To be sure, those general educational values are described in a particularly martial fashion in VMI's mission statement, in accordance with the military, adversative, and all-male character of the institution. But imparting those values *in that fashion—i.e.,* in a military, adversative, all-male environment—is the *distinctive* mission of VMI.

And as I have discussed (and both courts below found), *that* mission is *not* "great enough to accommodate women.". . .

5. The Court argues that VMI would not have to change very much if it were to admit women. The principal response to that argument is that it is irrelevant: If VMI's single-sex status is substantially related to the government's important educational objectives . . . , that concludes the inquiry. There should be no debate in the federal judiciary over "how much" VMI would be required to change if it admitted women and whether that would constitute "too much" change.

But if such a debate were relevant, the Court would certainly be on the losing side. . . . Changes that the District Court's detailed analysis found would be required include new allowances for personal privacy in the barracks, such as locked doors and coverings on windows, which would detract from VMI's approach of regulating minute details of student behavior, "contradict the principle that everyone is constantly subject to scrutiny by everyone else," and impair VMI's "total egalitarian approach" under which every student must be "treated alike"; changes in the physical training program, which would reduce "[t]he intensity and aggressiveness of the current program"; and various modifications in other respects of the adversative training program which permeates student life. . . .

6. Finally, the absence of a precise "all-women's analogue" to VMI is irrelevant. . . .

Although there is no precise female-only analogue to VMI, Virginia has created during this litigation the Virginia Women's Institute for Leadership (VWIL), a state-funded all-women's program run by Mary Baldwin College. I have thus far said nothing about VWIL because it is, under our established test, irrelevant, so long as VMI's all-male character is "substantially related" to an important state goal. But VWIL now exists, and the Court's treatment of it shows how far-reaching today's decision is.

VWIL was carefully designed by professional educators who have long experience in educating young women. The program . . . is designed to "provide an all-female program that will achieve substantially similar outcomes [to VMI's] in an all-female environment." After holding a trial where voluminous evidence was submitted and making detailed findings of fact, the District Court concluded that "there is a legitimate pedagogical basis for the different means employed [by VMI and VWIL] to achieve the substantially similar ends." [Citing 1994 district court opinion.] The Court of Appeals undertook a detailed review of the record and affirmed. (1995). . . . It is worth noting that none of the United States' own experts in the remedial phase of this case was willing to testify that VMI's adversative method was an appropriate methodology for educating women. This Court, however, does not care. Even though VWIL was carefully designed by professional educators who have tremendous experience in the area, and survived the test of adversarial litigation, the Court simply declares, with no basis in the evidence, that these professionals acted on " 'overbroad' generalizations."

C

A few words are appropriate in response to the concurrence, which finds VMI unconstitutional on a basis that is more moderate than the Court's but only at the expense of being even more implausible. The concurrence offers three reasons: First, that there is "scant evidence in the record" that diversity of educational offering was the real reason for Virginia's maintaining VMI. "Scant" has the advantage of being an imprecise term. I have cited the clearest statements of diversity as a goal for higher education in the 1990 Report of the Virginia Commission on the University of the 21st Century to the Governor and General Assembly, the 1989 Virginia Plan for Higher Education, the Budget Initiatives prepared in 1989 by the State Council of Higher Education for Virginia, the 1974 Report of the General Assembly Commission on Higher Education, and the 1969 Report of the Virginia Commission on Constitutional Revision. There is *no* evidence to the contrary, once one rejects (as the concurrence rightly does) the relevance of VMI's founding in days when attitudes towards the education of women were different. . . .

Second, the concurrence dismisses out of hand what it calls Virginia's "second justification for the single-sex admissions policy: maintenance of the adversative method." The concurrence reasons that "this justification does not serve an important governmental objective" because, whatever the record may show about the pedagogical benefits of *single-sex* education, "there is no similar evidence in the record that an adversative method is pedagogically beneficial or is any more likely to produce character traits than other methodologies." That is simply wrong. . . . In reality, the pedagogical benefits of VMI's adversative approach were not only proved, but were a given in this litigation. The reason the woman applicant who prompted this suit wanted to enter VMI was assuredly not that she wanted to go to an all-male school; it would cease being all-male as soon as she entered. She wanted the distinctive adversative education that VMI provided, and the battle was joined (in the main) over whether VMI had a basis for excluding women from that approach. . . .

A third reason the concurrence offers in support of the judgment is that the Commonwealth and VMI were not quick enough to react to the "further developments" in this Court's evolving jurisprudence. . . . If only, the concurrence asserts, Virginia had "made a genuine effort to devote comparable public resources to a facility for women, and followed through on such a plan, it might well have avoided an equal protection violation." That is to say, the concurrence believes that after our decision in *Hogan* . . . the Commonwealth should have known that what this Court expected of it was . . . yes!, the creation of a state all-women's program. Any lawyer who gave that advice to the Commonwealth ought to have been either disbarred or committed. . . . And any Virginia politician who proposed such a step when there were already 4 4-year women's colleges in Virginia . . . ought to have been recalled. . . .

IV

. . . [T]he Court's decision today will have consequences that extend far beyond the parties to the case. . . .

A

Under the constitutional principles announced and applied today, single-sex public education is unconstitutional. By going through the motions of applying a balancing test . . . the Court creates the illusion that government officials in some future case will have a clear shot at justifying some sort of single-sex public education. Indeed, the Court seeks to create even a greater illusion than that: It purports to have said nothing of relevance to *other* public schools at all. "We address specifically and only an educational opportunity recognized . . . as 'unique' . . . . " [Citing a footnote in the Court's opinion.]. . .

. . . [T]he rationale of today's decision is sweeping: for sex-based classifications, a redefinition of intermediate scrutiny that makes it indistinguishable from strict scrutiny. Indeed, the Court indicates that if any program restricted to one sex is "uniqu[e]," it must be opened to members of the opposite sex "who have the will and capacity" to participate in it. I suggest that the single-sex program that will not be capable of being characterized as "unique" is not only unique but nonexistent. In any event, regardless of whether the Court's rationale leaves some small amount of room for lawyers to argue, it ensures that single-sex public education is functionally dead. The costs of litigating the constitutionality of a single-sex education program, and the risks of ultimately losing that litigation, are simply too high to be embraced by public officials. . . . The enemies of single-sex education have won; by persuading only seven Justices (five would have been enough) that their view of the world is enshrined in the Constitution, they have effectively imposed that view on all 50 States.

This is especially regrettable because, as the District Court here determined, educational experts in recent years have increasingly come to "suppor[t] [the] view that substantial educational benefits flow from a single-gender environment, be it male or female, that cannot be replicated in a coeducational setting.". . . Until quite recently, some public officials have attempted to institute new single-sex programs, at least as experiments. In 1991, for example, the Detroit Board of Education announced a program to establish three boys-only schools for inner-city youth; it was met with a lawsuit, a preliminary injunction was swiftly entered by a District Court that purported to rely on *Hogan,* and the Detroit Board of Education voted to abandon the litigation and thus abandon the plan. Today's opinion assures that no such experiment will be tried again.

B

There are few extant single-sex public educational programs. The potential of today's decision for widespread disruption of existing institutions lies in its application to private single-sex education. Government support is immensely important to private educational institutions. Mary Baldwin College—which designed and runs VWIL—notes that private institutions of higher education in the 1990–1991 school year derived approximately 19 percent of their budgets from federal, state, and local government funds, *not including financial aid to students.* Charitable status under the tax laws is also highly significant for private educational institutions, and it is certainly not beyond the Court that rendered today's decision to hold that a donation to a single-sex college should be deemed contrary to public policy and therefore not deductible if the college discriminates on the basis of sex. The Court adverts to private single-sex education only briefly, and only to make the assertion (mentioned above) that "[w]e address specifically and only an educational opportunity recognized by the District Court and the Court of Appeals as 'unique.' " . . . [T]hat assurance assures nothing, unless it is to be taken as a promise that in the future the Court will disclaim the reasoning it has used today to destroy VMI. The Government, in its briefs to this Court, at least purports to address the consequences of its attack on VMI for public support of private single-sex education. It contends that private colleges which are the direct or indirect beneficiaries of government funding are not thereby necessarily converted into state actors to which the Equal Protection Clause is then applicable. That is true. It is also virtually meaningless.

The issue will be not whether government assistance turns private colleges into state actors, but whether the government *itself* would be violating the Constitution by providing state support to single-sex colleges. For example, in *Norwood* v. *Harrison* (1973), we saw no room to distinguish between state operation of racially segregated schools and state support of privately run segregated schools. . . .

The only hope for state-assisted single-sex private schools is that the Court will not apply in the future the principles of law it has applied today. That is a substantial hope, I am happy and ashamed to say. After all, did not the Court today abandon the principles of law it has applied in our earlier sex-classification cases? And does not the Court positively invite private colleges to rely upon our ad-hocery by assuring them this case is "unique"? I would not advise the foundation of any new single-sex college (especially an all-male one) with the expectation of being allowed to receive any government support; but it is too soon to abandon in despair those single-sex colleges already in existence. It will certainly be possible for this Court to write a future opinion that ignores the broad principles of law set forth today, and that characterizes as utterly dispositive the opinion's perceptions that VMI was a uniquely prestigious all-male institution, conceived in chauvinism, etc., etc. I will not join that opinion. . . .

□ □ □

Nos. 95-124 and 95-227

Denver Area Educational Telecommunications Consortium, Inc., et al., Petitioners v. Federal Communications Commission et al.

Alliance for Community Media, et al., Petitioners v. Federal Communications Commission et al.

On writs of certiorari to the United States Court of Appeals
for the District of Columbia Circuit

[June 28, 1996]

JUSTICE BREYER announced the judgment of the Court and delivered the opinion of the Court with respect to Part III, an opinion with respect to

Parts I, II, and V, in which JUSTICE STEVENS, JUSTICE O'CONNOR, and JUSTICE SOUTER join, and an opinion with respect to Parts IV and VI, in which JUSTICE STEVENS and JUSTICE SOUTER join.

These cases present First Amendment challenges to three statutory provisions that seek to regulate the broadcasting of "patently offensive" sex-related material on cable television. Cable Television Consumer Protection and Competition Act of 1992 §§10(a), 10(b), and 10(c), 47 U.S.C. §§532(h), 532(j), and note following §531. The provisions apply to programs broadcast over cable on what are known as "leased access channels" and "public, educational, or governmental channels." Two of the provisions essentially permit a cable system operator to prohibit the broadcasting of "programming" that the "operator reasonably believes describes or depicts sexual or excretory activities or organs in a patently offensive manner." §10(a); see §10(c). The remaining provision requires cable system operators to segregate certain "patently offensive" programming, to place it on a single channel, and to block that channel from viewer access unless the viewer requests access in advance and in writing. §10(b).

We conclude that the first provision—that *permits* the operator to decide whether or not to broadcast such programs on leased access channels—is consistent with the First Amendment. The second provision, that requires leased channel operators to segregate and to block that programming, and the third provision, applicable to public, educational, and governmental channels, violate the First Amendment, for they are not appropriately tailored to achieve the basic, legitimate objective of protecting children from exposure to "patently offensive" material.

I

Cable operators typically own a physical cable network used to convey programming over several dozen cable channels into subscribers' houses. Program sources vary from channel to channel. Most channels carry programming produced by independent firms, including "many national and regional cable programming networks that have emerged in recent years," *Turner Broadcasting System, Inc.* v. *FCC* (1994), as well as some programming that the system operator itself (or an operator affiliate) may provide. Other channels may simply retransmit through cable the signals of over-the-air broadcast stations. Certain special channels here at issue, called "leased channels" and "public, educational, or governmental channels," carry programs provided by those to whom the law gives special cable system access rights.

A "leased channel" is a channel that federal law requires a cable system operator to reserve for commercial lease by unaffiliated third parties. About 10 to 15 percent of a cable system's channels would typically fall into this category. "[P]ublic, educational, or governmental channels" (which we shall call "public access" channels) are channels that, over the years, local governments have required cable system operators to set aside for public, educational, or governmental purposes as part of the consideration an operator gives in return for permission to install cables under city streets and to use public rights-of-way. Between 1984 and 1992 federal law . . . prohibited cable system operators from exercising any editorial control over the content of any program broadcast over either leased or public access channels.

In 1992, in an effort to control sexually explicit programming conveyed over access channels, Congress enacted the three provisions before us. The first two provisions relate to leased channels. The first says:

> "This subsection shall permit a cable operator to enforce prospectively a written and published policy of prohibiting programming that the cable operator reasonably believes describes or depicts sexual or excretory activities or organs in a patently offensive manner as measured by contemporary community standards." §10(a)(2).

The second provision applicable only to leased channels requires cable operators to segregate and to block similar programming if they decide to permit, rather than to prohibit, its broadcast. The provision tells the Federal Communications Commission (FCC) to promulgate regulations that will (a) require "programmers to inform cable operators if the program[ming] would be indecent as defined by Commission regulations"; (b) require "cable operators to place" such material "on a single channel"; and (c) require "cable operators to block such single channel unless the subscriber requests access to such channel in writing." §10(b)(1). The Commission issued regulations defining the material at issue in terms virtually identical to those we have already set forth, namely as descriptions or depictions of "sexual or excretory activities or organs in a patently offensive manner" as measured by the cable viewing community. The regulations require the cable operators to place this material on a single channel and to block it (say, by scrambling). They also require the system operator to provide access to the blocked channel "within 30 days" of a subscriber's written request for access and to reblock it within 30 days of a subscriber's request to do so.

The third provision is similar to the first provision, but applies only to public access channels. The relevant statutory section instructs the FCC to promulgate regulations that will

> "enable a cable operator of a cable system to prohibit the use, on such system, of any channel capacity of any public, educational, or governmental access facility for any programming which contains obscene material, sexually explicit conduct, or material soliciting or promoting unlawful conduct." §10(c).

The FCC, carrying out this statutory instruction, promulgated regulations defining "sexually explicit" in language almost identical to that in the statute's leased channel provision, namely as descriptions or depictions of "sexual or excretory activities or organs in a patently offensive manner" as measured by the cable viewing community.

The upshot is . . . the federal law before us (the statute as implemented through regulations) now permits cable operators either to allow or to forbid the transmission of "patently offensive" sex-related materials over both leased and public access channels, and requires those operators, at a minimum, to segregate and to block transmission of that same material on leased channels.

Petitioners, claiming that the three statutory provisions, as implemented by the Commission regulations, violate the First Amendment, sought judicial review of the Commission's First Report and Order and its Second Report and

Order in the United States Court of Appeals for the District of Columbia Circuit. A panel of that Circuit agreed with petitioners that the provisions violated the First Amendment. (1993). The entire Court of Appeals, however, heard the case en banc and reached the opposite conclusion. It held all three statutory provisions (as implemented) were consistent with the First Amendment. (1995). Four of the eleven en banc appeals court judges dissented. Two of the dissenting judges concluded that all three provisions violated the First Amendment. Two others thought that either one, or two, but not all three of the provisions, violated the First Amendment. We granted certiorari to review the en banc Court's First Amendment determinations.

II

We turn initially to the provision that *permits* cable system operators to prohibit "patently offensive" (or "indecent") programming transmitted over leased access channels. . . .

We recognize that the First Amendment, the terms of which apply to governmental action, ordinarily does not itself throw into constitutional doubt the decisions of private citizens to permit, or to restrict, speech—and this is so *ordinarily* even where those decisions take place within the framework of a regulatory regime such as broadcasting. . . .

Nonetheless, petitioners . . . point to circumstances that, in their view, make the analogy with private broadcasters inapposite and make this case a special one, warranting a different constitutional result. As a practical matter, they say, cable system operators have considerably more power to "censor" program viewing than do broadcasters, for individual communities typically have only one cable system, linking broadcasters and other program providers with each community's many subscribers. . . . Moreover, concern about system operators' exercise of this considerable power originally led government—local and federal—to insist that operators provide leased and public access channels free of operator editorial control. To permit system operators to supervise programming on leased access channels will create the very private-censorship risk that this anticensorship effort sought to avoid. At the same time, petitioners add, cable systems have two relevant special characteristics. They are unusually involved with government, for they depend upon government permission and government facilities (streets, rights-of-way) to string the cable necessary for their services. And in respect to leased channels, their speech interests are relatively weak because they act less like editors, such as newspapers or television broadcasters, than like common carriers, such as telephone companies.

Under these circumstances, petitioners conclude, Congress' "permissive" law, *in actuality*, will "abridge" their free speech. And this Court should treat that law as a congressionally imposed, content-based, restriction unredeemed as a properly tailored effort to serve a "compelling interest." They further analogize the provisions to constitutionally forbidden content-based restrictions upon speech taking place in "public forums" such as public streets, parks, or buildings dedicated to open speech and communication. And, finally, petitioners say that the legal standard the law contains (the "patently offensive" standard) is unconstitutionally vague.

Like the petitioners, JUSTICES KENNEDY and THOMAS would have us decide this case simply by transferring and applying literally categorical standards this Court has developed in other contexts. For JUSTICE KENNEDY, leased access channels are like a common carrier, cablecast is a protected medium, strict scrutiny applies, §10(a) fails this test, and, therefore, §10(a) is invalid. For JUSTICE THOMAS, the case is simple because the cable operator who owns the system over which access channels are broadcast, like a bookstore owner with respect to what it displays on the shelves, has a predominant First Amendment interest. Both categorical approaches suffer from the same flaws: they import law developed in very different contexts into a new and changing environment, and they lack the flexibility necessary to allow government to respond to very serious practical problems without sacrificing the free exchange of ideas the First Amendment is designed to protect.

The history of this Court's First Amendment jurisprudence, however, is one of continual development, as the Constitution's general command that "Congress shall make no law . . . abridging the freedom of speech, or of the press," has been applied to new circumstances requiring different adaptations of prior principles and precedents. The essence of that protection is that Congress may not regulate speech except in cases of extraordinary need and with the exercise of a degree of care that we have not elsewhere required. At the same time, our cases have not left Congress or the States powerless to address the most serious problems.

Over the years, this Court has restated and refined these basic First Amendment principles, adopting them more particularly to the balance of competing interests and the special circumstances of each field of application. [Citation of cases omitted.]

This tradition teaches that the First Amendment embodies an overarching commitment to protect speech from Government regulation through close judicial scrutiny, thereby enforcing the Constitution's constraints, but without imposing judicial formulae so rigid that they become a straightjacket that disables Government from responding to serious problems. This Court, in different contexts, has consistently held that the Government may directly regulate speech to address extraordinary problems, where its regulations are appropriately tailored to resolve those problems without imposing an unnecessarily great restriction on speech. JUSTICES KENNEDY and THOMAS would have us further declare which, among the many applications of the general approach that this Court has developed over the years, we are applying here. But no definitive choice among competing analogies (broadcast, common carrier, bookstore) allows us to declare a rigid single standard, good for now and for all future media and purposes. . . . [A]ware as we are of the changes taking place in the law, the technology, and the industrial structure, related to telecommunications, we believe it unwise and unnecessary definitively to pick one analogy or one specific set of words now. . . .

. . . [W]e can decide this case more narrowly, by closely scrutinizing §10(a) to assure that it properly addresses an extremely important problem, without imposing, in light of the relevant interests, an unnecessarily great restriction on speech. The importance of the interest at stake here — protecting children from exposure to patently offensive depictions of sex; the accommodation of the interests of programmers in maintaining access channels and of cable operators in editing the contents of their channels; the similarity of the problem and its solution to those at issue in [*FCC v.*] *Pacifica* [*Foundation* (1978)]; and the flexibility inherent in an approach that permits private cable operators to make editorial decisions, lead us to conclude that §10(a) is a sufficiently tailored response to an extraordinarily important problem.

First, the provision before us comes accompanied with an extremely important justification, one that this Court has often found compelling—the need to protect children from exposure to patently offensive sex-related material.

Second, the provision arises in a very particular context—congressional *permission* for cable operators to regulate programming that, but for a previous Act of Congress, would have had no path of access to cable channels free of an operator's control. The First Amendment interests involved are therefore complex, and involve a balance between those interests served by the access requirements themselves (increasing the availability of avenues of expression to programmers who otherwise would not have them) and the disadvantage to the First Amendment interests of cable operators and other programmers (those to whom the cable operator would have assigned the channels devoted to access).

Third, the problem Congress addressed here is remarkably similar to the problem addressed by the FCC in *Pacifica*, and the balance Congress struck is commensurate with the balance we approved there. In *Pacifica* this Court considered a governmental ban of a radio broadcast of "indecent" materials. . . . The Court found this ban constitutionally permissible primarily because "broadcasting is uniquely accessible to children" and children were likely listeners to the program there at issue—an afternoon radio broadcast. In addition, the Court wrote, "the broadcast media have established a uniquely pervasive presence in the lives of all Americans," "[p]atently offensive, indecent material . . . confronts the citizen, not only in public, but also in the privacy of the home," generally without sufficient prior warning to allow the recipient to avert his or her eyes or ears; and "[a]dults who feel the need may purchase tapes and records or go to theaters and nightclubs" to hear similar performances.

All these factors are present here. Cable television broadcasting, including access channel broadcasting, is as "accessible to children" as over-the-air broadcasting, if not more so. Cable television systems, including access channels, "have established a uniquely pervasive presence in the lives of all Americans.". . . "Patently offensive" material from these stations can "confron[t] the citizen" in the "privacy of the home" with little or no prior warning. . . . There is nothing to stop "adults who feel the need" from finding similar programming elsewhere, say, on tape or in theaters. In fact, the power of cable systems to control home program viewing is not absolute. Over-the-air broadcasting and direct broadcast satellites already provide alternative ways for programmers to reach the home, and are likely to do so to a greater extent in the near future.

Fourth, the permissive nature of §10(a) means that it likely restricts speech less than, not more than, the ban at issue in *Pacifica*. The provision removes a restriction as to some speakers—namely, cable operators. Moreover, although the provision does create a risk that a program will not appear, that risk is not the same as the certainty that accompanies a governmental ban. . . . Finally, the provision's permissive nature brings with it a flexibility that allows cable operators, for example, not to ban broadcasts, but, say, to rearrange broadcast times, better to fit the desires of adult audiences while lessening the risks of harm to children. . . .

The existence of this complex balance of interests persuades us that the permissive nature of the provision, coupled with its viewpoint-neutral application, is a constitutionally permissible way to protect children from the type of sexual material that concerned Congress, while accommodating both the First Amendment interests served by the access requirements and those served in restoring to cable operators a degree of the editorial control that Congress removed in 1984. . . .

Finally, petitioners argue that the definition of the materials subject to the challenged provisions is too vague, thereby granting cable system operators too broad a program-screening authority. . . . That definition, however, uses language similar to language previously used by this Court for roughly similar purposes. . . .

III

The statute's second provision significantly differs from the first, for it does not simply permit, but rather requires, cable system operators to restrict speech—by segregating and blocking "patently offensive" sex-related material appearing on leased channels (but not on other channels). In particular . . . this provision and its implementing regulations require cable system operators to place "patently offensive" leased channel programming on a separate channel; to block that channel; to unblock the channel within 30 days of a subscriber's written request for access; and to reblock the channel within 30 days of a subscriber's request for reblocking. Also, leased channel programmers must notify cable operators of an intended "patently offensive" broadcast up to 30 days before its scheduled broadcast date.

These requirements have obvious restrictive effects. The several up-to-30-day delays, along with single channel segregation, mean that a subscriber cannot decide to watch a single program without considerable advance planning and without letting the "patently offensive" channel in its entirety invade his household for days, perhaps weeks, at a time. These restrictions will prevent programmers from broadcasting to viewers who select programs day by day (or, through "surfing," minute by minute); to viewers who would like occasionally to watch a few, but not many, of the programs on the "patently offensive" channel; and to viewers who simply tend to judge a program's value through channel reputation, *i.e.,* by the company it keeps. Moreover, the "written notice" requirement will further restrict viewing by subscribers who fear for their reputations should the operator, advertently or inadvertently, disclose the list of those who wish to watch the "patently offensive" channel. Further, the added costs and burdens that these requirements impose upon a cable system operator may encourage that operator to ban programming that the operator would otherwise permit to run, even if only late at night.

The Government argues that, despite these adverse consequences, the "segregate and block" requirements are lawful because they are "the least restrictive means of realizing" a "compelling interest," namely "protecting the physical and psychological well-being of minors.". . .

We agree with the Government that protection of children is a "compelling interest." But we do not agree that the "segregate and block" requirements properly accommodate the speech restrictions they impose and the legitimate objective they seek to attain. . . .

Several circumstances lead us to this conclusion. For one thing, the law, as recently amended, uses other means to protect children from similar "patently offensive" material broadcast on *un*leased cable channels, *i.e.*, broadcast over any of a system's numerous ordinary, or public access, channels. The law, as recently amended, requires cable operators to "scramble or . . . block" such programming on any (unleased) channel "*primarily dedicated* to sexually-oriented programming." Telecommunications Act of 1996 (emphasis added). In addition, cable operators must honor a subscriber's request to block any, or all, programs on any channel to which he or she does not wish to subscribe. And manufacturers, in the future, will have to make television sets with a so-called "V-chip"—a device that will be able automatically to identify and block sexually explicit or violent programs.

Although we cannot, and do not, decide whether the new provisions are themselves lawful . . . , we note that they are significantly less restrictive than the provision here at issue. They do not force the viewer to receive (for days or weeks at a time) all "patently offensive" programming or none; they will not lead the viewer automatically to judge the few by the reputation of the many; and they will not automatically place the occasional viewer's name on a special list. . . .

The record does not . . . explain why, under the new Act, blocking alone— without written access-requests—adequately protects children from exposure to regular sex-dedicated channels, but cannot adequately protect those children from programming on similarly sex-dedicated channels that are leased. It does not explain why a simple subscriber blocking request system, perhaps a phone-call based system, would adequately protect children from "patently offensive" material broadcast on ordinary non-sex-dedicated channels (*i.e.*, almost all channels) but a far more restrictive segregate/block/written-access system is needed to protect children from similar broadcasts on what (in the absence of the segregation requirement) would be non-sex-dedicated channels that are leased. Nor is there any indication Congress thought the new ordinary channel protections less than adequate. . . .

We recognize . . . that Congress need not deal with every problem at once; and Congress also must have a degree of leeway in tailoring means to ends. But in light of the 1996 statute, it seems fair to say that Congress now has tried to deal with most of the problem. At this point, we can take Congress' different, and significantly less restrictive, treatment of a highly similar problem at least as *some indication* that more restrictive means are not "essential" (or will not prove very helpful). . . .

The record's description and discussion of a different alternative—the "lockbox"—leads, through a different route, to a similar conclusion. The Cable Communications Policy Act of 1984 required cable operators to provide

> "upon the request of a subscriber, a device by which the subscriber can prohibit viewing of a particular cable service during periods selected by the subscriber."

This device — the "lockbox" — would help protect children by permitting their parents to "lock out" those programs or channels that they did not want their children to see. The FCC, in upholding the "segregate and block" provisions, said that lockboxes protected children (including, say, children with inattentive parents) less effectively than those provisions. But it is important to understand why that is so. The Government sets forth the reasons as follows:

> "In the case of lockboxes, parents would have to discover that such devices exist; find out that their cable operators offer them for sale; spend the time and money to buy one; learn how to program the lockbox to block undesired programs; and, finally, exercise sufficient vigilance to ensure that they have, indeed, locked out whatever indecent programming they do not wish their children to view."

We assume the accuracy of this statement. But, the reasons do not show need for a provision as restrictive as the one before us. Rather, they suggest a set of provisions very much like those that Congress placed in the 1996 Act.

No provision, we concede, short of an absolute ban, can offer certain protection against assault by a determined child. . . . But . . . the Solicitor General's list of practical difficulties would seem to call, not for "segregate and block" requirements, but, rather, for informational requirements, for a simple coding system, for readily available blocking equipment (perhaps accessible by telephone), for imposing cost burdens upon system operators (who may spread them through subscription fees); or perhaps even for a system that requires lockbox defaults to be set to block certain channels (say, sex-dedicated-channels). These kinds of requirements resemble those that Congress has recently imposed upon all but leased channels. For that reason, the "lockbox" description and the discussion of its frailties reinforces our conclusion that the leased channel provision is overly restrictive when measured against the benefits it is likely to achieve. . . .

Consequently, we cannot find that the "segregate and block" restrictions on speech are a narrowly, or reasonably, tailored effort to protect children. Rather, they are overly restrictive, "sacrific[ing]" important First Amendment interests for too "speculative a gain." For that reason they are not consistent with the First Amendment.

IV

The statute's third provision, as implemented by FCC regulation, is similar to its first provision, in that it too permits a cable operator to prevent transmission of "patently offensive" programming, in this case on public access channels. But there are four important differences.

The first is the historical background. As JUSTICE KENNEDY points out, cable operators have traditionally agreed to reserve channel capacity for public, governmental, and educational channels as part of the consideration they give municipalities that award them cable franchises. In the terms preferred by JUSTICE THOMAS, the requirement to reserve capacity for public access channels is similar to the reservation of a public easement, or a dedication of land for streets and parks, as part of a municipality's approval of a subdivision of land. Significantly, these are channels over which cable operators have not historically exercised editorial control. Unlike §10(a) therefore, §10(c) does not restore to cable operators editorial rights that they once had, and the countervailing First Amendment interest is nonexistent, or at least much diminished.

The second difference is the institutional background that has developed as a result of the historical difference. When a "leased channel" is made available by the operator to a private lessee, the lessee has total control of programming during the leased time slot. Public access channels, on the other hand, are normally subject to complex supervisory systems of various sorts, often with both public and private elements. . . .

This system of public, private, and mixed nonprofit elements, through its supervising boards and nonprofit or governmental access managers, can set programming policy and approve or disapprove particular programming services. And this system can police that policy by, for example, requiring indemnification by programmers, certification of compliance with local standards, time segregation, adult content advisories, or even by prescreening individual programs. . . . Whether these locally accountable bodies prescreen programming, promulgate rules for the use of public access channels, or are merely available to respond when problems arise, the upshot is the same: there is a locally accountable body capable of addressing the problem, should it arise, of patently offensive programming broadcast to children, making it unlikely that many children will in fact be exposed to programming considered patently offensive in that community.

Third, the existence of a system aimed at encouraging and securing programming that the community considers valuable strongly suggests that a "cable operator's veto" is less likely necessary to achieve the statute's basic objective, protecting children, than a similar veto in the context of leased channels. Of course, the system of access managers and supervising boards can make mistakes, which the operator might in some cases correct with its veto power. Balanced against this potential benefit, however, is the risk that the veto itself may be mistaken; and its use, or threatened use, could prevent the presentation of programming, that, though borderline, is not "patently offensive" to its targeted audience. . . . And this latter threat must bulk large within a system that already has publicly accountable systems for maintaining responsible programs.

Finally, our examination of the legislative history and the record before us is consistent with what common sense suggests, namely that the public/nonprofit programming control systems now in place would normally avoid, minimize, or eliminate any child-related problems concerning "patently offensive" programming. We have found anecdotal references to what seem isolated instances of potentially indecent programming, some of which may well have occurred on leased, not public access channels. [Citations omitted.]

But these few examples do not necessarily indicate a significant nationwide pattern. . . . The Commission itself did not report any examples of "indecent" programs on public access channels. . . . Moreover, comments submitted to the FCC undermine any suggestion that prior to 1992 there were significant problems of indecent programming on public access channels. . . .

At most, we have found borderline examples as to which people's judgment may differ, perhaps acceptable in some communities but not others, of the type that petitioners fear the law might prohibit. [Citations omitted.] It is difficult to see how such borderline examples could show a compelling need, nationally, to protect children from significantly harmful materials. . . .

The upshot, in respect to the public access channels, is a law that could radically change present programming-related relationships among local community and nonprofit supervising boards and access managers, which relationships are established through municipal law, regulation, and contract. In doing so, it would not significantly restore editorial rights of cable operators, but would greatly increase the risk that certain categories of programming (say, borderline offensive programs) will not appear. At the same time, given present supervisory mechanisms, the need for this particular provision, aimed directly at public access channels, is not obvious. . . .

[W]e conclude that the Government cannot sustain its burden of showing that §10(c) is necessary to protect children or that it is appropriately tailored to secure that end. Consequently, we find that this third provision violates the First Amendment.

V

Finally, we must ask whether §10(a) is severable from the two other provisions. [Breyer concluded that the leased-access channel provision was severable and could stand even if the other two provisions were invalidated.]

VI

For these reasons, the judgment of the Court of Appeals is affirmed insofar as it upheld §10(a); the judgment of the Court of Appeals is reversed insofar as it upheld §10(b) and §10(c).

It is so ordered.

[Concurring opinions of JUSTICE STEVENS and JUSTICE SOUTER omitted.]

JUSTICE O'CONNOR, concurring in part and dissenting in part.
I agree that §10(a) is constitutional and that §10(b) is unconstitutional, and I join Parts I, II, III, and V, and the judgment in part. I am not persuaded, however, that the asserted "important differences" between §§10(a) and 10(c) are sufficient to justify striking down §10(c). I find the features shared by §10(a), which covers leased access channels, and §10(c), which covers public access channels, to be more significant than the differences. For that reason, I would find that §10(c) too withstands constitutional scrutiny. . . .

JUSTICE KENNEDY, with whom JUSTICE GINSBURG joins, concurring in part, concurring in the judgment in part, and dissenting in part.
The plurality opinion, insofar as it upholds §10(a) of the 1992 Cable Act, is adrift. The opinion treats concepts such as public forum, broadcaster, and common carrier as mere labels rather than as categories with settled legal significance; it applies no standard, and by this omission loses sight of existing First Amendment doctrine. When confronted with a threat to free speech in the context of an emerging technology, we ought to have the discipline to ana-

lyze the case by reference to existing elaborations of constant First Amendment principles. This is the essence of the case-by-case approach to ensuring protection of speech under the First Amendment, even in novel settings. Rather than undertake this task, however, the plurality just declares that, all things considered, §10(a) seems fine. I think the implications of our past cases for this one are clearer than the plurality suggests, and they require us to hold §10(a) invalid. Though I join Part III of the opinion (there for the Court) striking down §10(b) of the Act, and concur in the judgment that §10(c) is unconstitutional, with respect I dissent from the remainder.

I

Two provisions of the 1992 Act, §§10(a) and (c), authorize the operator of a cable system to exclude certain programming from two different kinds of channels. [Further description of the sections omitted.]

Sections 10(a) and (c) are unusual. They do not require direct action against speech, but do authorize a cable operator to deny the use of its property to certain forms of speech. As a general matter, a private person may exclude certain speakers from his or her property without violating the First Amendment, and if §§10(a) and (c) were no more than affirmations of this principle they might be unremarkable. Access channels, however, are property of the cable operator dedicated or otherwise reserved for programming of other speakers or the government. A public access channel is a public forum, and laws requiring leased access channels create common carrier obligations. When the government identifies certain speech on the basis of its content as vulnerable to exclusion from a common carrier or public forum, strict scrutiny applies. These laws cannot survive this exacting review. However compelling Congress' interest in shielding children from indecent programming, the provisions in this case are not drawn with enough care to withstand scrutiny under our precedents.

[II omitted]

III

[A omitted]

B

. . . Public access channels meet the definition of a public forum. We have recognized two kinds of public forums. The first and most familiar are traditional public forums, like streets, sidewalks, and parks, which by custom have long been open for public assembly and discourse. "The second category of public property is the designated public forum, whether of a limited or unlimited character—property that the State has opened for expressive activity by part or all of the public." *International Soc. for Krishna Consciousness, Inc.* v. *Lee* (1992).

Public access channels fall in the second category. Required by the franchise authority as a condition of the franchise and open to all comers, they are a designated public forum of unlimited character. . . . Public forums do not have to be physical gathering places, nor are they limited to property owned by the government. Indeed, in the majority of jurisdictions, title to some of the most traditional of public forums, streets and sidewalks, remains in private hands. . . . Public access channels are analogous; they are public forums even though they operate over property to which the cable operator holds title.

. . . In providing public access channels under their franchise agreements, cable operators therefore are not exercising their own First Amendment rights. They serve as conduits for the speech of others. Section 10(c) thus restores no power of editorial discretion over public access channels that the cable operator once had; the discretion never existed. It vests the cable operator with a power under federal law, defined by reference to the content of speech, to override the franchise agreement and undercut the public forum the agreement creates. . . .

The plurality refuses to analyze public access channels as public forums because it is reluctant to decide "the extent to which private property can be designated a public forum.". . .

Treating access channels as public forums does not just place a label on them, as the plurality suggests. It defines the First Amendment rights of speakers seeking to use the channels. When property has been dedicated to public expressive activities, by tradition or government designation, access is protected by the First Amendment. Regulations of speech content in a designated public forum, whether of limited or unlimited character, are "subject to the highest scrutiny" and "survive only if they are narrowly drawn to achieve a compelling state interest." Unless there are reasons for applying a lesser standard, §10(c) must satisfy this stringent review.

C

Leased access channels . . . are those the cable operator must set aside for unaffiliated programmers who pay to transmit shows of their own without the cable operator's creative assistance or editorial approval. In my view, strict scrutiny also applies to §10(a)'s authorization to cable operators to exclude indecent programming from these channels. . . .

Laws requiring cable operators to provide leased access are the practical equivalent of making them common carriers, analogous in this respect to telephone companies: They are obliged to provide a conduit for the speech of others. . . .

Laws removing common-carriage protection from a single form of speech based on its content should be reviewed under the same standard as content-based restrictions on speech in a public forum. . . . A common-carriage mandate . . . serves the same function as a public forum. It ensures open, nondiscriminatory access to the means of communication. . . . The functional equivalence of designating a public forum and mandating common carriage suggests the same scrutiny should be applied to attempts in either setting to impose content discrimination by law. Under our precedents, the scrutiny is strict. . . .

. . . [T]he plurality's unwillingness to consider our public-forum precedents does not relieve it of the burden of explaining why strict scrutiny should not apply. Except in instances involving well-settled categories of proscribable speech, strict scrutiny is the baseline rule for reviewing any content-based discrimination against speech. . . .

. . . It is no answer to say Congress does not have to create access channels at all, so it may limit access as it pleases. . . . [E]ven if Congress has no obligation to impose common carriage rules on cable operators or retain them forever, it is not at liberty to exclude certain forms of speech from their protection on the suspect basis of content. . . .

[D omitted]

IV

At a minimum, the proper standard for reviewing §§10(a) and (c) is strict scrutiny. The plurality gives no reason why it should be otherwise. I would hold these enactments unconstitutional because they are not narrowly tailored to serve a compelling interest.

The Government has no compelling interest in restoring a cable operator's First Amendment right of editorial discretion. As to §10(c), Congress has no interest at all, since under most franchises operators had no rights of editorial discretion over PEG [public, educational, and governmental] access channels in the first place. As to §10(a), any governmental interest in restoring operator discretion over indecent programming on leased access channels is too minimal to justify the law. . . .

Congress does have, however, a compelling interest in protecting children from indecent speech. So long as society gives proper respect to parental choices, it may, under an appropriate standard, intervene to spare children exposure to material not suitable for minors. This interest is substantial enough to justify some regulation of indecent speech even under, I will assume, the indecency standard used here.

Sections 10(a) and (c) nonetheless are not narrowly tailored to protect children from indecent programs on access channels. First, to the extent some operators may allow indecent programming, children in localities those operators serve will be left unprotected. Partial service of a compelling interest is not narrow tailoring. . . .

Second, to the extent cable operators prohibit indecent programming on access channels, not only children but adults will be deprived of it. . . . It matters not that indecent programming might be available on the operator's other channels. The Government has no legitimate interest in making access channels pristine. A block-and-segregate requirement similar to §10(b), but without its constitutional infirmity of requiring persons to place themselves on a list to receive programming, protects children with far less intrusion on the liberties of programmers and adult viewers than allowing cable operators to ban indecent programming from access channels altogether. . . .

Sections 10(a) and (c) present a classic case of discrimination against speech based on its content. There are legitimate reasons why the Government might wish to regulate or even restrict the speech at issue here, but §§10(a) and 10(c) are not drawn to address those reasons with the precision the First Amendment requires.

[V omitted]

VI

In agreement with the plurality's analysis of §10(b) of the Act, insofar as it applies strict scrutiny, I join Part III of its opinion. Its position there, however, cannot be reconciled with upholding §10(a). In the plurality's view, §10(b), which standing alone would guarantee an indecent programmer some access to a cable audience, violates the First Amendment, but §10(a), which authorizes exclusion of indecent programming from access channels altogether, does not. There is little to commend this logic or result. I dissent from the judgment of the Court insofar as it upholds the constitutionality of §10(a).

JUSTICE THOMAS, joined by THE CHIEF JUSTICE and JUSTICE SCALIA, concurring in the judgment in part and dissenting in part.

I agree with the plurality's conclusion that §10(a) is constitutionally permissible, but I disagree with its conclusion that §§10(b) and (c) violate the First Amendment. For many years, we have failed to articulate how and to what extent the First Amendment protects cable operators, programmers, and viewers from state and federal regulation. I think it is time we did so, and I cannot go along with the plurality's assiduous attempts to avoid addressing that issue openly.

I

The text of the First Amendment makes no distinction between print, broadcast, and cable media, but we have done so. In *Red Lion Broadcasting Co.* v. *FCC* (1969), we held that, in light of the scarcity of broadcasting frequencies, the Government may require a broadcast licensee "to share his frequency with others and to conduct himself as a proxy or fiduciary with obligations to present those views and voices which are representative of his community and which would otherwise, by necessity, be barred from the airwaves.". . .

In contrast, we have not permitted that level of government interference in the context of the print media. . . .

Our First Amendment distinctions between media . . . placed cable in a doctrinal wasteland in which regulators and cable operators alike could not be sure whether cable was entitled to the substantial First Amendment protections afforded the print media or was subject to the more onerous obligations shouldered by the broadcast media. . . . Over time, however, we have drawn closer to recognizing that cable operators should enjoy the same First Amendment rights as the nonbroadcast media.

Two Terms ago, in *Turner Broadcasting System, Inc.* v. *FCC* (1994), we stated expressly: The *Red Lion* standard does not apply to cable television. . . . While Members of the Court disagreed about whether the must-carry rules imposed by Congress were content-based, and therefore subject to strict scrutiny, there was agreement that cable operators are generally entitled to much the same First Amendment protection as the print media. . . .

In *Turner*, by adopting much of the print paradigm, and by rejecting *Red Lion*, we adopted with it a considerable body of precedent that governs the respective First Amendment rights of competing speakers. In *Red Lion*, we had legitimized consideration of the public interest and emphasized the rights of viewers, at least in the abstract. Under that view, "[i]t is the right of the viewers and listeners, not the right of the broadcasters, which is paramount." After *Turner*, however, that view can no longer be given any credence in the cable context. It is the operator's right that is preeminent. . . . [W]hen there is a conflict, a programmer's asserted right to transmit over an operator's cable system must give way to the operator's editorial discretion. . . .

By recognizing the general primacy of the cable operator's editorial rights over the rights of programmers and viewers, *Turner* raises serious questions about the merits of petitioners' claims. None of the petitioners in these cases are cable operators; they are all cable viewers or access programmers or their representative organizations. . . .

JUSTICE BREYER's detailed explanation of why he believes it is "unwise and unnecessary" to choose a standard against which to measure petitioners' First Amendment claims largely disregards our recent attempt in *Turner* to define that standard. . . .

In the process of deciding not to decide on a governing standard, JUSTICE BREYER purports to discover in our cases an expansive, general principle permitting government to "directly regulate speech to address extraordinary problems, where its regulations are appropriately tailored to resolve those problems without imposing an unnecessarily great restriction on speech." This heretofore unknown standard is facially subjective and openly invites balancing of asserted speech interests to a degree not ordinarily permitted. . . .

In any event, even if the plurality's balancing test were an appropriate standard, it could only be applied to protect speech interests that, under the circumstances, are themselves protected by the First Amendment. But, by shifting the focus to the balancing of "complex" interests, JUSTICE BREYER never explains whether (and if so, how) a programmer's ordinarily unprotected interest in affirmative transmission of its programming acquires constitutional significance on leased and public access channels. . . .

II

A

. . . There is no getting around the fact that leased and public access are a type of forced speech. Though the constitutionality of leased and public access channels is not directly at issue in these cases, the position adopted by the Court in *Turner* ineluctably leads to the conclusion that the federal access requirements are subject to some form of heightened scrutiny. . . .

It is one thing to compel an operator to carry leased and public access speech, . . . but it is another thing altogether to say that the First Amendment forbids Congress to give back part of the operators' editorial discretion, which all recognize as fundamentally protected, in favor of a broader access right. It is no answer to say that leased and public access are content neutral and that §§10(a) and (c) are not, for that does not change the fundamental fact . . . that it is the operators' journalistic freedom that is infringed, whether the challenged restrictions be content neutral or content based. . . .

B

It makes no difference that the leased access restrictions may take the form of common carrier obligations. . . . That the leased access provisions may be described in common-carrier terms does not demonstrate that access programmers have obtained a First Amendment right to transmit programming over leased access channels. Labeling leased access a common carrier scheme has no real First Amendment consequences. It simply does not follow from common carrier status that cable operators may not, with Congress' blessing, decline to carry indecent speech on their leased access channels. Common carriers are private entities and may, consistent with the First Amendment, exercise editorial discretion in the absence of a specific statutory prohibition. . . .

C

Petitioners argue that public access channels are public fora in which they have First Amendment rights to speak and that §10(c) is invalid because it imposes content-based burdens on those rights. . . . I do not agree with petitioners' antecedent assertion that public access channels are public fora. . . .

Cable systems are not public property. Cable systems are privately owned and privately managed, and petitioners point to no case in which we have held that government may designate private property as a public forum. . . . [T]he nature of the regulatory restrictions placed on cable operators by local franchising authorities are not consistent with the kinds of governmental property interests we have said may be formally dedicated as public fora. Our public forum cases have involved property in which the government has held at least some formal easement or other property interest permitting the government to treat the property as its own in designating the property as a public forum. . . . That is simply not true in these cases. . . .

Similarly, assertion of government control over private property cannot justify designation of that property as a public forum. We have expressly stated that neither government ownership nor government control will guarantee public access to property. . . . [W]e have never even hinted that regulatory control, and particularly direct regulatory control over a private entity's First Amendment speech rights, could justify creation of a public forum. . . .

. . . Public access channels are not public fora, and, therefore, petitioners' attempt to redistribute cable speech rights in their favor must fail. For this reason, and the other reasons articulated earlier, I would sustain both §10(a) and §10(c).

III

. . . The parties agree that Congress has a "compelling interest in protecting the physical and psychological well-being of minors" and that its interest "extends to shielding minors from the influence of [indecent speech] that is not obscene by adult standards.". . . Because §10(b) is narrowly tailored to achieve that well-established compelling interest, I would uphold it. I therefore dissent from the Court's decision to the contrary. . . .

The Court strikes down §10(b) by pointing to alternatives, such as reverse-blocking and lockboxes, that it says are less restrictive than segregation and

blocking. . . . [T]hese methods . . . do not effectively support parents' authority to direct the moral upbringing of their children. The FCC recognized that
leased-access programming comes "from a wide variety of independent
sources, with no single editor controlling [its] selection and presentation."
Thus, indecent programming on leased access channels is "especially likely to
be shown randomly or intermittently between non-indecent programs." Rather
than being able to simply block out certain channels at certain times, a subscriber armed with only a lockbox must carefully monitor all leased-access programming and constantly reprogram the lockbox to keep out undesired programming. . . .

Petitioners argue that §10(b)'s segregation and blocking scheme is not sufficiently narrowly tailored because it requires the viewer's "written consent"; it
permits the cable operator 30 days to respond to the written request for access;
and it is impermissibly underinclusive because it reaches only leased access programming.

. . . [P]etitioners' allegations of an official list "of those who wish to watch
the 'patently offensive' channel," as the majority puts it, are pure hyperbole.
The FCC regulation implementing §10(b)'s written request requirement says
nothing about the creation of a list, much less an official government list. It
requires only that the cable operator receive written consent. Other statutory
provisions make clear that the cable operator may not share that, or any other,
information with any other person, including the Government. . . .

Though making an oral request for access, perhaps by telephone, is slightly less bothersome than making a written request, it is also true that a written
request is less subject to fraud "by a determined child." Consequently, despite
the fact that an oral request is slightly less restrictive in absolute terms, it is also
less effective in supporting parents' interest in denying enterprising, but
parentally unauthorized, minors access to blocked programming.

The segregation and blocking requirement was not intended to be a
replacement for lockboxes, V-chips, reverse-blocking, or other subscriber-ini-
tiated measures. Rather, Congress enacted in §10(b) a default setting under
which a subscriber receives no blocked programming without a written request.
Thus, subscribers who do not want the blocked programming are protected,
and subscribers who do want it may request access. Once a subscriber requests
access to blocked programming, however, the subscriber remains free to use
other methods, such as lockboxes, to regulate the kind of programming shown
on those channels in that home. . . .

The United States has carried its burden of demonstrating that §10(b) and
its implementing regulations are narrowly tailored to satisfy a compelling governmental interest. Accordingly, I would affirm the judgment of the Court of
Appeals in its entirety. I therefore concur in the judgment upholding §10(a)
and respectfully dissent from that portion of the judgment striking down
§§10(b) and (c).

□ □ □

How the Court Works

The Constitution makes the Supreme Court the final arbiter in "cases" and "controversies" arising under the Constitution or the laws of the United States. As the interpreter of the law, the Court often is viewed as the least mutable and most tradition-bound of the three branches of the federal government. But the Court has undergone innumerable changes in its history, some of which have been mandated by law. Some of these changes are embodied in Court rules; others are informal adaptations to needs and circumstances.

The Schedule of the Term

Annual Terms

By law the Supreme Court begins its regular annual term on the first Monday in October, and the term lasts approximately nine months. This session is known as the October term. The summer recess, which is not determined by statute or Court rules, generally begins in late June or early July of the following year. This system—staying in continuous session throughout the year, with periodic recesses—makes it unnecessary to convene a special term to deal with matters arising in the summer.

The justices actually begin work before the official opening of the term. They hold their initial conference during the last week in September. When the justices formally convene on the first Monday in October, oral arguments begin.

Arguments and Conferences

At least four justices must request that a case be argued before it can be accepted. Arguments are heard on Monday, Tuesday, and Wednesday for seven two-week sessions, beginning in the first week in October and ending in mid-April. Recesses of two weeks or longer occur between the sessions of oral arguments so that justices can consider the cases and deal with other Court business.

The schedule for oral arguments is 10:00 a.m. to noon and 1 p.m. to 3 p.m. Because most cases receive one hour apiece for argument, the Court can hear up to twelve cases a week.

The Court holds conferences on the Friday just before the two-week oral argument periods and on Wednesday and Friday during the weeks when oral arguments are scheduled. The conferences are designed for consideration of cases already heard in oral argument.

Before each of the Friday conferences, the chief justice circulates a "discuss" list—a list of cases deemed important enough for discussion and a vote. Appeals are placed on the discuss list almost automatically, but as many as three-quarters of the petitions for certiorari are dismissed. No case is denied review during conference, however, without an initial examination by the justices and their law clerks. Any justice can have a case placed on the Court's conference agenda for review. Most of the cases scheduled for the discuss list also are denied review in the end but only after discussion by the justices during the conference.

Although the last oral arguments have been heard by mid-April each year, the conferences of the justices continue until the end of the term to consider cases remaining on the Court's agenda. All conferences are held in secret, with no legal assistants or other staff present. The attendance of six justices constitutes a quorum. Conferences begin with handshakes all around. In discussing a case, the chief justice speaks first, followed by each justice in order of seniority.

Decision Days

Opinions are released on Tuesdays and Wednesdays during the weeks that the Court is hearing oral arguments; during other weeks, they are released on Mondays. In addition to opinions, the Court also releases an "orders" list—the summary of the Court's action granting or denying review. The orders list is posted at the beginning of the Monday session. It is not announced orally but can be obtained from the clerk and the public information officer. When urgent or important matters arise, the Court's summary orders may be made available on a day other than Monday.

Unlike its orders, decisions of the Court are announced orally in open Court. The justice who wrote the opinion announces the Court's decision, and justices writing concurring or dissenting opinions may state their views as well. When more than one decision is to be rendered, the justices who wrote the opinion make their announcements in reverse order of seniority. Occasionally, all or a large portion of the opinion is read aloud. More often the author summarizes the opinion or simply announces the result and states that a written opinion has been filed.

Reviewing Cases

In determining whether to accept a case for review, the Court has considerable discretion, subject only to the restraints imposed by the

Visiting the Supreme Court

The Supreme Court building has six levels, two of which—the ground and main floors—are accessible to the public. The basement contains a parking garage, a printing press, and offices for security guards and maintenance personnel. On the ground floor are the John Marshall statue, the exhibition area, the public information office, and a cafeteria. The main corridor, known as the Great Hall, the courtroom, and justices' offices are on the main floor. The second floor contains dining rooms, the justices' reading room, and other offices; the third floor, the Court library; and the fourth floor, the gym and storage areas.

From October to mid-April, the Court hears oral arguments Monday through Wednesday for about two weeks a month. These sessions begin at 10 a.m. and continue until 3 p.m., with a one-hour recess starting at noon. They are open to the public on a first-come, first-served basis.

Visitors may inspect the Supreme Court chamber any time the Court is not in session. Historical exhibits and a free motion picture on how the Court works also are available throughout the year. The Supreme Court building is open from 9 a.m. to 4:30 p.m. Monday through Friday, except for legal holidays. When the Court is not in session, lectures are given in the courtroom every hour on the half hour between 9:30 a.m. and 3:30 p.m.

Constitution and Congress. Article III, section 2, of the Constitution provides that "In all Cases affecting Ambassadors, other public Ministers and Consuls, and those in which a State shall be Party, the supreme Court shall have original Jurisdiction. In all the other Cases ... the supreme Court shall have appellate Jurisdiction, both as to Law and Fact, with such Exceptions, and under such Regulations as the Congress shall make."

Original jurisdiction refers to the right of the Supreme Court to hear a case before any other court does. Appellate jurisdiction is the right to review the decision of a lower court. The vast majority of cases reaching the Supreme Court are appeals from rulings of the lower courts; generally only a handful of original jurisdiction cases are filed each term.

After enactment of the Judiciary Act of 1925, the Supreme Court gained broad discretion to decide for itself what cases it would hear. In 1988 Congress virtually eliminated the Court's mandatory jurisdiction, which obliged it to hear most appeals. Since then that discretion has been nearly unlimited.

Methods of Appeal

Cases come to the Supreme Court in several ways: through petitions for writs of certiorari, appeals, and requests for certification.

In petitioning for a writ of certiorari, a litigant who has lost a case in a lower court sets out the reasons why the Supreme Court should review the case. If a writ is granted, the Court requests a certified record of the case from the lower court.

The main difference between the certiorari and appeal routes is that the Court has complete discretion to grant a request for a writ of certiorari but is under more obligation to accept and decide a case that comes to it on appeal.

Most cases reach the Supreme Court by means of the writ of certiorari. In the relatively few cases to reach the Court by means of appeal, the appellant must file a jurisdictional statement explaining why the case qualifies for review and why the Court should grant it a hearing. Often the justices dispose of these cases by deciding them summarily, without oral argument or formal opinion.

Those whose petitions for certiorari have been granted must pay the Court's standard $300 fee for docketing the case. The U.S. government does not have to pay these fees, nor do persons too poor to afford them. The latter may file in forma pauperis (in the character or manner of a pauper) petitions. Another, seldom used, method of appeal is certification, the request by a lower court—usually a court of appeals—for a final answer to questions of law in a particular case. The Court, after examining the certificate, may order the case argued before it.

Process of Review

In the 1995–1996 term the Court was asked to review about 7,600 cases. All petitions are examined by the staff of the clerk of the Court; those found to be in reasonably proper form are placed on the docket and given a number. All cases, except those falling within the Court's original jurisdiction, are placed on a single docket, known simply as "the docket." Only in the numbering of the cases is a distinction made between prepaid and in forma pauperis cases on the docket. The first case filed in the 1996–1997 term, for example, would be designated 96–1. In forma pauperis cases contain the year and begin with the number 5001. The second in forma pauperis case filed in the 1996–1997 term would thus be number 96–5002.

Each justice, aided by law clerks, is responsible for reviewing all cases on the docket. In recent years a number of justices have used a "cert pool" system in this review. Their clerks work together to examine cases, writing a pool memo on several petitions. The memo then is given to the justices who determine if more research is needed. Other justices may prefer to review each petition themselves or have their clerks do it.

Petitions on the docket vary from elegantly printed and bound documents, of which multiple copies are submitted to the Court, to single sheets of prison stationery scribbled in pencil. The decisions to grant or deny review of cases are made in conferences, which are held in the conference room adjacent to the chief justice's chambers. Justices are summoned to the conference room by a buzzer, usually between 9:30 and 10:00 a.m. They shake hands with each other and take their appointed seats, and the chief justice then begins the discussion.

Discuss and Orders Lists

A few days before the conference convenes, the chief justice compiles the discuss list of cases deemed important enough for discussion and a vote. As many as three-quarters of the petitions for certiorari are denied a place on the list and thus rejected without further consideration. Any justice can have a case placed on the discuss list simply by requesting that it be placed there.

Only the justices attend conferences; no legal assistants or staff are present. The junior associate justice acts as doorkeeper and messenger, sending for reference material and receiving messages and data. Unlike with other parts of the federal government, few leaks have occurred about what transpires during the conferences.

At the start of the conference, the chief justice makes a brief statement outlining the facts of each case. Then each justice, beginning with the senior associate justice, comments on the case, usually indicating in the course of the comments how he or she intends to vote. A traditional but unwritten rule is that four affirmative votes puts a case on the schedule for oral argument.

Petitions for certiorari, appeals, and in forma pauperis motions that are approved for review or denied review during conference are placed on a certified orders list to be released the next Monday in open court.

Arguments

Once the Court announces it will hear a case, the clerk of the Court arranges the schedule for oral argument. Cases are argued roughly in the order in which they were granted review, subject to modification if more time is needed to acquire all the necessary documents. Cases generally are heard not sooner than three months after the Court has agreed to review

The Supreme Court's law library contains about 300,000 volumes and houses the most complete available set of the printed briefs, appendices, and records of Court cases.

them. Under special circumstances the date scheduled for oral argument can be advanced or postponed.

Well before oral argument takes place, the justices receive the briefs and records from counsel in the case. The measure of attention the brief receives—from a thorough and exhaustive study to a cursory glance—depends both on the nature of the case and the work habits of the justice.

As one of the two public functions of the Court, oral arguments are viewed by some as very important. Others dispute the significance of oral arguments, contending that by the time a case is heard most of the justices already have made up their minds.

Time Limits

The time allowed each side for oral argument is thirty minutes. Because the time allotted must accommodate any questions the justices may wish to ask, the actual time for presentation may be considerably shorter than thirty minutes. Under the current rules of the Court, one counsel only will be heard for each side, except by special permission.

An exception is made for an amicus curiae, a "friend of the court," a person who volunteers or is invited to take part in matters before a court but is not a party in the case. Counsel for an amicus curiae may participate in oral argument if the party supported by the amicus allows use of part of its argument time or the Court grants a motion permitting argument by this counsel. The motion must show, the rules state, that the amicus's argument "is thought to provide assistance to the Court not otherwise available." The Court is generally unreceptive to such motions.

Court rules provide advice to counsel presenting oral arguments before the Court: "Oral argument should emphasize and clarify the written arguments appearing in the briefs on the merits." That same rule warns—with italicized emphasis—that the Court "looks with disfavor on oral argument read from a prepared text." Most attorneys appearing before the Court use an outline or notes to make sure they cover the important points.

Circulating the Argument

The Supreme Court has tape-recorded oral arguments since 1955. In 1968 the Court, in addition to its own recording, began contracting with private firms to tape and transcribe all oral arguments. The contract stipulates that the transcript "shall include everything spoken in argument, by Court, counsel, or others, and nothing shall be omitted from the transcript unless the Chief Justice or Presiding Justice so directs." But "the names of Justices asking questions shall not be recorded or transcribed; questions shall be indicated by the letter 'Q.' "

The marshal of the Court keeps the tapes during the term, and their use usually is limited to the justices and their law clerks. At the end of the term, the tapes are sent to the National Archives. Persons wishing to listen to the tapes or buy a copy of a transcript can apply to the Archives for permission to do so.

Transcripts made by a private firm can be acquired more quickly. These transcripts usually are available a week after arguments are heard. Transcripts can be read in the Court's library or public information office. Those who purchase the transcripts must agree that they will not be photographically reproduced. In addition, transcripts of oral arguments are available on the Westlaw electronic data retrieval system.

Proposals have been made to tape arguments for television and radio use or to permit live broadcast coverage of arguments. The Court has rejected these proposals.

Use of Briefs

The brief of the petitioner or appellant must be filed within forty-five days of the Court's announced decision to hear the case. Except for in forma pauperis cases, forty copies of the brief must be filed with the Court. For in forma pauperis proceedings, the Court requires only that documents be legible. The opposing brief from the respondent or appellee is to be filed within thirty days of receipt of the brief of the petitioner or appellant. Either party may appeal to the clerk for an extension of time in filing the brief.

Court Rule 24 sets forth the elements that a brief should contain. These are: the questions presented for review; a list of all parties to the proceeding; a table of contents and table of authorities; citations of the opinions and judgments delivered in the lower courts; "a concise statement of the grounds on which the jurisdiction of this Court is invoked"; constitutional provisions, treaties, statutes, ordinances, and regulations involved; "a concise statement of the case containing all that is material to the consideration of the questions presented"; a summary of argument; the argument, which exhibits "clearly the points of fact and of law being presented and citing the authorities and statutes relied upon"; and a conclusion "specifying with particularity the relief which the party seeks."

The form and organization of the brief are covered by rules 33 and 34. The rules limit the number of pages in various types of briefs. The rules also set out a color code for the covers of different kinds of briefs. Petitions are white; motions opposing them are orange. Petitioner's briefs on the merits are light blue, while those of respondents are red. Reply briefs are yellow; amicus curiae, green; and documents filed by the United States, gray.

Questioning

During oral argument the justices may interrupt with questions or remarks as often as they wish. Unless counsel has been granted special permission extending the thirty-minute limit, he or she can continue talking after the time has expired only to complete a sentence.

The frequency of questioning, as well as the manner in which questions are asked, depends on the style of the justices and their interest in a particular case. Of the current justices, all but Clarence Thomas participate, more or less actively, in questioning during oral arguments; Thomas asks questions very, very rarely.

Questions from the justices may upset and unnerve counsel by interrupting a well-rehearsed argument and introducing an unexpected element. Nevertheless, questioning has several advantages. It serves to alert counsel about what aspects of the case need further elaboration or more information. For the Court, questions can bring out weak points in an argument—and sometimes strengthen it.

Conferences

Cases for which oral arguments have been heard are then dealt with in conference. During the Wednesday afternoon conference, the cases that

The Supreme Court's bench, angled at the ends, allows justices to see each other during oral arguments.

were argued the previous Monday are discussed and decided. At the all-day Friday conference, the cases argued on the preceding Tuesday and Wednesday are discussed and decided. Justices also consider new motions, appeals, and petitions while in conference.

Conferences are conducted in complete secrecy. No secretaries, clerks, stenographers, or messengers are allowed into the room. This practice began many years ago when the justices became convinced that decisions were being disclosed prematurely.

The justices meet in an oak-paneled, book-lined conference room adjacent to the chief justice's suite. Nine chairs surround a large rectangular table, each chair bearing the nameplate of the justice who sits there. The chief justice sits at the east end of the table, and the senior associate justice at the west end. The other justices take their places in order of seniority. The junior justice is charged with sending for and receiving documents or other information the Court needs.

On entering the conference room the justices shake hands with each other, a symbol of harmony that began in the 1880s. The chief justice begins the conference by calling the first case to be decided and discussing it. When the chief justice is finished, the senior associate justice speaks, followed by the other justices in order of seniority.

The justices can speak for as long as they wish, but they practice restraint because of the amount of business to be completed. By custom each justice speaks without interruption. Other than these procedural arrangements, little is known about what transpires in conference. Although discussions generally are said to be polite and orderly, occasionally they can be acrimonious. Likewise, consideration of the issues in a particular case may be full and probing, or perfunctory, leaving the real debate on the question until later when the written drafts of opinions are circulated up and down the Court's corridors between chambers.

Generally the discussion of the case clearly indicates how a justice plans to vote on it. A majority vote is needed to decide a case—five votes if all nine justices are participating.

Opinions

After the justices have voted on a case, the writing of the opinion or opinions begins. An opinion is a reasoned argument explaining the legal issues in the case and the precedents on which the opinion is based. Soon after a case is decided in conference, the task of writing the majority opinion is assigned. When in the majority, the chief justice designates the writer. When the chief justice is in the minority, the senior associate justice voting with the majority assigns the job of writing the majority opinion.

Any justice may write a separate opinion. If in agreement with the Court's decision but not with some of the reasoning in the majority opinion, the justice writes a concurring opinion giving his or her reasoning. If in disagreement with the majority, the justice writes a dissenting opinion or simply goes on record as a dissenter without an opinion. More than one justice can sign a concurring opinion or a dissenting opinion.

The amount of time between the vote on a case and the announcement of the decision varies from case to case. In simple cases where few points of law are at issue, the opinion sometimes can be written and cleared by the other justices in a week or less. In more complex cases, especially those with several dissenting or concurring opinions, the process can take six months or more. Some cases may have to be reargued or the initial decision reversed after the drafts of opinions have been circulated.

The assigning justice may consider the points made by majority justices during the conference discussion, the workload of the other justices, the need to avoid the more extreme opinions within the majority, and expertise in the particular area of law involved in a case.

The style of writing a Court opinion—majority, concurring, or dissenting—depends primarily on the individual justice. In some cases, the justice may prefer to write a restricted and limited opinion; in others, he or she may take a broader approach to the subject. The decision likely is to be influenced by the need to satisfy the other justices in the majority.

When a justice is satisfied that the written opinion is conclusive or "unanswerable," it goes into print. Draft opinions are circulated, revised, and printed on a computerized typesetting system. The circulation of the drafts—whether computer-to-computer or on paper—provokes further discussion in many cases. Often the suggestions and criticisms require the writer to juggle opposing views. To retain a majority, the author of the draft opinion frequently feels obliged to make major emendations to satisfy justices who are unhappy with the initial draft. Some opinions have to be rewritten several times.

One reason for the secrecy surrounding the circulation of drafts is that some of the justices who voted with the majority may find the majority draft opinion so unpersuasive—or one or more of the dissenting drafts so convincing—that they change their vote. If enough justices alter their votes, the majority may shift, so that a former dissent becomes the majority opinion. When a new majority emerges from this process, the task of writing, printing, and circulating a new majority draft begins all over again.

When the drafts of an opinion—including dissents and concurring views—have been written, circulated, discussed, and revised, if necessary, the final versions then are printed. Before the opinion is produced the reporter of decisions adds a "headnote" or syllabus summarizing the decision and a "lineup" showing how the justices voted.

Two hundred copies of the "bench opinion" are made. As the decision is announced in Court, the bench opinion is distributed to journalists and others in the public information office. Another copy, with any necessary corrections noted on it, is sent to the U.S. Government Printing Office, which prints 3,397 "slip" opinions, which are distributed to federal and state courts and agencies. The Court receives 400 of these, and they are available to the public free through the Public Information Office as long as supplies last. The Government Printing Office also prints the opinion for inclusion in *United States Reports,* the official record of Supreme Court opinions.

The Court also makes opinions available electronically, through its so-called Hermes system, to a number of large legal publishers, the Government Printing Office, and other information services. These organizations allow redistribution of the opinions to their own subscribers and users. Opinions are available on the Internet through Case Western Reserve University. The Hermes system was established as a pilot project in 1991 and expanded and made permanent in 1993.

In 1996 the Court also established its own electronic bulletin board system (BBS) that provides anyone with a personal computer online access to the Court's opinions, docket, argument calendar, and other information and publications. The telephone number for the Court's BBS is (202) 554-2570.

The public announcement of opinions in Court probably is the Court's most dramatic function. It may also be the most expendable.

Depending on who delivers the opinion and how, announcements can take a considerable amount of the Court's time. Opinions are given simultaneously to the public information officer for distribution. Nevertheless, those who are in the courtroom to hear the announcement of a ruling are participating in a very old tradition. The actual delivery may be tedious or exciting, depending on the nature of the case, the eloquence of the opinion, and the style of its oral delivery.

Brief Biographies

William Hubbs Rehnquist

Born: October 1, 1924, Milwaukee, Wisconsin.

Education: Stanford University, B.A., Phi Beta Kappa, and M.A., 1948; Harvard University, M.A., 1949; Stanford University Law School, LL.B., 1952.

Family: Married Natalie Cornell, 1953; died, 1991; two daughters, one son.

Career: Law clerk to Justice Robert H. Jackson, U.S. Supreme Court, 1952–1953; practiced law, 1953–1969; assistant U.S. attorney general, Office of Legal Counsel, 1969–1971.

Supreme Court Service: Nominated as associate justice of the U.S. Supreme Court by President Richard Nixon, October 21, 1971; confirmed, 68–26, December 10, 1971; nominated as chief justice of the United States by President Ronald Reagan, June 17, 1986; confirmed, 65–33, September 17, 1986.

President Reagan's appointment of William H. Rehnquist as chief justice in 1986 was a deliberate effort to shift the Court to the right. Since his

early years as an associate justice in the 1970s, Rehnquist had been the Court's strongest conservative voice. And as chief justice, Rehnquist has helped move the Court to the right in a number of areas, including criminal law, states' rights, civil rights, and church-state issues.

Rehnquist, the fourth associate justice to become chief, argues that the original intent of the Framers of the Constitution and the Bill of Rights is the proper standard for interpreting those documents today. He also takes a literal approach to individual rights. These beliefs have led him to dissent from the Court's rulings protecting a woman's privacy-based right to abortion, to argue that no constitutional barrier exists to school prayer, and to side with police and prosecutors on questions of criminal law. In 1991 he wrote the Court's decision upholding an administration ban on abortion counseling at publicly financed clinics. The next year he vigorously dissented from the

Court's affirmation of *Roe v . Wade* , the 1973 opinion that made abortion legal nationwide.

A native of Milwaukee, Rehnquist attended Stanford University, where he earned both a B.A. and an M.A. He received a second M.A. from Harvard before returning to Stanford for law school. His classmates there recalled him as an intelligent student with already well-entrenched conservative views.

After graduating from law school in 1952, Rehnquist came to Washington, D.C., to serve as a law clerk to Supreme Court justice Robert H. Jackson. There he wrote a memorandum that later came back to haunt him during his Senate confirmation hearings. In the memo Rehnquist favored separate but equal schools for blacks and whites. Asked about those views by the Senate Judiciary Committee in 1971, Rehnquist repudiated them, declaring that they were Justice Jackson's, not his own.

Following his clerkship, Rehnquist decided to practice law in the Southwest. He moved to Phoenix and immediately became immersed in Arizona Republican politics. From his earliest days in the state, he was associated with the party's conservative wing. A 1957 speech denouncing the liberalism of the Warren Court typified his views at the time.

During the 1964 presidential race, Rehnquist campaigned ardently for Barry Goldwater. It was then that Rehnquist met and worked with Richard G. Kleindienst, who later, as President Richard Nixon's deputy attorney general, appointed Rehnquist to head the Justice Department's Office of Legal Counsel as an assistant attorney general. In 1971 Nixon nominated him to the Supreme Court.

Rehnquist drew opposition from liberals and civil rights organizations before winning confirmation and again before being approved as chief justice in 1986. The Senate voted to approve his nomination in December 1971 by a vote of 68–26 at the same time that another Nixon nominee, Lewis F. Powell Jr., was winning nearly unanimous confirmation.

In 1986 Rehnquist faced new accusations of having harassed voters as a Republican poll watcher in Phoenix in the 1950s and 1960s. He was also found to have accepted anti-Semitic restrictions in a property deed to a Vermont home. Despite the charges, the Senate approved his appointment as chief justice 65–33. Liberal Democratic senators cast most of the no votes in both confirmations.

Despite his strong views, Rehnquist is popular among his colleagues and staff. When he was nominated for chief justice, Justice William J. Brennan Jr., the leader of the Court's liberal bloc, said Rehnquist would be "a splendid chief justice." After becoming chief justice, Rehnquist was credited with speeding up the Court's conferences, in which the justices decide what cases to hear, vote on cases, and assign opinions.

Rehnquist was married to Natalie Cornell, who died in 1991. They had two daughters and a son. Recent news reports said that Rehnquist was dating Cynthia Holcomb Hall, a judge on the Ninth U.S. Circuit Court of Appeals.

John Paul Stevens

Born: April 20, 1920, Chicago, Illinois.

Education: University of Chicago, B.A., Phi Beta Kappa, 1941; Northwestern University School of Law, J.D., 1947.

Family: Married Elizabeth Jane Sheeren, 1942; three daughters, one son; divorced 1979; married Maryan Mulholland Simon, 1980.

Career: Law clerk to Justice Wiley B. Rutledge, U.S. Supreme Court, 1947–1948; practiced law, Chicago, 1949–1970; judge, U.S. Court of Appeals for the Seventh Circuit, 1970–1975.

Supreme Court Service: Nominated as associate justice of the U.S. Supreme Court by President Gerald R. Ford, November 28, 1975; confirmed, 98–0, December 17, 1975.

When President Gerald R. Ford nominated federal appeals court judge John Paul Stevens to the Supreme Court seat vacated by veteran liberal William O. Douglas in 1975, Court observers struggled to pin an ideological label on the new nominee. The consensus that finally emerged was that Stevens was neither a doctrinaire liberal nor conservative, but a judicial centrist. His subsequent opinions bear out this description, although in recent years he has moved steadily toward the liberal side.

Stevens is a soft-spoken, mild-mannered man who often sports a bow tie under his judicial robes. A member of a prominent Chicago family, he had a long record of excellence in scholarship, graduating Phi Beta Kappa from the University of Chicago in 1941. He earned the Bronze Star during a wartime stint in the navy and then returned to Chicago to enter Northwestern University Law School, from which he was graduated magna cum laude in 1947. From there Stevens left for Washington, where he served as a law clerk to Supreme Court justice Wiley B. Rutledge. He returned to Chicago to join the prominent law firm of Poppenhusen, Johnston, Thompson & Raymond, which specialized in antitrust law. Stevens developed a reputation as a pre-eminent antitrust lawyer and three years later in 1952 formed his own firm, Rothschild, Stevens, Barry & Myers. He remained there, engaging in private practice and teaching part-time at Northwestern and the University of Chicago law schools, until his appointment by President Richard Nixon in 1970 to the U.S. Court of Appeals for the Seventh Circuit.

Stevens developed a reputation as a political moderate during his undergraduate days at the University of Chicago, then an overwhelmingly liberal campus. Although he is a registered Republican, he has never been active in partisan politics. Nevertheless, Stevens served as Republican counsel in 1951 to the House Judiciary Subcommittee on the Study of Monopoly Power. He also served from 1953 to 1955, during the Eisenhower administration, as a member of the attorney general's committee to study antitrust laws.

In his five years on the federal appeals court, Stevens earned a reputation as an independent-minded judicial craftsman. President Ford, who took office after Nixon's forced resignation, wanted to nominate a moderate of impeccable legal reputation to help restore confidence in government after the Watergate scandals. Stevens was confirmed without dissent, 98–0, on December 17, 1975, and took office two days later.

Stevens has frequently dissented from the most conservative rulings of the Burger and Rehnquist Courts. For example, he dissented from the Burger Court's 1986 decision upholding state antisodomy laws and the Rehnquist Court's 1989 decision permitting states to execute someone for committing a murder at the age of sixteen or seventeen. He has taken liberal positions on abortion rights, civil rights, and church-state issues.

In his second full term on the Court, Stevens wrote the main opinion in a case upholding the right of the Federal Communications Commission to penalize broadcasters for airing indecent material at times when children are in the audience. Among his other noteworthy opinions is a 1985 decision striking down an Alabama law that allowed a moment of silence for prayer or silent meditation at the beginning of each school day. In 1996 he wrote the majority opinion in an important punitive damages case that threw out a $2 million award in an Alabama case and set guidelines for reviewing punitive damage awards in the future.

In 1942 Stevens married Elizabeth Jane Sheeren. They have four children. They were divorced in 1979. Stevens subsequently married Maryan Mulholland Simon, a longtime neighbor in Chicago.

Sandra Day O'Connor

Born: March 26, 1930, El Paso, Texas.

Education: Stanford University, B.A., 1950; Stanford University Law School, LL.B., 1952.

Family: Married John J. O'Connor III, 1952; three sons.

Career: Deputy county attorney, San Mateo, California, 1952–1953; assistant attorney general, Arizona, 1965–1969; Arizona state senator,

1969–1975; Arizona Senate majority leader, 1972–1975; judge, Maricopa County Superior Court, 1974–1979; judge, Arizona Court of Appeals, 1979–1981.

Supreme Court Service: Nominated as associate justice of the U.S. Supreme Court by President Ronald Reagan August 19, 1981; confirmed, 99–0, September 21, 1981.

Sandra Day O'Connor was the Court's first woman justice, and in 1992, after a decade on the Court, she emerged as a coalition builder in the Court's legal doctrine on abortion and other controversial issues.

Pioneering came naturally to O'Connor. Her grandfather left Kansas in 1880 to take up ranching in the desert land that eventually became the state of Arizona. O'Connor, born in El Paso, Texas, where her mother's parents lived, was raised on the Lazy B Ranch, the 198,000-acre spread that her grandfather founded in southeastern Arizona near Duncan. She spent her school years in El Paso, living with her grandmother. She graduated from high school at age sixteen and then entered Stanford University.

Six years later, in 1952, Sandra Day had won degrees with great distinction, both from the university, in economics, and from Stanford Law School. At Stanford she met John J. O'Connor III, her future husband, and William H. Rehnquist, a future colleague on the Supreme Court. While in law school, Sandra Day was an editor of the *Stanford Law Review* and a member of Order of the Coif, the academic honor society.

Despite her record, O'Connor had difficulty finding a job as an attorney in 1952 when relatively few women were practicing law. She applied, among other places, to the firm in which William French Smith—first attorney general in the Reagan administration—was a partner, only to be offered a job as a secretary.

After she completed a short stint as deputy county attorney for San Mateo County (California) while her new husband completed law school at Stanford, the O'Connors moved with the U.S. Army to Frankfurt, Germany. There Sandra O'Connor worked as a civilian attorney for the army, while John O'Connor served his tour of duty. In 1957 they returned to Phoenix, where, during the next eight years, their three sons were born. O'Connor's life was a mix of parenthood, homemaking, volunteer work, and some "miscellaneous legal tasks" on the side.

In 1965 she resumed her legal career on a full-time basis, taking a job as an assistant attorney general for Arizona. After four years in that post she was appointed to fill a vacancy in the state Senate, where she served on the judiciary committee. In 1970 she was elected to the same body and two years later was chosen its majority leader, the first woman in the nation to hold such a post. O'Connor was active in Republican Party politics, serving as co-chair of the Arizona Committee for the Re-election of the President in 1972.

In 1974 she was elected to the Superior Court for Maricopa County, where she served for five years. Then in 1979 Democratic governor Bruce Babbitt appointed O'Connor to the Arizona Court of Appeals. It was from that post that President Reagan chose her as his first nominee to the Supreme Court, succeeding Potter Stewart, who retired. Reagan described her as "a person for all seasons." The Senate confirmed her on September 21, 1981, by a vote of 99–0.

O'Connor has helped push the Court in conservative directions in a number of areas, including criminal law and affirmative action. In 1989 she wrote the Court's opinion striking down a local minority contractor set-aside program. The same year she also wrote the Court's opinion permitting the death penalty for mentally retarded defendants. O'Connor has also been a strong voice for restricting state prisoners' ability to use federal habeas corpus to overturn criminal convictions or sentences.

Throughout the 1980s, O'Connor voted to uphold state laws regulating abortion procedures or restricting government funding of abortions. In 1992, however, she joined with two other Republican-appointed justices, Anthony M. Kennedy and David H. Souter, to form a majority for preserving a modified form of the Court's original abortion rights ruling, *Roe v. Wade*. In a jointly authored opinion the three justices said that Roe's "essential holding"—guaranteeing a woman's right to an abortion during most of her pregnancy—should be reaffirmed. But the joint opinion also said that states could regulate abortion procedures as long as they did not impose "an undue burden" on a woman's choice—a test that O'Connor had advocated in previous opinions.

Antonin Scalia

Born: March 11, 1936, Trenton, New Jersey.

Education: Georgetown University, A.B., 1957; Harvard University Law School, LL.B., 1960.

Family: Married Maureen McCarthy, 1960; five sons, four daughters.

Career: Practiced law, Cleveland, 1960–1967; taught at the University of Virginia, 1967–1971; general counsel, White House Office of Telecommunications Policy, 1971–1972; chairman, Administrative Conference of the United States, 1972–1974; head, Justice Department Office of Legal Counsel, 1974–1977; taught at the University of Chicago Law School,

1977–1982; judge, U.S. Court of Appeals for the District of Columbia Circuit, 1982–1986.

Supreme Court Service: Nominated as associate justice of the U.S. Supreme Court by President Ronald Reagan June 17, 1986; confirmed, 98–0, September 17, 1986.

After Warren E. Burger retired from the Court and Ronald Reagan named William H. Rehnquist to succeed him as chief justice, the president's next move—appointing Antonin Scalia as associate justice—was not surprising. On issues dear to Reagan, Scalia clearly met the president's tests for conservatism. Scalia, whom Reagan had named to the U.S. Court of Appeals for the District of Columbia Circuit in 1982, became the first Supreme Court justice of Italian ancestry. A Roman Catholic, he opposes abortion. He has also strongly opposed "affirmative action" preferences for minorities.

In contrast to the heated debate over Rehnquist's nomination as chief justice, only a few, brief speeches were given before the Senate confirmed the equally conservative Scalia, 98–0. He has since become the scourge of some members of Congress because of his suspicion of committee reports, floor speeches, and other elements of legislative history that courts traditionally use to interpret statutes.

Born in Trenton, New Jersey, March 11, 1936, Scalia grew up in Queens, New York. His father was a professor of Romance languages at Brooklyn College, and his mother was a schoolteacher. He was first in his graduating class at an all-male military academy in Manhattan, St. Francis Xavier, and class valedictorian at Georgetown University, where he graduated in 1957. He received his law degree in 1960 from Harvard Law School, where he served as note editor of the *Harvard Law Review*. He worked for six years for the firm of Jones, Day, Cockley & Reavis in Cleveland and then taught contract, commercial, and comparative law at the University of Virginia Law School.

Scalia was a specialist in administrative law and a strong advocate of deregulation. He served as general counsel of the White House Office of Telecommunications Policy from 1971 to 1972. He then headed the Administrative Conference of the United States, a group that advises the government on questions of administrative law and procedure. From 1974 through the Ford administration he headed the Justice Department's Office of Legal Counsel, a post Rehnquist had held three years earlier. Scalia then returned to academia to teach at the University of Chicago Law

School. From 1977 to 1982 he was editor of the magazine *Regulation,* published by the American Enterprise Institute for Public Policy Research.

President Ronald Reagan appointed Scalia to the U.S. Court of Appeals for the District of Columbia Circuit in 1982. There, Scalia showed himself to be a hard worker, an aggressive interrogator, and an articulate advocate. He had a marked impatience with what he saw as regulatory or judicial overreaching. In 1983 he dissented from a ruling requiring the Food and Drug Administration (FDA) to consider whether drugs used for lethal injections met FDA standards as safe and effective. The Supreme Court agreed, reversing the appeals court in 1985.

Scalia was thought to be the principal author of an unsigned decision in 1986 that declared major portions of the Gramm-Rudman-Hollings budget-balancing act unconstitutional. The Supreme Court upheld the decision later in the year.

On the Supreme Court Scalia quickly became a forceful voice for conservative positions. He joined in conservative decisions limiting procedural rights in criminal cases and in a series of rulings in 1989 limiting remedies in employment discrimination cases. He also strongly dissented from rulings upholding affirmative action and reaffirming abortion rights.

In many of his constitutional law opinions, Scalia argued for an "original intent" approach that limited rights to those intended when the Constitution was adopted. He also sharply challenged the use of legislative history in interpreting statutes. He argued that judges should look only to the words of the statute itself.

Scalia expressed his conservative views in aggressive questioning from the bench and in frequently acerbic opinions, especially in dissent.

Anthony McLeod Kennedy

Born: July 23, 1936, Sacramento, California.

Education: Stanford University, A.B., Phi Beta Kappa, 1958; Harvard University Law School, LL.B., 1961.

Family: Married Mary Davis, 1963; two sons, one daughter.

Career: Practiced law, San Francisco, 1961–1963, Sacramento, 1963–1975; professor of constitutional law, McGeorge School of Law, University of the Pacific, 1965–1988; judge, U.S. Court of Appeals for the Ninth Circuit, 1975–1988.

Supreme Court Service: Nominated as associate justice of the U.S. Supreme Court by President Ronald Reagan November 11, 1987; confirmed, 97–0, February 3, 1988.

Quiet, scholarly Anthony M. Kennedy, President Reagan's third choice for his third appointment to the Supreme Court, helped form a conservative majority on many issues in his initial years after joining the Court in 1988. While he adheres to generally conservative views, Kennedy has taken moderate stands on some issues that often make him a pivotal vote between the Court's conservative and liberal blocs.

Before Kennedy's nomination in November 1987, the Senate and the country had agonized through Reagan's two unsuccessful attempts to replace retiring Justice Lewis F. Powell Jr., first with Robert H. Bork and then with Douglas H. Ginsburg. The Senate rejected Bork's nomination after contentious hearings, where opponents depicted the federal appeals court judge as a conservative ideologue. Reagan then turned to Ginsburg, a colleague of Bork's on the federal appeals court in Washington, but he withdrew his name amid controversy about his admitted past use of marijuana.

A quiet sense of relief prevailed when Reagan finally selected a nominee who could be confirmed without another wrenching confrontation. Kennedy spent twelve years as a judge on the U.S. Court of Appeals for the Ninth Circuit. But unlike Bork, who wrote and spoke extensively for twenty years, Kennedy's record was confined mostly to his approximately five hundred judicial opinions, where he generally decided issues narrowly instead of using his opinions as a testing ground for constitutional theories. The Senate voted to confirm him without dissent, 97–0, on February 3, 1988.

A native Californian, Kennedy attended Stanford University from 1954 to 1957 and the London School of Economics from 1957 to 1958. He received an A.B. from Stanford in 1958 and an LL.B. from Harvard Law School in 1961. Admitted to the California bar in 1962, he was in private law practice until 1975, when President Gerald R. Ford appointed him to the appeals court. From 1965 to 1988 he taught constitutional law at McGeorge School of Law, University of the Pacific.

In his first full term on the Court, Kennedy provided a crucial fifth vote for the Court's conservative wing in a number of civil rights cases. He generally favored law enforcement in criminal cases. And in a closely watched abortion-rights case, he voted along with Chief Justice William H. Rehnquist and Justices Byron R. White and Antonin Scalia to overturn the 1973 ruling, *Roe v. Wade*, that first established a constitutional right to abortion.

Many observers viewed Kennedy's arrival as ushering in a new conservative era. But in 1992 he sorely disappointed conservatives in two major cases. In one he provided the critical fifth vote and wrote the majority opinion in a decision barring officially sponsored prayers at public high school graduation ceremonies. In the other he reversed himself on the abortion issue, joining with Justices Sandra Day O'Connor and David H. Souter in an opinion that upheld a modified version of *Roe v. Wade.*

Kennedy has proved to be a strong free speech advocate in First Amendment cases. In 1989 he helped form the 5–4 majority that overturned state laws against burning or desecrating the U.S. flag. The former constitutional law professor has also displayed a special interest in equal protection and federalism issues. He has voted with other conservatives in rulings that limited racially motivated congressional districting and backed states in disputes over federal power. But he was the swing vote in a 1995 decision to bar the states from imposing term limits on members of Congress. And in 1996 he wrote the opinion striking down Colorado's anti–gay rights amendment prohibiting enactment of any laws to bar discrimination against homosexuals.

David Hackett Souter

Born: September 17, 1939, Melrose, Massachusetts.

Education: Harvard College, B.A., 1961; Rhodes scholar, Oxford University, 1961–1963; Harvard University Law School, LL.B., 1966.

Family: Unmarried.

Career: Private law practice, Concord, New Hampshire, 1966–1968; assistant attorney general, New Hampshire, 1968–1971; deputy attorney general, New Hampshire, 1971–1976; attorney general, New Hampshire, 1976–1978; associate justice, New Hampshire Superior Court, 1978–1983; associate justice, New Hampshire Supreme Court, 1983–1990; judge, U.S. Court of Appeals for the First Circuit, 1990.

Supreme Court Service: Nominated as associate justice of the U.S. Supreme Court by President George Bush July 23, 1990; confirmed, 90–9, October 2, 1990.

At first the Senate did not know what to make of David H. Souter, a cerebral, button-down nominee who was President Bush's first appointment to the Court. Souter was little known outside his home state of New Hampshire, where he had been attorney general, a trial judge, and a state supreme court justice. He had virtually no scholarly writings to dissect and little federal court experience to scrutinize. Only three months earlier Bush had appointed him to the U.S. Court of Appeals for the First Circuit. Souter had yet to write a legal opinion on the appeals court.

During his confirmation hearings, the Harvard graduate and former Rhodes scholar demonstrated intellectual rigor and a masterly approach to constitutional law. His earlier work as state attorney general and New Hampshire Supreme Court justice had a conservative bent, but he came across as more moderate during the hearings.

Under persistent questioning from Democratic senators, Souter refused to say how he would vote on the issue of abortion rights. Abortion rights supporters feared he would provide a fifth vote for overturning the 1973 *Roe v. Wade* decision. Senators in both parties, however, said they were impressed with his legal knowledge. He was confirmed by the Senate 90–9; dissenting senators cited his refusal to take a stand on abortion.

On the bench Souter proved to be a tenacious questioner but reserved in his opinions. He generally voted with the Court's conservative majority in his first term. But in the 1991–1992 term he staked out a middle ground with Justices Sandra Day O'Connor and Anthony M. Kennedy in two crucial cases. In a closely watched abortion case Souter joined with the other two Republican-appointed justices in writing the main opinion reaffirming the "essential holding" of *Roe v. Wade*. The three also joined in forming a 5–4 majority to prohibit school-sponsored prayers at public high school graduation ceremonies.

In the Court's next several terms Souter moved markedly to the left. He joined with liberals in dissenting from cases that restricted racial redistricting. He also voted with the Court's liberal bloc on church-state and some criminal law issues.

Despite his experience in state government, Souter has proved to be a strong supporter of federal power in cases affecting states' rights. He joined the dissenters in a 1995 decision striking down on states' rights grounds a federal law banning the possession of guns near schools. And in 1996 he wrote a massive and scholarly dissent from the Court's decision limiting Congress's power to authorize private citizens to sue states in federal courts to enforce federal law.

Souter is known for his intensely private, ascetic life. He was born September 17, 1939, in Melrose, Massachusetts. An only child, he moved with his parents to Weare, New Hampshire, at age eleven. Except for college, he lived in Weare until 1990.

Graduating from Harvard College in 1961, Souter attended Oxford University on a Rhodes Scholarship from 1961 to 1963, then returned to Cambridge for Harvard Law School. Graduating in 1966, he worked for two years in a Concord law firm. In 1968 he became an assistant attorney general, rose to deputy attorney general in 1971, and in 1976 was appointed attorney general. Souter served as attorney general until 1978, when he was named to the state's trial court. Five years later Gov. John H. Sununu appointed Souter to the state supreme court. Sununu was Bush's chief of staff when Souter was named to the U.S. Supreme Court.

Souter, a bachelor, is a nature enthusiast and avid hiker.

Clarence Thomas

Born: June 23, 1948, Savannah, Georgia.

Education: Immaculate Conception Seminary, 1967–1968; Holy Cross College, B.A., 1971; Yale University Law School, J.D., 1974.

Family: Married Kathy Grace Ambush, 1971; one son; divorced 1984; married Virginia Lamp, 1987.

Career: Assistant attorney general, Missouri, 1974–1977; attorney, Monsanto Co., 1977–1979; legislative assistant to Sen. John C. Danforth, R-Mo., 1979–1981; assistant secretary of education for civil rights, 1981–1982; chairman, Equal Employment Opportunity Commission, 1982–1990; judge, U.S. Court of Appeals for the District of Columbia Circuit, 1990–1991.

Supreme Court Service: Nominated as associate justice of the U.S. Supreme Court by President George Bush July 1, 1991; confirmed, 52–48, October 15, 1991.

Clarence Thomas won a narrow confirmation to the Supreme Court in 1991 after surviving dramatic accusations of sexual harassment. He generated continuing controversy with outspoken conservative views as a justice.

The Senate's 52–48 vote on Thomas was the closest Supreme Court

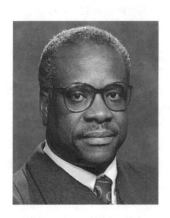

confirmation vote in more than a century. It followed a tumultuous nomination process that included close scrutiny of Thomas's judicial philosophy and sensational charges of sexual harassment brought by a former aide. Thomas denied the charges and accused the Senate Judiciary Committee of conducting a "high-tech lynching."

President George Bush nominated Thomas to succeed Thurgood Marshall, the Court's first black justice and a pioneer of the civil rights movement. Thomas came to prominence as a black conservative while serving as chairman of the Equal Employment Opportunity Commission during the Reagan and Bush administrations. Bush appointed him to the U.S. Court of Appeals for the District of Columbia Circuit in 1990.

Thomas was only forty-three at the time of his nomination to the Court, and senators noted that he likely would be affecting the outcome of major constitutional rulings well into the twenty-first century. Democratic senators closely questioned him on a range of constitutional issues—in particular, abortion. Thomas declined to give his views on abortion, saying he had never discussed the issue.

The committee decided to end its hearings even though it had received an allegation from a University of Oklahoma law professor, Anita Hill, that Thomas had sexually harassed her while she worked for him at the U.S. Department of Education and the EEOC. When the accusation leaked out, the Judiciary Committee reopened the hearing to take testimony from Hill, Thomas, and other witnesses.

In the end most senators said they could not resolve the conflict between Hill's detailed allegations and Thomas's categorical denials. Instead, senators fell back on their previous positions. Supporters praised his determined character and rise from poverty in rural Georgia. Opponents questioned whether Thomas had been candid with the committee in discussing his judicial philosophy.

After joining the Court, Thomas became one of the Court's most conservative members. He closely aligned himself with fellow conservative Antonin Scalia, voting with Scalia about 90 percent of the time. In 1992 he voted as his opponents had warned to overturn the 1973 abortion rights ruling, *Roe v. Wade,* but the Court reaffirmed the decision by a 5–4 vote.

In later cases Thomas wrote lengthy opinions sharply challenging existing legal doctrines. In 1994 he called for scrapping precedents that allowed courts to order the creation of majority-black districts for legislative or congressional seats. In 1995 he authored opinions that called for restricting the basis for Congress to regulate interstate commerce and for re-examining federal courts' role in desegregating public schools. In a campaign finance case in 1996, he urged the Court to overturn all laws limiting political contributions as an infringement on the First Amendment.

Thomas graduated from Yale Law School in 1974 and became an assistant attorney general of Missouri and, three years later, a staff attorney for Monsanto Company. He worked for Sen. John C. Danforth, R-Mo., as a legislative assistant and served in the Department of Education as assistant secretary for civil rights for one year before being named chairman of the EEOC.

Thomas's wife, the former Virginia Lamp, is a lawyer who served as a legislative official with the U.S. Department of Labor during the Bush administration and since 1993 as a senior policy analyst with the House Republican Conference. They were married in 1987. He has a son from his first marriage, which ended in divorce in 1984.

Ruth Bader Ginsburg

Born: March 15, 1933, Brooklyn, New York.
Education: Cornell University, B.A., 1954; attended Harvard University Law School, 1956–1958; graduated Columbia Law School, J.D., 1959.
Family: Married Martin D. Ginsburg, 1954; one daughter, one son.

Career: Law clerk to U.S. District Court Judge Edmund L. Palmieri, 1959–1961; Columbia Law School Project on International Procedure, 1961–1963; professor, Rutgers University School of Law, 1963–1972; director, Women's Rights Project, American Civil Liberties Union, 1972–1980; professor, Columbia Law School, 1972–1980; judge, U.S. Court of Appeals for the District of Columbia Circuit, 1980–1993.

Supreme Court Service: Nominated as associate justice of the U.S. Supreme Court by President Bill Clinton, June 22, 1993; confirmed, 96–3, August 3, 1993.

Ruth Bader Ginsburg's path to the U.S. Supreme Court is a classic American story of overcoming obstacles and setbacks through intelligence,

persistence, and quiet hard work. Her achievements as a student, law teacher, advocate, and judge came against a background of personal adversity and institutional discrimination against women. Ginsburg not only surmounted those hurdles for herself but also charted the legal strategy in the 1970s that helped broaden opportunities for women by establishing constitutional principles limiting sex discrimination in the law.

Born into a Jewish family of modest means in Brooklyn, Ruth Bader was greatly influenced by her mother, Celia, who imparted a love of learning and a determination to be independent. Celia Bader died of cancer on the eve of her daughter's high school graduation in 1948.

Ruth Bader attended Cornell University, where she graduated first in her class and met her future husband, Martin Ginsburg, who became a tax lawyer and later a professor at Georgetown University Law Center in Washington.

At Harvard Law School Ruth Bader Ginsburg made law review, cared for an infant daughter, and then helped her husband complete his studies after he was diagnosed with cancer. He recovered, graduated, and got a job in New York, and she transferred to Columbia for her final year of law school.

Although she was tied for first place in her class when she graduated, Ginsburg was unable to land a Supreme Court clerkship or job with a top New York law firm. Instead, she won a two-year clerkship with a federal district court judge. She then accepted a research position at Columbia that took her to Sweden, where she studied civil procedure and began to be stirred by feminist thought.

Ginsburg taught at Rutgers law school in New Jersey from 1963 to 1972. She also worked with the New Jersey affiliate of the American Civil

Liberties Union (ACLU), where her caseload included several early sex discrimination complaints. In 1972 Ginsburg became the first woman to be named to a tenured position on the Columbia Law School faculty. As director of the national ACLU's newly established Women's Rights Project, she also handled the cases that over the course of several years led the Supreme Court to require heightened scrutiny of legal classifications based on sex. Ginsburg won five of the six cases she argued before the Court.

President Jimmy Carter named Ginsburg to the U.S. Court of Appeals for the District of Columbia Circuit in 1980. There she earned a reputation as a judicial moderate on a sharply divided court. When Justice Byron R. White announced plans for his retirement in March 1993, Ginsburg was among the large field of candidates President Bill Clinton considered for the vacancy. Clinton considered and passed over two other leading candidates for the position before deciding to interview Ginsburg. White House aides told reporters later that Clinton had been especially impressed with Ginsburg's life story. Reaction to the nomination was overwhelmingly positive.

In three days of confirmation hearings before the Senate Judiciary Committee, Ginsburg depicted herself as an advocate of judicial restraint, but she also said courts sometimes had a role to play in bringing about social change. On specific issues she strongly endorsed abortion rights, equal rights for women, and the constitutional right to privacy. But she declined to give her views on many other issues, including capital punishment. Some senators said that she had been less than forthcoming, but the committee voted unanimously to recommend her for confirmation. The full Senate confirmed her four days later by a vote of 96–3.

Ginsburg was sworn in August 10, 1993, as the Court's second female justice — joining Justice Sandra Day O'Connor — and the first Jewish justice since 1969.

In her first weeks on the bench, Ginsburg startled observers and drew some criticism with her unusually active questioning, but she eased up later. In her voting, she took liberal positions on women's rights, civil rights, church-state, states' rights, and First Amendment issues, but she had a more mixed record in other areas, including criminal law. In 1996 she wrote the Court's opinion in an important sex discrimination case, requiring the all-male Virginia Military Institute to admit women or give up its public funding.

Stephen Gerald Breyer

Born: August 15, 1938, San Francisco, California.

Education: Stanford University, A.B., Phi Beta Kappa, 1959; Oxford University, B.A. (Marshall scholar), 1961; Harvard Law School, LL.B., 1964.

Family: Married Joanna Hare, 1967; two daughters, one son.

Career: Law clerk to Justice Arthur J. Goldberg, U.S. Supreme Court, 1964–1965; assistant to assistant attorney general, antitrust, U.S. Justice Department, 1965–1967; professor, Harvard Law School, 1967–1981; assistant special prosecutor, Watergate Special Prosecution Force, 1973; special counsel, Senate Judiciary Committee, 1974–1975; chief counsel, Senate Judiciary Committee, 1979–1980; judge, U.S. Court of Appeals for the First Circuit, 1980–1994.

Supreme Court Service: Nominated as associate justice of the U.S. Supreme Court by President Bill Clinton May 17, 1994; confirmed, 87–9, July 29, 1994.

When President Bill Clinton introduced Stephen G. Breyer, his second Supreme Court nominee, at a White House ceremony on May 16, 1994, he described the federal appeals court judge as a "consensus-builder." The reaction to the nomination proved his point. Senators from both parties quickly endorsed Breyer. The only vocal dissents came from a few liberals and consumer advocates, who said Breyer was too probusiness.

Breyer, chosen to replace the retiring liberal justice Harry A. Blackmun, won a reputation as a centrist in fourteen years on the federal appeals court in Boston and two earlier stints as a staff member for the Senate Judiciary Committee. Breyer's work crossed ideological lines. He played a critical role in enacting airline deregulation in the 1970s and writing federal sentencing guidelines in the 1980s.

Born in 1938 to a politically active family in San Francisco, Breyer earned degrees from Stanford University and Harvard Law School. He clerked for Supreme Court Justice Arthur J. Goldberg and helped draft Goldberg's influential opinion in the 1965 case establishing the right of

married couples to use contraceptives. Afterward he served two years in the Justice Department's antitrust division and then took a teaching position at Harvard Law School in 1967.

Breyer took leave from Harvard to serve as an assistant prosecutor in the Watergate investigation in 1973, special counsel to the Judiciary Committee's Administrative Practices Subcommittee from 1974 to 1975, and the full committee's chief counsel from 1979 to 1980. He worked for Sen. Edward Kennedy, D-Mass., but also had good relationships with Republican committee members. His ties to senators paid off when President Jimmy Carter nominated him for the federal appeals court in November 1980. Even though Ronald Reagan had been elected president, GOP senators allowed a vote on Breyer's nomination.

As a judge, Breyer was regarded as scholarly, judicious, and open-minded, with generally conservative views on economic issues and more liberal views on social questions. He wrote two books on regulatory reform that criticized economic regulations as anticompetitive and questioned priorities in some environmental and health rulemaking. He also served as a member of the newly created United States Sentencing Commission from 1985 to 1989. Later he defended the commission's guidelines against criticism from judges and others who viewed them as overly restrictive.

President Clinton interviewed Breyer before his first Supreme Court appointment in 1993 but chose Ruth Bader Ginsburg instead. He picked Breyer in 1994 after Senate Majority Leader George Mitchell took himself out of consideration and problems developed with two other leading candidates.

In his confirmation hearings before the Senate Judiciary Committee, Breyer defused two potential controversies by saying that he accepted Supreme Court precedents upholding abortion rights and capital punishment. The only contentious issue in the confirmation process concerned Breyer's investment in the British insurance syndicate Lloyd's of London. Some senators said Breyer should have recused himself from several environmental pollution cases because of the investment. Breyer told the committee that the cases could not have affected his holdings but also promised to get out of Lloyd's as soon as possible. The panel went on to recommend the nomination unanimously.

One Republican senator, Indiana's Richard Lugar, raised the Lloyd's issue during debate, but Breyer was strongly supported by senators from both parties. The Senate voted to confirm Breyer 87–9. Breyer disposed of his investment in Lloyd's shortly after taking office.

In his first two terms, Breyer compiled a moderately liberal record. He dissented from several conservative rulings on race and religion and wrote the dissenting opinion for the four liberal justices in a decision that struck down a federal law prohibiting the possession of firearms near schools. But he had a more conservative record on criminal law issues and joined the Court's 1995 opinion permitting random drug testing of high school athletes.

Breyer joined Ginsburg as the Court's second Jewish justice. The Court had two Jewish members only once before, in the 1930s when Louis Brandeis and Benjamin Cardozo served together for six years.

Glossary of Legal Terms

Accessory. In criminal law, a person not present at the commission of an offense who commands, advises, instigates, or conceals the offense.

Acquittal. A person is acquitted when a jury returns a verdict of not guilty. A person also may be acquitted when a judge determines that insufficient evidence exists to convict him or that a violation of due process precludes a fair trial.

Adjudicate. To determine finally by the exercise of judicial authority, to decide a case.

Affidavit. A voluntary written statement of facts or charges affirmed under oath.

A fortiori. With stronger force, with more reason.

Amicus curiae. Friend of the court; a person, not a party to litigation, who volunteers or is invited by the court to give his or her views on a case.

Appeal. A legal proceeding to ask a higher court to review or modify a lower court decision. In a civil case, either the plaintiff or the defendant can appeal an adverse ruling. In criminal cases a defendant can appeal a conviction, but the Double Jeopardy Clause prevents the government from appealing an acquittal. In Supreme Court practice an appeal is a case that falls within the Court's mandatory jurisdiction as opposed to a case that the Court agrees to review under the discretionary writ of certiorari. With the virtual elimination of the Court's mandatory jurisdiction in 1988, the Court now hears very few true appeals, but petitions for certiorari are often referred to imprecisely as appeals.

Appellant. The party who appeals a lower court decision to a higher court.

Appellee. One who has an interest in upholding the decision of a lower court and is compelled to respond when the case is appealed to a higher court by an appellant.

Arraignment. The formal process of charging a person with a crime, reading that person the charge, asking whether he or she pleads guilty or not guilty, and entering the plea.

Attainder, Bill of. A legislative act pronouncing a particular individual guilty of a crime without trial or conviction and imposing a sentence.

Bail. The security, usually money, given as assurance of a prisoner's due appearance at a designated time and place (as in court) to procure in the interim the prisoner's release from jail.

Bailiff. A minor officer of a court, usually serving as an usher or a messenger.

Brief. A document prepared by counsel to serve as the basis for an argument in court, setting out the facts of and the legal arguments in support of the case.

Burden of proof. The need or duty of affirmatively providing a fact or facts that are disputed.

Case law. The law as defined by previously decided cases, distinct from statutes and other sources of law.

Cause. A case, suit, litigation, or action, civil or criminal.

Certiorari, Writ of. A writ issued from the Supreme Court, at its discretion, to order a lower court to prepare the record of a case and send it to the Supreme Court for review.

Civil law. Body of law dealing with the private rights of individuals, as distinguished from criminal law.

Class action. A lawsuit brought by one person or group on behalf of all persons similarly situated.

Code. A collection of laws, arranged systematically.

Comity. Courtesy, respect; usually used in the legal sense to refer to the proper relationship between state and federal courts.

Common law. Collection of principles and rules of action, particularly from unwritten English law, that derive their authority from longstanding usage and custom or from courts recognizing and enforcing these customs. Sometimes used synonymously with case law.

Consent decree. A court-sanctioned agreement settling a legal dispute and entered into by the consent of the parties.

Contempt (civil and criminal). Civil contempt arises from a failure to follow a court order for the benefit of another party. Criminal contempt occurs when a person willfully exhibits disrespect for the court or obstructs the administration of justice.

Conviction. Final judgment or sentence that the defendant is guilty as charged.

Criminal law. The branch of law that deals with the enforcement of laws and the punishment of persons who, by breaking laws, commit crimes.

Declaratory judgment. A court pronouncement declaring a legal right or interpretation but not ordering a specific action.

De facto. In fact, in reality.

Defendant. In a civil action, the party denying or defending itself against charges brought by a plaintiff. In a criminal action, the person indicted for commission of an offense.

De jure. As a result of law or official action.

De novo. Anew; afresh; a second time.

Deposition. Oral testimony from a witness taken out of court in response to written or oral questions, committed to writing, and intended to be used in the preparation of a case.

Dicta. *See* Obiter dictum.

Dismissal. Order disposing of a case without a trial.

Docket. A calendar prepared by the clerks of the court listing the cases set to be tried.

Due process. Fair and regular procedure. The Fifth and Fourteenth amendments guarantee persons that they will not be deprived of life, liberty, or property by the government until fair and usual procedures have been followed.

Error, Writ of. A writ issued from an appeals court to a lower court requiring it to send to the appeals court the record of a case in which it has entered a final judgment and which the appeals court will review for error.

Ex parte. Only from, or on, one side. Application to a court for some ruling or action on behalf of only one party.

Ex post facto. After the fact; an ex post facto law makes an action a crime after it already has been committed, or otherwise changes the legal consequences of some past action.

Ex rel. Upon information from; the term is usually used to describe legal proceedings begun by an official in the name of the state but at the instigation of, and with information from, a private individual interested in the matter.

Grand jury. Group of twelve to twenty-three persons impanelled to hear, in private, evidence presented by the state against an individual or persons accused of a criminal act and to issue indictments when a majority of the jurors find probable cause to believe that the accused has committed a crime. Called a "grand" jury because it comprises a greater number of persons than a "petit" jury.

Grand jury report. A public report, often called "presentments," released by a grand jury after an investigation into activities of public officials that fall short of criminal actions.

Guilty. A word used by a defendant in entering a plea or by a jury in returning a verdict, indicating that the defendant is legally responsible as charged for a crime or other wrongdoing.

Habeas corpus. Literally, "you have the body"; a writ issued to inquire whether a person is lawfully imprisoned or detained. The writ demands that the persons holding the prisoner justify the detention or release the prisoner.

Immunity. A grant of exemption from prosecution in return for evidence or testimony.

In camera. In chambers. Refers to court hearings in private without spectators.

In forma pauperis. In the manner of a pauper, without liability for court costs.

In personam. Done or directed against a particular person.

In re. In the affair of, concerning. Frequent title of judicial proceedings in which there are no adversaries but instead where the matter itself—such as a bankrupt's estate—requires judicial action.

In rem. Done or directed against the thing, not the person.

Indictment. A formal written statement, based on evidence presented by the prosecutor, from a grand jury. Decided by a majority vote, an indictment charges one or more persons with specified offenses.

Information. A written set of accusations, similar to an indictment, but filed directly by a prosecutor.

Injunction. A court order prohibiting the person to whom it is directed from performing a particular act.

Interlocutory decree. A provisional decision of the court before completion of a legal action that temporarily settles an intervening matter.

Judgment. Official decision of a court based on the rights and claims of the parties to a case that was submitted for determination.

Jurisdiction. The power of a court to hear a case in question, which exists when the proper parties are present and when the point to be decided is within the issues authorized to be handled by the particular court.

Juries. *See* Grand jury; Petit jury.

Magistrate. A judicial officer having jurisdiction to try minor criminal cases and conduct preliminary examinations of persons charged with serious crimes.

Majority opinion. An opinion joined by a majority of the justices explaining the legal basis for the Court's decision and regarded as binding precedent for future cases.

Mandamus. "We command." An order issued from a superior court directing a lower court or other authority to perform a particular act.

Moot. Unsettled, undecided. A moot question also is one that no longer is material; a moot case is one that has become hypothetical.

Motion. Written or oral application to a court or a judge to obtain a rule or an order.

Nolo contendere. "I will not contest it." A plea entered by a defendant at the discretion of the judge with the same legal effect as a plea of guilty, but it may not be cited in other proceedings as an admission of guilt.

Obiter dictum. Statements by a judge or justice expressing an opinion and included with, but not essential to, an opinion resolving a case before the court. Dicta are not necessarily binding in future cases.

Parole. A conditional release from imprisonment under conditions that, if the prisoner abides by the law and other restrictions that may be imposed, the prisoner will not have to serve the remainder of the sentence.

Per curiam. "By the court." An unsigned opinion of the court, or an opinion written by the whole court.

Petit jury. A trial jury, originally a panel of twelve persons who tried to reach a unanimous verdict on questions of fact in criminal and civil proceedings. Since 1970 the Supreme Court has upheld the legality of state juries with fewer than twelve persons. Fewer persons serve on a "petit" jury than on a "grand" jury.

Petitioner. One who files a petition with a court seeking action or relief, including a plaintiff or an appellant. But a petitioner also is a person who files for other court action where charges are not necessarily made; for example, a party may petition the court for an order requiring another person or party to produce documents. The opposite party is called the respondent.

When a writ of certiorari is granted by the Supreme Court, the parties to the case are called petitioner and respondent in contrast to the appellant and appellee terms used in an appeal.

Plaintiff. A party who brings a civil action or sues to obtain a remedy for injury to his or her rights. The party against whom action is brought is termed the defendant.

Plea bargaining. Negotiations between a prosecutor and the defendant aimed at exchanging a plea of guilty from the defendant for concessions by the prosecutor, such as reduction of the charges or a request for leniency.

Pleas. *See* Guilty; Nolo contendere.

Plurality opinion. An opinion supported by the largest number of justices but less than a majority. A plurality opinion typically is not regarded as establishing a binding precedent for future cases.

Precedent. A judicial decision that may be used as a basis for ruling on subsequent similar cases.

Presentment. *See* Grand jury report.

Prima facie. At first sight; referring to a fact or other evidence presumably sufficient to establish a defense or a claim unless otherwise contradicted.

Probation. Process under which a person convicted of an offense, usually a first offense, receives a suspended sentence and is given freedom, usually under the guardianship of a probation officer.

Quash. To overthrow, annul, or vacate; as to quash a subpoena.

Recognizance. An obligation entered into before a court or magistrate requiring the performance of a specified act—usually to appear in court at a later date. It is an alternative to bail for pretrial release.

Remand. To send back. When a decision is remanded, it is sent back by a higher court to the court from which it came for further action.

Respondent. One who is compelled to answer the claims or questions posed in court by a petitioner. A defendant and an appellee may be called respondents, but the term also includes those parties who answer in court during actions where charges are not necessarily brought or where the Supreme Court has granted a writ of certiorari.

Seriatim. Separately, individually, one by one.

Stare decisis. "Let the decision stand." The principle of adherence to settled cases, the doctrine that principles of law established in earlier judicial decisions should be accepted as authoritative in similar subsequent cases.

Statute. A written law enacted by a legislature. A collection of statutes for a particular governmental division is called a code.

Stay. To halt or suspend further judicial proceedings.

Subpoena. An order to present oneself before a grand jury, court, or legislative hearing.

Subpoena duces tecum. An order to produce specified documents or papers.

Tort. An injury or wrong to the person or property of another.

Transactional immunity. Protects a witness from prosecution for any offense mentioned in or related to his or her testimony, regardless of independent evidence against the witness.

Use immunity. Protects a witness from the use of his or her testimony against the witness in prosecution.

Vacate. To make void, annul, or rescind.

Writ. A written court order commanding the designated recipient to perform or not perform specified acts.

United States Constitution

We the People of the United States, in Order to form a more perfect Union, establish Justice, insure domestic Tranquility, provide for the common defence, promote the general Welfare, and secure the Blessings of Liberty to ourselves and our Posterity, do ordain and establish this Constitution for the United States of America.

Article I

Section 1. All legislative Powers herein granted shall be vested in a Congress of the United States, which shall consist of a Senate and House of Representatives.

Section 2. The House of Representatives shall be composed of Members chosen every second Year by the People of the several States, and the Electors in each State shall have the Qualifications requisite for Electors of the most numerous Branch of the State Legislature.

No Person shall be a Representative who shall not have attained to the age of twenty five Years, and been seven Years a Citizen of the United States, and who shall not, when elected, be an Inhabitant of that State in which he shall be chosen.

[Representatives and direct Taxes shall be apportioned among the several States which may be included within this Union, according to their respective Numbers, which shall be determined by adding to the whole Number of free Persons, including those bound to Service for a Term of Years, and excluding Indians not taxed, three fifths of all other Persons.][1] The actual Enumeration shall be made within three Years after the first Meeting of the Congress of the United States, and within every subsequent Term of ten Years, in such Manner as they shall by Law direct. The Number of Representatives shall not exceed one for every thirty Thousand, but each State shall have at Least one Representative; and until such enumeration shall be made, the State of New Hampshire shall be entitled to chuse three, Massachusetts eight, Rhode-Island and Providence Plantations one, Connecticut five, New-York six, New Jersey four, Pennsylvania eight, Delaware one, Maryland six, Virginia ten, North Carolina five, South Carolina five, and Georgia three.

When vacancies happen in the Representation from any State, the Executive Authority thereof shall issue Writs of Election to fill such Vacancies.

The House of Representatives shall chuse their Speaker and other Officers; and shall have the sole Power of Impeachment.

Section 3. The Senate of the United States shall be composed of two Senators from each State, [chosen by the Legislature thereof,][2] for six Years; and each Senator shall have one Vote.

Immediately after they shall be assembled in Consequence of the first Election, they shall be divided as equally as may be into three Classes. The Seats of the Senators of the first Class shall be vacated at the Expiration of the second Year, of the second Class at the Expiration of the fourth Year, and of the third Class at the Expiration of the sixth Year, so that one third may be chosen every second Year; [and if Vacancies happen by Resignation, or otherwise, during the Recess of the Legislature of any State, the Executive thereof may make temporary Appointments until the next Meeting of the Legislature, which shall then fill such Vacancies.][3]

No Person shall be a Senator who shall not have attained to the Age of thirty Years, and been nine Years a Citizen of the United States, and who shall not, when elected, be an Inhabitant of that State for which he shall be chosen.

The Vice President of the United States shall be President of the Senate, but shall have no Vote, unless they be equally divided.

The Senate shall chuse their other Officers, and also a President pro tempore, in the Absence of the Vice President, or when he shall exercise the Office of President of the United States.

The Senate shall have the sole Power to try all Impeachments. When sitting for that Purpose, they shall be on Oath or Affirmation. When the President of the United States is tried, the Chief Justice shall preside: And no Person shall be convicted without the Concurrence of two thirds of the Members present.

Judgment in Cases of Impeachment shall not extend further than to removal from Office, and disqualification to hold and enjoy any Office of honor, Trust or Profit under the United States: but the Party convicted shall nevertheless be liable and subject to Indictment, Trial, Judgment and Punishment, according to Law.

Section 4. The Times, Places and Manner of holding Elections for Senators and Representatives, shall be prescribed in each State by the Legislature thereof; but the Congress may at any time by Law make or alter such Regulations, except as to the Places of chusing Senators.

The Congress shall assemble at least once in every Year, and such Meeting shall [be on the first Monday in December],[4] unless they shall by Law appoint a different Day.

Section 5. Each House shall be the Judge of the Elections, Returns and Qualifications of its own Members, and a Majority of each shall constitute a Quorum to do Business; but a smaller Number may adjourn from day to day, and may be authorized to compel the Attendance of absent Members, in such Manner, and under such Penalties as each House may provide.

Each House may determine the Rules of its Proceedings, punish its Members for disorderly Behaviour, and, with the Concurrence of two thirds, expel a Member.

Each House shall keep a Journal of its Proceedings, and from time to time publish the same, excepting such Parts as may in their Judgment require Secrecy; and the Yeas and Nays of the Members of either House on any question shall, at the Desire of one fifth of those Present, be entered on the Journal.

Neither House, during the Session of Congress, shall, without the Consent of the other, adjourn for more than three days, nor to any other Place than that in which the two Houses shall be sitting.

Section 6. The Senators and Representatives shall receive a Compensation for their Services, to be ascertained by Law, and paid out of the Treasury of the United States. They shall in all Cases, except Treason, Felony and Breach of the

Peace, be privileged from Arrest during their Attendance at the Session of their respective Houses, and in going to and returning from the same; and for any Speech or Debate in either House, they shall not be questioned in any other Place.

No Senator or Representative shall, during the Time for which he was elected, be appointed to any civil Office under the Authority of the United States, which shall have been created, or the Emoluments whereof shall have been encreased during such time; and no Person holding any Office under the United States, shall be a Member of either House during his Continuance in Office.

Section 7. All Bills for raising Revenue shall originate in the House of Representatives; but the Senate may propose or concur with Amendments as on other Bills.

Every Bill which shall have passed the House of Representatives and the Senate, shall, before it become a Law, be presented to the President of the United States; If he approve he shall sign it, but if not he shall return it, with his Objections to that House in which it shall have originated, who shall enter the Objections at large on their Journal, and proceed to reconsider it. If after such Reconsideration two thirds of that House shall agree to pass the Bill, it shall be sent, together with the Objections, to the other House, by which it shall likewise be reconsidered, and if approved by two thirds of that House, it shall become a Law. But in all such Cases the Votes of both Houses shall be determined by yeas and Nays, and the Names of the Persons voting for and against the Bill shall be entered on the Journal of each House respectively. If any Bill shall not be returned by the President within ten Days (Sundays excepted) after it shall have been presented to him, the Same shall be a Law, in like Manner as if he had signed it, unless the Congress by their Adjournment prevent its Return, in which Case it shall not be a Law.

Every Order, Resolution, or Vote to which the Concurrence of the Senate and House of Representatives may be necessary (except on a question of Adjournment) shall be presented to the President of the United States; and before the Same shall take Effect, shall be approved by him, or being disapproved by him, shall be repassed by two thirds of the Senate and House of Representatives, according to the Rules and Limitations prescribed in the Case of a Bill.

Section 8. The Congress shall have Power To lay and collect Taxes, Duties, Imposts and Excises, to pay the Debts and provide for the common Defence and general Welfare of the United States; but all Duties, Imposts and Excises shall be uniform throughout the United States;

To borrow Money on the credit of the United States;

To regulate Commerce with foreign Nations, and among the several States, and with the Indian Tribes;

To establish an uniform Rule of Naturalization, and uniform Laws on the subject of Bankruptcies throughout the United States;

To coin Money, regulate the Value thereof, and of foreign Coin, and fix the Standard of Weights and Measures;

To provide for the Punishment of counterfeiting the Securities and current Coin of the United States;

To establish Post Offices and post Roads;

To promote the Progress of Science and useful Arts, by securing for limited Times to Authors and Inventors the exclusive Right to their respective Writings and Discoveries;

To constitute Tribunals inferior to the supreme Court;

To define and punish Piracies and Felonies committed on the high Seas, and Offences against the Law of Nations;

To declare War, grant Letters of Marque and Reprisal, and make Rules concerning Captures on Land and Water;

To raise and support Armies, but no Appropriation of Money to that Use shall be for a longer Term than two Years;

To provide and maintain a Navy;

To make Rules for the Government and Regulation of the land and naval Forces;

To provide for calling forth the Militia to execute the Laws of the Union, suppress Insurrections and repel Invasions;

To provide for organizing, arming, and disciplining, the Militia, and for governing such Part of them as may be employed in the Service of the United States, reserving to the States respectively, the Appointment of the Officers, and the Authority of training the Militia according to the discipline prescribed by Congress;

To exercise exclusive Legislation in all Cases whatsoever, over such District (not exceeding ten Miles square) as may, by Cession of particular States, and the Acceptance of Congress, become the Seat of the Government of the United States, and to exercise like Authority over all Places purchased by the Consent of the Legislature of the State in which the Same shall be, for the Erection of Forts, Magazines, Arsenals, dock-Yards, and other needful Buildings; — And

To make all Laws which shall be necessary and proper for carrying into Execution the foregoing Powers, and all other Powers vested by this Constitution in the Government of the United States, or in any Department or Officer thereof.

Section 9. The Migration or Importation of such Persons as any of the States now existing shall think proper to admit, shall not be prohibited by the Congress prior to the Year one thousand eight hundred and eight, but a Tax or duty may be imposed on such Importation, not exceeding ten dollars for each Person.

The Privilege of the Writ of Habeas Corpus shall not be suspended, unless when in Cases of Rebellion or Invasion the public Safety may require it.

No Bill of Attainder or ex post facto Law shall be passed.

No Capitation, or other direct, Tax shall be laid, unless in Proportion to the Census or Enumeration herein before directed to be taken.[5]

No Tax or Duty shall be laid on Articles exported from any State.

No Preference shall be given by any Regulation of Commerce or Revenue to the Ports of one State over those of another; nor shall Vessels bound to, or from one State, be obliged to enter, clear, or pay Duties in another.

No Money shall be drawn from the Treasury, but in Consequence of Appropriations made by Law; and a regular Statement and Account of the Receipts and Expenditures of all public Money shall be published from time to time.

No Title of Nobility shall be granted by the United States: And no Person holding any Office of Profit or Trust under them, shall, without the Consent of the

Congress, accept of any present, Emolument, Office, or Title, of any kind whatever, from any King, Prince, or foreign State.

Section 10. No State shall enter into any Treaty, Alliance, or Confederation; grant Letters of Marque and Reprisal; coin Money; emit Bills of Credit; make any Thing but gold and silver Coin a Tender in Payment of Debts; pass any Bill of Attainder, ex post facto Law, or Law impairing the Obligation of Contracts, or grant any Title of Nobility.

No State shall, without the Consent of the Congress, lay any Imposts or Duties on Imports or Exports, except what may be absolutely necessary for executing it's inspection Laws: and the net Produce of all Duties and Imposts, laid by any State on Imports or Exports, shall be for the Use of the Treasury of the United States; and all such Laws shall be subject to the Revision and Controul of the Congress.

No State shall, without the Consent of Congress, lay any Duty of Tonnage, keep Troops, or Ships of War in time of Peace, enter into any Agreement or Compact with another State, or with a foreign Power, or engage in War, unless actually invaded, or in such imminent Danger as will not admit of delay.

Article II

Section 1. The executive Power shall be vested in a President of the United States of America. He shall hold his Office during the Term of four Years, and, together with the Vice President, chosen for the same Term, be elected, as follows

Each State shall appoint, in such Manner as the Legislature thereof may direct, a Number of Electors, equal to the whole Number of Senators and Representatives to which the State may be entitled in the Congress: but no Senator or Representative, or Person holding an Office of Trust or Profit under the United States, shall be appointed an Elector.

[The Electors shall meet in their respective States, and vote by Ballot for two Persons, of whom one at least shall not be an Inhabitant of the same State with themselves. And they shall make a List of all the Persons voted for, and of the Number of Votes for each; which List they shall sign and certify, and transmit sealed to the Seat of the Government of the United States, directed to the President of the Senate. The President of the Senate shall, in the Presence of the Senate and House of Representatives, open all the Certificates, and the Votes shall then be counted. The Person having the greatest Number of Votes shall be the President, if such Number be a Majority of the whole Number of Electors appointed; and if there be more than one who have such Majority, and have an equal Number of Votes, then the House of Representatives shall immediately chuse by Ballot one of them for President; and if no Person have a Majority, then from the five highest on the list the said House shall in like Manner chuse the President. But in chusing the President, the Votes shall be taken by States, the Representation from each State having one Vote; A quorum for this Purpose shall consist of a Member or Members from two thirds of the States, and a Majority of all the States shall be necessary to a Choice. In every Case, after the Choice of the President, the Person having the greatest Number of Votes of the Electors shall be the Vice President. But if there should remain two or more who have equal Votes, the Senate shall chuse from them by Ballot the Vice President.][6]

The Congress may determine the Time of chusing the Electors, and the Day on which they shall give their Votes; which Day shall be the same throughout the United States.

No Person except a natural born Citizen, or a Citizen of the United States, at the time of the Adoption of this Constitution, shall be eligible to the Office of President; neither shall any Person be eligible to that Office who shall not have attained to the Age of thirty five Years, and been fourteen Years a Resident within the United States.

In Case of the Removal of the President from Office, or of his Death, Resignation, or Inability to discharge the Powers and Duties of the said Office,[7] the Same shall devolve on the Vice President, and the Congress may by Law provide for the Case of Removal, Death, Resignation or Inability, both of the President and Vice President, declaring what Officer shall then act as President, and such Officer shall act accordingly, until the Disability be removed, or a President shall be elected.

The President shall, at stated Times, receive for his Services, a Compensation, which shall neither be encreased nor diminished during the Period for which he shall have been elected, and he shall not receive within that Period any other Emolument from the United States, or any of them.

Before he enter on the Execution of his Office, he shall take the following Oath or Affirmation:—"I do solemnly swear (or affirm) that I will faithfully execute the Office of President of the United States, and will to the best of my Ability, preserve, protect and defend the Constitution of the United States."

Section 2. The President shall be Commander in Chief of the Army and Navy of the United States, and of the Militia of the several States, when called into the actual Service of the United States; he may require the Opinion, in writing, of the principal Officer in each of the executive Departments, upon any Subject relating to the Duties of their respective Offices, and he shall have Power to grant Reprieves and Pardons for Offences against the United States, except in Cases of Impeachment.

He shall have Power, by and with the Advice and Consent of the Senate, to make Treaties, provided two thirds of the Senators present concur; and he shall nominate, and by and with the Advice and Consent of the Senate, shall appoint Ambassadors, other public Ministers and Consuls, Judges of the supreme Court, and all other Officers of the United States, whose Appointments are not herein otherwise provided for, and which shall be established by Law: but the Congress may by Law vest the Appointment of such inferior Officers, as they think proper, in the President alone, in the Courts of Law, or in the Heads of Departments.

The President shall have Power to fill up all Vacancies that may happen during the Recess of the Senate, by granting Commissions which shall expire at the End of their next Session.

Section 3. He shall from time to time give to the Congress Information of the State of the Union, and recommend to their Consideration such Measures as he shall judge necessary and expedient; he may, on extraordinary Occasions, convene both Houses, or either of them, and in Case of Disagreement between them, with Respect to the Time of Adjournment, he may adjourn them to such Time as he shall think proper; he shall receive Ambassadors and other public Ministers; he shall take Care that the Laws be faithfully executed, and shall Commission all the Officers of the United States.

Section 4. The President, Vice President and all civil Officers of the United States, shall be removed from Office on Impeachment for, and Conviction of, Treason, Bribery, or other high Crimes and Misdemeanors.

Article III

Section 1. The judicial Power of the United States, shall be vested in one supreme Court, and in such inferior Courts as the Congress may from time to time ordain and establish. The Judges, both of the supreme and inferior Courts, shall hold their Offices during good Behaviour, and shall, at stated Times, receive for their Services, a Compensation, which shall not be diminished during their Continuance in Office.

Section 2. The judicial Power shall extend to all Cases, in Law and Equity, arising under this Constitution, the Laws of the United States, and Treaties made, or which shall be made, under their Authority; — to all Cases affecting Ambassadors, other public Ministers and Consuls; — to all Cases of admiralty and maritime Jurisdiction; — to Controversies to which the United States shall be a Party; — to Controversies between two or more States; — between a State and Citizens of another State;[8] — between Citizens of different States; — between Citizens of the same State claiming Lands under Grants of different States, and between a State, or the Citizens thereof, and foreign States, Citizens or Subjects.[8]

In all Cases affecting Ambassadors, other public Ministers and Consuls, and those in which a State shall be Party, the supreme Court shall have original Jurisdiction. In all the other Cases before mentioned, the supreme Court shall have appellate Jurisdiction, both as to Law and Fact, with such Exceptions, and under such Regulations as the Congress shall make.

The Trial of all Crimes, except in Cases of Impeachment, shall be by Jury; and such Trial shall be held in the State where the said Crimes shall have been committed; but when not committed within any State, the Trial shall be at such Place or Places as the Congress may by Law have directed.

Section 3. Treason against the United States, shall consist only in levying War against them, or in adhering to their Enemies, giving them Aid and Comfort. No Person shall be convicted of Treason unless on the Testimony of two Witnesses to the same overt Act, or on Confession in open Court.

The Congress shall have Power to declare the Punishment of Treason, but no Attainder of Treason shall work Corruption of Blood, or Forfeiture except during the Life of the Person attainted.

Article IV

Section 1. Full Faith and Credit shall be given in each State to the public Acts, Records, and judicial Proceedings of every other State. And the Congress may by general Laws prescribe the Manner in which such Acts, Records and Proceedings shall be proved, and the Effect thereof.

Section 2. The Citizens of each State shall be entitled to all Privileges and Immunities of Citizens in the several States.

A Person charged in any State with Treason, Felony, or other Crime, who shall flee from Justice, and be found in another State, shall on Demand of the executive Authority of the State from which he fled, be delivered up, to be removed to the State having Jurisdiction of the Crime.

[No Person held to Service or Labour in one State, under the Laws thereof, escaping into another, shall, in Consequence of any Law or Regulation therein, be discharged from such Service or Labour, but shall be delivered up on Claim of the Party to whom such Service or Labour may be due.][9]

Section 3. New States may be admitted by the Congress into this Union; but no new State shall be formed or erected within the Jurisdiction of any other State; nor any State be formed by the Junction of two or more States, or Parts of States, without the Consent of the Legislatures of the States concerned as well as of the Congress.

The Congress shall have Power to dispose of and make all needful Rules and Regulations respecting the Territory or other Property belonging to the United States; and nothing in this Constitution shall be so construed as to Prejudice any Claims of the United States, or of any particular State.

Section 4. The United States shall guarantee to every State in this Union a Republican Form of Government, and shall protect each of them against Invasion; and on Application of the Legislature, or of the Executive (when the Legislature cannot be convened) against domestic Violence.

Article V

The Congress, whenever two thirds of both Houses shall deem it necessary, shall propose Amendments to this Constitution, or, on the Application of the Legislatures of two thirds of the several States, shall call a Convention for proposing Amendments, which, in either Case, shall be valid to all Intents and Purposes, as Part of this Constitution, when ratified by the Legislatures of three fourths of the several States, or by Conventions in three fourths thereof, as the one or the other Mode of Ratification may be proposed by the Congress; Provided [that no Amendment which may be made prior to the Year One thousand eight hundred and eight shall in any Manner affect the first and fourth Clauses in the Ninth Section of the first Article; and][10] that no State, without its Consent, shall be deprived of its equal Suffrage in the Senate.

Article VI

All Debts contracted and Engagements entered into, before the Adoption of this Constitution, shall be as valid against the United States under this Constitution, as under the Confederation.

This Constitution, and the Laws of the United States which shall be made in Pursuance thereof; and all Treaties made, or which shall be made, under the Authority of the United States, shall be the supreme Law of the Land; and the Judges in every State shall be bound thereby, any Thing in the Constitution or Laws of any State to the Contrary notwithstanding.

The Senators and Representatives before mentioned, and the Members of the several State Legislatures, and all executive and judicial Officers, both of the United States and of the several States, shall be bound by Oath or Affirmation, to support this Constitution; but no religious Test shall ever be required as a Qualification to any Office or public Trust under the United States.

Article VII

The Ratification of the Conventions of nine States, shall be sufficient for the Establishment of this Constitution between the States so ratifying the Same.

Done in Convention by the Unanimous Consent of the States present the Seventeenth Day of September in the Year of our Lord one thousand seven hundred and Eighty seven and of the Independence of the United States of America the Twelfth. IN WITNESS whereof We have hereunto subscribed our Names,

George Washington,
President and
deputy from Virginia.

New Hampshire: John Langdon,
Nicholas Gilman.

Massachusetts: Nathaniel Gorham,
Rufus King.

Connecticut: William Samuel Johnson,
Roger Sherman.

New York: Alexander Hamilton.

New Jersey: William Livingston,
David Brearley,
William Paterson,
Jonathan Dayton.

Pennsylvania: Benjamin Franklin,
Thomas Mifflin,
Robert Morris,
George Clymer,
Thomas FitzSimons,
Jared Ingersoll,
James Wilson,
Gouverneur Morris.

Delaware:	George Read, Gunning Bedford Jr., John Dickinson, Richard Bassett, Jacob Broom.
Maryland:	James McHenry, Daniel of St. Thomas Jenifer, Daniel Carroll.
Virginia:	John Blair, James Madison Jr.
North Carolina:	William Blount, Richard Dobbs Spaight, Hugh Williamson.
South Carolina:	John Rutledge, Charles Cotesworth Pinckney, Charles Pinckney, Pierce Butler.
Georgia:	William Few, Abraham Baldwin.

[The language of the original Constitution, not including the Amendments, was adopted by a convention of the states on September 17, 1787, and was subsequently ratified by the states on the following dates: Delaware, December 7, 1787; Pennsylvania, December 12, 1787; New Jersey, December 18, 1787; Georgia, January 2, 1788; Connecticut, January 9, 1788; Massachusetts, February 6, 1788; Maryland, April 28, 1788; South Carolina, May 23, 1788; New Hampshire, June 21, 1788.

Ratification was completed on June 21, 1788.

The Constitution subsequently was ratified by Virginia, June 25, 1788; New York, July 26, 1788; North Carolina, November 21, 1789; Rhode Island, May 29, 1790; and Vermont, January 10, 1791.]

Amendments

Amendment I

(First ten amendments ratified December 15, 1791.)

Congress shall make no law respecting an establishment of religion, or prohibiting the free exercise thereof; or abridging the freedom of speech, or of the press; or the right of the people peaceably to assemble, and to petition the Government for a redress of grievances.

Amendment II

A well regulated Militia, being necessary to the security of a free State, the right of the people to keep and bear Arms, shall not be infringed.

Amendment III

No Soldier shall, in time of peace be quartered in any house, without the consent of the Owner, nor in time of war, but in a manner to be prescribed by law.

Amendment IV

The right of the people to be secure in their persons, houses, papers, and effects, against unreasonable searches and seizures, shall not be violated, and no Warrants shall issue, but upon probable cause, supported by Oath or affirmation, and particularly describing the place to be searched, and the persons or things to be seized.

Amendment V

No person shall be held to answer for a capital, or otherwise infamous crime, unless on a presentment or indictment of a Grand Jury, except in cases arising in the land or naval forces, or in the Militia, when in actual service in time of War or public danger; nor shall any person be subject for the same offence to be twice put in jeopardy of life or limb; nor shall be compelled in any criminal case to be a witness against himself, nor be deprived of life, liberty, or property, without due process of law; nor shall private property be taken for public use, without just compensation.

Amendment VI

In all criminal prosecutions, the accused shall enjoy the right to a speedy and public trial, by an impartial jury of the State and district wherein the crime shall have been committed, which district shall have been previously ascertained by law, and to be informed of the nature and cause of the accusation; to be confronted with the witnesses against him; to have compulsory process for obtaining witnesses in his favor, and to have the Assistance of Counsel for his defence.

Amendment VII

In Suits at common law, where the value in controversy shall exceed twenty dollars, the right of trial by jury shall be preserved, and no fact tried by a jury, shall be otherwise re-examined in any Court of the United States, than according to the rules of the common law.

Amendment VIII

Excessive bail shall not be required, nor excessive fines imposed, nor cruel and unusual punishments inflicted.

Amendment IX

The enumeration in the Constitution, of certain rights, shall not be construed to deny or disparage others retained by the people.

Amendment X

The powers not delegated to the United States by the Constitution, nor prohibited by it to the States, are reserved to the States respectively, or to the people.

Amendment XI

(Ratified February 7, 1795)

The Judicial power of the United States shall not be construed to extend to any suit in law or equity, commenced or prosecuted against one of the United States by Citizens of another State, or by Citizens or Subjects of any Foreign State.

Amendment XII

(Ratified June 15, 1804)

The Electors shall meet in their respective states and vote by ballot for President and Vice-President, one of whom, at least, shall not be an inhabitant of the same state with themselves; they shall name in their ballots the person voted for as President, and in distinct ballots the person voted for as Vice-President, and they shall make distinct lists of all persons voted for as President, and of all persons voted for as Vice-President, and of the number of votes for each, which lists they shall sign and certify, and transmit sealed to the seat of the government of the United States, directed to the President of the Senate; — The President of the Senate shall, in the presence of the Senate and House of Representatives, open all the certificates and the votes shall then be counted; — The person having the greatest number of votes for President, shall be the President, if such number be a majority of the whole number of Electors appointed; and if no person have such majority, then from the persons having the highest numbers not exceeding three on the list of those voted for as President, the House of Representatives shall choose immediately, by ballot, the President. But in choosing the President, the votes shall be taken by states, the representation from each state having one vote; a quorum for this purpose shall consist of a member or members from two-thirds of the states, and a majority of all the states shall be necessary to a choice. [And if the House of Representatives shall not choose a President whenever the right of choice shall devolve upon them, before the fourth day of March next following, then the Vice-President shall act as President, as in the case of the death or other constitutional disability of the President. —][11] The person having the greatest number of votes as Vice-President, shall be the Vice-President, if such number be a majority of the whole number of Electors appointed, and if no person have a majority, then from the two highest numbers on the list, the Senate shall choose the Vice-President; a quorum for the purpose shall consist of two-thirds of the whole number of Senators, and a majority of the whole number shall be necessary to a choice. But no person constitutionally ineligible to the office of President shall be eligible to that of Vice-President of the United States.

Amendment XIII

(Ratified December 6, 1865)

Section 1. Neither slavery nor involuntary servitude, except as a punishment for crime whereof the party shall have been duly convicted, shall exist within the United States, or any place subject to their jurisdiction.

Section 2. Congress shall have power to enforce this article by appropriate legislation.

Amendment XIV

(Ratified July 9, 1868)

Section 1. All persons born or naturalized in the United States, and subject to the jurisdiction thereof, are citizens of the United States and of the State wherein they reside. No State shall make or enforce any law which shall abridge the privileges or immunities of citizens of the United States; nor shall any State deprive any person of life, liberty, or property, without due process of law; nor deny to any person within its jurisdiction the equal protection of the laws.

Section 2. Representatives shall be apportioned among the several States according to their respective numbers, counting the whole number of persons in each State, excluding Indians not taxed. But when the right to vote at any election for the choice of electors for President and Vice President of the United States, Representatives in Congress, the Executive and Judicial officers of a State, or the members of the Legislature thereof, is denied to any of the male inhabitants of such State, being twenty-one years of age,[12] and citizens of the United States, or in any way abridged, except for participation in rebellion, or other crime, the basis of representation therein shall be reduced in the proportion which the number of such male citizens shall bear to the whole number of male citizens twenty-one years of age in such State.

Section 3. No person shall be a Senator or Representative in Congress, or elector of President and Vice President, or hold any office, civil or military, under the United States, or under any State, who, having previously taken an oath, as a member of Congress, or as an officer of the United States, or as a member of any State legislature, or as an executive or judicial officer of any State, to support the Constitution of the United States, shall have engaged in insurrection or rebellion against the same, or given aid or comfort to the enemies thereof. But Congress may by a vote of two-thirds of each House, remove such disability.

Section 4. The validity of the public debt of the United States, authorized by law, including debts incurred for payment of pensions and bounties for services in suppressing insurrection or rebellion, shall not be questioned. But neither the United States nor any State shall assume or pay any debt or obligation incurred in aid of insurrection or rebellion against the United States, or any claim for the loss or emancipation of any slave; but all such debts, obligations and claims shall be held illegal and void.

Section 5. The Congress shall have power to enforce, by appropriate legislation, the provisions of this article.

Amendment XV

(Ratified February 3, 1870)

Section 1. The right of citizens of the United States to vote shall not be denied or abridged by the United States or by any State on account of race, color, or previous condition of servitude.

Section 2. The Congress shall have power to enforce this article by appropriate legislation.

Amendment XVI

(Ratified February 3, 1913)

The Congress shall have power to lay and collect taxes on incomes, from whatever source derived, without apportionment among the several States, and without regard to any census or enumeration.

Amendment XVII

(Ratified April 8, 1913)

The Senate of the United States shall be composed of two Senators from each State, elected by the people thereof, for six years; and each Senator shall have one vote. The electors in each State shall have the qualifications requisite for electors of the most numerous branch of the State legislatures.

When vacancies happen in the representation of any State in the Senate, the executive authority of such State shall issue writs of election to fill such vacancies: *Provided,* That the legislature of any State may empower the executive thereof to make temporary appointments until the people fill the vacancies by election as the legislature may direct.

This amendment shall not be so construed as to affect the election or term of any Senator chosen before it becomes valid as part of the Constitution.

Amendment XVIII

(Ratified January 16, 1919) [13]

Section 1. After one year from the ratification of this article the manufacture, sale, or transportation of intoxicating liquors within, the importation thereof into, or the exportation thereof from the United States and all territory subject to the jurisdiction thereof for beverage purposes is hereby prohibited.

Section 2. The Congress and the several States shall have concurrent power to enforce this article by appropriate legislation.

Section 3. This article shall be inoperative unless it shall have been ratified as an amendment to the Constitution by the legislatures of the several States, as provided in the Constitution, within seven years from the date of the submission hereof to the States by the Congress.

Amendment XIX

(Ratified August 18, 1920)

The right of citizens of the United States to vote shall not be denied or abridged by the United States or by any State on account of sex.

Congress shall have power to enforce this article by appropriate legislation.

Amendment XX

(Ratified January 23, 1933)

Section 1. The terms of the President and Vice President shall end at noon on the 20th day of January, and the terms of Senators and Representatives at noon on the 3d day of January, of the years in which such terms would have ended if this article had not been ratified; and the terms of their successors shall then begin.

Section 2. The Congress shall assemble at least once in every year, and such meeting shall begin at noon on the 3d day of January, unless they shall by law appoint a different day.

Section 3.[14] If, at the time fixed for the beginning of the term of the President, the President elect shall have died, the Vice President elect shall become President. If a President shall not have been chosen before the time fixed for the beginning of his term, or if the President elect shall have failed to qualify, then the Vice President elect shall act as President until a President shall have qualified; and the Congress may by law provide for the case wherein neither a President elect nor a Vice President elect shall have qualified, declaring who shall then act as President, or the manner in which one who is to act shall be selected, and such person shall act accordingly until a President or Vice President shall have qualified.

Section 4. The Congress may by law provide for the case of the death of any of the persons from whom the House of Representatives may choose a President whenever the right of choice shall have devolved upon them, and for the case of the death of any of the persons from whom the Senate may choose a Vice President whenever the right of choice shall have devolved upon them.

Section 5. Sections 1 and 2 shall take effect on the 15th day of October following the ratification of this article.

Section 6. This article shall be inoperative unless it shall have been ratified as an amendment to the Constitution by the legislatures of three-fourths of the several States within seven years from the date of its submission.

Amendment XXI

(Ratified December 5, 1933)

Section 1. The eighteenth article of amendment to the Constitution of the United States is hereby repealed.

Section 2. The transportation or importation into any State, Territory, or possession of the United States for delivery or use therein of intoxicating liquors, in violation of the laws thereof, is hereby prohibited.

Section 3. This article shall be inoperative unless it shall have been ratified as an amendment to the Constitution by conventions in the several States, as provided in the Constitution, within seven years from the date of the submission hereof to the States by the Congress.

Amendment XXII

(Ratified February 27, 1951)

Section 1. No person shall be elected to the office of the President more than twice, and no person who has held the office of President, or acted as President, for more than two years of a term to which some other person was elected President shall be elected to the office of the President more than once. But this Article shall not apply to any person holding the office of President when this Article was proposed by the Congress, and shall not prevent any person who may be holding the office of President, or acting as President, during the term within which this Article become operative from holding the office of President or acting as President during the remainder of such term.

Section 2. This article shall be inoperative unless it shall have been ratified as an amendment to the Constitution by the legislatures of three-fourths of the several States within seven years from the date of its submission to the States by the Congress.

Amendment XXIII

(Ratified March 29, 1961)

Section 1. The District constituting the seat of Government of the United States shall appoint in such manner as the Congress may direct:
A number of electors of President and Vice President equal to the whole number of Senators and Representatives in Congress to which the District would be entitled if it were a State, but in no event more than the least populous State; they shall be in addition to those appointed by the States, but they shall be considered, for the purposes of the election of President and Vice President, to be electors

appointed by a State; and they shall meet in the District and perform such duties as provided by the twelfth article of amendment.

Section 2. The Congress shall have power to enforce this article by appropriate legislation.

Amendment XXIV

(Ratified January 23, 1964)

Section 1. The right of citizens of the United States to vote in any primary or other election for President or Vice President, for electors for President or Vice President, or for Senator or Representative in Congress, shall not be denied or abridged by the United States or any State by reason of failure to pay any poll tax or other tax.

Section 2. The Congress shall have power to enforce this article by appropriate legislation.

Amendment XXV

(Ratified February 10, 1967)

Section 1. In case of the removal of the President from office or of his death or resignation, the Vice President shall become President.

Section 2. Whenever there is a vacancy in the office of the Vice President, the President shall nominate a Vice President who shall take office upon confirmation by a majority vote of both Houses of Congress.

Section 3. Whenever the President transmits to the President pro tempore of the Senate and the Speaker of the House of Representatives his written declaration that he is unable to discharge the powers and duties of his office, and until he transmits to them a written declaration to the contrary, such powers and duties shall be discharged by the Vice President as Acting President.

Section 4. Whenever the Vice President and a majority of either the principal officers of the executive departments or of such other body as Congress may by law provide, transmit to the President pro tempore of the Senate and the Speaker of the House of Representatives their written declaration that the President is unable to discharge the powers and duties of his office, the Vice President shall immediately assume the powers and duties of the office as Acting President.

Thereafter, when the President transmits to the President pro tempore of the Senate and the Speaker of the House of Representatives his written declaration that no inability exists, he shall resume the powers and duties of his office unless the Vice President and a majority of either the principal officers of the executive department or of such other body as Congress may by law provide, transmit within four days to the President pro tempore of the Senate and the Speaker of the House of Representatives their written declaration that the President is unable to discharge the powers and duties of his office. Thereupon Congress shall decide the issue, assembling within forty-eight hours for that purpose if not in session. If the Congress, within twenty-one days after receipt of the latter written declaration, or, if Congress is not in session, within twenty-one days after Congress is required to assemble, determines by two-thirds vote of both Houses that the President is unable to discharge the powers and duties of his office, the Vice President shall continue to discharge the same as Acting President; otherwise, the President shall resume the powers and duties of his office.

Amendment XXVI

(Ratified July 1, 1971)

Section 1. The right of citizens of the United States, who are eighteen years of age or older, to vote shall not be denied or abridged by the United States or by any State on account of age.

Section 2. The Congress shall have power to enforce this article by appropriate legislation.

Amendment XXVII

(Ratified May 7, 1992)

No law varying the compensation for the services of the Senators and Representatives shall take effect, until an election of Representatives shall have intervened.

Notes

1. The part in brackets was by section 2 of the Fourteenth Amendment.
2. The part in brackets was changed by the first paragraph of the Seventeenth Amendment.
3. The part in brackets was changed by the second paragraph of the Seventeenth Amendment.
4. The part in brackets was changed by section 2 of the Twentieth Amendment.
5. The Sixteenth Amendment gave Congress the power to tax incomes.
6. The material in brackets has been superseded by the Twelfth Amendment.
7. This provision has been affected by the Twenty-fifth Amendment.
8. These clauses were affected by the Eleventh Amendment.
9. This paragraph has been superseded by the Thirteenth Amendment.
10. Obsolete.
11. The part in brackets has been superseded by section 3 of the Twentieth Amendment.
12. See the Nineteenth and Twenty-sixth Amendments.
13. This Amendment was repealed by section 1 of the Twenty-first Amendment.
14. See the Twenty-fifth Amendment.

Source: U.S. Congress, House, Committee on the Judiciary, *The Constitution of the United States of America, as Amended*, 100th Cong., 1st sess., 1987, H Doc 100–94.

Index

Abortion, 25, 112–113
  parental notification, 69
  protests, 126–127, 138–139
Abrams v. Johnson, 135
Abstention, 78
ACLU. *See* American Civil Liberties
  Union
Acquittals, 82–83
Admissions policies
  affirmative action, 69
  state military schools, 2, 6, 9, 12, 15,
    38–42, 115
Advertising
  agricultural marketing orders,
    137
  Central Hudson test, 58–60
  liquor prices, 10, 12, 20*t*, 21, 23,
    57–61, 108–109
Affirmative action, 69
Age discrimination, 24–25, 113
Age Discrimination in Employment
  Act, 113
Agent Orange, 23, 106
Agricultural laborers, 117
Agricultural marketing orders, 137
Ahmar, Akil, 9, 13–14
Alabama, 103–104, 123–124
Alcohol billboards, 60
Allied-Bruce Terminix Cos. v. Dobson
  (1995), 79
Allstate Insurance Co., 78
American Civil Liberties Union
  (ACLU), 3, 24–25, 128
American Intellectual Property Law
  Association, 133
Antiterrorism and Effective Death
  Penalty Act of 1996, 91
Antitrust law, 14
  exemption, 115–116
Appeals, 78–79, 133
Arbitration, 79
Arizona, 9, 27, 94–95, 139
Arizonans for Official English v. Arizona,
  139
Arkansas, 25
Arlt, Charles Wesley, 63, 90

Association of Trial Lawyers of Ameri-
  ca, 49
*Atherton v. Federal Deposit Insurance Cor-
  poration*, 133
*Auciello Iron Works, Inc. v. National Labor
  Relations Board* (1996), 116–117
Auer v. Robbins, 140–141
Austin v. United States (1993), 62, 64

Bailey, Roland, 85
Bailey v. United States (1995), 85
Baltimore, Maryland, 60
*Bank One Chicago, N.A. v. Midwest Bank
  & Trust Co.* (1996), 71
Banking, 22, 71–72
  savings and loans, 13, 18, 107, 133
Bankruptcy, 10, 72–74
Baran, Jan, 57
Barnes, Michael, 26, 28, 64
*Barnett Bank of Marion County, N.A. v.
  Nelson, Florida Insurance Commissioner*
  (1996), 71
Bartholomew, Dwayne, 87–88
Bartholomew, Rodney, 87–88
Bayless, Jeffrey, 35
Behrens v. Pelletier (1996), 78–79
Bell Atlantic Co., 112
Bender, Paul, 41
Bennett v. Spear, 136
Bennis, John, 61
Bennis, Tina, 61–64
Bennis v. Michigan (1996), 61–63,
  88–89
Bergman, Barbara, 26
Berry, William, 40
Birth, Elizabeth, 37
Blessing v. Freestone, 140
BMW, 21
BMW of North America, Inc. v. Gore
  (1996), 43, 46–49, 123–124
*Board of County Commissioners, Wabaun-
  see County, Kansas v. Umbehr* (1996),
  109–110
*Board of County Commissioners of Bryan
  County, Okla. v. Brown*, 140
Bokat, Stephen, 2–3, 18, 21, 49

Medical Devices Act, 105
Medtronic, Inc. v. Lohr (1996), 105–106
Meghrig v. KFC Western, Inc. (1996), 104
Melendez v. United States (1996), 98–99
Mental competency, 28
Military justice, capital punishment system, 27
Military schools, single-sex admissions policies, 2, 6, 9, 12, 15, 19, 24, 38–42
Miller v. Johnson (1995), 101
Minnesota, 136
Miranda warnings, 15, 28, 93
Mississippi, 121
Mississippi University for Women v. Hogan (1982), 39
M.L.B. v. S.L.G., 133
Mofford, Rose, 139
Montana, 14
Montana v. Egelhoff (1996), 85–86
Moore, Charles Edward, Jr., 91
Morse v. Republican Party of Virginia (1996), 102–104
Mosbacher, Robert, 105
Multiemployer bargaining, 116
Multiple-party nominations, 136
Municipal liability, 140

National Football League, 22, 116
National Football League Players Association, 116
National Labor Relations Act, 116, 118
National Labor Relations Board (NLRB), 21, 116–117
National Labor Relations Board v. Town & Country Electric, Inc. (1995), 117–118
National Rifle Association, 129
National Sheriffs Association, 131
Neal v. United States (1996), 99
New Party, 136
New York, 50, 138
New York v. United States (1992), 43, 129
NFL. *See* National Football League
Nixon, Richard M., 16, 127
NLRB. *See* National Labor Relations Board
Norfolk & Western Railway Co. v. Hiles (1996), 120–121
North Carolina
  redistricting, 2, 20, 20*t*, 29–31, 33–34, 101–102
  taxation, 122–123
Norton, Gale, 36

O'Connor, Sandra Day, 11, 16–17
  on abstention, 78
  on cable indecency, 49, 51–52, 110–111
  on campaign finance, 56, 100
  on commercial speech, 109
  on copyright software, 75
  on criminal law, 85–86, 89
  on disability rights, 113–114
  dissenting votes, 4, 4*t*
  on federal regulation, 105–106
  on forfeitures, 62, 64, 89
  on free speech, 109–110
  on gay rights, 2, 37
  on government contracts, 106–107
  on interstate commerce, 129, 132
  on jury trials, 94
  on labor law, 117, 119, 121
  on liquor price advertising, 59
  on punitive damages, 6, 47–48, 124
  on redistricting, 2, 6, 19, 28, 31–33, 100–101
  on sentencing, 98–99
  on single-sex schools, 6
  on states' rights, 43–44
  on taxation, 77
  on toxic waste, 104
  on Virginia Military Institute's defense, 41
  voting pattern, 5–6, 7*t*
  on voting rights, 103
  on women's rights, 2
O'Connor v. Consolidated Coin Caterers Corp. (1996), 113
Official English law, 127, 139
O'Gilvie v. United States, 133
O'Hair, John, 61
O'Hare Truck Service, Inc. v. City of Northlake (1996), 109–110
Ohio, 58, 134
Ohio v. Robinette, 134
Oklahoma, 27, 105
Olson, Theodore, 10, 41, 67
Oregon, 136
Ornelas v. United States (1996), 95–96
Overtime pay, 140–141

Pacific Mutual Life Insurance Co. v. Haslip (1991), 47
Pan Am Flight 103, 124
Parents' rights, 67, 69
Patents, 13, 76–77, 132–133
Peacock v. Thomas (1996), 79–80